You Are Here Traveling with JohnnyJet.com

Eric Leebow with John E. DiScala

Yahbooks Publishing

You Are Here Traveling with JohnnyJet.com
PRINTED IN THE UNITED STATES OF AMERICA

All of the sites listed in this publication were visited and functional at the time of this writing. Great efforts have been made to make this book a complete compilation and as accurate as possible. Please be aware the Internet will continue to change. The authors have provided this book ensuring its usefulness, but are not responsible for any information that may have changed since publication.

ISBN: 0-9713991-4-X

Library of Congress Control Number: 2002113206

Leebow, Eric Leebow
Traveling with JohnnyJet.com / Eric Leebow with John E. DiScala. - 1st ed.
p. cm. -- (You are here ; 5)
Includes index.
LCCN 2002113206
ISBN 0-9713991-4-X

1. Travel-Computer network resources. 2. Internet.
2. World Wide Web. I. DiScala, John E. II. Title.

G155.AIL44 2003 025.06'91
QBI02-200831
Cover photos: Superstock and John E. DiScala
Book Design: Janice Phelps
Editing: Dachell McSween

Dedication

Jeanne Hansen DiScala
1927–2000

"Her Life Was Her Family, and Her Family Was Her Life"

Preface

On October 14, 2000, I lost the most important person to me. My mother and I were extremely close. In fact, I can proudly say I was the "Ultimate Momma's boy." Every other weekend, I would travel from California to Connecticut to visit her. As a tribute, this book is dedicated in memory of my mother.

My real name isn't Johnny Jet, it's John Einar DiScala, and I was almost the "Ultimate Italian,"-- "John Anthony DiScala." Thank God, I was delivered two weeks early on my grandfather Hansen's Birthday. Although I never met grandpa, my mom would always tell stories about him. Grandpa came over from Denmark, and was a very strong man, who loved fish. Mom always dreamed of going to see the country where Dad was born. My mother chose not to go because she did not want to leave her kids. The one positive thing to come out of my mom's cancer was that I was able to give that dream to her. Cancer made my mom realize that life isn't forever and to seize every moment. When she recovered from her first nine hour operation, I said to my mom in the hospital bed, "Mom, when you get better, we are going to Denmark." She said, "No, I can't. I'm in chemo." I pressured her and finally my mother asked the doctor to give her a week off from the chemo. She was very excited about the trip and began packing a month earlier. I redeemed some miles and treated us to our dream trip.

Our seats were First Class to places we only dreamed about visiting including London for shopping and going to the theatre. We also visited Paris, where my mom would've studied if she took that scholarship from Parsons School of Design. The most important place was The Island of Fyn in Denmark. When we were landing in Copenhagen, I glanced over at my mom and I watched her staring out of the window, with tears rolling down her face. We toured the house where my grandfather grew up and even took home a piece of the brick! We had the greatest time meeting long lost relatives and exploring Denmark. My mom was so cute and appreciative. She kept thanking me, but I was really thanking her.

Upon our return home, my mom's cancer came back spreading to her liver, esophagus, and gall bladder. She went through another grueling nine hour operation. Every time she would go into that operating room at Sloan Kettering Hospital, she looked like a soldier ready for the front line. When she came out, I said, "Mom, you need to get well soon, because I just ordered two more tickets to go back to Europe." Although she couldn't talk, she had a sparkle in her eye. That summer, my mom and I returned to Europe. She even made her first plane ride alone! She flew from New York to DC to meet me.

Mom had this special presence about her or maybe it was her way with words. As we waited for our flight in the stuffy, but plush first class lounge, I noticed that everyone in there was pretentious. I put my bags down, and then showed my mom all the gourmet food. I went to the bathroom and found all of the workers surrounding her. They were listening to her stories about how she was beating cancer, and how lucky she was to be flying first class. When I walked over, they told me how great my mom was, and how lucky she was to have a son like me. I said, "You are right! She is great, but she's not the lucky one - I am." It was so amazing that in just a few minutes, she had all these ladies laughing and bringing her gifts.

Our trip to Frankfurt, Strasbourg, Paris, Denmark, and Sweden was great. Although she still had the cancer, my mom managed to do this itinerary all in two weeks. She loved it! When we came home, we found out the cancer came back again, this time spreading to her lungs, but she didn't lose faith. She never gave up hope. She said to her doctor, "Do what ever it takes because I want to see my 3-year-old granddaughter's wedding." She had chemo every week for ten months.

While my mom was in the hospital, she was in tremendous pain. I would always ask her if she wanted me to spend the night with her. I would stay by her side every night. However, this particular time, she said, “It might not be a good idea, it could be a rough night." I brought the cot in and while we were lying on our beds, we could hear all those terrible sounds that take place in a hospital. Across the hall, there was a lady screaming and moaning in pain. The nurses were cleaning my mother's other neighbor because she just passed away. I said, “Mom, we need to get you out of this horrible place. Where do you want to go?" She said “Let's go back to Europe... tonight." I said, “Great! Let's go! She turned out the light and I said, “Close your eyes. I can feel it, can you?" She said, “Oh yeah." I said, “Where are we?" My mom said, “We're in Strasbourg going up the canal in the tour boat." I said, “Yes we are!" She said, “Look at the picture perfect blue sky with all those soft puffy white clouds." I said, “Doesn't the sun feel so warm?" She said, “Yes it does and those flowers are so beautiful, and look at that magnificent church located on the right." I said, “This is such a beautiful place. Where do you want to go after Strasbourg?" She said, “Let's take the train to Paris." I said, “Great, I can't wait!" That night we both went to sleep --not in the hospital-- but in a much better place.

I'm not worried about my mom. I know her world is so much better now. The first thing we did when we got home after my mom died is throw away all of her medication and pain pills because she doesn't need them anymore. As Martin Luther King once said, “Free at Last, Free at Last, Thank God Almighty [She's] Free At Last." My mom is in Heaven now dancing with God, the Saints, her parents, her brothers, sister, niece, nephew, and many others. One day I will be with her. And mom, I am looking forward to our dance. I LOVE YOU!

If you would like to make a contribution to The American Cancer Society in her honor, please log on to *www.cancer.org* or call the American Cancer Society at 1-800-ACS-2345.

Introduction

It's funny how things happen and businesses are created. I started Johnny Jet all for fun. It began by emailing a few of my traveling friends who were not earning the miles and points. We would compete with one another to see who would accrue the most miles. However, I felt like I wasn't a true friend if I didn't help them get the most out of their mileage programs. Besides, I was kicking their butts so badly that there was no way they would catch up! My points accumulated and I had learned a lot while traveling 125,000 miles a year. From reading the Sunday travel sections, to travel magazines and the frequent flier sites, I gained knowledge about traveling. First I started emailing my buddies important numbers and pin numbers so they could earn double or triple miles/points. As the weeks went by, I became more creative with the travel information. Weekly features such as tips, specials, Webcams, a helpful travel Web site of the week, and a story including exotic travel pictures were added. My list of subscribers continued to grow and I would get emails from new people asking to be added to my email list.

When my list grew to about 5,000 names, I decided it was time to create JohnnyJet.com. I felt there were so many helpful and cool sites out there, but not one of them provided all the essential travel information. I had so many travel bookmarks/favorites. I laid them all out and organized them with a couple of friends (Thanks Kevin and Bojan). Then… voila!... The Johnny Jet Portal was born!

JohnnyJet.com is designed to help travelers discover everything about traveling. It doesn't matter if you travel once every five years or if you travel five days a week. It's for everyone! It really is your first stop to travel. My big break came when Laura Bly from USA Today found out about JohnnyJet.com and named it Web site of the week. From that point on, the press wrote about Johnny Jet and it was then featured in over 100 major news organizations including Time, Fortune, Los Angeles Times, New York Times, Washington Post, CNBC and, MSNBC. It's amazing how a personal site has grown as one of the most visited destinations on the Web!

Eventually, I started getting emails from readers around the world who wanted to know if I had a book. I never even thought of writing one until the emails became more frequent. That's where Eric came in. Around the same time, I started to receive many emails, I received a book proposal from Eric and his company, Yahbooks Publishing. I checked out his past books and liked them. I quickly learned that Eric was the savviest Internet guy out there, and he had three books and a weekly newsletter to prove it. What I liked about Eric was his enthusiasm and commitment. With these two positive qualities combined with mine, we could put together the ultimate Internet travel guide for people wanting quick and easy information. That's what we hope you'll find in this book.

We recommend referring to the Johnny Jet Codes listed in this book, while accessing the Johnny Jet Web site. This book was designed as a companion to JohnnyJet.com, to make the site easier to navigate and more beneficial to travelers. So keep it near your computer.

Thanks for you support and we hope you like our hard work! Happy Travels!

Eric and Johnny
Please visit the You Are Here Books site at
www.yahbooks.com

About the Authors

Eric Leebow

Eric Leebow was born in Livingston, New Jersey on November 11, 1977. The numbers, 11/11/77, have always been known to be lucky. Eric's creativity started as a kid trying to use blocks to create buildings.

He is the second of four boys and one sister. He was always motivated by his brothers-- Jonathan, Matthew, and Todd, and his little sister Joni. Eric always worked hard in school and knew he could achieve his goals. He attended Lehigh University and graduated with a Bachelor of Science in Marketing. Throughout his college years, he has found the Internet to be a tremendous learning tool and a great place to surf. After visiting JohnnyJet.com, Eric became fascinated with the site and contacted Johnny about creating a book based on the site.

When Eric is not on the Internet, he enjoys running, basketball, juggling, reading, and art. He is always interested in trying out new things and believes that there is no limit to creativity. Eric resides in Cleveland, Ohio.

John Einar DiScala

John Einar DiScala was born in Norwalk, Connecticut on May 31, 1969, on his grandfather, Einar Hansen's birthday. "When man first landed on the moon on the day of his christening, you knew he was going to be someone special," said his father, Francis J. DiScala Sr., a poet and a criminal trial lawyer. John's dad encouraged him to put his thoughts on paper and helped him learn to read at a young age. He found his most important lesson was being exposed to his mother's love and commitment to family. Although she was once awarded a fellowship to Paris after graduating from Parsons School of Design, Jeanne traded her career as a fashion designer to "design a family." She was the most influential person in John's life, and she possessed an unyielding belief that family and love is paramount.

John is the youngest of four children. Nurtured and pushed by his older siblings, he was surrounded by his sisters, Georgette and Carol, and his brother Frank. Through their circle of friends, he learned to get along well with people of all ages, and made many friends outside of his age group. During his high school years, he lost interest in academics. However, he became interested in education again and attended college. He went from having poor grades in high school to becoming an honor student and Student Body President at Marymount College in Palos Verdes, California. He later transferred to Loyola Marymount where he graduated with a Bachelor of Arts degree in History and excelled in athletics.

Although John travels 150,000 miles a year, traveling didn't always come easy to him. At 18, while at JFK Airport with his mother, he refused to board a plane headed to Australia to visit his sisters. He suddenly became afraid to fly because he had asthma and the doctor put a great fear in him by saying, "The planes are pressurized only to 8,000 feet so you might have a tough time breathing." Three years later, he conquered his fear of flying when he decided to attend college in California. His attitude towards flying changed rapidly. After graduating college, John accepted a job as a recruiter for his alma mater; Marymount College. Due to his job duties, he was required to fly around the country, including 26 states and Hawaii. He soon became impatient with long lines, poor seating, delays and other frequent flying problems. John wanted to find better ways to reduce general misery and uncertainty that often accompanied his travel experience. He noticed that some people never waited in lines and enjoyed great perks like sitting in one of those comfortable seats, eating a gourmet dinner, and having their baggage off the plane first. This is also where he became fascinated with accruing miles and points. He studied these people, read a lot of travel books and magazines. Soon John began to email his circle of friends with what he had learned, along with weekly specials, webcams, the travel news and the coolest travel web sites. Everyone looked forward to receiving John's weekly stories with great traveling pictures.

Johnny Jet was born, a name he acquired as a teenager riding his jet ski (Johnny Jetski) on Long Island Sound. Today, he and JohnnyJet.com have received critical acclaim from various newspapers, magazines, and radio and television personalities, as one of the best travel sites on the Internet. According to MSNBC, "This site should be on every desktop." He resides in Los Angeles with his girlfriend Amber (AKA: Amber Airplane).

Table of Contents

*Denotes Johnny Jet Code

Chapter 1

Steals and Deals on Fares

There are many ways to get deals on fares, you can go the charter flight route, shop at consolidators, be a courier, shop at many of the online sites, try travel auctions, or go straight to the airlines. The end result is getting your ticket. Here you will find the sites that will assist you in getting the best deals on fares.

*Online Flights

Johnny Jet Code: Travel Flights

To get the cheapest fares, shop around. Check all of these Web sites and compare prices. It's recommended that you check the information provided in this chapter first to see about the market, and if you are flexible, check the Travel Auctions chapter. Orbitz, and Qixo are the controversial sites that search multiple companies. Or if you like, you could try downloading Sidestep to do some comparison shopping. Remember, if you book your flight online, print out the confirmation page to keep track of your reservation.

Here are twelve tips on getting low fares on flights for both online and offline:

1. Stay current with the news and newspaper on airfares.
2. Stay over on Saturdays because less business travelers tend to stay on Saturdays, airlines can charge less for tickets when people stay over the weekend.
3. Be flexible with your flight schedule. Tuesdays, Wednesdays, and Saturdays are typically the cheapest days to fly when airports aren't as busy.
4. Consider traveling through a smaller sized airport or at off-peak times.
5. If you can make the late-night flights known as "red-eyes" or take a stop or two, you are likely to get lower fares.
6. It's recommended to ask the airline about package deals in other areas such as rental car or hotel rooms available with your ticket. Sometimes you can get miles by doing this.
7. Check a few Web sites to find lower fares, or use a fare comparison site.
8. Ask about standby fares when flying off-season.
9. You can save by purchasing tickets from consolidators who buy in blocks.
10. Book your flight at least 3-4 weeks in advance.
11. Utilize your frequent flier miles on longer trips.
12. Check out the low fare or budget airlines like Southwest, Jet Blue, Spirit, ATA, and others. These airlines usually have the cheapest fares.

Air Courier Association

http://www.aircourier.org

Airline tickets are costly and Air Courier believes on giving lower ticket prices for its members. Prices are guaranteed to be the lowest, or your money is either refunded or the price is matched.

Air Tech Ltd.

http://www.airtech.com

Air Tech's Flight Pass was designed for people who have flexibility with their travel. Through its unique Flight Pass, it is able to offer budget flight prices to travelers.

Air Fares

http://www.air-fare.com

This site will help you find cruise and air fares throughout major destinations in the U.S. and Canada. Click on a city and find the lowest published airfares between cities.

American Express Travel

http://www.americanexpress.com/travelservices

American Express offers air, car, and hotel reservation resources for the corporate business traveler and personal travel alike. There are some added travel resources here as well.

4 Airlines Tickets

http://www.4airlines.com

Find discount airline tickets, car rental, cruises, and hotel accommodations at this one stop ticket source.

AirTreks.com

http://www.airtreks.com

Specializing in international travel, AirTreks offers excellent prices on traveling around the world. The unique Trip Planner enables you to create a customized itinerary and receive prices on the spot.

Atevo Travel

http://www.atevo.com

Atevo offers full service online booking of air, hotel, car, and cruises along with travel news, a photo gallery, destination recommendations, a guide to U.S. National Parks, a place for you to create your own travel page, e-postcards to send and more.

Tom Parsons' Best Fares

http://www.bestfares.com

Tom Parsons' Best Fares started out as a newsletter in 1982 and ever since it has been offering great fares and travel secrets. A group of over twenty full-time researchers are looking for the best fares for you, and the site offers a variety of travel resources. The magazine has become a well-known name in the travel industry.

Cheap Tickets

http://www.cheaptickets.com

They call it "The Best Kept Secret in Travel." And with a name like "Cheap Tickets" you could only expect to get a discount. The site specializes in discounted airfares, rental cars, hotels, cruises, last minute travel, and specials.

Discount Airfare

http://www.discountairfare.com

These travel agents offer discount fares for international travel, group travel, and identity travel for all age groups.

EconomyTravel.com

http://www.economytravel.com

Traveling internationally doesn't have to be so expensive and Economy Travel, as a consolidator understands this. Specializing in low airfares internationally, you can be sure to find some good deals here. Also offered are European Rail Passes and Travel Insurance.

Flights.com

http://www.flights.com

Flights.com is a leading European travel booking site that provides deals on flights throughout the world.

Expedia Travel

http://www.expedia.com

Expedia offers simple and easy to use one stop shopping for airline tickets, hotels and car reservations, vacation packages, cruises, and more for any traveler who likes the aspect of do-it-yourself travel planning. You'll find maps, driving directions, and other traveler tools here. The site offers 360 degree virtual walking tours of hotels, tourist attractions, and more which can be found in the site map. The "Book Together and Save" feature allows you to arrange ground transportation, hotels, and tickets for your travel itinerary before you choose your flight. You can expect to find a greater quantity of trips offered this way.

FareChase.com

http://www.farechase.com

This site searches fares at over one hundred major travel sites. If your goal is to find some cheap tickets, this may be a good starting point.

FlyCheap.com

http://www.flycheap.com

As part of the My Travel Group, FlyCheap.com offers booking services at the best possible prices. The program searches through dozens of airlines, finding the lowest fares without sacrificing quality seats.

Go-Today.com

http://www.go-today.com

Go-Today and have fun tomorrow at this site that specializes in discount independent last minute getaways and vacation packages to Europe as well as advanced trips. Go-Today also offers family travel packages, themed vacations, and unique tours. Go-Today.com is affiliated with the European Express, www.europeexpress.com that offers more customized European vacations.

Hotwire

http://www.hotwire.com

Hotwire works with major travel partners and caters to the leisure traveler by providing a quick and easy way to get deals on travel with its unique "Hot-Fares" and "Hot-Rates." You can save up to 40% or more with discount airline tickets, hotel reservations, car rentals, and last minute travel deals found at Hotwire. You can expect to pay similar prices to an auction site like Priceline.com, so this could help you in determining bidding amounts, if you choose to go the bidding route.

Lowestfare.com

http://www.lowestfare.com

Get discount fares on vacation packages for leisure travel and business travel alike. Lowestfare.com offers cruises, vacation packages, hotels, car rentals, and special tour packages along with a toll-free customer service line.

OneTravel.com

http://www.onetravel.com

Known for its one stop travel services, offering low prices, and travel advice, OneTravel.com can confirm reservations at worldwide hotels, rent cars, and save on vacation packages. Its unique "White Label" airfares allow you to get low prices on flights without knowing the name of the airline. You can book travel bargains from over 500 airlines, 54,000 hotels, and 48 car rental companies for domestic and global travel.

Orbitz.com

http://www.orbitz.com

This one stop shopping discount travel giant is known to get flights, hotels, car rentals, package deals, and more. It was established by five of the world's leading airlines including: American, Continental, Delta, Northwest, and United. Orbitz.com is keeping the traveler in mind and today you can access over 450 airlines scanning two billion possibilities resulting in some of the lowest airfares on the Internet. If you like, you can look into alternative airports within 25 to 100 miles of your destination.

Qixo.com

http://www.qixo.com

Qixo is an airfare search engine that integrates multiple travel sites in one. Over twenty major travel Web sites are compared at once, and you can choose your price. Although flights may be lower priced, you may expect some stops.

Side Step

http://www.sidestep.com

Side Step is an award-winning and unique low-fare travel tool that you can download and comparison shop for the best travel prices for flights, hotels, and rental cars. In addition to going to sites to check fares, this is a great tool to download.

TravelHero.com

http://www.travelhero.com

This is a full service Internet Travel agency offering discounts on accommodations, air flights, and rental car reservations throughout the world. You'll find the largest database of hotels, motels, bed and breakfasts, and inns on the Internet.

TravelHUB

http://www.travelhub.com

This travel agency directory has hundreds of travel agencies for specialized travel. You'll find worldwide tour packages, a newsletter, ask an expert section, cruise finder, hotel finder, and more.

TravelNow.com

http://www.travelnow.com

Travel Now offers global one stop travel shopping for staying, driving, and flying. There is a large selection of hotels here to choose from and some great savings. One unique feature enables searching by type of jet.

Travelocity.com

http://www.travelocity.com

The Sabre company travel giant has one stop travel shopping for air, car, cruise, hotel and vacation. You'll find maps, a video gallery, and other guides built within making it quite unique with travel planning assistance. For more about Sabre visit *www.sabre.com*.

Trip.com

http://www.trip.com

This premier one stop travel site helps business professionals and leisure travelers alike find some great deals on flights, lodging, cars, vacation packages, and cruises. It offers a variety of other travel resources including a trip coach, maps, flight tracker, and more.

Vacation Together

http://www.vacationtogether.com

Vacation Together provides all accommodations to travelers with a one stop shopping appeal. Vacation packages include leading brand name vacation packagers. Features include email specials, and hot deals, along with around the clock customer service.

*Air Passes

Airpasses.com

http://www.airpasses.com

To see more on Air Passes visit *Johnny Jet Code: Air Passes*

*Charter Flights

For a listing of charter flight sites, check out *Johnny Jet Code: Charter Flights*

*Consolidators

Johnny Jet Code: Consolidator

Consolidators are companies who buy airline tickets in bulk (at wholesale) and sell them below the airline retail prices. You can get great deals especially for last minute travel, round-the-world tickets, taking the whole family, and traveling during the high season (Europe in the summer- Caribbean in the winter). You might not get frequent flyer miles, an advance seat assignment, or a refundable ticket. And it's best to pay with a credit card even if it costs more. For answers to frequently asked questions about consolidators visit *www.travel-library.com/air-travel/consolidators.html*

USACA

http://www.usaca.com

The United States Air Consolidators Association is the national trade association for the air consolidator business.

Pacific Gateway

http://www.pacificgateway.com

With the motto "We Sell the World," Pacific Gateway is a wholesaler of international airline tickets sold to travel agents.

Rebel Tours Consolidator

http://www.rebeltours.com

Since 1975, Rebel Tours has offered low priced tickets on international air consolidation, ground transportation, individual and group tours, ski packages, and hotel accommodations.

Air Plan

http://www.airplan.com

Air Plan is an airline ticket consolidator for discounted international airfares for travel agents. It has contracts for Europe, Asia, Middle East, Australia, New Zealand, and Africa.

Levon Travel

http://www.levontravel.com

Since 1960, Levon has serviced the travel industry providing wholesale fares to travel agencies and retail fares to travelers visiting Europe and the Middle East.

Redwood Sky Tours

http://www.skytours.com

Established in 1977, Redwood Sky Tours is a travel company located in downtown San Rafael a few minutes north of San Francisco. Today it is one of the largest sellers of discounted tickets in California, with a philosophy of exceptional customer care with the best possible price.

Mena Tours

http://www.menatours.net

Mena Tours and Travel was established in Chicago in 1965 and offers a highly trained bilingual staff, providing personalized, affordable, and efficient services to Central and South America and Domestic and International destinations.

Destination Europe Resources

http://www.der.com

DER offers discounts on travel with a selection of over 23 scheduled airlines including every major U.S. gateway to your selected destination.

Dollar Saver Travel

http://www.dstravel.com

Dollar Saver is a consolidator and discount retailer for international flights flying on major airlines worldwide.

Kutrubes Travel

http://www.kutrubestravel.com

If you are looking for an adventurous exotic vacation, Kutrubes Travel offers this kind of trip to many destinations including Albania, Lebanon, Northern Ireland, Russia, Croatia, Macedonia, Bulgaria, Tunisia and South America. Kutrubes specializes in offering low airfares to these destinations.

AESU Discount Fares

http://www.aesu.com

Since 1977, AESU has offered complete services as a travel company. The site presents European tours for those between the ages of 18-35, discount airfares known as price busters from over 200 U.S. cities going to over 180 international cities, and small and large group incentives.

Asia Cheap Fares

http://www.asiacheapfares.com

Specializing in trips to Asia, this site offers lower fares to Asia from around the world.

Kristensen International Travel & Tours, Ltd.

http://www.kitt-travel.com

Since 1985, KITT has been a full-service travel agency with a team of skilled travel professionals, offering travel for corporations, groups, students, and leisure travel.

Azure Travel Bureau Inc.

http://www.azuretravel.com/airticket.htm

Azure provides both international and domestic airfares with major airlines. It specializes in discounts in the international sector, traveling to every major continent.

Holiday Travel International

http://www.holidaytvl.com

Since 1971, Holiday Travel International is a full-service travel agency innovator specializing in leisure, corporate, and wholesale travel.

Travac

http://www.travac.com

Here travel agents will find consolidator fares from the USA to Europe, Africa, Mid East, Mexico, Central and Southern America, and the Pacific and Orient.

Travel Team

http://www.travelteam.com

Travel Team began near the University of Washington campus in 1978. Today it is known as the leading travel agency of Puget Sound, saving you money on your travel destinations. The Travel Team offers specials on all sorts of travel.

D-FW Tours

http://www.dfwtours.com

Established in 1978, D-FW Tours remains one of the largest volume airline consolidators, offering discounts for travel agents and the general public.

Solar Tours

http://www.solartours.com
Solar Tours offers economical and customized vacation packages and air travel for groups going to Latin America, Mexico, and Spain.

Travel Network

http://www.travel-network.com
The Travel Network specializes in discount domestic airfare and discount Mexico and Hawaiian vacations to exotic destinations such as Puerto Vallarta, Cabo San Lucas, and San Jose del Cabo, Mazatlan, Cancun, and more.

*Courier Travel

These companies buy tickets so they can use the cargo space to deliver important packages. The only way they can use the space and not pay astronomical fees is to have someone accompany a shipment. Don't worry, you don't have to carry anything and seldom do you ever touch the packages. A representative from the freight company will meet you at the airport when you arrive and another one will meet you when you land. All you need to do is sign some forms. You're not responsible for the shipment (the airlines know you didn't pack it). These flights are typically used for International flights and depart from major cities. Length of stay varies. These flights aren't just for last minute travel. Although you can book months in advance, the closer to departure will provide you with a cheaper flight. Most of the time you can't check bags and there is only one courier per flight. If you want your companion to go with you, ask if they can book you on a successive courier flight (you will arrive and depart a day apart). For more information on courier travel, you may want to visit the International Association of Air Travel Couriers at *www.courier.org,* the Air Courier Association at *www.aircourier.org* or Courier Travel *www.couriertravel.org*. For more information on couriers, check out *Johnny Jet Code: Courier Travel*

*European Budget Airlines

Johnny Jet Code: Budget Air Euro

Europe By Air

http://www.europebyair.com

Available in different languages, Europe By Air offers Intra-Europe FlightPass connecting 22 individual airline route systems, spanning thirty nations in one European network of more than 150 cities. FlightPass price is $99 per one-way flight to any destination (plus airport tax). It features extensive route network, reservations in advance or on-the-go, no charge for itinerary changes, "open" tickets, no blackout dates, no fare zones, start anywhere, and end anywhere in Europe.

Aero Lloyd

http://www.aerolloyd.de

This German airline provides information on flight news, reservations, and air schedules.

Air Europa

http://www.air-europa.com

This Spanish airline provides domestic and international flight reservations.

Air One

http://www.air-one.it/it

Air One operates in Italy with flights between Rome Fiumicino and Milan Linate.

BMI British Midland

http://www.iflybritishmidland.com

BMI British Midland is a leading UK full service airline with its main operational base at London Heathrow.

Buzz

http://www.buzzaway.com

Buzz offers affordable flights to popular European destinations.

Condor

http://www.condor.de

Condor is a German airline with news and flight offerings.

Easy Jet

http://www.easyjet.com

Available in different languages, Easy Jet is a UK airline offering flights to Europe.

Euro Wings

http://www.eurowings.de

Euro Wings is a German charter airline with news and flight offerings.

Go Fly

http://www.go-fly.com

This UK airline offers low fares from London, Bristol, East Midlands, Belfast and Scotland to various European destinations.

LTU International Airways

http://www.ltu.com

LTU offers a travel guide to Germany along with discount scheduled fares from the United States.

Ryan Air

http://www.ryanair.com

Ryan Air is a London company offering low fares for Irish and European flights.

Sky Ways

http://www.skyways.se

Sky Ways is a Swedish airline flying to destinations in Sweden on smaller airplanes.

Spanair

http://www.spanair.com/es
Spanair offers low airfare in Spain to many destinations including Barcelona and Madrid.

Virgin Express

http://www.virgin-express.com
Virgin Express offers low fares to various destinations in Europe.

Aer Fares

http://aerfares.net
Aer Fares is an advanced search engine for European Budget airlines.

*Late and Last Minute Travel

Johnny Jet Code: Last Minute

Do you have a last minute trip to take? Finding good deals at the last minute isn't always easy, but these sites may come in handy.

11th Hour Vacations

http://www.11thhourvacations.com
It's the 11th hour and you have nowhere to find ticket bargains? With tens of thousands of packages, you may find this site useful when you are looking for a last minute deal on flights, hotels, cruises, or vacation packages within four weeks of the trip.

Last Minute Travel

http://www.lastminutetravel.com
Book last minute, pay less. This site may come in use when you need it and is very good for those who are last minute travelers. You can book a trip within a four week lead time and still get a great deal. Whether you are looking for an extra night at a hotel, a vacation package, or car rentals at the last minute, this site will save you.

Moments-Notice

http://www.moments-notice.com

If you are looking to travel out of the country on a moments notice, this site has plenty of trips available. Becoming a member entitles you to some greater deals on trips to the Caribbean or some deserted island.

Smarter Living

http://www.smarterliving.com

This is a consumer community of budget minded travelers with a weekly newsletter on last minute travel promotions and deals on hotels, car rentals, cruises, and vacation packages. The site includes some great travel tips and articles. You'll find airfares compiled from Expedia, Trip.com, SkyAuction.com, and Hotels.com, in addition to individual airlines and hotels. It provides an email service that will send you email notices customized for your departure city.

Site 59

http://www.site59.com

Looking for a great weekend getaway within fourteen days of the trip? Site 59 offers excellent last minute travel getaway packages. Hotel, flights, and rental cars are combined together; you can save up to 60% here at times. Trips are mostly in the U.S. and the Caribbean. You may see some overlap with Travelocity.com and Orbitz.com since Site59.com provides them with last minute deals. Site 59 is owned by Travelocity.

Travel Zoo

http://www.travelzoo.com/lastminute

Travel Zoo provides a list of random last minute getaways from major cities. Although the selection may be limited, you're likely to find some of the best unexpected deals here.

*London Bucket Shops

Johnny Jet Code: London Bucket

This is a great place to look for fares originating in London. Let's say you want to go from New York to India. You can save a lot of money buying a Round Trip ticket to London, and then buying a ticket from one of these agencies to go to India. You will not only save money but you will be able to break up your trip and stay in London both ways. You can also use these Shops for tickets for inter Europe and Africa.

ATAB Air Travel Advisory Bureau

http://www.atab.co.uk
Since 1982, the Air Travel Advisory Bureau has provided millions of travelers with discount flight fares from all major UK airports.

Cheapflights.com

http://www.cheapflights.com
Since 1996, Cheapflights.com has been a UK travel portal location to find some of the lowest fares in the industry.

TFI Tours

http://www.lowestairprice.com
Founded in 1981, TFI Tours is known for pioneering low cost negotiated fares. Its clients include a variety of travel sites, corporations, travel agencies, tour operators, cruise lines, and other organizations looking for low fares.

Trail Finders

http://www.trailfinders.com
Trail Finders is a well known independent UK travel company known for its custom itineraries and great selection of discounted flights, tours, hotels, insurance, and car hire throughout the world.

Lupus Travel

http://www.lupustravel.com

Since 1983, Lupus Travel has dealt with leisure and holiday travel with a focus on major London West End hotels and local businesses. Lupus Travel offers competitive rates to major suppliers including airlines, hotels, car rental companies, and travel insurance.

Benz Travel

http://www.benztravel.co.uk

Benz Travel specializes in discounted flights on all scheduled airlines to all destinations worldwide including places such as Amsterdam, Paris, Barcelona, Madrid, New York, Chicago, Los Angeles, and more.

Airline Network

http://www.airline-network.co.uk

Airline Network specializes in discounted airfare among other travel including hotels, holiday getaways, car hire, insurance, and cruises.

Travel Scene

http://www.travelscene.co.uk

Travel Scene specializes in city break holidays to Europe and worldwide. The site offers air travel and self-drive breaks and 360-degree virtual city tours.

Charter Flight Center

http://www.charterflights.co.uk

Charter Flight Center specializes in charters from the UK with destinations worldwide. The site offers parking, car hire, insurance, city breaks, charters, and scheduled flights.

*Travel Auctions

Johnny Jet Code: Your Bid

Auction site tips:

Before you start bargain hunting at any travel site, you'll need to research prices on various travel services in order to avoid bidding too high. It's recommended you test the market at traditional online flight sites. Remember, with a lot of these auction sites you can't choose flight times, airline, or how many stops you will have. Also keep in mind, you most likely will not get frequent flyer miles or hotel points. Auctions have strict refund policies where they have you initial a page agreeing to the terms of service. If you have the time, bid in small amounts until the price is right, and so you don't bid too much. You can choose a date, but you may not get the preferred time. Another caveat is that sometimes you will fly a "red-eye" or at odd hours for lower priced fares. For a comprehensive online article on bidding sites, visit www.cnet.com and type in the search "going cheap" for a great feature story with tips on bidding. Good luck bidding!

BidTripper.com Vacation Auctions

http://www.bidtripper.com

Vacation travel auctions and straight purchases of trips, tours, excursions, and package deals can be found here. Read up on some travel reviews, and check out the postcard gallery and send one to a friend.

Bidding For Travel

http://www.biddingfortravel.com

Those interested in strategizing their Priceline.com bidding will find this message board useful. You can research what deals others are getting, post your own and become well informed on the auction side of travel.

EbayTravel.com

http://www.ebay.com/travel

Known for its auctions, Ebay.com has a variety of auctioneers auctioning travel, trips, vacations, and much more.

Bid4Vacations.com

http://www.bid4vacations.com

With many vacant hotel rooms and unfilled cruises, Bid4Vacations.com offers a business-to-consumer vacation auction site where people can purchase vacation packages with great discounts and properties can become more occupied.

Generous Adventures

http://www.generousadventures.com

Generous Adventures is an auction site offering award-winning accommodations, unusual trips and eco tours from around the world. The profits from the auctions benefit different organizations and people around the world.

Sky Auction

http://www.skyauction.com

Here you will find auctions on hotels, tours, cruises, and all-inclusive packaged vacation deals. The company is based on the idea that consumers shouldn't have to pay more than they feel their travel is worth, and that purchasing travel should be easy and exciting.

Priceline.com

http://www.priceline.com

Known as a pioneer in "demand collection," where you can save money as you "name your own price" on airline tickets, hotel rooms, rental cars, and more. You can also find packaged deals to over 1,200 destinations in North America and Europe. Although it boasts you can save as much as 20% lower than competing online travel sites, you may be getting different hotel selections. If you are in the UK, check out www.priceline.co.uk to bid. If you are looking to see some past winning deals won on Priceline.com you may want to check out www.pricelinedeals.com.

*USA Budget Airlines

Johnny Jet Code: Budget Air USA

Air Tran

http://www.airtran.com

Air Tran provides economical air travel throughout the Southeast and Eastern Coast of the United States with most flights connecting in Atlanta.

ATA

http://www.ata.com

American Trans Air has scheduled air flights from Chicago-Midway and Indianapolis International Airport.

Frontier Airlines

http://www.flyfrontier.com

This Western airline services the Denver airport.

Jet Blue

http://www.jetblue.com

Jet Blue was the first budget airline to offer free live satellite television programming in-flight. Jet Blue travels throughout the United States in Airbus A320s. You'll find flights from New York to Las Vegas and California.

Mesa Air Group

http://www.mesa-air.com

Mesa Air Group provides flights throughout Canada and Mexico. In the West and Midwest it is America West Express, and known in the East as US Airways Express.

Pan Am Airways

http://www.flypanam.com

Known as the first American airline to use radio communications, and carry emergency lifesaving equipment, Pan Am is recognized in New England, Canada, Florida, and the Caribbean.

Shuttle America

http://www.shuttleamerica.com

Shuttle America is a regional airport in the Northeastern United States that operates as US Airways Express.

Southwest Airlines

http://www.iflyswa.com

Since 1971, Southwest Airlines has provided short haul air travel throughout the United States.

Spirit Air

http://www.spiritair.com

Spirit Air offers discount rates serving the Eastern United States.

Sun Country

http://www.suncountry.com

Sun Country has a terminal in Minneapolis and offers chartered and scheduled flights to Dallas, Denver, Las Vegas, Laughlin, Los Angeles, Orlando, Phoenix, San Diego, San Francisco, and Seattle.

Chapter 2

Lodging

*Bed and Breakfasts

Johnny Jet Code: BB

A bed and breakfast can be a good alternative to a large commercial hotel chain. Many of them provide more personalized service, and private places to stay. And of course, breakfast is included, and that's where the name began. We have plenty of selections for you.

BB Directory

http://www.bbdirectory.com

Looking for a romantic bed and breakfast? This site lists the bed and breakfasts by state with a picture of the bed and breakfast. Clicking on the picture takes you to a descriptive write up of the bed and breakfast along with specifics such as rates, amenities, minimum stay, and surrounding attractions.

Bed and Breakfast Directory

http://www.bedandbreakfast.com

Thousands of bed and breakfasts can be found here and this site was founded by a bed and breakfast enthusiast. Search by city, map, keywords, and more. Get great gifts for bed and breakfast travelers. Find out which ones are for sale, and more at this comprehensive site.

Best Inns

http://www.bestinns.net

This directory covers bed and breakfasts and inns in the U.S., Canada, Mexico, and the Caribbean. The site includes color pictures, a write up about the inn along with features. There is a great section on recipes, too.

Bed and Breakfast Country Inns List

http://www.bnblist.com

This site is large listing of bed and breakfasts in the U.S. along with a description and a few color pictures. Links for the bed and breakfasts are provided.

BB Online

http://www.bbonline.com

This colorful site informs you of bed and breakfast locations in the U.S., Canada, Mexico, and the Caribbean. Search by specific geographic locations within country or state. Provides color photos, along with a description and recipes.

Educators Bed and Breakfast

http://www.edubabnet.com

This membership site was created for the budget conscious traveler and consists of a private travel network of more than 5,000 educators who share their homes in North America and throughout the world. For a small annual membership and registration fee, you can access these bed and breakfasts.

Go-Native's Guide to Bed & Breakfast and Inns

http://www.go-native.com

Click on one of the 50 states and you are taken to an alphabetical listing of cities with bed and breakfasts and inns within each of the states. A short description of the city, along with address and telephone information on the inn or bed and breakfast is shown.

iLoveInns.com

http://www.iloveinns.com

If you love inns, you will likely love this award-winning site that is a creation of guidebook publisher American Historic Inns. Covering thousands of inns and bed and breakfasts within the U.S., Canada, Puerto Rico, and the Virgin Islands, this is a great starting place for seeing pictures, reviews, and more details.

International Bed and Breakfast

http://www.ibbp.com

Since 1995, International Bed and Breakfasts features bed and breakfasts and inns throughout the United States and internationally around the world. Review a bed and breakfast, see which ones are rated, and find some recipes at this great site.

InnSite: The Internet Directory of Bed & Breakfasts

http://www.innsite.com

This is one of the more interesting directories of bed and breakfasts. Simply choose an activity and you see different bed and breakfasts within proximity of that activity. You can also browse by state, country or keyword. Another plus is that each inn links to a mapping site.

The Inn Keeper Bed & Breakfast finder

http://www.theinnkeeper.com

Search for inns in all 50 states and worldwide at this site. You can search by keyword, amenities, region, association, or by location on the map. See some of the most popular inn hot spots. Check out some of the special packages.

Travel Assist

http://www.travelassist.com

This is a quick directory of links to bed and breakfasts that is categorized by region.

111 Travel Directory

http://www.triple1.com

This site specializes in basic listing of bed and breakfasts and hotels, but there are many different specialized travel resources including car rental, one stop travel booking and more. Check it out.

*Body and Soul

For a listing of lodging satisfying both the body and the soul, check out Johnny Jet Code: Body Soul

*Classic Motels

Here's a list of some of the Classic Motels in America. Check out Johnny Jet Code: Classic Motels

*Condos

Johnny Jet Code: Condos

Condo Saver

http://www.condosaver.com

Looking for a discount on your condo vacation place? Book a condo and see how you can get "more room for your money" on this site. If you have a condo, you can add it to this site.

*Deserted Islands

Have you ever wanted to get away from it all? I mean it all! If you have the money, we have the islands for you!
Check out Johnny Jet Code: Deserted Islands

*Dude Ranches

Johnny Jet Code: Dude Ranch

Horse 101

http://www.horse101.com

This is one of the most comprehensive sites relating to horses. It contains a directory of dude ranches and horse places.

Arizona Dude Ranch Association

http://www.arizonaranches.com

This association includes more traditional to smaller, rural ranches where riding and ranching are the main focus. The site offers extraordinary western lifestyle trips where you can ride with cowboys and cowgirls. Trips are good for corporate retreats, family reunions, and intimate getaways.

Bandera Cowboy Capital

http://www.banderacowboycapital.com

Known as the "Cowboy Capital of the World," Bandera County in Texas offers dude ranching experiences where visitors can enjoy a taste of Old Western lifestyle with a backdrop of the amazing scenery of Texas Hill County.

C Lazy U Ranch

http://www.clazyu.com

Since 1946, the C Lazy U Ranch has offered a family Western hospitality ranching atmosphere. There are plenty of activities for both winter and fall including hiking, riding, fly fishing, tennis, skiing, sleighing, and more.

Colorado Dude and Guest Ranch

http://www.coloradoranch.com

This site offers "Old Western Hospitality" dude ranch vacations for all. There are horses, mountains, activities for kids and families, and more for the entire family to enjoy.

Double JJ Resort

http://www.doublejj.com

The Double JJ is surrounded by a 1,000 acre horse ranch and offers family, adults-only, or business conference packages with horseback riding, golfing, and much more.

Dude Ranch Association

http://www.duderanch.org

Since 1926, the Dude Ranch Association has helped people find vacations pertaining to dude ranches. It provides approved dude ranches in Western states and Canadian provinces. Find a dude ranch by state or province, helpful vacation information, and the latest dude ranch news.

Dude Ranches of North America

http://www.duderanches.com

Here is your resource guide to dude and guest ranches across North America. The site contains hundreds of listings, and you can check out some of your favorites or add your ranch.

Flying L Guest Ranch

http://www.flyingl.com

The Flying L is in the heart of Texas, an hour Northwest of San Antonio, and two hours Southwest of Austin. It offers a variety of activities for the whole family including horseback riding, golf, hiking, and swimming.

Mayan Ranch

http://www.mayanranch.com

The Mayan Dude Ranch is in Bandera, Texas, the "Cowboy Capital of the World." The ranch has picturesque trails with over 340 acres from the lowlands of the Medina River.

Pine Grove Dude Ranch and Resort

http://www.pinegrove-ranch.com

This is a family-owned and operated dude ranch nestled in the Shawangunk Mountains on 600 acres rambling over fields, brooks, and woodlands. In addition to horse riding, there is tennis, archery, horseshoes, ping-pong, bocce, mini golf, basketball, softball, volleyball, and much more.

Rancho de los Caballeros

http://www.sunc.com

Here is a premier historic guest ranch in Arizona. There is a golf club with 20,000 acres or desert trail horseback rides to enjoy. If you like you can lounge in the pool, play tennis, shoot skeet, or enjoy the nature program and watch birds.

Ranch Web

http://www.ranchweb.com

Looking to take a vacation on a ranch? You'll find all sorts of ranches on this site, including: dude, guest, resort, spa, luxury, fly-fishing, and white-water rafting. Make a reservation, get guest reviews, explore interactive maps, find ranches for sale, and more at this comprehensive ranch site.

White Stallion Ranch

http://www.wsranch.com

This ranch in Tucson, Arizona offers old western vacations for the whole family to enjoy. With 3,000 acres of wide-open land at the foot of the Tucson Mountains adjacent to the Saguaro National Park, you'll enjoy western-style horseback riding among its scenic trails.

*Holistic Vacations

http://www.healingchild.com

http://www.hoho.co.uk

http://www.sacredheritage.com

http://www.solunatours.com/st-about.htm

Here you will find some holistic vacations.
Check out Johnny Jet Code: Holistic

*Home Exchanges

Did you know you could swap homes with other families? You can stay for cheap as long as you're willing to open your home.

For a listing of home exchange related sites, check out Johnny Jet Code: Home Exchange

*Hostels

Johnny Jet Code: Hostel Stay

Hostels are unique inexpensive ways of living, as you share space with other guests. Many students travel in this way, but anyone can try it. Similar to a college dorm room with bunk beds, this site will explain where to find them to everything you could want to know about them.

Hostels

http://www.hostels.com

The site includes a message board, stories, hostel news, and articles.

Hostelling International

http://www.hihostels.ca

If you are looking for a hostel in Canada, this is a good place to look.

Hostelling International - American Youth Hostels

http://www.hiayh.org

This directory facilitates finding a youth hostel in the United States and internationally. You'll find programs, ways to give back to the hostels, 360-degree virtual tours of the hostels, and ways to schedule a hostel reservation.

Hostel Watch

http://www.hostelwatch.com

Find some of the best hostels in Europe at this directory, pinpoint them on the map, make a reservation, and access some great hostel resources.

Hostelweb

http://www.hostelweb.com

The American Youth Hostels Western Region focuses on the western United States hostels and is part of the Hostelling International - American Youth Hostels (HI-AYH). This nonprofit organization offers memberships, reservations, and a directory of hostels.

International Youth Hostel Federation

http://www.iyhf.org

Joining this organization entitles you to stay at youth hostels around the world and thousands of other discounts.

*International Hotels

Here's a list of the most popular International Hotel discount brokers.
Check out Johnny Jet Code: International Hotels

*Legendary Hideaways

Have you ever wanted to stay where the rich and famous stay?
Now you can, as we list some of the most legendary hideaways.
Check out Johnny Jet Code: Legendary Hideaways

*Lighthouse Inns

Did you know you could sleep in a lighthouse? Well, now you do!
Check out Johnny Jet Code: Lighthouse

*Lodges in National Parks

Get close to nature. Check out Johnny Jet Code: Lodge Parks

*Resorts

Johnny Jet Code: Resort Travel

Atlantis Paradise Island Resort

http://www.atlantis.com

The Atlantis in Paradise Island, Bahamas is a world renowned beach resort with everything from beach vacationing and water slides, to casino gaming, caving adventures, and sports and recreation facilities.

Beaches Resorts

http://www.beaches.com

Beaches Resorts by Sandals provides some of the most comprehensive all-inclusive resort stays for kids and families, singles, couples, and just about everyone. From gourmet meals, to water sports, spas, and more, there is something for everyone at these Caribbean locations.

Club Med

http://www.clubmed.com

"Hands up, baby hands up, give me your heart." Okay that's the theme song. And here is the site where you can find out about all the Club Med locations. Now you can look online to find your Club Med hot spot, book trip, and get Club Med News. They have great places for family travel, singles, or adults traveling. For Club Med discounts, check out www.clubhandsupdiscounts.com and you could save at least 10% on your Club Med vacation.

Couples Resorts

http://www.couples.com

Couples Resorts offers romantic vacations in Jamaica. It was founded in 1948 as Tower Isle Resort in Ocho Rios and in 1978 it was named Couples. It was the first all-inclusive resort in Jamaica. Resorts are in Ocho Rios and Negril.

Disney Vacation Club-Resorts

http://www.dvc-resorts.com

Disney has some fabulous Vacation Club-Resorts including: Vero Beach, Hilton Head Island, Old Key West, Boardwalk Villas, Villas at Disney's Wilderness Lodge, and Beach Club Villas. You'll find information on membership, the resorts, and how to book your reservation.

Divi Resorts

http://www.diviresorts.com

Divi Resorts are located in the Caribbean on the islands of Aruba, Barbados, Bonaire, Cayman Brac, St. Croix, and St. Maarten. You'll find information on the resorts and casinos, and online reservations.

Resorts and Lodges

http://www.resortsandlodges.com

Here is the definitive directory of resorts online. You can search by location, resort type, or by activity. Each resort is shown with a brief summary describing the resort and a link to the resort's site.

Promo Caribe Mexico

http://www.promocaribe.com

Here you will find travel options in over 50 of the finest resort tourist destinations in Mexico, Cuba, Guatemala, Belize, and the Dominican Republic.

RCI Holiday Network

http://www.rciholidaynetwork.com

This network provides specialty holiday and resort vacation stays throughout the United States and Canada. You can do a Resort Quick Search by specifying the month, location, and length of stay.

Resorts Online

http://www.resortsonline.com

Luxury travelers will find some of the world's top resorts here. Resorts chosen are mostly 4 and 5 star ratings. Simply pick an activity and you will be linked to some of the top resorts.

Resort Source

http://www.resortsource.com

This is a great resource for resort information and unique property information in North America and the Caribbean. The site has listings with photos and videos on accommodations, the rates, and recreational information and meetings held at the resorts.

Sandals Resorts

http://www.sandals.com

Sandals Resorts are award winning and renowned for its luxury resorts and romantic getaways in the Caribbean. Sandals can best be described as "paradise at last," with accommodations which include gourmet dining to diving and golfing. These resorts provide a great getaways providing a beautiful setting on the beach, or resting on a lazy hammock.

Super-Clubs

http://www.superclubs.com

Super Clubs offers what is known as "super inclusive" packages to the Caribbean with everything included in the vacation price at the Breezes Resorts in Jamaica, Curacao, The Bahamas, and Brazil. The resorts provide a Camp Breezes for children.

*Retreats

Johnny Jet Code: Retreats

Find the Divine

http://www.findthedivine.com

If you are looking for a religious retreat, something spiritual, here you will find 1,000 retreats searchable by region, information on the centers, workshops, a spiritual directory, and a retreat listing service.

Retreats International

http://www.retreatsintl.org

At Retreats International, the emphasis is on setting aside enough time for yourself in this busy world. Retreats offered here consist of quiet time to step aside from everyday concerns at an inn-like facility within driving distance from the city.

NARDA Centers

http://www.nardacenters.org

NARDA is a connected network of Christian retreat and educational centers and people who inform, support, and collaborate with the centers.

Our Lady of Florida

http://www.ourladyofflorida.org

Our Lady of Florida offers an ideal setting for retreats seminars, workshops, and conference meetings. The Spiritual Center consists of a peaceful and prayerful environment for those visiting to share the life of the Passionists. It features 75 single rooms, conference rooms, and a fountain garden.

Jesuit Retreat House of Cleveland

http://www.jrh-cleveland.org

The Jesuit Retreat House of Cleveland is for people interested in spending time with their Jesuit faith. With over 100 years, this retreat provides a sacred setting for people in the contemporary Church and society.

Ghost Ranch

http://www.ghostranch.org

Offering guests the best of New Mexico, the Ghost Ranch is own by the Presbyterian Church welcoming people of diverse faiths and racial origins and creating a unique experience for all visitors.

Living Water Retreat Center

http://www.livingwaterretreatcenter.com

In the heart of the desert mountains of Arizona, this retreat is an oasis for relaxing and recharging your life. Living Water is a place where Christians from all denominations can gather and become closer with their faith.

Powell House Quaker House Retreat

http://www.powellhouse.org

This Quaker conference and retreat center hosts adult, family, and youth programs with a mission to foster the spiritual growth of Friends or Quakers and to strengthen the application of the Friends' testimonies in the world.

Camp Kulaqua

http://www.campkulaqua.com

Here you will find Florida Christian retreats for adults, children and youth ages 8-16.

*Set me up in that Hotel

Johnny Jet Code: Hotel Stay

About Hotel Brokers

These companies buy excess inventory in bulk. They get great deals on hotel rooms where you can save up to 70% off! The only kicker is you have to pay for everything upfront, but if you cancel you get refunded for everything but a cancellation fee. If you are certain that you are going, it's a great deal, I use them all the time. However, there is no doubt you need to always research to get the best deals. Check with hotel brokers, individual hotel Web sites, Hotel 800 numbers and call the hotel direct. You cannot guarantee a certain way to get the cheapest rate. It takes time and research to find the best deals. For instance there may be times when the hotel Web site mentions rooms are not available and tells you when you can find room vacancies on the hotel broker sites or just by calling the hotel. Sometimes the hotels rates may be less than the hotel broker rates or vice versa. You may find it helpful to download a program like Travelaxe at www.travelaxe.com to do some comparison shopping of hotels. It's almost a game to find the best deal, and you need to WIN!

About.com Hotels

http://hotels.about.com

What would you like to know about hotels that you don't already know? This site is an excellent gateway to the many hotels worldwide. It provides articles, and a directory of hotel sites, hotel reviews, hotel saving tips, hotel photos, and much more.

Airport Hotel Guide

http://www.airporthotelguide.com

This site will find you a hotel that is near a specific airport.

Asia Travel Hotels

http://www.asiatravel.com

This site specializes in discounts on hotels in Asia. It boasts you can save up to 75% on hotels in Asia. You also may want to check out www.english.ctrip.com.

Hotels with High Speed Internet Access

http://www.expedia.com/wiredhotels

http://www.geektools.com/geektels

More hotels have high speed Internet access, but these sites will make sure for you.

1800 USA Hotels

http://www.1800usahotels.com

Book your hotel and save money with over 15,000 hotels worldwide at this member site. Interesting featured links on the site include: calendar, world clock, weather, currency conversions, travel news, and travel alerts.

American Accommodations Network

http://www.americanhotelnetwork.com

Make a hotel reservation online and get some great rates. This site covers many of the popular city destinations in the United States. One plus is that they carry rooms for sold out dates in many hotels by ordering in advance.

Hip Hotels

http://www.hiphotels.net

This site features links to some of the "hippest" hotels with the latest trends and developments worldwide. If you are into fashion, style, or what's in vogue, this is the site for you.

Hotel Directories and Brokers

http://www.all-hotels.com
http://www.andbook.co.uk
http://www.betterhotelrates.com
http://www.cheapestdeals.com
http://www.bookmyroom.com
http://www.cheapnights.com
http://www.hotelworld.com
http://www.hotels-london.co.uk
http://www.localhotels.com
http://www.lodging.com
http://www.roomsaver.com
http://www.travelweb.com
http://www.turbotrip.com
http://www.worldhotel.com
http://www.quikbook.com

Find hotels and book your stay at hotels around the world at these hotel search engines.

LateRooms.com

http://www.laterooms.com

If you are booking a hotel room at the last minute, this site may come in handy when you need to find a hotel and would like to get excellent savings.

Leading Hotels of the World

http://www.lhw.com

When you have to stay at only the best 5 star luxury hotels, this site certainly proves its point. These hotels have to apply for admissions. So if you are just curious to see where they are or what they look like, head on over to this site. Check for price, availability, and then make your reservation at some of the most extravagant hotels in the world.

Small Luxury Hotels of the World

http://www.slh.com

Looking for a small resort place or a small luxury hotel? This site puts them all in one directory so you can easily get to them.

Travelaxe

http://www.travelaxe.com

This site offers a downloadable application that searches and compares multiple travel Web sites to assist you with finding the lowest hotel rates.

Venere European Hotel Reservations

http://www.venere.com

Booking a hotel, finding a bed and breakfast or lodging in Europe can be fun with this site that offers the most comprehensive European hotel booking online. This site is available in English, Italian, Deutsch, French, and Spanish.

Wotif

http://www.wotif.com

"What if?" This site specializes in booking last minute hotels at a discount in Australia, New Zealand, Asia, Ireland, and Europe. It has expanded to the U.K. and the U.S.

Hotel Motel and Condo Finder

http://www.motels.com

Motels.com is a motel, hotel and condo finder. Search by state, or city. Find low rates, discounts, accessories, and more.

Hotels Online Directory

http://www.hotelsonline.com

This hotels directory consists of direct links to thousands of hotels throughout the world. You'll find featured hotels, deals, discounts, and almost any site for hotels.

Hotel Discounts

http://www.hoteldiscounts.com

Reserving a hotel at the last minute, is possible at this site where you can book a hotel and save up to 70% off domestic and international hotels. The site is so confident about your savings that the rates are guaranteed.

Hotel Guide

http://www.hotelguide.com

This online directory will direct you to booking almost any hotel in any country. With over 65,000 worldwide hotels in its database, you can find hotel locations, and latest rates, amenities, and numerous hotels offering online reservations. There is also a subscription to a hotel discussion newsletter. This site is also available in mobile and PDA versions at http://mobile.hotelguide.com. It's also available in nine different languages.

Hotels.com

http://www.hotels.com

If booking a hotel separately is what you desire, this site is worth a visit. Simply type in your destination and dates of stay, and you will be shown some of the best prices on hotel accommodations. They even guarantee the lowest rates. They are able to do this because hotel rooms are purchased in blocks.

Hotels and Travel on the Net

http://www.hotelstravel.com

Hotels, travel, and rental cars are all here. Book a hotel, a flight, and a car all at once. The travel news section is a plus and so are the hot deals.

Hotel View

http://www.hotelview.com

If you want to watch a video of the hotel room before you stay there, this site provides a search of hotels by name or location.

Octopus Travel

http://www.octopustravel.com

Offering over 15,000 discounted hotels worldwide, this site may save you some time and money when you are traveling internationally.

Places to Stay

http://www.placestostay.com

This site focuses on reservations at various places including romantic bed and breakfasts, unique hotels and resorts.

Trip Advisor

http://www.tripadvisor.com

This site has unbiased reviews of thousands of hotels, resorts, and vacation packages.

World Hotel Reservations

http://www.worldres.com

Make your hotel reservations at this network that connects you to member hotels worldwide.

*Spas, Time to Relax

Johnny Jet Code: Spa Relax

Sometimes you might just like to unwind, relax, and go to a spa that offers massages, facials, or other pampering services. When you travel, this is a great time to do it. A good place to start your search for spas is www.spafinder.com and the others are recommended individual spas to check out. Many spas offer gift certificates that make great gifts, and you can treat yourself with one too.

Canyon Ranch Health Spa and Resort

http://www.canyonranch.com

Since 1979, Canyon Ranch has set the lifestyle standard by offering world-class fitness and wellness programs along with spa pampering, and gourmet dining. Canyon Ranch offers the finest amenities of spa services, fitness and outdoor sports, medical and behavioral services, nutrition consultations and workshops, spiritual pursuits, and gourmet cuisine.

Destination Spa Group

http://www.destinationspagroup.com

The group promotes healthy vacations for self-improvement in the areas of health, fitness, and beauty. Whether you are looking for a massage, bath, weight loss, skin treatment, or other self-pampering, DSG offers it. Visitors can choose from a variety of member spas and gain information having a better overall spa getaway experience.

Golden Door Spa

http://www.goldendoor.com

Health, beauty, mind body, and fitness are the focuses of this Southern California spa. Consisting of a hidden valley surrounded by sun-soaked hills, and organic gardens, this impeccable spa offers week long escapes combining total mind and body rejuvenation with 40 guests each week.

Healing Retreats & Spas Online

http://www.healingretreats.com

This magazine is devoted to providing information on the spa industry along with information on alternative healing and health. You will find a directory of spas in the United States, along with articles.

Miraval Resort

http://www.miravalresort.com

Offering life in balance, Miraval is a luxury resort off Arizona's desert land providing "mindfulness" as a way of life, and promoting health. Miraval offers a variety of activities, pampering guest services, and innovative dining experiences, This is a resort destination where you can connect to life, health, meaning and purpose.

Nemacolin Woodlands Resort and Spa

http://www.nwlr.com

Offering a distinct pampering experience whether it may be in the plush chateau, a rustic lodge, or cozy townhouses, Nemacolin Woodlands possesses elegance, variety, and more in a spa vacation. Whether you are looking for golf or riding as your sport, the Woodlands Spa, provides treatments that will heal your mind, body, and soul.

Resorts to Wellness Escapes

http://www.resortstowellness.com

These escapes promote wellness of the mind, body, and spirit with quality destination spas worldwide. Choose from lifestyle escapes, wellness escapes, or city escapes with a unique all-inclusive package.

Royal Spas of Europe

http://www.royal-spas.com

Known for its spas and meeting the highest quality requirements, this site provides a picturesque description of prominent European spas that have been rich in tradition. Countries covered include: Italy, Spain, Austria, Germany, Great Britain, Hungary, Czech Republic, Greece, and Finland.

About.com Spas

http://www.spas.about.com

What would you like to know about spas that you don't already know? This site is an excellent gateway to the many spas worldwide. It provides articles and a directory of spa sites. Some of the categories include: Top Spas, U.S. Day Spas, Spa News, Spa Bookstore, Aromatherapy, Massage Therapy, Spa Magazines, and much more.

Spa Finder

http://www.spafinder.com

This site is an online magazine for the spa aficionado. With a comprehensive database of spas, spa products, spa consultations and spa reservations and deals, this site is a spa enthusiast's haven.

Spas Only

http://www.spasonly.com

Specializing in spas only, this spa vacation planning site finds some of the best spas in the world. Look for spas by your interest or by destination. If you need help with spa words, you can visit the spa dictionary. It's taking you to some of the finest spas in Italy, France, Switzerland, Germany, Austria, Hungary, U.S., Mexico, and the Caribbean.

Great Spas of the World

http://www.spatime.com

This directory shows you the great spas of the world, and what they offer their customers. Click on a country or a state and you are directed to various spa facilities. Whether you are looking for an individual spa or resort or a group getaway package, you can most likely find something here.

Mario's International Spas and Hotels

http://www.marios-spa.com

Mario's Spa is located throughout the Cleveland, Ohio area and provides a full service spa with everything from facials to pedicures and massages. It also has a hotel in Ohio and an inn located in North Head on Grand Manan Island in New Brunswick, Canada.

Spa View

http://www.spaview.com

Spas in the United States, Caribbean, and Europe are presented on this site. You can book hotel and resort spas online, and take an interactive virtual tour with spa pictures and descriptions.

Spawish

http://www.spawish.com

Would you like to get someone a gift certificate for a spa? This is the site to do it. You can wish someone a happy spa trip here, and get him or her a gift of a massage, or other spa treatment. See which spas offer the spa wish certificates.

The Wyndham Peaks Resort and Spa

http://www.thepeaksresort.com

The Wyndham Peaks Resort Golden Spa is found nestled within 14,000 feet of Rocky Mountain peaks, overlooking the historic Telluride and is surrounded by natural wonders. The spa presents a reviving and life enhancing experience with 40 guests weekly.

The Spas Directory

http://www.thespasdirectory.com

This spa directory finds spas or health resorts within the UK. You can search by region and use the map, or use a more detailed search to find set parameters on your spa interests.

*Time Share

Johnny Jet Code: Time Shares

Here are some definitions to help you understand what time shares are. For more definitions, you can visit *www.timesharetransfers.com* and you will find a dictionary of time share related words.

Timeshare: A unit at a resort that is sold on a week slot of time. Owners pay maintenance fees for yearly upkeep.

Exchange: This is trading an interval week at one resort for an interval week at another resort. Or you can trade for a different week at the home resort. This allows owners to vacation anywhere worldwide.

Exchange Company: A company that facilitates the exchange process between two owners who want to exchange their unit. Owners deposit their unit with the exchange company, which then finds an appropriate match based on availability.

Time Share Users Group

http://www.tug2.net

TUG is a self-help organization composed of timeshare owners and others who are interested in learning about timeshare. The site provides an unbiased resource for consumers on timeshare. There is a section for members with resort reviews and ratings and various classified ads, advice, a top ten resorts section and more.

Time Sharing Today

http://www.timesharing-today.com

This is a magazine that informs consumers about timeshares. It features many classified ads and timeshares available for buying, selling, or renting.

RCI.com

http://www.rci.com

This is the world's largest vacation exchange company. It increases the value of your vacation ownership with more than 3,700 premier resorts worldwide. At this site you can explore the resorts and reap the other benefits of RCI membership.

Interval World International

http://www.intervalworld.com

Here you will find timeshare and exchange travel options throughout the year. As a part of the Quality Exchange Network, Interval International consists of 2,000 resorts and over a million members worldwide.

Marriot Vacation Club International

http://www.vacationclub.com

Known as a premier vacation club, MVCI presents a worldwide list of vacation ownership and rental villas with destinations ranging from Paradise Island to Breckenridge and Disney World. Guests enjoy vacations surrounded by luxuries within escape atmospheres.

Vacation Home Unlimited

http://www.vhurentals.com

This leading home exchange has been offering a variety of quality vacation rentals worldwide. All bookings are made directly with the owners and contacting them is easy within a click of your mouse.

*Vacation Rentals

Johnny Jet Code: Vacation Renting

1st Choice Vacation Rentals

http://www.choice1.com

This is a guide to distinct vacation rentals, time shares, villas, condominiums, ski cabins, and B&Bs worldwide. You can list your property or search for other properties by popular locations and worldwide destinations.

Beach Vacation Rentals

http://www.4beachnuts.com

Specializing in beach rentals, this site has cottages, cabanas on a mountainside, and ocean view rentals for all tastes and beach dwellers.

Beach Houses to Rent

http://www.beachhouse.com

If you ever wanted to live in a beach house, or wanted to rent one for a getaway, this is a site that will assist you with your beach house rental needs.

Cyber Rental Vacation Rentals

http://www.cyberrentals.com

This directory features vacation rentals worldwide. You can search by continent for homes for sale, or add your own rentals. The site has pictures with everything from private homes, and cottages, to condos.

Ebay Real Estate

http://www.ebayrealestate.com

Ebay offers a venue for real estate with many vacation rentals offerings.

GreatRentals.com Vacation Rentals

http://www.greatrentals.com

This venue offers great places to stay in over 50 countries and has a compilation of thousands of vacation rental homes, condos, villas, cabins, B&Bs, and more offerings all listed by their owners. You can select a destination by the map or by clicking on one of the destinations.

Goin 2 Travel

http://www.goin2travel.com

Here you can experience the joy of your own vacation home without ownership costs. This site offers a wide variety of vacation homes, villas, condos and apartments in the world's highly sought after resorts areas.

Holi-Swaps

http://www.holi-swaps.com

Buy, rent, or exchange vacation homes worldwide.

Holiday Bank

http://www.holidaybank.com

Here you can search thousands of holiday properties worldwide and find some of the best villas, cottages, and chalets. Search by destination, activity or accommodations.

Home Exchange

http://www.homeexchange.com

At this site, you can search for homes worldwide from Anguilla to Zambia.

Home Link International

http://www.homelink.org

This is the world's largest home exchange membership organization.

iVacations.com

http://www.ivacation.com

International Vacation Homes is an award-winning site featuring vacation home rentals, villas, condos, time share, and properties for sale. The site is searchable by state, region or country worldwide.

Maverick Real Estate

http://www.maverickrealestate.net

Maverick offers a few distinctive home vacation rentals in Mount Snow, Sugar Bush, and Newport Rhode Island. This site belongs to Johnny Jet's brother.

OceanFrontProperties.com

http://www.oceanfrontproperties.com

Here you will find some of the most pristine oceanfront and beach properties for sale, lease, rent, or exchange around the world. The site includes oceanfront estates, homes, condos, land and businesses for sale, lease, rent, and exchange.

Disney World Vacation Homes

http://www.disneyvacationhomes.com

http://www.familiesfirst.com

http://www.orlandovacationhomes.com

If you are looking for a vacation home near the land of Mickey Mouse, then these are great places to look.

Resort Quest Vacations

http://www.resortquest.com

Since 1998, this site has offered quality online vacation and condominium rentals booking and real estate in various destination resorts.

Stay 4 Free

http://www.stay4free.com

This membership site was made for those who travel much and like to meet people from different countries and cultures. Founded by a group of travelers, you can find addresses of people offering free accommodations throughout the world.

Vacation Rental Managers Association

http://www.vrma.com

This professional trade association for the short-term property management industry offers a vacation rental directory including rental companies in North America offering over 100,000 homes, townhouses, and condos. As a member of the association, the vacation rental company aspires to a code of standards indicating professionalism.

Vacation Spot

http://www.vacationspot.com

In conjunction with Expedia, Vacation Spot offers specialty lodging in condos, villas, inns, and hotel suites worldwide. The site includes photos, descriptions, rates, and bookings for thousands of searchable properties.

Vacation Homes

http://www.vacationhomes.com

At this directory you'll find one of the largest online compilations of privately held rental properties searchable by location. There are over 1,200 vacation destinations with over a million of registered users.

Vacation Rentals by Owner

http://www.vrbo.com

This large vacation rental site has property listings worldwide available throughout the year. Those looking to sell timeshare or other rental properties can visit this site and advertise a single specific time frame. Those looking to buy can search by time share.

10K Vacation Rentals

http://www.10kvacationrentals.com

You will find vacation rentals throughout the world by clicking on the map. Each vacation rental has a short description with pricing and availability. You can also add your own property and vacation rentals and put them up for sale.

Armed Forces Savings Network

http://www.afvclub.com

You will find condo rentals, hotel and airline discounts, car rentals, and more travel deals.

International Chapters Villa-Rentals

http://www.villa-rentals.com

This site specializes in offering quality holiday villa rentals throughout Europe and the Caribbean. It includes over 2000 properties that can be found in the world's most desirable and exotic locations.

Unusual Villa Rentals

http://www.unusualvillarentals.com

If you'd like to rent a castle or an island, then this is the site to visit. It includes rentals of over 3,000 private villas and 30 islands worldwide,

Chapter 3

Ground Transportation

Need a taxi? No need to worry, just find a local taxi company and give them a call. You can also check out all local ground transportation and Greyhound Bus schedules.

*Catch a Train in Time

Johnny Jet Code: Rail Trains

I think taking Amtrak between NY and DC is much more convenient and time efficient than an airline. I also love taking the train in Europe. Check out the schedules and buy your EuroRail passes.

Yahoo! Train Travel

http://dir.yahoo.com/Recreation/Travel/Train_Travel
Yahoo provides a directory listing of a few train travel sites.

The European Railway Server

http://mercurio.iet.unipi.it

http://mercurio.iet.unipi.it/misc/timetabl.html
If you are looking for information on the European railways, this is one site that will tell you about it.

MTA Metro-North Railroad Schedules Long Island and Connecticut

http://www.mta.nyc.ny.us/lirr/html/ttn/lirrtt.htm

http://www.mta.nyc.ny.us/mnr/html/planning/schedules/sched_form.cfm

Whether you are looking for Long Island train schedules or Connecticut train schedules East of the Hudson River, you can find them at this site.

American Orient Express

http://www.americanorientexpress.com

At American Orient Express you will find week long deluxe vintage luxury train trips throughout the United States and transcontinental U.S. and Canada. These scenic trips are taken through cultural experiences, exploring history, wildlife, and geography guided by experts and guest lecturers through parks such as Yellowstone and Grand Teton.

Amtrak Trains

http://www.amtrak.com

Amtrak is a leading rail service that offers a satisfaction guarantee on your train trip. At the site you can plan your trip and find out where you would like to go on an Amtrak train, and check out the schedules.

Bay Area Rapid Transit

http://www.bart.gov

If you are traveling in the San Francisco Bay Area, this is the train you will ride. The site offers a schedule, tickets, rider's guides, news, and more.

Blue Train

http://www.bluetrain.co.za

The Blue Train is perhaps the most luxurious train in South Africa and the world combined with the luxuries of the world's leading hotels providing an elegant experience for both recreational and business travel.

Cape Cod Central Railroad

http://www.capetrain.com

Taking a scenic rail trip excursion along Cape Cod Bay is what this site offers. Whether you are looking for a train trip with dinner, lunch, or for a special occasion, you can find it when you are in Cape Cod.

Eurail

http://www.eurail.com

This community started as a joint venture of European railroad companies and European shipping lines. It now offers Eurail Passes and Eurail tickets, which makes many train travel experiences in Europe. The site offers news, train info, and tickets and passes purchasing information.

Europe Rail International

http://www.europrail.net

This is a North American source for Eurorail and Eurail passes providing you a site to find fares, schedules, a European rail trip planner, and maps of the European rails.

Eurostar

http://www.eurostar.com

Looking to travel from London to Paris or London to Brussels? The Eurostar offers a modern day train experience that will take you there within a few hours. Eurostar remains a leader in train travel in Europe.

Transport for London

http://www.londontransport.co.uk

Transport for London is one of the largest transportation systems in the world. Whether you are traveling by bus, tram, or river, this site provides tourist information, interactive maps, ticket rates, and more.

Massachusetts Bay Transportation Authority

http://www.mbta.com

The MBTA provides schedules and route maps of rapid transit and bus services. You can shop for passes, and read the latest transit news.

Orient Express Trains

http://www.orient-expresstrains.com

For years, the Orient Express Trains have offered travelers luxury train trips around the world. It's known for their historic passage from London through Paris to Venice. Places traveled include: South Pacific Australia, Asia, UK, and Continental Europe.

Paris Metro Le Metropolitan

http://www.paris.org/Metro

Would you like to know more about the Metro in Paris? If so, here you will find line maps of the Metro and bus routes, history, and a few other links.

Rail Europe

http://www.raileurope.com

Those looking to ride the rails in Europe will find some great information on the European railways here. Rail Europe is committed to offering Eurail, Europass, France Rail and British Rail fares and schedules.

Europe by Eurail

http://www.railpass.com

You can order rail passes to Europe and Britain. The site offers other guides as well as maps.

Rail Connection

http://www.railconnection.com

Here you will find one-stop shopping for European rail passes. With its unique conductor service RailConnection.com will help you decide on which passes are best for you to get based on your trip and passes are delivered to you within a couple of business days.

Rail Serve

http://www.railserve.com

This comprehensive railroad directory has a mission to "provide the world with the best resource for finding rail-related content on the Internet." Whatever you are looking for related to the railroad is likely to be found on this site.

Rail Travel Center

http://www.railtravelcenter.com

Specializing in scenic train tours in the United States, Canada, Mexico, and Europe, the Rail Travel Center offers some of the most unique train touring trips for railroad fans. Check out some of the photos of these trains and it is likely you would want to go on one of them.

Rick Steve's Guide to European Rail Pass

http://www.ricksteves.com/rail

Rick Steve's guide features some of the basics to rail passes. How do rail passes work, itinerary planning, choosing your rail pass, how to order, and using your rail pass are all explained.

Rocky Mountaineer Railtours

http://www.rkymtnrail.com

Take a luxury rail tour on the Rocky Mountaineer and experience the greatness of the Canadian Rockies. The site explains the various tours that can be taken in either small or large groups. Everything from history to scenery can be seen here.

Subway Navigator

http://www.subwaynavigator.com

You will find direct access to the world's subways with maps, general information on the Official Transport Authority, a route finder, and more.

Grand Canyon Railway and Resort

http://www.thetrain.com

Hop about and view the scenic Grand Canyon by rail. This historic train goes through Ponderosa forests, desert plains, and it eventually takes you to the canyon. Check out the great history of the great Grand Canyon Railway, view packages, tour specials, and watch a video clip.

Great Little Trains of Wales

http://www.greatlittletrainsofwales.co.uk

Take a train tour of Wales and see some of the best scenery in the British Isles. Each train is an old steam train with plenty of polished paintwork and brass.

The Tube

http://www.thetube.com

The Tube is the home of the London Underground railway. The site contains history, a journey planner, online tickets, maps of rail travel, and live updates. If you are going out, you will find the event information quite helpful as it shows you the closest station to the events.

Train Italy

http://www.trenitalia.com

Looking to catch a train in Italy? This train may take you to Florence or Rome and tickets, news, and information can be found online.

Trains on the Web

http://www.trainweb.com

This is where you look to find trains on the Web. In addition to a rail Web directory, you'll find travel and passenger info on where to locate a rail car, photos of trains, forums, industry news, and more about the railroads in the United States and worldwide.

Adventures by Rail

http://www.trippexplorer.com

Tripp Explorer takes first class rail travelers all over the world to some of the best rail traveling places. Take a nostalgic journey and explore Dickens Christmas, ride in the sky through Copper Canyon, explore Europe, Britain, Germany, and more while riding on the train.

VIA Rail Canada

http://www.viarail.ca

Riding the railways in Canada is easy with this site. Whether traveling as a family, student, senior, for business, or adventure and leisure, VIA Rail Canada has something for you. Plan your journey, learn about the trains, and get relevant train travel information at this Canadian railway.

Virgin Trains

http://www.virgintrains.co.uk

This UK train operator operates West Coast Trains and Cross Country Trains. Traveling from London Euston to the West Midlands, the North West, North Wales, and Scotland, you can be sure to find a train when visiting the UK. You can get your tickets online.

*Gas it Up

Johnny Jet Code: Get Gas

Before you plan a road trip, it's a good idea to check out the gas station locations and current gas prices.

Fuel Gauge Report

http://www.fuelgaugereport.com
Find out the national unleaded fuel average prices for the current day, yesterday, a month ago, and a year ago.

Gas Price Watch

http://www.gaspricewatch.com
Do you want to find the lowest prices on gas in your neighborhood? Visit this site and you will know where to get your gas deals before filling up.

Gas Wars Online

http://www.gaswars.com
Looking for the lowest fuel prices? Gas wars Online is where you can voice your knowledge about the best prices for gas.

*Gas Stations

http://www.arco.com
http://www.bp.com
http://www.chevron.com/prodserv/map/locator
http://www.citgo.com
http://www.hess.com
http://www.localshell.com
http://www.exxon.com
http://www.mobil.com
http://www.marathon.com
http://www.phillips66.com
http://www.texaco.com
http://www.unocal.com
Here are some known gas stations you may stop at along the way during a road trip. *Johnny Jet Code: Gas Stations*

*Rental Cars

Johnny Jet Code: Rent Cars

Hawaiian Riders

http://www.hawaiianriders.com

While you are in Hawaii, you can rent some luxury roadsters, motorcycles, and more. Car rentals include exotic cars like Ferrari, Porsche, and Vipers. You can rent Harleys, Jeeps, beach gear, and more.

Harleys

http://www.harleys.com

Rent a Harley motorcycle or scooter on some of the islands in Hawaii, including Kona and the Big Island.

Breezenet's Rental Car Guide

http://www.bnm.com

http://www.rentalcarguide.com

Looking for a rental car? This award-winning site allows you to compare rental car rates and make a reservation for a rental car. Find discounts, SUV/Van rentals, luxury rentals, where to rent a car if you are under 25, rental car tips, and luxury and exotic rentals.

Manual of Traffic Signs

http://www.members.aol.com/rcmoeur/signman.html

http://www.mto.gov.on.ca/english/traveller/signs

Hopefully, you know what these signs mean if you are a driver, but these sites do a good job of explaining them with pictures.

Ride Board

http://www.rideboard.com

Need a ride? If so, check out this board where road travelers can match up with rides. You can easily search for a ride or post your own ride.

*Road Trips

Johnny Jet Code: Hit the Road

DriveinMovie.com Drive-in Movie Theatres

http://www.driveinmovie.com

DriveinMovie.com is dedicated to the culture, history, preservation and promotion of Drive-in theatres. Drive-in theatres offer a nostalgic alternative and a good deal on movies. This site is a directory of Drive-in movie theatres in the United States and throughout the world.

4 Road Trips

http://www.4roadtrips.4anything.com

The 4 Anything Network brings us their road trip section. You'll find a lot of road travel related resources. Site includes: U.S. Highways and Byways, Roadside attractions, Maps and Road Reports, Hitchhiking, Car Games, and more.

Historic Route 66

http://www.historic66.com

This is the oldest site on route 66. Find out what's happening on route 66, get the facts, read some books and maps, check out the photo gallery, watch some movies on the route, and more about the famous route 66.

I-95 Guide

http://www.usastar.com/i95/homepage.htm

This site is a comprehensive guide for interstate-95 travelers. It covers Florida to Maine with information on exit services, rest areas, attractions, road construction, weather, gas, and more.

Roadside America

http://www.roadsideamerica.com

This is your online guide to offbeat tourist attractions. If you are a tourist or just planning a road trip, this is one site that you should check out to find some unique touring ideas. There is an electric map that will guide you to the great roadside attractions.

Roadside Peek

http://www.roadsidepeek.com

Take a peek of what roadside attractions can be found on the side of the road. You'll see nostalgic architecture, automobile drive ins, old motels and hotels, gas stations, and other road side tourist attractions. This site is filled with great pictures.

World's Largest Roadside Attractions

http://www.wlra.us

Think big before visiting this unique site where you will find the largest sightseeing attractions throughout the world. You will be amazed at what you see. See the largest catsup bottle, the largest shoe, the largest airplane, the largest flag, and many more.

Road Trip America

http://www.roadtripamerica.com

The philosophy here is that "Life is a journey. Take the Scenic route!" At this travelogue, you will find updates on road trips. There is a forum where road trippers can discuss road trips, road trip resources, stories, photos, maps, a collection of weird road signs, and more.

Road Trip USA

http://www.roadtripusa.com

This site gives you a map of the USA and covers basic information about the various routes in the USA. It's also available in a book series format.

Route 66

http://www.route66.com

Enjoy the route before you take it. Here you will find what's happening on route 66, where to stay, and general points of interest before you drive.

Route 66 Magazine

http://www.route66magazine.com

The official magazine for the route is great way to enjoy the route and stay current on what's new.

The Mother Road

http://www.themotherroad.com
Here you can take a tour of route 66, then and now.

SmarTraveler

http://www.smartraveler.com
What's the traffic like on the road? Here you will find up to the minute traffic reports for a handful of major cities in the U.S. Information on weather conditions and construction is also available.

Traffic.com

http://www.traffic.com
Click on one of the major U.S. cities and find out about the traffic. Whether you are in New York, Chicago, Detroit, Phoenix, Philadelphia, or one of the others, you can visually picture the traffic.

Internet Traffic Report

http://www.internettrafficreport.com
You've seen the traffic on the road, now how is the traffic on the information superhighway? Check it out.

*RVing and Camping in Style

RVs or Recreational Vehicles are designed for recreational as in camping. They are usually equipped with living quarters to make traveling fun and easy. This section you will find all the sites you will need to make your trip across the country or the next town a breeze.

4 Camping

http://www.4camping.com
The 4 Anything Network brings us their camping section. You'll find a bunch of travel and backpacking related resources. Site includes: Resource for campers and backpackers, organizations, equipment, and gear.

Campsites 411

http://www.campsites411.com

Looking for a campsite in the U.S. or Canada? This site can help you find a campground, RV Parks, camping resources, and more. There is tourism info, camping resources, classified ads, and travel articles for the well prepared camper.

American Camping Association

http://www.acacamps.org

The ACA is an online community of camp professionals devoted to enriching the lives of children and adults through camping experiences in the United States. You'll find a huge database of accredited camps along with resources for camp counselors, directors, and staff.

Camping World

http://www.campingworld.com

Shopping for RV parts and accessories is easy at this site that has almost everything imaginable for an RV. You'll find on-the-road gear to systems, upkeep, interiors, and more.

Camping and Campground Reservation

http://www.reserveamerica.com

This site offers a reservation service for camping and campgrounds.

Cruise America: RV Rentals

http://www.cruiseamerica.com

Looking to rent or buy an RV? With over 150 Cruise America rental centers in the United States, Canada, and Alaska, you will most likely find something here.

Destiny RV

http://www.destinyrv.com

Going RVing? Begin your journey by clicking on the road signs and plan a trip to some of the most popular RV resorts. You can tour RV spots in Vegas, Anaheim, Colorado River, Phoenix, and Dallas.

Campgrounds and Trailer Parks in Canada

http://www.myvacationguide.com

Finding a campground or trailer park is easy at this comprehensive picturesque directory. This site covers all provinces of Canada including: Alberta, British Columbia, Manitoba, New Brunswick, Newfoundland & Labrador, Nova Scotia, Ontario, Prince Edward Island, Québec, and Saskatchewan.

Go Camping America

http://www.gocampingamerica.com

The official site of the National Association of RV Parks provides a directory of RV parks and campgrounds. The search options are easy with a clickable map of the U.S. and Canada, state and province search, park search, and more advanced search options. Each state or province has some information on parks and some have trivia and facts. Check out the message board and the camper travel tips.

Free Camp Grounds

http://www.freecampgrounds.com

This site offers information on free RV parks and campgrounds in the American West. It is also a printed book.

KOA: Campgrounds of America

http://www.koa.com

KOA has been in the camping business for years, offering camping getaways in safe, clean, and fun environments. KOA has campgrounds throughout the U.S., Canada, Japan, and Mexico.

Mountain Travel Sobek

http://www.mtsobek.com

With many years of travel adventures, you'll find travel adventures are plentiful at this adventure company's site that offers many different customized and private worldwide adventure trips including: camping, backpacking, climbing, safaris, and more.

National Recreation Reservation Service (NRRS)

http://www.reserveusa.com

You can reserve your place at over 49,500 campsites. This service is provided by the Corps of Engineers and USDA Forest Service. The state site is organized in camping and cabins.

New RVer

http://www.newrver.com

If you are new to RVing you will find this site very useful. It contains a guide with reviews to RV specific magazines, provides articles, great advice, and much more for the beginner.

Go RVing

http://www.gorving.com

The Go RVing Coalition was created in 1994 and consists of RV manufacturers, suppliers of accessories, dealers, and campgrounds. The coalition provides the general public with information on the benefits of RV travel. You'll find out why you should be RVing.

RV USA

http://www.rvusa.com

This is the largest online portal for RV and motor home related information. You'll find manufactures, dealers, parts and accessories, rentals, a classifieds section, and much more.

RV America

http://www.rvamerica.com

Here is a complete directory of RV related information. Find associations, dealers, manufacturers, chat rooms, and message boards.

RV Bookshelf

http://www.rvbookshelf.com

You will find books, magazines, camping guides, and more for the RVer.

RV Site

http://www.rvsite.com

The RV Site is a portal for Camping and RV information. If you are looking for phone numbers, addresses and Web resources for campgrounds, RV dealers and manufacturers, RV Clubs, National Park reservations, Tourism Bureaus, Road Services, and more, this is one comprehensive resource.

RV Zone

http://www.rvzone.com

This Internet camping guide is a basic directory of RV rentals, RV clubs, dealers, manufacturers, campgrounds and resorts, and more for the RV enthusiast.

Trailer Life Directory Online

http://www.tldirectory.com

Specializing in campground and RV information the Trailer Life Directory has an online version of its popular print edition. The site offers facts and travel tidbits, state trivia, scenic byways and highways, tourism hotlines and much more. Great products for the RV traveler offered on the site include: directories, magazines, books and more.

USA Camp Sites

http://www.usacampsites.com

Where are all the camp sites in the USA? This site provides the most comprehensive list of campgrounds in the U.S. Click on a state and start camping.

Woodall's

http://www.woodalls.com

This publisher has presented complete information about campgrounds since 1935. There is a searchable database of campgrounds, RV parks, and outdoor activities. Whether you are looking for tenting or want to know a little more about RVs, Woodall's explains it.

*Taxis, Limos, and Buses

Johnny Jet Code: Ground Transport

AAA Foundation for Traffic Safety

http://www.aaafoundation.org

This non-profit, publicly supported charitable research organization is dedicated to keeping people safe on the highways, saving lives, and reducing injuries by preventing crashes. Since 1947 the AAA Foundation has developed road safety educational materials for drivers and pedestrians.

American Public Transportation Association

http://www.apta.com

The APTA is a site to find the latest information on public transportation, including press releases, government legislation, statistics, publications, and membership services. For information on the United States Bus Transit Systems with 200 or more buses visit www.apta.com/sites/transus/bus.htm and you will be directly linked to the bus sites.

Association for Safe International Road Travel

http://www.asirt.org

ASIRT was established after the tragic death of a medical student in a bus accident while traveling abroad. Today it educates the public about the risks involved with international road travel. You will find travel news, reports, tips, and more about keeping safe when traveling. There are some staggering statistics to see also.

Airport Service

http://www.airportservice.com

The Worldwide Airport Limousine Directory is a directory for limousine transportation to and from airports. You can select the location of the airport you are traveling to or from and then find a transportation company within the area.

Bureau of Transportation Department

http://www.bts.gov

The BTS site provides statistics on transportation.

Bus About in Europe

http://www.busabout.com

Bus throughout Europe with scheduled hop on and off bus transportation linking from major European cities.

Big Bus Company

http://www.bigbus.co.uk

You'll find sight seeing tours of London with over 80 traditional London double-decker open-top sight seeing buses.

GoByCoach.com

http://www.gobycoach.com

GoByCoach.com provides booking services for National Express, Eurolines, and European flight link coach and bus transportation services.

American Bus Association

http://www.buses.org

The ABA is a trade association for the bus industry, representing the motorcoach industry, and facilitating the relationship between the motorcoach and tour companies in North America. Members include motorcoach operators, tour operators, companies in the travel industry, and associates.

Busses on the Web

http://www.busweb.com

This site is a directory of buses, coaches and motorcoach starting pages on the Web. If there is something you didn't already know about buses or bus companies you can find it on this site.

Canadian Automobile Association

http://www.caa.ca

Similar to the AAA, the CAA provides travelers with emergency road services. Other services include travel tips, travel agencies, maps, tour books, weather forecasts, highway conditions, and more.

Coach USA

http://www.coachusa.com

If you are looking for bus ground transportation, you may find your nearest Coach bus to fulfill that need. Coach offers charter bus tours, airport shuttles, sightseeing and group tours, taxi services, and more.

U.S. Department of Transportation

http://www.dot.gov

This is the main governing body for transportation in the United States. You will find information on customer satisfaction, national traffic and road closure, and more. Since 1967, their mission has been to "serve the United States by ensuring a fast, safe, efficient, accessible and convenient transportation system that meets our vital national interests and enhances the quality of life of the American people, today and into the future."

Insurance Institute for Highway Safety

http://www.hwysafety.org

This site is dedicated to automobile safety. Features include the crash-test dummies, car recalls news, and automobile safety technology. You will also find information on child seats, teen and senior drivers. For vehicle crash tests check out http://www.hwy.org/vehicle_ratings/ratings.htm. You will see vehicle crash test ratings.

National Highway Traffic Safety Administration

http://www.nhtsa.gov

This site provides everything you can imagine about car safety. This site starts with popular topics such as airbags and safety belts, to passenger safety and crash test statistics. Read the latest news on safety issues and new safety laws.

National Transportation Safety Board

http://www.ntsb.gov

The NTSB is an independent Federal agency that investigates civil aviation accidents in the U.S. and significant accidents in other forms of transportation.

Cartalk Got A Car?

http://cartalk.cars.com/Got-A-Car

Your famous radio car talk guys are talking about cars online. Before you take your next road trip and want to travel, this would be a good site. From car safety to traveling in your car is all on this site. Get your questions answered before you leave for that long road trip.

Gray Line Worldwide

http://www.grayline.com

Gray Line is a tour operator that offers sightseeing tour packages to over 150 destinations, charter services, airport shuttle transfers, and convention services on six continents. Tours can be booked online.

Greyhound Lines, Inc.

http://www.greyhound.com

Known as the largest provider of intercity bus transportation, this site serves thousands of destinations throughout the world. The site provides bus fares, schedules, and ticketing information. Travel planning, tours and charters, information for students, seniors, and more about traveling on a bus.

Horizon Tours

http://www.horizonsbuses.com

Located in Florida, Alliance Motor Coaches offers charter bus transportation. The buses are equipped with air conditioning, a P.A. system, audio and video stereo equipment.

1-800-TAXICAB

http://www.1800taxicab.com

This is the North American taxicab network. You can call the number or check out the site about 1-800-TAXICAB.

Limos.com Limousine Search Directory

http://www.limos.com

Finding a limo is easy with this directory. Just click on where you are, the type of limo service, and when you are going and it will bring up different limo companies. You can request a quote online, too. Other sites within the same network consist of *www.limousinesonline.com* and *www.limo-search.com*.

Motorcoach Tours Directory

http://www.motorcoach.com

This site provides consumer protection tips for chartering a motorcoach, and a national directory of motorcoach tour operators and affiliates.

Connecticut Limo

http://www.ctlimo.com

Since 1960, Connecticut Limo has provided scheduled airport transportation to Bradley International, Newark International, John F. Kennedy, and LaGuardia airports.

New York Airport Limos

http://www.jerusalemcar.com

http://www.carmelcarservice.com

http://www.telavivlimo.com

At these New York limousine services you will find reasonable rates on transportation.

Airport Shuttle New Orleans

http://www.airportshuttleneworleans.com

The shuttle makes an easier commute to your destination from Louis Armstrong International Airport.

Mears Transportation

http://www.mearstransportation.com

Since 1939, Mears has provided ground transportation in Florida. Vehicles include buses, taxicabs, shuttle vans, Lincoln Town cars and stretch limos.

Oakland International Airport Shuttles

http://www.flyoakland.com/shuttles.shtml

You will find a listing of shuttle services commuting from the Oakland International Airport.

Prime Time Shuttle

http://www.primetimeshuttle.com

Prime Time has shuttle services in California and Connecticut, serving airport commuters in the Ground Net nationwide network of quality airport transportation.

Super Shuttles International

http://www.supershuttle.com

Throughout the United States, Super Shuttles provide door-to-door airport ground transportation at major airports. At this site, you can make online reservations and find out about fares.

Trailways Transportation Systems

http://www.trailways.com

Serving Travelers since 1936, this franchise organization is comprised of independent transportation companies that serve as tour and charter tour operators. They provide shuttle, transit on ground, air, rail, and sea.

Traveling America

http://www.travelingamerica.com

This is the only company in the United States that offers fully coordinated driving trips for independent travelers. Traveling America has done the research for you by fully researching the various road destinations.

Urban Ride

http://www.urbanride.com

Urban Ride provides chauffeured luxury sedan and limousine services throughout the world. The company offers corporate, group event, road, and ground transportation along with quality transportation services in many cities worldwide.

Chapter 4

Boat Travel

Want to get away and see multiple places without packing and unpacking? Well, then take a cruise! We have every cruise line listed and other methods of traveling by boat, such as Ferry's, Yachts, Barges, Canalling and much more...

*Barges

Did you know about the world of luxury through hotel barging? Expect to be pampered as you glide through rivers on these 5 star barges. *Check out Johnny Jet Code: Barges*

*Boating and Sailing Away

Johnny Jet Code: Boat Rides

1800 Sailaway Yacht Charters

http://www.1800sailaway.com

This award winning site and company has been sailing away since 1976 and has provided on the water travel a pleasurable experience. Choose to go on a chartered powered or sail yacht to the Bahamas, Caribbean, Mediterranean, or South Pacific with or without the crew.

*Boating Magazines

http://www.boatbiz.com
http://www.boatingworldonline.com
http://www.floridasportsman.com
http://www.goboatingamerica.com
http://www.motorboatingandsailing.com
http://www.saltwatersportsman.com
http://www.soundingsonline.com

Here are some boating magazines including Boating Industry, Boating World, Florida Sportsman, Go Boating and Sea, Motorboats & Sailing, Saltwater Sportsman, and Soundings. *Johnny Jet Code: Boating Magazines*

Charter a Boat

http://www.charteraboat.com

Olson Nautical Charters will take you on boats to the Caribbean, Virgin Islands, and the Mediterranean. Boats available are sailboats, catamarans, and motor powered yachts. Whether you are looking for a skipper, your own bareboat tour of the ocean or to take a captain-guided tour, you can find it on this site.

Caribbean Yacht Vacations

http://www.whidbey.com/cyv

CYV offers both privately crewed and bareboat sailing on yacht charters. This main site leads you to other catalog brochure sites that show in detail some of the yachts, along with pictures and itineraries.

H2O Performance Boats

http://www.h2operformance.com

Are you looking to buy or sell a performance boat? H2O Performance makes buying and selling performance boats easy. Find out what's hot in performance boating, enter the boating forum, and get the latest performance boat news and see a calendar, at this great performance boat marketing site.

Paradise Adventures and Cruises

http://www.paradiseadventures.com.au

Established in 1977, Paradise Adventures and Cruises is a tour and yacht wholesaler and broker in Sydney, Australia. Offering personalized service, and trips to ocean destinations such as sailing in the Mediterranean, Caribbean, and Indian Ocean. Also offers other trips, including romantic getaways, motor yacht trips, and more.

Sailing Point

http://www.sailingpoint.com

Whether you are looking for a yacht to charter or a boat to buy, this site presents you with the best. This convenient site offers a one stop shop for sailing yachts, news, and information for sailors.

Ship Guide

http://www.shipguide.com

Since 1992, this guide has provided delivery and contact information within the container ship industry. Today, it has all the North American and European container ship schedules and various international schedules.

Sunsail Worldwide Sailing Holidays

http://www.sunsail.com

Sunsail provides a variety of sailing and water sport holidays in countries throughout the world. From yacht charters, sailing vacations, yachts for sale, water sporting, clubs, and corporate sailing, this site offers plenty of sailing opportunities and vacations for the sailing enthusiast and beginning sailor alike.

*Boating Safety

Johnny Jet Code: Boat Safe

Office of Boating Safety

http://www.uscgboating.org

The mission of the Office of Boating Safety is to reduce fatalities, personal injuries, and property damage involving recreational boats and to improve boating safety while encouraging the development and enjoyment of all U.S. waters.

Boat Safe

http://www.boatsafe.com

Here is a nationally approved online boating safety course. It includes boating tips, boating quizzes, a section for kids, and more.

United States Coast Guard

http://www.uscg.mil

This is the official site of the U.S. Coast Guard, a federal agency that is a part of the Department of Transportation, serving the waterways as a national defense role. To search for vessels you can visit http://psix.uscg.mil/psix2/vesselsearch.asp and you can search by vessel name, number, flag, service, or year.

United States Power Squadrons

http://www.usps.org

The USPS was established in 1914 as a non-profit educational organization devoted to making boating safer and more enjoyable by teaching classes in seamanship, navigation and related subjects.

*Canal Boating

Johnny Jet Code: Canal Boater

Britain Afloat

http://www.britain-afloat.com

If you are going to Britain and floating away on a canal boat is something you hope to do, this site offers a variety of different canal boat getaways for the holidays in the UK.

Canalia.com

http://www.canalia.com

This online magazine is dedicated to Britain's historic canals and waterways. You will find listings of canal holidays, boats for sales, books on the canals, events, stoppages, and more.

European Water Ways

http://www.europeanwaterways.com

Floating Country Inns offers canal and luxury cruises on the rivers in Burgundy, Loire Valley, and Provence areas of France. The site also explores England and Ireland. Find out more about the company at www.ewaterways.com.

H2O France and Barging Vacations

http://www.h2ofrance.com

http://www.barginginfrance.com

Barging and canalling in France could be quite an experience at these sites that offer trips to cruise the waterways of Europe. See the different types of boats, and marinas, and learn about the canal system in France and Continental Europe.

*Cruise Lines

Major Cruise lines

http://www.carnival.com

http://www.celebritycruises.com

http://www.costacruises.com

http://www.crystalcruises.com

http://www.cunardline.com

http://www.disneycruise.com

http://www.hollandamerica.com

http://www.ncl.com

http://www.orientlines.com

http://www.princess.com

http://www.regalcruises.com

http://www.royalcarribean.com

http://www.royalolympiccruises.com

http://www.rssc.com

http://www.seabourn.com

http://www.silversea.com

These are some of the larger and more known cruise lines. Included: Carnival, Celebrity, Crystal, Cunard, Disney, Holland America, Norwegian, Orient Lines, Princess, Regal, Royal Olympic, Radisson Seven Seas, Seabourn, and Silver Sea. If you don't see one listed, that you are looking for, you may want to check out *www.cruisepage.com* which links to almost every cruise line in the world. *Johnny Jet Code: Cruise Lines*

*International Ferry Schedules

Find out the international ferry schedules, including ferries of the British Isles, Mediterranean, and Scandinavia.

Check out: Johnny Jet Code: International Ferries

*Just Cruise It

Johnny Jet Code: Just Cruising

Looking to go on a cruise? We have every cruise Web site, phone number, reviews, and discount brokers. You can also check out the history and the cleanliness of the ship. We also have small charters and barges too.

About.com Cruises

http://www.cruises.about.com

What would you like to know about cruises that you don't already know? Find it here, including: cruise lines, destinations, cruise shopping, cruise jobs, cruise cams, cruising with kids, and more for the cruiser.

7 Blue Seas

http://www.7blueseas.com

At 7 Blue Seas, you can find some of the latest and greatest deals on cruise lines at this musically enhanced and picturesque site. There is information for first time cruisers, cruising with kids, finding a cruise, and the best cruises. Cruise lines include: Carnival, Celebrity, Crystal, Disney, Holland America, Norwegian, Princess, and Royal Caribbean.

Tips on taking a cruise

1. Plan your cruise with a company that specializes in cruises and you are more likely to get a better deal on your cruise vacation.
2. Decide where you want to cruise and from what port. Some cruises are seasonal so plan ahead. For instance, Alaskan cruises deport during the summer, as well as many European cruises. Cruise trips through the Panama Canal embark in the fall and spring.
3. Plan the onboard and off board activities that interest you before you set sail
4. Decide on a large or small cruise. A larger cruise can be more entertaining, yet a small cruise may offer more personalized services.
5. Book ahead, the earlier you book, the greater discount you may receive.
6. Inquire about what age group will go on the cruise. This will give you an idea about your fellow passengers.
7. Choose a cruise where you feel comfortable about the attire. While some cruises require formal dress and business attires for dinners, others allow for casual dress.
8. Pack light and bring along all your necessary toiletries.

All Cruise

http://www.allcruise.com

Discounting everything that sales, this travel agency site offers a variety of different cruises. Lines include: Crystal, Carnival, Celebrity, Cunard, Holland America, Princess, Seven Seas, and Royal Caribbean.

All Cruise Auction

http://www.allcruiseauction.com

All Cruise Auction is the first name in cruise auctions on the Web. You may be able to find some of the best cruise deals on this auction site. Bidding on a cruise is a little different from purchasing a cruise, but there could be some challenges as more people bid on a particular cruise. The top 10 list provides some of the more popular auctions.

American Safari Cruises

http://www.amsafari.com

American Safari Cruises specializes in intimate, active, deluxe cruises on four yachts to Alaska, Mexico's Sea of Cortes, Belize, and Costa Rica. The itineraries are focused on viewing wildlife, fine dining, and various activities including kayaking, beachcombing, hiking, snorkeling, sailing and motorized inflatable rafts.

Cruise.com

http://www.cruise.com

A subsidiary of Omega World Travel, Inc. this site is a popular destination for discount deals on cruises providing discounts for 2 for 1 or great deals on cruises. Linking you to ship reviews, this site offers an abundance of cruises. Another plus is the low price guarantee where you can counter match advertised cruise prices.

Cruise2.com

http://www.cruise2.com

Cruise2.com is the largest non-profit cruise portal on the Web created for those who love to cruise. You will find ship reviews and ratings, sample menus, cruise agents, and much more at this comprehensive cruise site.

Cruise411.com

http://www.cruise411.com

Cruise411.com offers a large database of every major cruise line with search capabilities that include side-by-side comparisons of the cruise. You can search for last minute cruise deals, or view pictures and deck plans. Check out Cruise Buzz to find out the latest news on cruises and see a comparison of special interest cruises like Art History, Golf, and Wine Lectures. Travel info will keep you updated with trip info, weather, and more. A plus is the low price guarantee. Check out www.cruise-news.com to see some of the latest news powered by Cruise411.com.

Cruise Mates

http://www.cruisemates.com

This magazine on cruises is independently operated and has an unbiased Web site dedicated to the cruise enthusiast. You'll find cruise critiques, cruise ship news and information, advice on cruising, and more on getting the best deals on cruise trips. Participate in a cruise message board and chat with fellow cruisers at this online meeting place.

Cruise Net Golden Bear Travel

http://www.cruisenet.com

Golden Bear Travel is a wholly owned subsidiary of American Express. Cruises offered here include extended world cruises typically longer cruise trips around three to four months in length. They also offer shorter Mariner Club cruises.

Cruise Opinion

http://www.cruiseopinion.com

Cruise Opinion is one of the top places to go and find opinions and reviews on cruises. Submit your own review and read reviews on different cruise lines.

Cruise @ddicts

http://www.cruise-addicts.com

Those addicted to cruising will find this site helpful. It features the latest cruise news, cruise ship reviews, a message board, photos and postcards, Web resources, and much more.

Cruise Critic

http://www.cruisecritic.com

This community of cruise lovers contains an online guide to most of your cruise traveling needs along with cruise ship reviews, message boards, weekly cruise bargains, the latest cruise industry news, trip planning, a reader's poll on cruises, and more.

Cruise Diva Linda Coffman's Cruise Planner

http://www.cruisediva.com

Linda is a freelance cruise travel writer or "cruise-aholic" who provides a wide variety of resources on cruise travel. She provides a cruise newsletter, helpful cruise packing tips, reviews and information on cruise lines, a cruise diary, and much more.

Cruise Reviews

http://www.cruisereviews.com

These cruise ship reviews are written by passengers and separated by cruise line and each individual cruise ship. These reviews are based on personal cruising experiences and are available for search by destination.

Internet Cruise Travel Network

http://www.cruisetravel.com

Specializing in luxury cruise travel, this highly regarded online agency will help you pick your ideal cruise. Whether you are looking for suites, cruise specials, or ship itineraries, this site is here to help you find it. Create your own ideal cruise profile and go from there.

Cruise Lines International Association

http://www.cruising.org

CLIA was created in 1975 and it provides a forum for companies who market cruise and passenger lines in North America, so that they can meet, discuss, and raise awareness about the cruise experience. As a cruise consumer, you can find a cruise line, locate a cruise expert, find cruises for special interest, and get the latest cruise news.

Expedition Cruises

http://www.expeditioncruises.com

Expedition Cruises offers unbiased comparisons of different cruise destinations in Antarctica, Arctic, Latin America, Galapagos, Baja, and Alaska.

All Aboard Cruise Center

http://www.cruisingfun.com

All Aboard has agents that specialize in cruises and helps clients find the right cruise based on your interests and budget. Service is fully customized to match your cruising needs. The site takes you to the latest cruising news, Webcams from cruises, and more to make the most of your cruise.

Charter Network

http://www.charternet.com

This is a directory of charter companies. There are fishing charters, sailing charters, diving charters, yacht charters, charter brokers, marinas, yacht clubs, schools and lessons, and places to stay here.

Cruise Direct

http://www.cruisedirect.com

Cruise Direct provides online cruise reservations and information on major cruise lines, with information on pricing, schedules, and availability.

Cruise Week News

http://www.cruise-week.com

Get the latest breaking news on the cruise industry emailed or faxed to you from this site. You can also find archived copies of the newsletter on the site.

Cruise West

http://www.cruisewest.com

This cruise line specializes in small-ship cruises with destinations to Alaska, Canada's Inside Passage, California's Wine Country, and Columbia and Snake River.

Peter Dielmann Cruises

http://www.deilmann-cruises.com

Deilmann Cruises specialize in four and five star deluxe European river cruise vacations. With a group of different cruises on both rivers and oceans, you have a variety of different choices. The site includes tour packages and a news section.

Expedition Trips

http://www.expeditiontrips.com

Here is your small cruise ship expert tourist site that offers trips to Alaska, Antarctica, the Galapagos, and Baja. Expedition leaders are naturalists and the company is a member of the ecotourism society.

Freighter World Cruises

http://www.freighterworld.com

You'll find a different kind of cruising experience on a freighter ship. Freighter boats may not be the most exciting travel, yet they offer an informal and casual, but unpopulated surrounding. The only scheduled activity is mealtimes.

Lake Champlain Ferries

http://www.ferries.com

Lake Champlain is considered the "sixth great lake" next to HOMES (Huron, Ontario, Michigan, Erie, and Superior). Take a ferry or a cruise at this site that offers specialty cruises and charters through the convenient ferry crossings between Vermont and New York. The site has the history of Lake Champlain, and a visit to the Breakwater Café & Grille may be worthwhile.

Get Cruising Directory

http://www.getcruising.com

This directory will take you to a variety of different boating opportunities. See some cruise line comparisons with statistics, ferries, barges, charters, and much more. Check out the forum and the early cruise liners.

Glacier Bay Tours

http://www.glacierbaytours.com

You are probably thinking that this site will bring you a cold cruise visiting Alaska. However, visiting this site does offer some great photos, videos, and more that explain Glacier Bay's small ship cruising options. See humpback whales, glacier calving, and kayaking up north. Check out the guestbook and the fascinating photos.

icruise.com

http://www.icruise.com

This is a cruise search engine portal. So, if you cruise you may want to check this one out first. It leads the Internet in cruise vacation travel. The site includes a comprehensive database of cruise ships, great deals on selected vacations, along with a price-engine comparison of the best fares on the Web. Get the inside scoop on adventure, luxury, discount, and river cruises. Find out why cruising is great, read some articles, and get answers to your questions, and more.

Porthole Cruise Magazine

http://www.porthole.com

This magazine features vacationing tips, cruise trips, shopping, traveling, boating, and more at this online version of this top cruising information magazine.

Sea Letter Cruise Magazine

http://www.sealetter.com

This monthly cruise magazine specializes in the leisure and luxury cruise market, as it focuses on cruise reviews, cruise ships, cruise ports, cruise specials, shore excursions, and more. The articles are written by its readers and cruise enthusiasts alike.

Ship Stats

http://www.shipstats.com

Compare up to three different ship stats side by side. Stats include: sanitation, attire, cruise size, year refurbished, speed tipping, babysitting, beauty salon, and much more.

Small Ship Cruises

http://www.smallshipcruises.com

This is the "biggest website in the world on small ships." There are less than 500 hundred travelers aboard. However, if you are looking for a cruise with 5 to 500 travelers, it can also be found on this site. Search by cruise line or destination and check out the weekly deals.

Spirit Cruises

http://www.spiritcruises.com

Offering dinner cruises in Boston, Chicago, New Jersey, New York, Norfolk, D.C. Seattle, Richmond, and Philadelphia, Spirit Cruises has become an entertaining time for lunch and dinner.

The Cruise Outlet

http://www.thecruiseoutlet.com

This award winning cruise travel agency site may have the answers to your cruising needs. Expert cruisers, help you find cruise travel for the family or group, whether you are looking for theme cruises or business cruises. An incentive program is offered along with price guarantee. There are some great cruise travel tips, too.

World Explorer Cruises

http://www.wecruise.com

Since 1978, World Explorer Cruises has offered leisure travelers voyages of discovery and educational programs aboard ship in Alaska and Central America.

Windjammer Barefoot Cruises

http://www.windjammer.com

Sail away with Windjammer on a unique barefoot cruising experience in tall sail boats. You can catch a breeze at this site that is enjoyable to view as it could be a relaxing and enjoyable experience. Different from a motor yacht, you will find yourself cruising to Anguilla, St. John, St. Kitts, Martinique, Tobago, St. Vincent, and more. Be sure to check out the unique theme cruises.

Windstar Cruises

http://www.windstarcruises.com

Small Caribbean, European, and Polynesian cruises don't get much more luxurious than Windstar. This uniquely designed travel site takes you 180 degrees from the ordinary offering streaming videos. View excellent photos of the sailing yachts and take a look at the itineraries that take you from places like The Keys to the Bahamas to New Zealand.

Yahoo! Vacation Store

http://www.yahoovacationstore.com

Yahoo! Travel offers a great portal for cruises on this site. Whether you would like to browse by cruise line or shop by destination, it can be found on this site.

*Ports

Here is a list of the most popular ports in the United States. Find all kinds of info about a particular port. Check out Johnny Jet Code: Ports

*U.S. Ferry Schedules

For more information on international ferry schedules in the United States check out Johnny Jet Code: US Ferries

*Whale Watching

Johnny Jet Code: Whale Watchers

Anytime Charters Juneau Sports Fishing

http://www.1alaskafishing.com

If you are looking to whale watch in Alaska, this is a good starting place. This Alaska charter specializes in sport fishing and whale watching, and sightseeing in small group trips.

Mosquito Fleet-Seattle

http://www.whalewatching.com

This leading wildlife adventure company specializes in whale watching of orca whales. Tours create a memorable, educational, and safe whale experience and are naturalist-guided in the San Juan Islands, Puget Sound, and Seattle. The site also includes limited season gray whale tours.

Cape Cod Whale Watching

http://www.whalewatchingplymouth.com

Capt. John Boats offers an unforgettable Cape Cod and Stellwagen Bank whale watching experience. Some of the whales you will encounter include the Humpback Whale, Finback Whale, Minke Whale, Right Whale and Pilot whale, dolphins, porpoises, and seals.

Nova Scotia Whale Watching

http://www.novascotiawhalewatching.com

Lunenberg Whale Watching Tours provides an unmatched whale and ocean adventure off Nova Scotia's southern coast. Tours are typically three-hours in length, and depart four times daily. The site includes a photo gallery, and online booking info.

Seasmoke Whale Watching

http://www.seaorca.com

Since 1986 Seasmoke Whale Watching has provided personal and quality tours on the waters where the orca or killer whales reside in Johnstone Strait near Alert Bay and Telegraph Cove, providing some of the finest whale watching.

Sea World

http://www.seaworld.com

Sometimes you don't have to go to the ocean to watch the whales, but rather visit your closest Sea World theme park in Texas, California, or Florida. You can also watch a Shamu Whale Adventure at www.shamu.com.

Whale Net

http://www.whalenet.net

This site provides almost everything you would want to know about whales and information on whale watching. The site includes Whale Net Tours, information on how to find whales, questions for scientists, and much more.

*Yacht Charters

Now you know where to find the places to book a chartered yacht.
Check out Johnny Jet Code: Yacht Charter

Chapter 5

Outdoors and Adventures

Are you an outdoors traveler? If so, this chapter will entice you. We have everything from African Safaris, Bird Watching, Hiking, Camping, Rock Climbing, and even extreme sports like parachuting. You name it! If you like the outdoors, we have it here!

Outdoors

*Back Packing

Would you like to climb and hike with everything on your back?
Check out: Johnny Jet Code: Back Packer

*Bird Watchers

Johnny Jet Code: Bird Watcher

National Audubon Society

http://www.audubon.org
It's the National Audubon Society's mission is to conserve natural ecosystems, but a main part of it focuses on birds. Visit the "Watch List" to see species of birds that need our help in preservation. Find the latest news on the national campaigns here. Check out the travel section where you'll find worldwide Audubon Nature Odysseys.

Aves Travel

http://www.angelfire.com/biz/Avestravel

Birdwatchers looking for a tour operator specializing in bird watching will find these Ecuadorian bird watching experiences fascinating. The site has pictures of birds that you could click on to learn more information.

Big Bird Search

http://www.bigbirdsearch.com

This is a specific search engine for parrots and pet birds. If you have a particular feathered friend in mind, type its name in and click to find the information about it. A listing of resources will pop up and you can go to various sites. That exotic bird may be easier to find after all.

Birding.com

http://www.birding.com

If you ever wanted to know about birding, this site is your answer. Comprehensive resources include: birding for beginners, photos, identifying birds, products for bird watchers, a listing of the top birding places, and more.

Bird Tours

http://www.birdtours.co.uk

Where are the bird tours happening online? At this site you will find thousands of tours for bird aficionados. Spanning the continents, birdwatchers are reporting their birding experiences on this site. You'll find plenty of great bird books showcased here.

Bird Watching

http://www.birdwatching.com

Birdwatchers looking for software, videos, and books related to birds will like the offerings on this site. You will find information on birds, and bird sporting, along with birding tips, and frequently asked questions for bird watchers. There is also a selection of bird gifts here to check out.

Bird Watching Australia

http://www.birdwatching-australia.com

There are plenty of rainforest birds in Australia. The site is designed with a variety of birds from the Australian rainforests. Click on a bird and get a larger picture with more detailed information on it. You will find different bird watching resources as well.

Bird Studies of Canada

http://www.bsc-eoc.org

This non-profit organization is devoted to conservation and preserving wild birds and their habitats. There are plenty of other bird resources linked from this site, as well as the latest news on various programs.

Canadian Wild Bird Adventures

http://www.canadawildbirdwatching.com

Bird watchers looking to take a personalized guided bird watching adventure in Canada will find this site most interesting. Get a quick overview of the birds and see what bird watching vacations are offered in the Lake of the Woods.

Eagle-Eye Tours

http://www.eagle-eye.com

This site specializes in offering birding and nature tours throughout the world. Each tour has a page description along with tour dates, a trip report, and various bird sightings. Tours are typically a week to three weeks in length and cover the Americas, Mexico, the Caribbean, Africa, Europe, and Asia.

Fat Birder

http://www.fatbirder.com

This comprehensive birder directory caters to bird watching enthusiasts with links to birders all over. The site includes information on bird watching trip reports, guides, books, tours, clubs, facts on birds, and much more.

Wings Bird Watching Tours

http://www.wingsbirds.com

Fly away with wings on this site that contains a collection of worldwide bird watching tours. These trips are for the avid bird watcher, and are typically a week or two in length.

Project Bird Watch

http://www.projectbirdwatch.org

The project supports community conservation of birds and the natural world. The site offers a great variety of bird news, photos, and sounds. Ecotourism travels consist of bird watching trips that promote conservation in lands such as Bali, Indonesia, and New Guinea.

Surf Birds

http://www.surfbirds.com

A group of birding friends from Britain and America created this unique birding site that presents bird news articles, resources for birders, pictures, identification articles, trip reports, bird email postcards, and more at this great place for all bird enthusiasts.

*Camping Out

For more information on camping check out Johnny Jet Code: Go Camping

* Earth Friendly Tourism

Johnny Jet Code: Eco Tourism

Earthwatch Institute

http://www.earthwatch.org

Earthwatch's mission is to promote conservations of our natural resources by creating partnerships between scientists, educators, and the general public. For the traveler, they offer expeditions where you can go on an adventure and help make a difference with the research scientists. An Earthwatch expedition is different from a tour, but it is quite interesting.

Eco Travel Center

http://www.ecotour.org

Learn everything you would ever want to know about eco-travel and exploring conservation-oriented places. Destinations include communities in Bolivia, Brazil, Ghana, Guatemala, Indonesia, Mexico, and Panama.

Ecotravel.com

http://www.ecotravel.com

Ecotravel.com was founded by four friends who are passionate about nature based travel and preservation. At Ecotravel.com you will find some of the most environmentally friendly vacations in the EcoDirectory which contains a list of tour operators who specifically cater to the earth conscious traveler. You can then select your trip based on the location and activities offered. There are a variety of articles, a trip-planning guide with a packing list, to do lists, and a destination guide.

The International Ecotourism Society

http://www.ecotourism.org

This Society provides you with information on ecotourism and resources for the ecotourism professional. Find out more about this society and responsible travel to natural areas that conserves the environment and sustains the well-being of local people. It provides news, tour operators, and Web resources to conservation organizations.

Escape Artist

http://www.escapeartist.com

This site shows you how to restart your life in another country. Look for international real estate, learn about investing offshore, find out more about living and working in a particular country, and more at this site that offers references and helps you escape abroad.

Geographia

http://www.geographia.com

Increase your knowledge on various destinations throughout the world. Find out more about the history and culture while you virtually explore Africa, Asia, Caribbean, Europe, and Latin America. If you would like to know why you should go there, what accommodations are available, and where to go, this is one site that will help show you the way.

Green Travel

http://www.green-travel.com

Environmentally speaking, "green travel" is traveling that is good for our environment and nature. This site has an ecotourism theme that takes you to other environmentally responsible links focusing on traveling throughout Africa, Asia, Europe, and North America.

World Wildlife Fund Travel Program

http://www.worldwildlife.org/travel

The World Wildlife Fund takes you to some of the best places on Earth to see wildlife in its natural setting. Tours are adventurous and conservationist oriented. Each tour includes an expert tour guide. With over 200 destinations, this site is a great place for the ecotourism enthusiast.

InfoHub.com

http://www.infohub.com

InfoHub.com is a specialty travel guide that contains the largest selection of vacations with over 11,000 unique vacation opportunities listed, and guarantees the lowest price. Click on a category of interest or a destination of choice. Vacationers could now fulfill that dream of going wherever they want.

Planeta.com

http://www.planeta.com

You can join in online forums and conferences at this information clearinghouse for practical ecotourism throughout the world. Travel expert, Ron Mader focuses on environmental news and practical touring around the world. This site contains excellent resources on Latin America, including cybercafes, sports, study abroad, and more.

Journey File Travelogues

http://www.journeyfile.com

At Journey File you can read about and post your own personal journey experiences. Find out what others have to say about different destinations and more at this travelogue site.

Post Cards From America

http://www.postcardsfrom.com

How nice would it be to get a travel postcard sent directly to your email box? This site does just that, representing all 50 states. A couple actually quit their jobs, got an RV, and explored their dreams when they took pictures of the United States. It's quite an interesting story, and they have a fascinating diary as well. This is one of the most amazing postcard gallery travelogues online.

Our Trip Around the World

http://www.ourtrip.com

Joe and Cara put their careers on hold and took a trip around the world. It is documented on this travelogue site. Throughout the U.S. they traveled in a Volkswagen Eurovan, and throughout the world they traveled by planes, trains, buses, and by foot.

Terraquest

http://www.terraquest.com

Take a virtual expedition to Antarctic and the Galapagos at this award-winning design site. Explore the history, science, and ecology of Antarctica. See the wildlife, learn about the history and take a virtual reality tour of the Galapagos at this travelogue.

Rick Steves' Europe Through the Back Door

http://www.ricksteves.com

Rick has an adventurous site for you that will take you from A to Z when it comes to traveling in Europe. From tips to trips, it's here at this excellent site.

Travel Adventures: Around the World in 80 Clicks

http://www.traveladventures.org

Visiting this site will make you feel as though you have seen the world on one page. From the homepage you are led to all the continents and countries. Read travel stories by Boris Kester and look at some of the pictures of places he has visited. See how many clicks it takes you to make it around the world.

*Great Outdoors

Johnny Jet Code: Great Outdoors

Adventure Sports Online

http://www.adventuresports.com

Looking for outfitters and tour guides for your next adventure trip is easy with this site. It provides event calendars and downloadable applications. From someone new to the sport or an advanced performer, this site provides valuable resources whether you are biking, climbing, hiking, fishing, skiing, kayaking, canoeing, rafting, and more.

How to See the World

http://www.artoftravel.com

How to See the World is a travelogue presented in 25 chapters, or about 100,000 words, and 120 illustrations, this online book by John Gregory explains how you can see the world on $25 a day or less. It contains tips, personal experiences, and humor that will enlighten any traveler's day.

Backpack Europe on a Budget

http://www.backpackeurope.com

Going to Europe and backpacking doesn't have to be expensive, and this one time student created this site to explain how you can do it. You'll find backpack tips and hostelling information, along with information on the different kinds of transportations. There are plenty of Web related resources linked from this great site.

CampNet America

http://www.campnetamerica.com

This online camping library provides a database of campgrounds, travel clubs, RV suppliers, camping rentals, and resources.

Cave Directory of the United States

http://www.goodearthgraphics.com/showcave.html

This site is a complete directory to caves open to the U.S. public. It has cave photography tips and a virtual cave.

Cave Diving

http://www.cavediving.com

Combine caving and diving and get cave diving at this site where you can find out how to enjoy the underwater caves. Explore the breathtaking labyrinths of Mexico's Yucatan Peninsula. Each cave diving trip is lead by experienced group leaders and guides.

Gordon's Guide

http://www.gordonsguide.com

Specializing in outdoor adventures, this lively portal connects you to a variety of different activities. You'll find whale watching, skiing, kayaking, trekking, outdoor family travel, and more. There are some featured adventures and an excellent collection of Web resources. The printed Gordon's Guides are also available here.

GORP

http://www.gorp.com

The award-winning Great Outdoor Recreation Pages provide a portal where anybody can find something related to outdoor recreation and travel. Search by destination, activity, gear, or just come to this site to plan your trip. If you are looking for highly rated places in recreational travel, then you will find a wealth of information. Whether you are looking for some of the best skiing, hiking, or biking, the GORP has it.

Green Tortoise Adventure Travel

http://www.greentortoise.com

Take a 2 to 14 day bargain tour aboard sleeper coach buses throughout North and Central America with a group of adventure travelers. Each day, you will encounter another activity which will start with swimming, and continue with cave exploration, mountain climbing, whitewater rafting, scenic outlook views, in town tourism, forest meandering, building campfires, cooking meals, and more.

iExplore Adventure Travel

http://www.iexplore.com

In association with National Geographic, iExplore is an award-winning site offering over 3,000 trips worldwide from over 130 tour operators. It is a world leader in traveling off-the-beaten-path and adventurous outdoor travels with an emphasis on ecotourism, experiential trips, and more to offer the complete traveler. If you would like expert advice before you travel to anywhere from Australia or Zimbabwe, iExplore offers that as well as video clips to watch before you journey. In addition to the great services, iExplore offers various products and travel gear.

Backpack the Old Continent of Europe

http://www.oldcontinent.com

This site offers backpacking and budget travel information for travelers to Europe who would like to know about hostels and the European train system. You'll find info on lodging, flying, train schedules, tips, articles, a FAQ, and more Web resources on backpacking in Europe.

Cool Trails

http://www.cooltrails.com

This outdoor recreation site is 100% hiker-written with information on Pacific Northwest backcountry destinations. It is the site's mission is to increase hikers' enjoyment of the Northwest by sharing information on various destinations and hiker-created trip reports.

RecWorld Directory

http://www.recworld.com

This is an outdoor recreation directory of tour operators. It caters to the hunting trekker, fisherman, ecotourism traveler, and sea kayaking adventurous traveler type. If you are the rough outdoors traveler, then this site is for you. Check out the articles and explore the recreational world online.

Serious Sports

http://www.serioussports.com

Here is a great resource for top gear, adventure sports guides, serious sport schools, and more. Whether you are hang gliding, paragliding, skydiving, rock climbing, or mountaineering, you will likely find it here.

TheBackPacker.com

http://www.thebackpacker.com

If you are backpacking, this all-inclusive hiking and backpacking site is a great resource for you. You'll find articles, information for beginners, trails throughout the United States, some excellent pictures, and much more at this comprehensive backpacking resource.

The Backpacker Network

http://www.thebackpacker.net

This is resource is for new back packers and budget minded back packers alike. It contains a hostel database throughout Europe as well as other resources, travel tips, and a beer index.

Trails.com

http://www.trails.com

Finding a particular trail is quite easy here. Whether you are looking for hiking, mountain biking, skiing, or any other trail, it can be found on this site. Select an activity and find it among thousands of trails.

Wildernet

http://www.wildernet.com

At this directory, you can search for recreational activities in the U.S. Search for activities or by location. Whether you are looking for camping, hiking, fishing, backpacking, biking, climbing, or rafting, there is something here for your outdoor recreational needs. Through their mountain encyclopedia, you can check out www.peakware.com.

World Surface

http://www.worldsurface.com

Backpackers and independent travelers will find their niche on this site. They can explore the planet, read travel stories, travelogues, trip reviews, and more. There is a travel shop, news on tourism, and many places to explore. Becoming a member entitles you to write to other members.

*Great Safaris

Johnny Jet Code: Great Safaris

Abercrombie & Kent Luxury and Adventure Travel

http://www.abercrombiekent.com

Abercrombie & Kent specializes in luxury and adventure travel vacations. Take a hike up Kilimanjaro or exploring the Galapagos are options. It started as a safari company in Nairobi, Kenya, and now offers over one hundred destinations on every continent where you can take unique tours based on your activity interests.

Africa Adventure Consultants

http://www.adventuresinafrica.com

Here the consultants help you customize your travel experience in Africa when you go visit places in Eastern and Southern Africa. Places including: Tanzania, Kenya, Botswana, Namibia, Malawa, and Victoria Falls are featured. The site guides provides information on where to start your trip.

Africa Archipelago

http://www.africaarchipelago.com

If you are looking for a unique tailor made safari, this London based company has many years of experience touring Africa, and can make your trip an enjoyable one. Specializing in honeymoons, and safaris, this site tours Kenya, Zambia, Zimbabwe, Botswana, and the Indian Ocean.

Africa Tours Inc.

http://www.africasafaris.com

Going to Africa is an adventure and at Africa Tours Inc. it is an adventure with your interest in mind first. Customizing, tailor-made tours to fit your liking, this site provides trips to places like Kenya, Tanzania, South Africa, Zimbabwe, Botswana, Seychelles, Zambia, Namibia, and Egypt. An excellent frequently asked questions section is provided also.

Safaris.com

http://www.safaris.com

Africa Safari specialists have been taking people off the beaten path since 1987. This site is taking you to Kenya, Tanzania, Botswana, and Zimbabwe. Trips include detailed outlines of the ten day adventure, and more information can be requested on the site.

Australian Natural History Safari

http://www.anhs.com.au

This site shows you how to tour the Australian outback on a four-wheel drive through the rainforest. This site is ideal for a private, small group tour, low impact exploration of the natural rainforest, wildlife world, animals, and surrounding that only can be found down under.

Churchill Nature Tours

http://www.churchillnaturetours.com

Top quality tours are taking you to central Canada or Churchill, Riding Mountain National Park, southern Manitoba, and the Rockies. Offering a wildlife experience like no other, you can take a polar bear adventure tour, a summer safari with the whales, and watch birds.

Conservation Corporation Africa

http://www.ccafrica.com

One of Africa's most comprehensive touring companies, CC Africa offers a great selection of African tours. This site includes guided walking and mobile operated tours in Botswana, Kenya, Tanzania, Zimbabwe, and South Africa. There are travel tips for each country also.

Eco Africa

http://www.ecoafrica.com

Eco Africa is providing an overall basis of southern African eco-tourism with an environmentally minded conservation mission. It offers wildlife safaris with a specialist theme in mind. Features include directories of African national parks, African adventures, and more.

Rare Earth Explorations

http://www.gorp.com/rareearth

Rare Earth Explorations plans personalized and specialized guided wildlife safaris in India and Africa. Adventures included walking tours, hiking and trekking, canoeing, tiger conservation, exploration of eastern and southern Africa, and more traveling experiences.

Wildland Adventure Travel

http://www.wildland.com

These tour guides are exploring the natural and cultural world, this tour operator is geared for the active traveler, family traveling, and honeymoon travel experiences. This site specializes in camping and ecotourism in the Americas, Africa, Alaska, Middle East, Turkey, and Europe.

On Safari

http://www.onsafari.com

This comprehensive resource covers the world of safaris in Eastern to Southern Africa. From where to start to what you need to do to plan your safari can be found at On Safari. It has a search feature that makes it possible to search by region, country or activity. A team of travel agents takes a personalized approach to your safari.

Thomson Safaris

http://www.thomsonsafaris.com

The Thomson family specializes in safaris to Tanzania. Specializing in family and group itineries, at this comprehensive site you will find information on the Serengeti Park, Mt. Kilimanjaro, Selous, Tanganyika, and customized safaris. Other features include expert guides, all inclusive packages, and some great pictures that make this site something for any safari enthusiast to see.

Travcoa

http://www.travcoa.com

Travcoa specializes in luxury tours through the wild safaris in the world. With over 100 itineraries through 90 countries offered, you'll experience lost cities, restless sands, coveted treasures, and ancient religions of Africa and the Middle East.

Wilderness Safaris

http://www.wilderness-safaris.com

This great safari site specializes in safaris in Southern Africa, Botswana, Namibia, Zimbabwe, Malawi, and Zambia. Information is provided on various camps and lodges along with a paw rating on the safaris. Take a look at the collection of slide shows to see some of the more interesting pictures available for safaris.

Uncharted Outposts

http://www.unchartedoutposts.com

Uncharted Outposts offers unique and customized trip planning, taking you to private ranch destinations, stylish tents camps, small intimate lodges, and island hideaways in Africa, Australia, New Zealand, and Central and South America. Each trip is organized from start to finish in a personalized way.

Zimbabwe South Travel

http://www.zimbabwesouthtravel.com

Zimbabwe South Travel is a travel consultancy specializing in custom African safaris for adventurous travelers. Travelers consist of conservation minded families and small groups interested in an active experience with the wildlife and culture of southern Africa.

*Hiking There

Johnny Jet Code: Take a Hike

Backroads

http://www.backroads.com

Take a hike on the "back roads" with this company that offers active vacation packages throughout the world to over one hundred different destinations. In addition to hiking, you will bike, walk, kayak, and more. Check out the postcard gallery at this site.

BCT Scenic Walking Tours

http://www.bctwalk.com

Take a walking tour of the British Isles and Continental Europe with an experienced local leader. Destinations include: England, Scotland, Ireland, France, Spain, Italy, Greece, Germany, Austria, Czech Republic, and Norway. This site contains plenty of pictures and descriptions of the tours.

Bushwalking in Australia

http://www.bushwalking.org.au

This comprehensive site is a great place for anyone interested in bushwalking in Australia. Bushwalking clubs, information on Australia, and other online resources can be found here.

Country Walkers

http://www.countrywalkers.com

The trails on a Country Walkers tour lead to exhilarating encounters with our natural world with its worldwide walking tours. Each tour includes food, accommodations, and a guide.

Rails-to-Trails Conservancy

http://www.railtrails.org

This nonprofit organization features information on U.S. trails. You can read about the benefits of trails, find trails at www.traillink.com, check out the latest trail news, and more.

Scot Walk

http://www.scotwalk.co.uk

Take a walking tour in Scotland around and through the hills with gentle walking on average of 4-10 miles a day. You will view historic landmarks and Scotland heritage as you go on guided or self-guided tours.

Survival Sites

http://www.equipped.org/urls.htm

Here you will find a bunch of links to sites that focus on survival and ratings on the quality of information provided.

The Trail Master

http://www.thetrailmaster.com

One devoted hiker started this site to share his favorite walks with you. The site contains information on where to hike with recommendations for hiking products, accessories, and guided tours. There is a section with essential hiking tips.

Trail Place

http://www.trailplace.com

The Center for Appalachian Trail Studies is dedicated to hikers of this trail. The site includes a forum, online journals, photos, and hiker resources.

Tran Scotland Walking Holidays

http://www.transcotland.com

Known for its walking holidays in Scotland, this company started back in 1984 and it now organizes guided trips, self-guided trips, and independent holidays. Trips include hotel accommodations, baggage transfer, and route information.

European Walking Tours

http://www.walkingtours.com

You will find private European walking tours in groups of eight or more walkers. Whether you are a brisk walker or like to take it a little slow, EWT caters to you. Walkers stay at hotels and tours are taking you to France, Austria, and other European places.

*Visit a Park

Johnny Jet Code: Park Visitor

Yahoo! Parks

http://sports.yahoo.com/parks

Yahoo provides national and international information on the parks. Just click on a state, country, or an activity and a listing of the parks will show up. This is convenient to use when you are looking for a park in a specific location, but don't know the name.

American Park Network

http://www.americanparknetwork.com

The American Park Network provides a comprehensive resource on America's favorite National Parks that you can explore. Whether it's the great chasm of the Grand Canyon or the geysers of Yellowstone, it has been a leading publisher of visitor guide magazines for national parks for many years. The site contains information on activities, reservations and trip planning, a message board to talk about your park experience, and an online store.

L.L. Bean Park Search

http://www.llbean.com/parksearch

Parks are at your fingertips here. Whether you are looking for a national park or an international park, you can find it on this site. You can search by location, park name, or outdoor activity. There is a great section that has camping, cycling, fitness, fishing, hiking, paddling, and sports tips.

National Park Foundation

http://www.nationalparks.org

The NPF is chartered by congress to strengthen the connection between the American people and their national parks by raising funds, making grants, creating partnerships, and building awareness. The site has travel planning, information on kids programs, volunteering programs, pictures, and more.

National Park Service

http://www.nps.gov

This site leads you to the national parks covering over 80 million acres in the United States. You can visit the parks and get linked to specific national parks, find historical links to the past, explore the natural world online and see which parks are being preserved, and learn facts and figures on the parks. Visiting the national parks is the next step, but this site makes it easy to find out about them online.

National Parks and Conservation Association

http://www.npca.org

The NPCA is committed to protecting our scenic beauty, wildlife, and natural resources of the national parks. Here you can explore the parks, learn about park safety, take a virtual park tour, and learn how you can take action in preserving our great parks and the surrounding natural beauty.

Recreation

http://www.recreation.gov

Looking for government recreation areas is easy with this searchable by state site that contains information about recreation on federal lands in the United States.

Parks Canada

http://www.parkscanada.pch.gc.ca

The Canadian Parks can easily be viewed on this site available in both French and English. From historical information to virtual tours, you can find much of the information on Canadian parks here.

The NPS Grand Canyon

http://www.nps.gov/grca

The National Park Service provides information on the Grand Canyon along with a trip planner, park news, park guide, other online resources, and more.

The Canyon

http://www.thecanyon.com

This picturesque site is sponsored by the Grand Canyon Chamber of Commerce and provides information on lodging accommodations, dining, activities, surrounding attractions and more.

The Grand Canyon Explorer

http://www.kaibab.org

Those considering visiting the Grand Canyon will find this site very informative with some great pictures, maps, and much more. Check out the visitor's center, learn the basics with a virtual guided tour, and find out more about the Canyon in the news.

Grand Canyon National Park Lodges

http://www.grandcanyonlodges.com

Here on the south rim of the Grand Canyon you will find some great lodging, bus tours, nature walks, Native American artistry, unique shopping, wildlife, world famous scenery, and rafting and mule rides.

Central Park

http://www.centralpark.org

Central Park is probably the most well known park. There are 843 acres located in the heart of New York City. Take an online tour and learn about the park's history, sports, and more. There are some great pictures to see on this site.

Yellowstone National Park

http://www.yellowstone.net

Yellowstone Park is Americas first and foremost park in Wyoming. You will find information on the park and pictures of landscapes, animals, waterfalls, and geyser basins. Check out the interactive video tours and the top ten things to see at the park.

Yosemite Online

http://www.yosemite.org

Yosemite National Park and Yosemite Association is online at this site where you can see live pictures that reload every few minutes, find out about the park and plan a trip, and more. For more information on Yosemite Park Tours, visit *www.yosemiteparktours.com* and you will see a variety of tours.

*Solo Travel

Johnny Jet Code: Solo Travelers

Adventure Connections

http://www.adventure-connections.com

This is a tour-based company for single travelers offering a maximum of twelve travelers in an informal group atmosphere taking you to amazing places. Trips are historically and culturally driven to places including Barcelona, Spain, Rio de Janeiro, Brazil and San Jose, Costa Rica.

The World Outdoors

http://www.theworldoutdoors.com

This site specializes in a variety of outdoor recreation trips and adventure travel. In particular, there are sections on biking, hiking, sport vacations and parks. There is a section for solo travelers.

Independent Traveler

http://www.independenttraveler.com

This is a travel planning guide and community for independent travelers. It has tips on how to save money on travel, traveler reviews and tales, message boards, news and more travel tips.

Travel Companion Exchange

http://www.travelcompanions.com

The motto here is, "why travel alone when traveling together with a pre-selected, compatible partner and newly found friend is not only less costly but also more enjoyable and more practical." You can become a member and find a travel companion.

Connecting: Solo Travel Network

http://www.cstn.org

CSTN is a non-profit, international organization of people who enjoy sharing their solo trips. It includes the latest news about trips for singles, and it promotes hospitality among solo travelers throughout the world. The Web site provides information on lodging, cruises, resorts, clubs, and organizations. There is a special section for members offering networking with other solo travelers.

Travel Alone

http://www.travelaloneandloveit.com

Flight attendant and solo travel expert Sharon B. Wingler has created an online resource and book for those traveling alone. The site is dedicated to showing you how to safely and economically see the world on your own. It contains questions and answers, along with traveling solo tips and resources.

Travel Chums

http://www.travelchums.com

People with similar interests gather here and find someone to travel with. Travel Chums matches up solo travelers with others so you can travel with similar people while sharing the costs of a room, taxi, and other expenses.

Parents without Partners

http://www.parentswithoutpartners.org

This is a national non-profit educational organization devoted to single parents and their children. The mission of the site is to assist parents with the exchange of ideas of parenting techniques while furthering the common welfare and well being of children. The site contains information on memberships, chapters, news, and more.

Singles Travel International

http://www.singlestravelintl.com

Singles looking to go on fun trips and tour the world will find Singles Travel International very informative.

Go Solo Travel Club

http://www.gosolotravelclub.com

This travel club specializes in catering to travelers without a partner who would like to travel in an organized tour group. Everyone on the tour has a single room, but won't be charged the single room rate. Tours are available for both domestic and international.

Solo Dining

http://www.solodining.com

At Solo Dining, eating alone is a delightful experience. The site offers a subscription to a print and online newsletter, information on recommended restaurants, and more for a solo dining experience.

Theme Parks and Attractions

Johnny Jet Code: Theme Parks

Amusement Park Directory

http://www.123world.com/amusement

If you are looking for an amusement park in a particular state or country, this site will direct you to that park.

Theme Parks

http://www.themeparks.com

This is an informational site about theme parks in the United States. There are message boards and chats, information pages on the theme parks, pictures, and theme park voting feedback.

Theme Park Critic

http://www.themeparkcritic.com

This is a premier guide to theme parks and attractions. The site provides user reviews of rides and shows at some of America's popular theme parks including major theme parks such as Disney World, Universal's Adventure Island, Busch Gardens, and much more.

Roller Coasters

http://www.americanmidway.com

http://www.coastergallery.com

http://www.coasterquest.com

http://www.coasterville.com

http://www.joyrides.com

http://www.lifthill.com

http://www.rcdb.com

http://www.rollercoasterworld.com

http://www.thrillride.com

http://www.ultimaterollercoaster.com

Now that you've seen the amusement park directories, check out some roller coaster sites. These sites will provide you with information on the coasters, reviews, and photos. If you are looking for stats, be sure to check out the Roller Coaster Database at *www.rcdb.com*. If you are only looking for photos of roller coasters, check out the coaster gallery at *www.coastergallery.com*.

4 Adventure

http://www.4adventure.com

Adventure Island, Busch Gardens, Discovery Cove, Sea World, Sesame Street, and Water Country USA are all here. Take your pick at one of these great Anheuser Busch Adventure Parks.

*Disney Theme Parks

http://www.disneyland.com

http://www.disneyworld.com

http://www.disney.com

No introduction really needed here, but if you are looking for Mickey Mouse, Donald Duck, Goofy, or Pluto, you will be sure to find them here. Those looking to save on their Disney trips may want to check out the promotions and discounts at www.disneydollarless.com and www.mousesavers.com. For more on Disney Vacations, check out *Johnny Jet Code: Disney Vacations*

Hotel Orlando

http://www.hotelorlando.com

If a hotel near Disney World and the other major theme parks in Orlando is what you are looking for, then visit this site. You will find an aerial image of Orlando and you can scope out the best places to stay depending on which Orlando theme parks you would like to visit.

Mouse Planet: Unofficial Disney Park Guides

http://www.mouseplanet.com

This is your guide to all the Disney theme parks without going to the official Disney site. Do you want to know what hotels are closest to Disney, where the bathrooms are, or what else you never knew about Disney, that you have always wanted find out? Don't forget to hit up the "mouse pad" to go to a discussion board.

Hidden Mickeys

http://www.hiddenmickeys.org

Mickey Mouse fans will get a lot of joy out of this site where you can search for Mickey Mouse images or Mickey Silhouettes that are placed within Disney attractions. There are a lot of other Disney surprises you can find. A great place to go before you go to Disney, this site gets you prepared to see where he's hiding.

Knott's Berry Farm

http://www.knotts.com

Located in Southern California, Knott's Berry Farm is known as the "Friendliest Place in the West." From rides to attractions, this is quite an amusement park to see. Online you can see the latest attractions and a park guide.

World Waterpark Association

http://www.waterparks.org

Searching for waterparks is very easy with this site that lets you search for a park by name, city, state, or country. After you are done searching, you can get ready to jump in and get wet.

Yesterland

http://www.yesterland.com

Where do the old Disneyland attractions go after they are no longer the main attractions? You are here at Yesterland, a place on the Web to see all of the great old attractions and what Disneyland was like before you were born. Check it out!

Universal Studios

http://themeparks.universalstudios.com

http://www.universalkids.com

http://www.universalstudios.com

Universal Studios is the entertainment fun place where music, movies, television, theme parks, and more can be found. Kids will enjoy fun games, songs, and more from Universal home videos at the kids' site. Some of the all time favorite theme park attractions include: Jaws, Back to the Future, and Jurassic Park, Water World, and E.T.

Warner Bros.

http://www.kids.warnerbros.com

http://www.warnerbros.com

WB is the home of the Looney Tunes and a lot of other great television shows. There is so much to do at the main WB site. Categories include: originals, movies, DVD/Video releases, television, Looney Tunes, kids stuff, music, message boards, and shopping. Visit the WB kid site where you can sing, play games, and more.

MGM

http://www.mgm.com

Listen to the lions roar and find out the latest news with Metro Goldwyn Mayer and see the newest movie reviews and releases. Preview what's coming to the theaters with video clips and check the latest television happenings.

IMAX Theatres

http://www.imax.com

Learn about the IMAX technology, find out what is playing at your nearest IMAX theater, and more about this innovative film viewing experience. While you are here, watch some video clips, download a screensaver, look at the educational films, read about the corporation, and more. Find out where the closest IMAX theatre is located.

Six Flags

http://www.sixflags.com

Six Flags theme parks are all over the world! Don't miss this site if you are in for some great rides and would like to locate your closest Six Flags.

Cedar Point

http://www.cedarpoint.com

Cedar Point is a great amusement park in Sandusky, Ohio known as the Roller Coaster Capital of the World and is the second oldest amusement park in North America. It also has the most rides in the world. For more on Cedar Point, check out the unofficial sites at www.thepointol.com and www.guidetothepoint.com.

Dollywood

http://www.dollywood.com

Country music star Dolly Parton has here own amusement park in the Smoky Mountains of Tennessee. You'll find some crafts, rides, attractions, and dining at this site that brings you to Dolly's online.

Paramount's Kings Island

http://www.pki.com

Paramount has some great theme parks throughout North America and Kings Island is certainly no exception. Famous for its Drop Zone, Beast, and Nickelodeon rides, this park is a blast. Check out the other Paramount theme parks (www.paramountparks.com) including: Canada's Wonderland, Carowinds, Kings Dominion, Great America, and the Star Trek Experience.

Hershey Park

http://www.hersheypark.com

Hershey Park located in Hershey, Pennsylvania is the sweetest place on Earth. There are lots of rides and fun attractions at this magnificent chocolate world online.

Lego Land

http://www.legolandca.com

Lego Land in the United States is just a half an hour north of San Diego, California and it is where you can see and play with some of the best building blocks in the world. There are also other Lego Lands throughout the world that you can see at *www.legoland.com*.

Build-A-Bear Workshops

http://www.buildabear.com

These bear building workshops are located all over the United States. Find one near you and start creating your own personalized teddy bear. Check out the fun games and the cool "libeary" where you can have fun and learn a little about bears. Find out how you can throw a party at a Build-A-Bear Workshop.

Going to the Circus

http://www.bigapplecircus.org

http://www.circusweb.com

http://www.cirquedusoleil.com

http://www.ringling.com

It's where the lions are tamed, the jugglers throw flames, the contortionists twist, the trapeze artist swings so gracefully, and the clowns make you laugh. Check out and visit some of these well-known circuses.

Space Needle

http://www.spaceneedle.com

Visit Seattle, Washington and look up in the sky about 605 feet and you will see the top of the Space Needle. This building will show you the view of the whole city. It's quite an attraction to see and you can learn more about it online before you see it live.

Seattle Center

http://www.seattlecenter.com

Seattle Center is a 74-acre area in Seattle Washington that has some of the key attractions of the city. Within Seattle Center you will find the Space Needle, Key Arena, Memorial Stadium, Opera House, Pacific Science Center, and more. From award-winning theatre companies to pro sports teams, there is much to do in Seattle Center. The Center was originally created for the 1962 World's Fair.

Theme Park Insider

http://www.themeparkinsider.com

You don't have to visit every theme park to get the inside scoop on them. You'll find Busch Gardens, Disney, Legoland, Six Flags, Universal, and many more. This site sums it all up for you with reader's picks, discussion boards, ratings, reviews, and more.

Adventures

*Adventure Travel: Go Exploring

Johnny Jet Code: Adventure Travel

Around the Worlds

http://www.aroundtheworlds.com

Available in English and French, this site is packed with information from a traveling team that focuses on traveling tips, travelogues, photos, travel tools, travel news, and more.

Away.com

http://www.away.com

Away you go to extraordinary travel with this massive site. This site is nothing but the extraordinary trips and tours to offbeat destinations such as kangaroo watching in Australia, paddle boating in Ecuador, horseback riding in Zimbabwe, and skiing in Colorado. Search over 5,000 unique trips and travel adventures including: hiking, cruising, cycling, diving, horseback riding, skiing, and more. Check out the photo gallery, trip itineraries, destination guides, expert forums, and message boards.

Online Adventure

http://www.onlineadventure.com

If for some reason it's difficult to take the real adventure, this online adventure spot may be the next best virtual thing. Check out the travel videos, photos, and virtual reality tours of various nature related vacations. There are some great scenes on this site.

Adventure Travel

http://www.adventuretravel.com

This online consulting site will find adventures that are eco-friendly. Not sure if you want to go to a certain place, but would like more information or get some good ideas on a travel destination? This impressive portal with a great variety of adventurism may be your answer to traveling adventurously.

Dave's Travel Corner

http://www.davestravelcorner.com

Looking for some good travel articles, pictures, travel news, classifieds, and more? Dave has a great place on the Web.

Knots

http://www.realknots.com/knots

Some adventure trips may require you to learn the ropes. Here you'll learn step-by-step instructions on how to tie a knot. Stoppers, bends, hitches, single loops, and more are here to occupy the adventure traveler that may need to knot something.

*Bi-Plane Rides

For more information on Bi-Plane Rides and taking a ride in one, check out Johnny Jet Code: Bi-Plane Rides

*Blimp Rides

For more information on blimps and blimp rides, check out Johnny Jet Code: Blimp Rides

*Driving Courses

For more information on driving courses, check out Johnny Jet Code: Drive Course

*Hot Air Ballooning

Johnny Jet Code: Ballooning

Albuquerque International Balloon Fiesta

http://www.aibf.org

This fiesta in New Mexico is a well known ballooning event each year. You can find out more about the event, see pictures, find out about balloon rides, and more.

Balloon Federation of America

http://www.bfa.net

The BFA is a non-profit volunteer organization, which includes information on all aspects of ballooning, representing over 3,500 members, and serves as the official ballooning branch of the United States National Aeronautic Association.

Ballooning in Tuscany

http://www.ballooningintuscany.com

If you ever wanted to tour Tuscany, Italy there may be no better way to enjoy an exquisite hot air balloon ride program. Tours are provided near Siena and Montelpulciano and include ballooning, walking, eating, wine tasting, and views of everything from the farmyard to the kitchen. Watch a real time video, and find pricing and reservation info.

Sonoma Aerostat-Adventures

http://www.aerostat-adventures.com

Aerostat Adventures offers hot air ballooning in Sonoma County, California. Ballooning experiences include single flights without hopping, and experienced pilots. You can see a photo gallery and schedule a flight online.

Fair Winds Hot Air Balloon Flights

http://www.fairwindsinc.com

Located in Boulder, Colorado, Fair Winds offers private and large group hot air ballooning trips over the Rocky Mountains of Boulder.

Tanzania Serengeti Balloon Safaris

http://www.balloonsafaris.com

There is no other experience like flying up in a hot air balloon. Now this time around you will be flying over the Serengeti in Tanzania. View the itinerary, a gallery of photographs, and watch an online video presentation of what it's like to be up in this balloon.

Hot Air Australia

http://www.hotair.com.au

This Australian hot air balloon tour operator resides in Cairns, the most popular Australian ballooning local. It offers trips across the Atherton Tablelands providing unsurpassed panoramic views of Australian landscapes. You can choose from uniquely designed state of the art Australian balloons of koalas and kangaroos. Check out the photo gallery.

Hot Air Ballooning

http://www.launch.net

Take off in a hot air balloon. This site explains everything from the basics of how balloons fly, race, and ballooning clubs. There is a section on ballooning questions and answers, a pilot's corner and shop, a ride board, balloon festivals, and more for the ballooning enthusiast at this comprehensive site.

Community State Bank National Balloon Classic

http://www.nationalballoonclassic.com

See the scheduled flights of the National Balloon Classic.

*Murder Mystery Vacations

For more information on murder mystery vacations,
check out Johnny Jet Code: Murder Mystery

*Outdoor Thrills

Are you up for an outdoor thrill like bungee jumping?
Check out Johnny Jet Code: Outdoor Thrill

*Parachuting

Johnny Jet Code: Parachute Diver

Dropzone.com

http://www.dropzone.com
Experienced and novice skydivers worldwide will find this site to be very informative. It includes an events calendar, forums, safety tips, gear, classifieds, auctions, and other Web related resources for the skydiving enthusiast.

Skydiving

http://www.skydiving.com
Find a place to skydive throughout the United States and Canada.

Skydive Pepperell, Boston

http://www.skyjump.com
Near Boston, Pepperell offers some of the most advanced skydiving training programs in New England.

Mile-Hi Skydiving

http://www.mile-hi-skydiving.com
Near Denver Colorado in Longmont, this skydiving school offers diving opportunities and answers to your questions for first time divers and experienced divers alike.

United States Parachuting Association

http://www.uspa.org
Here is the official site of the United States Parachuting Association. This nonprofit organization finds the most updated information on skydiving events, competitions, and more for the novice and advance skydiver. The organization holds a strong emphasis on skydiving safety, and features its publication *Parachutist Magazine.*

Chapter 6

Sports and Attention Sports Fans

Are you an athlete or do you enjoy playing sports? If so, this chapter will give you the most of what you want out of sports and travel. We have everything from biking and cycling, Fantasy Sports Leagues, golf, horse-back riding, rock climbing, skiing, and more. If you are more into the recreational sports, there are some Johnny Jet Codes to check out that will lead you to everything from Driving Courses to Sports News.

Sports and Recreation

*Biking and Cycling

Johnny Jet Code: Go Cycling

Back Road Travel in Sweden

http://www.backroadtravel.com

Looking to cycle on the back roads of Sweden, or bicycle in the early day, and take a hike in the evenings? Take a tour of the island of Gotland, or bike on the coast of Denmark, this site takes you to some of the historical landmarks with this cycling adventure.

Bicycle Beano Cycle Tours and Vegetarian Cuisine

http://www.bicycle-beano.co.uk

Vegetarian cuisines and group bicycle tours have this tour operator taking you to the UK. Now, even if you aren't a vegetarian, but if you are a cycler, you will find this trip fascinating as you explore London, Wales, and the Welsh Borders of England.

Long Bicycle Packing List

http://www-math.science.unitn.it/Bike/General/Packing_List.html

If you want to know what you should pack on a biking trip, this site explains it in a nutshell.

Bike Riders Tours

http://www.bikeriderstours.com

Go take a bicycling vacation in New England, Canada, France, Italy, Spain, and Portugal. The tours are in small groups with a maximum of sixteen bikers. There are more options available for self-guided bikers.

Bike Treks Limited

http://www.angelfire.com/sk/biketreks

Established in 1989, this company is a biking and hiking tour operator taking you on hiking and mountain biking adventure safaris in the Kenyan game reserves and national parks. If you love Africa, and cycling, this trip may be the one for you.

Country Lanes British Cycling

http://www.dspace.dial.pipex.com/countrylanes

Here you will find an award-winning British cycling tour specialist. Whether you are looking for a classic tour in fine country house hotels, or a more customized tour, Country Lanes offers it. This site also offers one day getaways and bed and breakfast tours in Britain.

Cyber Cycling

http://www.cycling.org

Here is your online resource to cycling around the world. You will find email lists for cyclers, bicycle sites, forums, events, classifieds, and more. Start cycling over to this site.

Cycle America

http://www.cycleamerica.com

You can cycle across state and coast-to-coast with the bicycle tours here. The site also offers national park and bicycle camping vacations. Check out the tour info, and the schedule to see when bicyclers are heading across America.

Beach's Motorcycle Tours

http://www.beaches-mca.com

Specializing in motorcycle tours of the European Alps, Norway, and New Zealand, this tour bike company will take you on a scenic ride. You'll see the Alpine Mountains to your right and scenery to your left. It's quite an adventure for a motorcyclist.

Cycle Italy

http://www.cycleitalia.com

Do you like a cycling challenge? Why not do it in Italy, where you will see the green, white, and red flags waving at you? High performance cycling tours are within reach at this site that brings you an Italian atmosphere with the cultural spice of friends, food, wine, beauty, and the joy of cycling. Check out the photos, the tour details, and more.

Free Wheeling Adventures

http://www.freewheeling.ca

Take an adventure to Nova Scotia Canada and enjoy great guided bike tours exploring the countryside at your own pace. Trips are for various skill levels and include food, inns, and van support. Hiking and sea kayaking options are also available.

Hog Tracks

http://www.hogtracks.com

Here you'll find biker-friendly road planning and mapping of various food and restaurant stops within the United States.

Horizons Unlimited

http://www.horizonsunlimited.com

A couple of motorcyclists who have traveled by motorcycle around the world have created and documented this site for other adventurous motorcyclists to see. See their photo album, read about their great adventure, and check out the message board.

L.A. Bike Tours

http://www.labiketours.com

Take a biking tour through Hollywood and Beverly Hills California. Included with bike rentals are helmets, storage baskets, and bike locks. Find out the schedule, check out photos, and visit the bike shop.

MotoDirectory.com

http://www.moto-directory.com/touring.htm

This is perhaps the largest directory of domestic and international motorcycle tour companies.

Napa Valley Bike Tours

http://www.napavalleybiketours.com

Take a guided tour of the Napa Valley and check out the other featured bike tours available. The site has a tour calendar, online booking, accommodations, and more for the biker who likes a little bit of luxury.

Northeastern Motorcycle Tours

http://www.motorcycletours.com

These motorcycle tours take you to some of the most scenic places in America. Tour the natural mountains in New England. Ride through Vermont, New Hampshire, Massachusetts and the Adirondack Mountains. See the beautiful Maine seacoasts, Nova Scotia and the Gaspé Peninsula.

*Extreme Sports

Johnny Jet Code: Extreme Sports

EXPN.com

http://www.expn.com
Extreme sports such as in-line skating, BMX biking, motocross jumping, snowboarding, skiing, and snowmobiling can be found here at this ESPN affiliate site. The site features pictures and info on the X-Games.

Extreme Sports

http://www.extremesports.com
Here you will find news, photos, movies, a calendar, and more for the extreme sports enthusiast and those just new to learning about these sports.

*Fantasy Sports Leagues

Have you ever fantasized about being a pro sports player or would you like to make believe that you are on a professional team? Check out *Johnny Jet Code: Fantasy Camps*

*Golf

Johnny Jet Code: Golfing

BestCourses.com

http://www.bestcoursestoplay.com
Find where some of the best courses to play are in the United States, get tour schedules, tips, records and stats, and information on golf games.

GolfandTravel.com

http://www.golfandtravel.com
GolfandTravel.com will lead you to the most exquisite and picturesque courses around the world.

Golf-Travel

http://www.golf-travel.com

Golf-Travel will give you a directory of top destinations for golfers along with travel packages, golf schools, and more.

GolfWeb

http://www.golfweb.com/travel

At Golfweb, you will find a variety of golf vacations.

Golf Online

http://www.golfonline.com/travel

Golf Online combines with Sports Illustrated to help you plan your golf outing and golf vacations.

Golf 101

http://www.golf101.com

Search for a golf course, get some tips on improving your golf game, learn how to avoid sand traps, improve your score, and more.

Golf Score Keeper

http://www.golfscorekeeper.com

Serious golfers can keep track of each round of golf on this site. It keeps track of your stats and provides analysis of your scores.

Perry Golf

http://www.perrygolf.com

Perry Golf is a Scottish golf tour operator that is committed to providing the world's finest golf travel experiences and you can plan unique golf vacations to various places including: England, Wales, Scotland, Ireland, Spain, and Portugal.

The Golf Travel Company

http://www.e-golftravel.com

Find customized golf travel packages to Great Britain and Europe and the sites serves as a source for your international golf tour to Scotland, Ireland, England, Wales, Spain, Portugal, France, Italy, and the British Open.

The Golf Channel

http://www.thegolfchannel.com

Get the latest golf news, scores, instruction, and tournament coverage at this site. There is a golf tracker where you can track your games, shop for golf supplies, see golf travel packages, and more.

*Gym Locator

Does your workout regimen require gym equipment?
If so, you can find the closest gym.
Check out: Johnny Jet Code: Gym Locator

*Horseback Riding

Johnny Jet Code: Horseback Ride

Adventures on Horseback

http://www.adventuresonhorseback.com

Christine Chauvin's Adventures on Horseback offers exhilarating trips of terrain, cultures, and wildlife in Africa, Brazil, Ecuador, India, or Spain. Trips are for the experienced and less experienced rider.

Apache Stables

http://www.apachestables.com

Apache Stables offers are one and two-hour rides that are taken on a unique trail throughout the Grand Canyon. Horseback riders will enjoy their Grand Canyon vacation riding through the Kabab National forests in the Western United States. After the ride, get ready to roast some marshmallows. Check the age and weight restrictions before taking a trip out west.

Cross Country Equestrian Vacations

http://www.equestrianvacations.com

Take your horse and get away at this site that provides a great variety of horseback riding vacation programs throughout the world. Whether you're riding in Europe, Central or South America, or the United States, this company will provide you with private or group lessons and package deals. You will see different parts of the world and learn riding.

Drumgooland House Equestrian Centre

http://www.horsetrek-ireland.com

Taking a pony for a ride in Ireland, trekking on a trail, and enjoy a holiday riding the horses in the beautiful scenic Mourne Mountain are what is offered on this site. Read the itinerary and see how you can explore Ireland and take a riding trip of a lifetime. Prices are in British Pounds and Francs.

Equestrian Holidays Ireland

http://www.ehi.ie

This directory contains more resources and links to equestrian centers throughout Ireland can be found at this site. Based on interest, you can find centers that specialize in trail riding, cross country, show jumping, polo, and more.

Equitour Riding Tours

http://www.equitours.com

Equitours is "America's Oldest and Largest Riding Tour Company." People all over the world on six continents take international riding tours. All tours are environmentally friendly with well-maintained horses.

Equestrian Safaris Ltd.

http://www.safaririding.com

Riding in the lands of Africa, taking a horseback trip that goes through the slopes of Mt. Meru or towards the Kilmanjaro Mountains is quite a unique experience. Choose from a selection of either Tanzania or Argentina with various trips available in each country. The pictures alone make this site something to see.

France Riding Tours

http://www.france-ridingtours.com

Touring the Chateaux of the Loire Valley in France, these equestrian guided tours take you riding around the fascinating castle scenery. The site which is in French and English provides an impressive itinerary along with pictures, and information on taking a riding tour. Prices are available in Francs.

German Horse Holidays

http://www.horse-box.de

Here you will find worldwide addresses of farms, ranches, and tour operators that provide horse holidays.

Hidden Trails

http://www.hiddentrails.com

Hidden Trails offers international horseback riding vacations and trails in over 40 countries. Whether you are looking to gallop on beaches, through meandering rivers, green forests, or through old trails, you will find plenty of riding trips here.

Horse Travels

http://www.horsetravels.com

The theme here is "seeing the country from the back of your horse." The site offers pictures, a newsletter, information on various trails from a couple, and more on horse travels.

Horse and Mule Trail Guide USA

http://www.horseandmuletrails.com

This is a guide to horse and mule trails in the USA. Trails are organized by state. The site contains many links to other horse related sites.

Horseback Riding Australia

http://www.equitrek.com.au

Going down under to the land of the Australia Outback, and you won't expect to be riding kangaroos here. Jump on that saddle and start "EquiTrekking" or checking out some of the horse trekking rides here.

Riding World

http://www.ridingworld.com

At this site, there are horseback riding vacations for those who appreciate fine horses, enjoy horse travel, and have a passion for the history and culture of places. Trips can be found in the U.S., Europe, Asia, Latin America, Canada, and Australia.

Timber Mountain Tour of Alberta Rockies

http://www.timbermountain.com

Taking a trail ride in the remote Rockies of southwestern Alberta, Canada can be quite an experience. Trails include horseback camping, and professionally guided pack trips. It's awe-inspiring scenery, with its great online photographs of wildflowers, wildlife, wild places, and camping will make you feel as though you are there.

*Mountain Biking

Are you up for climbing mountains on your bike?
Check out: Johnny Jet Code: Mountain Bike

*Recreation Sports Instruction

Johnny Jet Code: Sports Instruction

My Sports Guru

http://www.mysportsguru.com

This site has the sports participant in mind. All the tools you need to play better in any sport can be found here. Technique, tactics, training, and troubleshooting are all emphasized. Whether you are on the road traveling or just want to find out more about a sport, this site will help.

SportsID.com

http://www.sportsid.com

Almost every sport imaginable is explained at this digital library of streaming sports videos. Click on a sport and watch a short video clip. This is a great place to go for sports instruction while you are on the go.

*Rock Climbing

Johnny Jet Code: Rock Climber

America's Roof

http://www.americasroof.com

Do you ever wonder about the height of the highest mountain? Or would you like to attempt to climb it? This is your guide to the peak points in the U.S.A. You will also find maps, 3D images, panoramas, and postcards.

Climbing Magazine

http://www.climbing.com

Since 1970 Climbing Magazine has been a reliable source for rock climbers. Read the latest climbing tips, equipment reviews, find gyms, and much more.

Rock and Ice

http://www.rockandice.com

This rock climbing magazine will help you get a grip on the latest news and stories in rock climbing, gear reviews, and help you find the best places to rock climb. A directory of rock climbing gyms can also be found here.

RockClimbing.com

http://www.rockclimbing.com

Serving climbers all over the world since 1995, this grassroots site promotes the various climbing sites online, as well as the climbing community. Plenty of photos give it a picturesque view from above. There's a climbing trivia section and forum that is great for any climbing enthusiast.

Rock Climbing Safety Tips

http://www.safetytips.com/html/sports/rock/index.htm

What does it take to be safe when climbing? This site explains it. Find out the basics of what gear to wear to the different styles of climbing.

*Skiing, Making the Download Easier

Johnny Jet Code: Skiing

Condé Nast's Top Ski Resort Poll

http://www.concierge.com/cntraveler/skipoll

Condé Nast Traveler provides an annual poll on the top ski resorts in North America. It provides a paragraph about the resort with contact information and info on degree of difficulty of the slopes.

World Ski Guide

http://www.worldskiguide.com

The World Ski Guide is a comprehensive and objective guide to ski and snowboard resorts worldwide. It provides essential information on choosing your ideal resort and making the most of your skiing holiday. Each resort includes information on local accommodations surrounding the resorts.

Canadian Mountain

http://www.canadianmountain.com

Skiing in Canada can be fun, and this site provides package deals to make it to Western Canada and the Canadian Rockies. Resorts and places to ski and snow reports can be found here.

Resort Sports Network

http://www.rsn.com

The Resort Sports Network covers mountains, lands, and water and has information on weather, trail conditions, events, and more for skiers, snowboarders, and bikers. Keep up with the conditions and check out the online cams where you can see some action packed pictures that you can send to others through email.

European Ski Slopes

http://www.bonski.com

http://www.lafantastique.com

http://www.monterosa.com

Here are some European ski slopes to check out. Bon Ski is in the French Alps, La Fantastique is in Switzerland, and Monterosa is in Stockholm.

Go Skiing

http://www.goski.com

Ski resorts and ski locations can easily be found on this site that offers a directory of ski resorts. Click on a state or a country and you will find the ski resorts in that location.

Moguls Mountain Travel

http://www.moguls.com

Moguls Mountain Travel provides customized ski vacations to skiers and snowboarders alike. You can build a trip, find deals, get vacation planning tips, and shop for skiing equipment. So if Vail, Beaver Creek, Breckenridge, or Keystone are in your travel plans, this is one site to check out.

Skinet

http://www.skinet.com

This site is a great place to start when you are looking for skiing information. It's a gateway to where, when, and what's happening in the skiing world. Whether you are looking for snow, or just want to find some ski events, or ski vacations, you'll likely find it here.

Ski Portillo Chile

http://www.skiportillo.com

Skiing in the Chilean Andes can be chilly, yet this site will point you in the right direction. At the site you can make reservations, sign up for ski school, read news and events, available in both group classes and private classes. The site is available in English, Spanish, and Portuguese.

Ski Vacation Planners

http://www.skivacationplanners.com

Ski Vacation Planners is a full service tour operator that caters to the individual or group skier looking to find their skiing travel destination in places including: Western U.S., Canada, South America, and New Zealand. You can customize your ski trip here.

Steamboat Snow Mobile Tours

http://www.stmbtsnowmobiletours.com

Ride the Continental Divide in two hours or take a full day tour. You can tour Rabbits Ears Pass and the Flat Tops Trail. Tours include dining and are geared for novice to experts.

Snowmobiling in Colorado

http://www.columbine.com

Take a snowmobile tour in Winter Park Colorado with Trailblazer Snowmobile Tours. This site offers one hour and two hour tours as well as half and full day adventures. There's much to do after snowmobiling and you will find a variety of links to nearby places here.

Mountainzone

http://www.mountainzone.com

Snowboarding, mountain biking, hiking, skiing, climbing, and great photography all can be found at this mountainous site. If it has to do with a mountain, it's on this site and you will find stories of real life experiences. From the climbing glossary to the latest adventure news, it can be found here.

*Tennis

For more information on tennis and tennis resorts, check out Johnny Jet Code: Tennis

*Winter Sports

Johnny Jet Code: Winter Sports

About.com Skiing

http://www.skiing.about.com

What would you like to know about skiing that you don't already know? This site is an excellent gateway to the many skiing resorts worldwide. It provides articles for alpine, backcountry, nordic, and telemark skiers along with a directory of skiing sites. Some of the categories include: Competitive, Equipment, Extreme Skiing, History of Skiing, Training, and much more.

Alpine Zone

http://www.alpinezone.com

Specializing in New England, this site has information on the resorts, ski reports, lodging, a great message forum, and image gallery. When you're not skiing on this site, it offers excellent resources for hikers.

Cross Country Ski World

http://www.xcskiworld.com

If you like cross country skiing, this site provides an abundance of information for you. News, training, technique, equipment, and other topics of interest can be found here.

GoSki.com

http://www.goski.com

GoSki.com is a comprehensive guide to skiing around the world. You can find the location where you want to ski worldwide and it will tell you all the necessary information, with country profiles, and ski information.

American Skiing Company

http://www.peaks.com

This ski operator has resorts from the east to the west of the U.S. offering savings on ski packages to Steamboat, the Canyons, Killington, Mount Snow, and more.

Kidz n' Snow

http://www.kidznsnow.com

This is your online guide to winter family fun. Downhill skiing, snowboarding, cross country skiing, sledding, ice skating, and other winter sports are on this site. Find resorts and where to travel, gear for kids, and more.

MountainReports.com

http://www.mountainreports.com

This site is your guide to various mountain regions worldwide. See featured mountain cams, get general information on the mountains, and a quick weather report.

OnTheSnow.com

http://www.onthesnow.com

What's happening on the snow? Here you will get snow reports, AMI Snow News, gear and equipment reviews, skiing information, ski cams, travel planning, and more.

Ski Conditions

http://www.realconditions.com

Get the inside scoop on the ski conditions in real time and have them emailed to you daily. With your WAP device you can get conditions sent to you wirelessly through www.skisite.com.

Ski.com

http://www.ski.com

Find discounted ski packages to resort, with last minute deals, to over thirty North American ski areas.

Skilovers.net

http://www.skilovers.net

Do you want to meet a compatible person who shares your skiing passion? This is where Skilovers.net comes into play. Here you can meet someone to ski and play in the snow.

SkiMaps.com

http://www.skimaps.com

Find the largest collection of ski trail maps online in addition to resort information, travel and lodging, gear, the magazine, videos of ski resorts, and message board forums.

Ski-Europe

http://www.ski-europe.com

Those looking to go to Europe and ski will find this comprehensive resource useful. Find out where you should go, resort info, skiing deals, and more.

Ski-Guide Resort Finder

http://www.ski-guide.com

This is the ultimate guide to ski resorts in U.S. and Canada. Each ski resort has a summary with information on lift tickets, lodging, ski shops, food, activities, directions, and more.

Ski Resorts

http://www.7springs.com
http://www.alpinemountain.com
http://www.altaskiarea.com
http://www.alyeskaresort.com
http://www.bearvalley.com
http://www.beavercreek.com
http://www.berthoudpass.com
http://www.breckenridge.com
http://www.brianhead.com
http://www.deervalley.com
http://www.hiddenvalleyresort.com
http://www.jacksonhole.com
http://www.keystoneresort.com
http://www.killington.com
http://www.lakeplacid.com
http://www.mammothmountain.com
http://www.mountsnow.com
http://www.parkcitymountain.com
http://www.shawneemt.com
http://www.skiaspen.com
http://www.skicamelback.com
http://www.skiheavenly.com
http://www.skiloveland.com
http://www.skitaos.org
http://www.skiwinterpark.com
http://www.snowbird.com
http://www.squaw.com
http://www.steamboat.com
http://www.sugarbush.com
http://www.sugarloaf.com
http://www.sundayriver.com
http://www.sunvalley.com
http://www.tanglwood.com
http://www.thecanyons.com

http://www.vail.com
http://www.whistler.com
http://www.whistlerblackcomb.com
If you are looking for a major ski resort, here are some major ski resort sites.

Skiershop.com

http://www.skiershop.com
Looking for skiing equipment? This site has almost any kind of skiing equipment you can imagine with great prices.

Ski Central

http://www.skicentral.com
This is an excellent search engine for skiers. Plan your next ski trip, find gear, lodging, snowcams, and much more.

SkiNet.com

http://www.skinet.com
When you're just looking for snow, or would like to find the latest gear reviews, news, skiing photos, ski resorts, ski instruction, and much more. This site provides a great avenue for skiing enthusiasts of all levels.

SkiTown.com

http://www.skitown.com
Known as "The Premier Virtual Mountain Resort Community on the Internet," at SkiTown.com you can find mountain, lodging, skiing services, resorts, and more throughout the U.S. and Canada.

Snowboarding.com

http://www.snowboarding.com
Snowboarding enthusiasts will find this site to be a great hangout with action photos, gear reviews, message boars, news, and more.

Snowlink.com

http://www.snowlink.com
Here is a complete source for snow sports. Whether you are skiing, snowboarding, or snowmobiling, this site provides you with all the information, gear, learning tips, events, clubs, weather reports, and more.

Attention Sports Fans

*Horse Racing

For more information on horse racing,
check out Johnny Jet Code: Horse Racing

*Olympics

For more information on the Olympic Games,
check out Johnny Jet Code: Olympics

*Sports Finals

For more information on sporting event finals,
check out Johnny Jet Code: Sport Finals

*Sports News

Johnny Jet Code: Sports News

News for Sports

http://www.cnnsi.com
http://www.foxsports.com
http://www.espn.com
http://www.sportingnews.com
http://www.sportsnetwork.com
Get the latest sports news from CNNSI, Fox Sports, ESPN, Sporting News, and The Sports Network.

Chapter 7

Airline Information

Before you rush out the door to the airport for your flight or to pick someone up, it's always very important check to see if the flight is on time and check the gate arrival and departure information. You may also watch a plane in route by checking out the flight trackers.

*Airline Club Rooms

Ah… the airline club rooms. If you travel a lot, I recommend that you buy a year membership to one of these airport havens. They are quiet, have snacks, drinks, business meeting space, wired with the Internet, and clean toilets! The price ranges depending on your Frequent Flyer Status and you can also pay by using miles. Using credit cards like AmEx Platinum and Diners could get you in for free. (Check with them directly.) Get a priority pass, if you frequent multiple airlines. Day passes are available too. Here are a variety of airline clubs that offer lounges to relax. *Johnny Jet Code: Air Clubs*

*Airline Seating Charts

Where do you like to sit on the plane?
For information on airline seating charts, check out Johnny Jet Code: Seating Charts

7 Tips on seating on the plane

1. The Seat Guru may have the answer to what is good, bad, and questionable on US planes. You can visit his site at *www.seatguru.com.*
2. For extra legroom request a seat behind a dividing wall or in an emergency exit aisle.
3. Request an aisle seat for easier accesses to your stored carry on overhead, the lavatories, or if you would like to disembark quicker.
4. Parents or guardians traveling with children may want to consider sitting near the lavatories
5. If you like to lie down or spread out, you may want to request a seat in the back of the plane, as there are usually fewer people on less booked flights.
6. Request a seat in the front if you want to get off the plane faster, or are trying to make a connecting flight. The front of the plane is usually quieter too.
7. If you are apt to get motion sickness, choose a seat towards the middle of the plane or near the wings.

*Airlines

Johnny Jet Code: Airlines

*Flight Paging

This is a great service. Just register at your airline site with your flight info (arrival or departure) and you will get paged hours and minutes before your flight with the departure/arrival time, gate and any delays or cancellations. It's free, so what are you waiting for? Go!

Johnny Jet Code: Flight Paging

Air Craft Cheat Sheet

http://www.airportcitycodes.com/aaa/ACCheatFrame.html

This is a quick reference guide to the popular aircraft manufacturer engines and planes. It lists planes by model with information on the version, aisles, engines, seating, range, and more.

Airport City Codes

http://www.airportcitycodes.com/aaa/index.html

This site features the airport city codes, runway length, an aircraft cheat sheet, airline codes, and more to entertain you about airlines, airports, and airplanes.

Airwise

http://www.airwise.com

In addition to offering flights and travel, Airwise.com provides information on the airports with listings for nearby restaurants, shops, and transportation for over 50 airports worldwide. Look here if you wanted to know, if your flight is on schedule, and which airports are the most highly trafficked. Other features on the site include: travel discussion, an airline Web site directory, currency converter, ATM locator, and international phone codes.

Yahoo! Flight Check Times

http://travel.yahoo.com/t/travelocity/air/yfinal_fltchk_simple.html

Check your flight and see if it's on time and when it's leaving. Hundreds of Airlines are shown.

Airport Delays

http://www.clickondetroit.com/sh/idi/news/airlines/delay-map.html
This site is a map of the U.S. Click on a major city and check to see if the airport is running on a delay.

Airline Toll-Free Numbers and Web sites

http://air-travel-center.net/airlines.htm

http://www.airlinenumbers.com
All the airlines and toll free numbers are listed here.

FlightArrivals.com

http://www.flightarrivals.com
What time does that flight arrive? You will get free real-time arrival, departures, delays, schedule changes, and airport status on commercial flights throughout the U.S. and Canada. Search options are available where you can find a flight without knowing the flight number.

Hartfield Atlanta Airport Arrivals and Departures

http://www.infax.com/WebFIDS/atl/fids.asp
Find out when flights are arriving and departing from Hartsfield Atlanta International Airport.

Flight Explorer

http://www.flightexplorer.com/fasttrack.asp
Flight Explorer is a leader in flight tracking and the Fast Track system is a real-time tracking system that tracks commercial air traffic in North America, Atlantic, and Pacific flights.

Flight Trackers

http://www4.passur.com/bos.html

http://www4.passur.com/lax.html

http://www4.passur.com/sdf.html

http://www.flyquietsfo.com/live
Here are some of the coolest flight trackers for Boston, Los Angeles, Louisville, and San Francisco airports.

Flight Track with Trip.com

http://www.trip.com/trs/trip/flighttracker/flight_tracker_home.xsl

A graphical and text version of flight tracking is available at this site.

FlightView.com

http://www.flightview.com

RLM software Inc. provides up to the minute flight information. This includes: position, speed, and departure and arrival information for U.S. and Canada flights. Radar based data is available on commercial airlines and general aviation with a current air traffic chart.

FlyteComm Real-Time Tracking

http://www.flytecomm.com

FlyteComm offers real-time tracking of flights arriving or departing in the United States or Canada. Get updates on arrivals and delays updated every five minutes. Additional flight info includes departure times, aircraft type, current altitude, current groundspeed, and forecasted weather for your destination.

Flight Watch America

http://www.flightwatchol.com

Flight Watch is dedicated to promoting safe travel by offering defensive and specialized flying training programs.

Landings

http://www.landings.com

This online news site is specifically made for pilots, but it has interesting information on air travel that almost any traveler would find useful. There is an aviation directory on the site.

Quickaid Airport Directory

http://www.quickaid.com

This site is a great resource for finding information about major U.S. airports, the lodging around the airports, ground transportation, airport services, and more.

*In-Flight Entertainment

Johnny Jet Code: Flight Entertainment

So you can't decide if you should bring head phones or a book? Check ahead to see what movie is playing on your flight. Some airports allow you to rent a DVD and player then return it when you land or return. If you have your own personal notebook computer with a DVD player you can bring your notebook and rent a DVD for the trip if the airline showings aren't what you are interested in watching.

Rent a Movie In The Airport

http://www.inmotionpictures.com

You can rent a portable DVD player with a movie and take it on the flight. This site offers affordable and personalized entertainment for your trip.

Air Canada In-Flight

http://www.aircanada.ca/services/entertainment

Some of the in-flight entertainment services offered by Air Canada include enRoute TV where you can view box office hits, enRoute FM, which allows you to listen to, tunes, and a multimedia kit.

Air India In-Flight Entertainment

http://www.airindia.com/inflight/entertainment.htm

Air India offers a variety of music, and some of the latest films onboard.

Air New Zealand In-Flight Entertainment

http://www.airnz.co.nz/travelinfo/ontheplane/inflightentertainment/defaul t.htm

With Air New Zealand you will be able choose your departure and destination while viewing the available in-flight entertainment.

Continental In-Flight Services

http://www.continental.com/travel/inflight/entertainment

Continental explains some of its complimentary in-flight entertainment features including: films, music, video music shows, its in-flight news known as "Journeys," its magazines, and video games.

Delta In-Flight Entertainment

http://www.delta.com/travel/during_flight/inflight_ent/index.jsp

Delta informs flyers about movies, television, radio programming, and other in-flight entertainment for its flights.

Japan Air In-Flight Entertainment

http://www.japanair.com/Inflight_Services/Entertainment/default.htm

Japan Air explains its state-or-the-art in-flight entertainment systems, and its programs to help you enjoy long flights. Some include its magic entertainment, an eye-trek video system, and its noise cancellation.

Northwest Airlines In-Flight Services

http://www.nwa.com/services/onboard/movies

Find out what movies are showing in-flight for Northwest Airlines.

United Entertainment

http://www.ual.com/page/article/0,1360,1070,00.html

See what United Airlines has to offer for in-flight films, television, and music.

Thai Airways In-Flight Services

http://www.thaiair.com/flying/inflight.htm

Find out how you can make your long flight more comfortable with Thai Airway's in-flight services.

US Airways In-Flight Entertainment

http://www.usairways.com/travel/inflight/entertainment/index.htm

See what movies are playing in US Airways flights.

Virgin Atlantic Entertainment

http://www.virgin-atlantic.com/flying_with_us_entertainment.view.do
Check out the latest entertainment on Virgin Atlantic flights including: movies, television, audio, video games, and sky map.

*Meal Requests

Johnny Jet Code: Meal Requests

Are you on a special diet? If so, you can order a wide range of special meals from Kosher to Vegetarian. Some airlines even have kid's meals. To ensure your special meal gets boarded, follow these five steps:

1. Get the name of the person making your reservation and a confirmation number.
2. Call 24 hours in advance to make sure that your request really is on file.
3. When you check in for the flight, ask once again to make sure. (If it is not in there by now, it may be too late.)
4. When you board the plane, ask the flight attendant if your special meal has been loaded and give him/her your name, seat number, and meal preference on a piece of paper.
5. If you still don't get your meal, don't freak out on the flight attendants. It's not their fault, just write a complaint letter to the company.

Airline Meals

http://www.airlinemeals.net

Entice your taste buds before you get on the plane, and see what various airlines are serving for meals. This site provides pictures of the actual trays provided by one graphic designer who is a little bit fanatical about cabin cuisine. Your favorite airline dinner may await you online. So check this out, find out what's being served before you fly away!

Continental Special Meals

http://www.continental.com/travel/inflight/dining/special

See what special meals are offered on Continental flights.

Delta Special Meals

http://www.delta.com/travel/during_flight/dining/sp_meals/index.jsp

See the special meal offerings on Delta flights.

Hawaiian Airlines In-Flight Meals

http://www.hawaiianair.com/about/services/menus.asp

Find out what meals are being served on Hawaiian Airlines.

Midwest Express Airlines Food Sample

http://www.midwestexpress.com/experience/foodSample.asp

See sample menus of breakfast, lunch, and dinner served on Midwest Express Airlines.

Northwest Airlines Onboard Food & Beverage Service

http://www.nwa.com/services/onboard/food

See what food is being served on Northwest flights.

United Meals

http://www.ual.com/page/middlepage/0,1454,1057,00.html

United offers a number of meals for special diets and you can find out what meals are served.

Aero Mexico Special Meals

http://www.aeromexico.com/ingles/de_viaje/serv_esp/serv_esp.htm#alimentos

Read about Aero Mexico's special meals.

Air Canada Special Meals

http://www.aircanada.ca/services/services
Air Canada offers special meals for religious and dietary needs.

British Airways Menu Planning Criteria

http://www.britishairways.com/catering/docs/signature.shtml
British Airways has a meal planning criteria for its flights.

Cathay Pacific Meals

http://www.cathaypacific.com/intl/inflight/meals/0,,,00.html
Read about Cathay Pacific's dining and special meals in flight.

Japan Airlines Special Meals

http://www.japanair.com/Inflight_Services/Special_Meals/default.htm
Japan Airlines offers a variety of special meals.

Northwest Airlines Nutritional Information

http://www.nwa.com/services/onboard/food/nutrition
Northwest provides nutritional information on special meals.

*Route Maps

What route does that airplane take?
Check out Johnny Jet Code: Route Maps

Chapter 8

Airport Information

If you want to make sure your trip can go as smooth as possible, do your homework. Know what the three letter airport codes are so you can watch the check-in agent put the correct baggage tag on your luggage. You can also find out how the terminals are designed, where to eat, shop, or where the closest ATM machines are located.

*Timetable Downloads

http://www2.alaskaair.com/flights/timetable.asp

http://www.americawest.com/traveltools/wireless/mobile.htm

http://www.british-airways.com/flights/timetables

http://www.brussels-airlines.com/fly_timetable.htm

http://www.continental.com/tis/tis_02_06.asp

http://www.finnair.com/filecontent/com/filecontent/common/flights/aywt8_01.txt

http://ibp.scandanavian.net/timetable/ts/timetab1.asp

http://www.japanair.com/Travel_Planning/Flight_Info/default.htm

http://www.nwa.com/travel/timetable

http://www.ual.com/site/primary/0,10017,1891,00.html

http://dps2.usairways.com/cgi-bin/fs

http://www.lufthansa.com/fly/en/pas/pas_downloads_timetable.html

Here are some timetables and airline schedule sites. *Johnny Jet Code: Timetables*

*Airport Terminal Maps

For airport terminal maps, check out Johnny Jet Code: Terminal Maps

*Flight Info: Planes Arrive and Depart

Johnny Jet Code: Flight Info

Airline Quality

http://www.airlinequality.com

You will find information on the quality and service rankings of various airlines.

*Airline and Airport Links

http://www.airlineandairportlinks.com

This is a directory to the airline and airport Web sites sorted alphabetically, geographically or by code. *Johnny Jet Code: All Airports*

Budget Traveler's Guide to Sleeping in Airports

http://www.sleepinginairports.net

If you are really on a budget and you have to sleep in an airport, this is the guide to check out. It has airport sleeping tips, a best and worst list, articles and more.

Salk's International Airport Transit Guide

http://www.airporttransitguide.com

Published annually since 1982, this is an airport directory for travel agents, corporate executives, travel managers, and frequent flyers.

World Airport Guide

http://www.worldairportguide.com

This is a guide to airports around the world with links to information about airports worldwide.

iPilot Airport Lookup

http://www.ipilot.com/airport

This is a comprehensive database to get familiar with surrounding airport facilities. It's searchable by zip code, city, state, airport identifier, identifier list or airport name. Search for an airport and you'll get general information.

*Airport Parking

Johnny Jet Code: Airport Parking

Don't go driving in circles trying to find a place to park when you are running late for a flight. Plan ahead and know where the garages are located and how much they charge.

Airport Parking Reservations

http://www.airportparkingreservations.com

This company has done the shopping and has negotiated great parking rates for you before you get to the airport.

Airport Discount Parking

http://www.airportdiscountparking.com

Start your trip with free airport parking with the discount parking network.

Avistar Parking

http://www.avistarparking.com

AvisStar offers convenient airport valet parking centers at LaGuardia, Newark, JFK, Chicago O'Hare, Philadelphia, and Bradley airports.

Airport Parking

http://www.airport-parking.com

This site provides links to the airport parking Web sites in the United States, Canada, and some international airports.

The Parking Spot

http://www.theparkingspot.com

This company specializes in airport parking at various locations throughout the United States, including Atlanta, Dallas, Houston, Kansas City, Los Angeles, and St. Louis.

Park 'N Fly

http://www.pnf.com

Park 'N Fly offers parking and transportation to and from the airport with pick-ups at over ten airports.

Park Air Express

http://www.parkairexpress.com

PAE is a parking management company providing airport parking services in Atlanta, Cleveland, Dayton, Denver, Houston, and Los Angeles.

Parking Company of America

http://www.parkingcompany.com

The PCA offers parking and transportation to and from the airport with pick-ups at airports including Atlanta, Dallas, Denver, Memphis, Oakland, Phoenix, Pittsburgh, and San Francisco.

Sun Park

http://www.sunpark.com

Known as the first alternative to airport parking, this company is offering an airport parking alternative in Buffalo, Columbus, Houston, Oklahoma City, Philadelphia, St. Louis, and Washington D.C. It offers a shuttle service and various other parking benefits.

Airport Fast Park

http://www.airportfastpark.com

Airport Fast Park offers airport parking in Albuquerque, Austin, Baltimore, Cincinnati, Memphis, and Miami.

Thrifty Airport Parking

http://www.thriftynorthwest.com/AIRPORTPRK/AIRPORT.htm

Known for its car rental services, Thrifty also offers parking and shuttle services to SeaTac and Portland Airports.

*Live Traffic Control

Johnny Jet Code: Traffic Control

Do you like to listen to live air traffic control when you're flying? If so, some airports allow you to listen from your computer at home. You can also check out all the current flights in the U.S. airspace on the radar.

Air Traffic Café

http://www.airtrafficcafe.com

This is the most comprehensive site on air traffic control. Its goal is to improve quality, safety, and awareness within the ATC system through education and discussion. Air Traffic Café hopes to provide a clearer and broader insight to the workings of air traffic control as it relates to aviation, air travel, and occupational duties.

JFK

http://realserver.brooklyn.cuny.edu:8080/ramgen/encoder/jfk.rm

Here is a live radio feed of New York's JFK air traffic control.

Dallas Fort Worth Air Traffic Control

http://www.broadcast.com/simuflite

Listen to Dallas Fort Worth's air traffic control.

Chicago O'Hare Air Traffic Control

http://cyberair.com/audio/chiapp/index.html

Listen to Chicago O'Hare's air traffic control.

Centennial Airport Tower

http://www.airparts.com/tower.html

Listen to a live feed from the Centennial Airport Tower.

Live Air Traffic Control at Bankstown Airport

http://www.basair.com.au/bktower.shtml

Listen to live air traffic control from Bankstown Airport in Australia.

NASA Space Center Video Feeds

http://science.ksc.nasa.gov/shuttle/countdown/video/video45.html

See live video feeds of NASA's Space Center.

Chapter 9

Aviation

Are you fascinated with planes like Johnny? Here you can check out all the different types of planes, current and past. You can also surf Aviation Organization sites find out the latest from the FAA to the AOPA.

***Aviation Organizations**

http://www.acpi.org
http://www.aiaa.org
http://www.airlines.org
http://www.airportnet.org
http://www.airsearchrescue.com
http://www.aopa.org
http://www.faa.gov
http://www.iata.org
http://www.icao.int
http://www.iswap.org
http://www.natca.org
http://www.nbba.org
http://www.nemspa.org
http://www.ninety-nines.org
http://www.rotor.com
http://www.ssa.org
http://www.vtol.org

Here are some aviation organizations. Some include the FAA, American Helicopter Society, American Association of Airport Executives, American Institute of Aeronautics, and more. Check out *Johnny Jet Code: Aviation Org*

*Airplanes

Johnny Jet Code: Airplanes

I like to know what size plane I am flying. Just ask the reservation agent or look on your itinerary to see what type of aircraft you will be traveling on and check here to see the seating arrangements and other info about your plane.

AeroLink.com

http://www.aerolink.com

Since 1995, AeroLink has been a commercial aviation portal and directory of the professional and commercial aviation industry. The site features over 10,000 airline and aviation sites.

Airliners

http://www.airliners.net

If you are looking for a plane, you won't have to look elsewhere. This site has a huge archive of airplane pictures, statistics on the airliners, and history to read. It's basically a search engine for aircrafts. The only thing missing is the flights.

Heliport Search

http://www.rotor.com/fox/heli-2.htm

If you are looking for a heliport, this site provided by the Helicopter Association International will certainly help you find it. You can search by heliport name, city, state, and facility type, whether it may be a heliport, balloonport, gliderport, seaplane base, ultralight, stolport, or gliderport.

*The Boeing Company

http://www.boeing.com

Boeing is an aerospace engineering company that manufacturers jet planes. *Johnny Jet Code: Boeing*

*Aviation History

The history of flight is quite fascinating.
There is so much you can learn about it. For a little history on aviation, check out Johnny Jet Code: Aviation History

*Aviation Publications

There are a variety of aviation publications available to read. For aviation publications, check out Johnny Jet Code: Aviation Pubs

*First Flight

The Wright brothers took the first flight in 1903. To learn more about this flight, check out Johnny Jet Code: First Flight

*Planes of the Past

It's amazing to see how many different planes there were in the past and check out the pictures of the evolution of airplanes. For information on airplanes of the past, check out Johnny Jet Code: Past Planes

*Record Flights

There are all sorts of records that can be found in the Guinness Book of World Records, but the records for flights are quite fascinating. For record breaking flights, check out Johnny Jet Code: Record Flights

Chapter 10

Bored In Your Hotel Room?

Are you bored in your hotel room? Don't just sit there and twiddle your thumbs. Go out! But if you rather hang out inside, then check out these sites. Online crossword puzzles, TV guides, in room online entertainment, and instructions on how to make paper airplanes are all here.

*Bible and Religious Reading

http://www.bartleby.com/108
Bartleby provides versions of both the Old and New Testament. You may be aware that there is probably a bible to be found somewhere in the hotel room. If not, you can always read the online prayers at *Johnny Jet Code: Bible Prayer*

*Horoscopes

What's your sign? Are you a Virgo, Leo, Scorpio, or one of the others? Check out your horoscope at Johnny Jet Code: Astrology Sign

*Online Games

If you would like to play some games while you are in the hotel. Check out Johnny Jet Code: Gaming

*Paper Airplanes

Making paper airplanes could be so much fun while you are bored when traveling. Johnny Jet Code: Paper Planes

*Really Bored?

You can do things when you are really bored, and the Internet is filled with them. Bored.com is of course a great boredom buster, yet there are plenty more. Check out Johnny Jet Code: Really Bored

*Travel Humor

Johnny Jet Code: Funny Travel

Air Toons

http://www.airtoons.com

You are familiar with those airline safety cards. At this site you will laugh about them with parodies of these safety tips. It's available in both clean and dirty versions.

Dumb Laws

http://www.dumblaws.com

Ohio has a law that states, "It's illegal to get a fish drunk." That's just one of the many dumb laws you will find here.

Flight Humor

http://www.flighthumor.org

Presented by the University of Dayton, this funny site celebrates humor in aviation with a special tribute to Erma Bombeck.

Improv

http://www.improv.com

If you are looking to laugh at live standup comedy, The Improv Comedy Clubs across the United States are great. You can find the nearest Improve here.

Jokes.com

http://www.jokes.com

You'll find thousands of jokes at this site.

Pogo.com

http://www.pogo.com

Pogo offers a variety of different games with everything from crosswords and word games to card and board games, trivia, casino games, and much more.

Salon.com

http://www.salon.com

There are some good articles, some humor, travel and much more to be found at Salon.

The Onion

http://www.theonion.com

The Onion offers some great humor while you are on the go. This "onion" may make you laugh more than cry. It's recommended for mature audiences.

The Smoking Gun

http://www.thesmokinggun.com

The Smoking Gun provides interesting and humorous documents with everything from confidential government resources to top-secret info.

Miniclip

http://www.miniclip.com

Waiting for room service? Play some free games and watch some mini animation clips.

National Lampoon

http://www.nationallampoon.com

If you are looking for a little wild and crazy humor, National Lampoon is here to provide it.

Watch a Movie

CinemaSpot.com

http://www.cinemaspot.com

You'll find almost everything related to movies at this movie portal. It includes reviews and show times as well as award winners, discussion groups, trivia, and much more.

Cinemascore.com

http://www.cinemascore.com

How is a movie doing in the box office or the theatre? This site scores the latest Hollywood films with a letter grades and shows you how much it made in the box office.

Entertainment

http://abcnews.go.com/sections/entertainment

http://www.cnn.com/SHOWBIZ

http://www.etonline.com

http://www.eonline.com

http://www.ew.com

Here are some sites that you will not pass up for entertainment news and more.

Internet Movie Database

http://www.imdb.com

The IMDB is the most comprehensive database of movies and actors on the Web. If you are looking for cartoons, check the Big Cartoon Database at www.bcdb.com.

Movie Show and Tickets

http://movies.yahoo.com/movies

http://www.moviefone.com

Find movie showings and tickets.

Feed Room

http://www.feedroom.com

Sometimes the best television may be found on your computer. The Feed Room combines television with your computer and you are good to go while you watch television feeds of everything from news to ads.

ForMovies.com

http://www.formovies.com

This is a directory of local video stores where you can search for titles in your area. There are rankings of the top rentals, and box office hits.

Flashcan Animator

http://www.flashcan.com

Enjoy watching and making some flash films.

Flash Comedy

http://www.flashcomedy.com

Enjoy some quick flash comedy produced by digital artists.

Apple QuickTime Movie Trailers

http://www.apple.com/trailers

Apple Computer offers a great selection of movie trailer previews to watch online.

Like Television

http://www.liketelevision.com

If it's not television, it's like television, and this site will entertain those subscribers looking for everything from downloadable classics and cartoons to science fiction and comedy.

IFILM.com

http://www.ifilm.com

IFILM is a leading provider of broadband Internet entertainment. You'll find the largest collection of short films and movie clips here.

I Want My Flash TV

http://www.iwantmyflashtv.com

Flash entertainment and short flash movies at its greatest can be found here where digital flash artists showcase their works.

MovieFlix.com

http://www.movieflix.com

MovieFlix.com was founded in 1998 and has become a leader in online movie entertainment. It has a library of well over 2,500 full-length movies that are free and premium short films, independent films, and television shows in thirty categories.

Movie Mistakes

http://www.moviemistakes.com

It might be safe to say that there is at least one mistake in every movie. Well, this site tells you almost all of them. You'll find all films, top films, and even some movie trivia to keep you entertained.

Ain't It Cool News

http://www.aintitcoolnews.com

This site by Harry Knowles provides unique and interesting movie reviews of upcoming films, without spoiling the endings. You'll find a message board, a live chat, multimedia clips, and more.

Rotten Tomatoes

http://www.rottentomatoes.com

This is a great place to find movie reviews for the movie aficionado or not. You can view show times, check reviews of hundreds of thousands of movies, and there are links to trailers. If you are interested in looking up the actors or directors, you'll find them here too.

Stupid Videos

http://www.stupidvideos.com

This site holds a collection of quick, but humorous and "stupid" videos to watch and rate.

Supercala

http://www.supercala.com

You'll find some of the most entertaining movie reviews at this site. This site is also *www.supercalafragalistic.com.*

Television Guide

http://www.tvguide.com

The TV Guide has some television, movie, and show guides to check out. For movies, visit www.tvguide.com/movies and you will see what's in the theatres.

Soon to be Released

http://www.comingsoon.net

http://www.upcomingmovies.com

At Coming Soon and Yahoo! Upcoming Movies you can read the latest on what movies are about to be released and more.

*Crossword Puzzles

http://www.crossword-puzzles.co.uk

You will find some of the best crossword puzzles on the Web. If you are looking for crossword clues and tips check out *www.oneacross.com* and for more crossword puzzles, check out *Johnny Jet Code: Word Puzzles*

Chapter 11

Crew and Pilots

For flight attendants, pilots and people who want to be one! We have all the sites you need to keep you up to date with your unions and ever changing industry. We also have all the best Interline Discount sites out there, so when you are traveling for fun you can do it for cheap!

*Calling All Flight Attendants

Johnny Jet Code: Flight Attendants

Airline Staff

http://www.airlinestaff.com

This is the online hangout for flight crew. There are airline vacancies, funny email jokes, cabin crew perks, employment info, and more for the staff.

Association of Flight Attendants

http://www.afanet.org

Here is the largest labor union created by flight attendants. The organization has over 50,000 flight attendants representing 26 airlines. The goal is to negotiate improved pay, benefits, better working conditions, and safety.

The Cockpit Forum

http://www.cockpitforum.com

This club was especially created to offer worldwide value vacations to airline employees and their friends and families.

Crash Pads

http://www.crashpads.com

This site has a crash pad listing service that includes places to stay for airline professionals.

Crew Start

http://www.crewstart.com

This is a directory portal for an airline crew. It has airline news, airbus news, Boeing news, travel news, top stories, and more.

Date A Pilot

http://www.dateapilot.com

Would you like to date a pilot? Those in the industry can find others to meet on this dating site.

Flight Attendants Organization

http://www.flightattendants.org

This professional organization for flight attendants has discussion forums, crew chat, resources for attendants, and more.

Flight Attendant Association of Australia

http://www.faaadomestic.org.au

Keep updated with the complex issues in the Australian aviation industry.

In-Flight Careers

http://www.inflightcareers.com

This site offers a flight attendant career training program.

Interline Discounts

http://www.interlinediscounts.com

Airline employees deserve a break, and can benefit from airline discounts on tours, hotels, and numerous travel packages. Savings also include deals on golf, scuba, and more.

Jet Angels

http://www.jetangels.org

This site provides information on health and safety issues for flight attendants, and people in the aviation industry. Topics covered include: occupational illness, travel incidents such as dizziness and nausea, workers compensation, and prevention of illness.

KLM UK Pilot

http://www.klmukpilot.co.uk

This is the official site for the KLM UK pilots.

Learn to Fly

http://www.aopaflighttraining.org

http://www.beapilot.com

http://www.learntofly.com

http://www.studentpilot.com

If learning to fly a plane is something you endeavor, then check out some of these sites that may help you fly better.

Airline Pilot's Security Alliance

http://www.secure-skies.org

The APSA is a grass roots organization devoted to improving airline security. It believes that combining improved security and aircrafts along with volunteering pilots with firearms will ensure maximum possible security.

Sky Hag

http://www.skyhag.net

This is an unofficial America West flight attendant bonding site created by a flight attendant.

Sky-Highs.com Hosiery

http://www.sky-highs.com

This site offers graduated compression hosiery designed for flight attendants.

*Crew Layovers

For information on crew layovers, check out Johnny Jet Code: Crew Layovers

*Interline Discounts

Airline employees deserve a break, and can benefit from airline discounts on tours, hotels, numerous travel packages, golf, scuba, and more. For more info on interline discounts, check out Johnny Jet Code: Interline

*Jobs in Travel

For information on jobs in the travel industry, check out Johnny Jet Code: Travel Jobs

*Pilot Info

If you're a pilot you won't want to miss out on these important pilot Web sites. Check out Johnny Jet Code: Pilot Info

*Pilot Unions

We list all of the pilot unions here. Check out Johnny Jet Code: Pilot Unions

Chapter 12

Food on the Road

Traveling to a city and not sure where to eat? Well, then log on to these dining guides and see what restaurants will satisfy your palate. You can also find out where all the fast food restaurant and chains are located so you don't have to keep driving around the block looking for them. If you are traveling abroad you may want to check out the Department of Food Safety at www.who.int/fsf where you can read an articles about food safety when traveling to foreign countries.

*Cooking Schools

Looking to go to cooking school?
Check out a few sites at Johnny Jet Code: Cooking School

*Fast Food Restaurant Chains

Johnny Jet Code: Chain Dine

A & W *http://www.awrestauranats.com*
Arby's *http://www.arby.com*
Boston Market *http://www.boston-market.com*
Burger King *http://www.burgerking.com/locator/search.asp*
Carl's Jr. *http://www.carlsjr.com*
Church's Chicken *http://www.churchs.com*
Eat 'N Park *http://www.eatnpark.com*
Fat Burger *http://www.fatburger.com*
Fudd Ruckers *http://www.fuddruckers.com*
Hot Dog On A Stick *http://www.hotdogonastick.com*
KFC *http://www.kfc.com*
Koo Koo Roo *http://www.kookooroo.com*
In-N-Out Burger *http://www.in-n-out.com*
Jack in the Box *http://www.jackinthebox.com*
McDonald's Restaurant Locator *http://www.vicinity.com/mcdonalds*
Panda Express *http://www.pandaexpress.com*
Popeyes *http://www.popeyes.com*
Roy Rogers *http://www.plamondonroyrogers.com*
Sonic Drive-In *http://www.sonicdrivein.com*
Steak and Ale *http://www.steakale.com*
Steak 'N Shake *http://www.steaknshake.com*
Wendy's *http://www.wendys.com*
White Castle *http://www.whitecastle.com*
Wienerschnitzel *http://www.wienerschnitzel.com*

Enjoy some of your fast food favorites.

Fast Food Nutrition

http://www.olen.com/food

Have you ever wondered how nutritious is the food from Pizza Hut, Burger King, McDonald's, Baskin and Robbins, and other fast food restaurants? Get some facts and figures on fast food.

Pizza

http://www.chuckecheese.com
http://www.cpk.com
http://www.dominos.com
http://www.littlecaesars.com
http://www.papajohns.com
http://www.pizzahut.com
http://www.roundtablepizza.com
http://www.sbarro.com

From Chuck E. Cheese's, California Pizza to Sbarro, there are some great pizza chains to enjoy.

Mexican Food

http://www.bajafresh.com
http://www.chevys.com
http://www.chi-chis.com
http://www.chipotle.com
http://www.cozymels.com
http://www.eltorito.com
http://www.lasalsa.com
http://www.rubios.com
http://www.tacobell.com
http://www.tacojohns.com
http://www.wahoos.com

Spice up your dinner with some tacos, beans, burritos, and more.

Bagels

http://www.brueggers.com

http://www.einsteinbros.com

http://www.manhattanbagel.com

http://www.noahs.com

Munch on a bagel with cream cheese, and more.

Sandwiches

http://www.blimpie.com

http://www.miamisubs.com

http://www.quiznos.com

http://www.schlotzkys.com

http://www.subway.com

http://www.togos.com

From Blimpie to Subway, you can catch a sub for the road.

Coffee Shops

http://www.cariboucoffee.com

http://www.coffeebean.com

http:://www.peets.com

http://www.starbucks.com

If you don't have enough "java" online, you will certainly find some at these places where quality coffee beans, tastefully brewed coffees, cold beverages, pastries, and more are served.

Juices and Smoothies

http://www.orangejulius.com

http://www.jambajuice.com

http://www.smoothieking.com

Enjoy some freshly squeezed juices or an ice-cold smoothie.

Donuts

http://www.dunkindonuts.com

http://www.krispykreme.com

http://www.winchells.com

Some of the best donuts or doughnuts can be found online at these delicious donut hangouts. Find where the closest donut shop is located, and start dunking and dipping.

Pretzels

http://www.auntieannes.com
http://www.wetzels.com
Enjoy some warm pretzels.

Desserts

http://www.candydirect.com
http://www.cinnabon.com
http://www.cookiesbydesign.com
http://www.godiva.com
http://www.hickoryfarms.com
http://www.mrsfields.com
http://www.nabiscogifts.com
Enjoy some delicious desserts.

Fruit

http://www.gotfruit.com
Get some great fruit platters.

Ice Cream

http://www.baskinrobbins.com
http://www.benjerry.com
http://www.carvel.com
http://www.dairyqueen.com
http://www.haagen-dazs.com
http://www.tcby.com
Enjoy some cool and refreshing ice cream.

*Recipes

http://www.allrecipes.com
http://www.bettycrocker.com
http://www.cdkitchen.com
http://www.cooksmuse.com
http://www.copykat.com
http://www.epicurious.com
http://www.foodtv.com
http://www.recipesource.com
http://www.topsecretrecipes.com
http://www.yumyum.com
If you are looking for recipes, these sites will certainly help you find some. *Johnny Jet Code: Recipes*

*Restaurant Discounts

Johnny Jet Code: Meal Deals

Diners Club

http://www.dinersclubnorthamerica.com
The Diners Club offers dining discounts for card members.

Dine for less

http://www.dine4less.com
Find great savings with online restaurant coupons for dining out. Save up your dining dollars and check out the discounts here. You may find that you are becoming a new dining dweller.

In Good Taste Card

http://www.igtcard.com
This card is honored at more than 2,000 restaurants giving you discounts each time you dine.

IDine

http://www.idine.com
IDine has a frequent restaurant program where you can save up to 20% on dining.

Diner City

http://www.dinercity.com

Steel and porcelain diners are classic and this site is a directory to some of the most known diners in the United States. Find your closest diner, take a diner photo tour, get some diner facts, and read and write some diner reviews.

Epiculinary Distinctive Cooking Journeys

http://www.epiculinary.com

Epiculinary is a unique culinary tour operating company. The purpose of this site is to attract people to tour another country and learn about cooking and different cultures. Programs are offered in France, Italy, Spain, and the U.S. Making tapas in Spain, bouillabaisse in France, or pasta in Italy, this site caters for all tastes and budgets.

Fat-Guy.com

http://www.fat-guy.com

Lawyer, food critic, and restaurant connoisseur Steven Shaw spends his time dining out and reviewing restaurants in New York City, France, and Canada. What does he think of these restaurants and which are his favorites? He has a different kind of reviewing philosophy. Visit this site to find out.

RoadFood.com

http://www.roadfood.com

You've been on the road looking for a good meal off the highway and this site provides that information. It's devoted to finding restaurants and other memorable local eateries on the road. You can submit your own reviews of road food, too.

Search Chicago

http://www.searchchicago.com

Chicago has some of the best restaurants and this site searches for them. You can search by location, price, cuisine, and restaurant name. There's also a section that has restaurant reviews.

Seattle Dining

http://www.seattledining.com
Seattle is a beautiful city and dining there is great. At this site, you can read articles, reviews, news, and get deals from restaurants and grocers located in Seattle.

Theme Restaurants

http://www.tgifridays.com
http://www.hardrock.com/locations/cafes
http://www.planethollywood.com
http://www.rainforestcafe.com
Check out the menus at some popular themed restaurants and see what the latest happenings are here.

*Restaurant Guides

Johnny Jet Code: Restaurant Guide

Don't know where to eat? Now you can check out these online guides and find out what they recommend and how much it costs. Some even allow you to make a reservation from your computer.

Zagat

http://www.zagat.com
Nina and Tim Zagat founded Zagat in 1979. Zagat's Survey is well known for its thousands of ratings of restaurants and hotels. The site gives you more than forty cities within the U.S. to visit along with searches under categories of restaurants, cuisine, popularity, and neighborhoods.

Open Table Restaurant Reservations

http://www.opentable.com
Open Table provides restaurant searches in major U.S. cities along with unique real-time online reservations. Search by region, restaurant, cuisine, and price.

SavvyDiner.com

http://www.savvydiner.com

Make your dinner reservations online with ease by clicking on the U.S. city. This site includes map directions to the restaurant, a menu, along with a picture of the restaurant.

Restaurant Row

http://www.restaurantrow.com

This is the world's largest dining guide with over 100,000 restaurants. You can find restaurants by restaurant name or zip. Other searches are done by proximity, neighborhood, county, or more advanced searches. Find out which restaurants are in the top ten by city. It is available to mobile Internet users and you can easily find the location and phone number of the restaurant, make reservations, and find information on the restaurant.

Global Dining

http://www.globaldining.com

Global Dining is a directory of over 500,000 restaurants around the world. You can search by state, country, and zip. It is available for mobile Internet users and you can easily find the location and phone number of the restaurant, make reservations, and find information on the restaurant.

The Sushi World Guide

http://www.sushi.to

Where can you find great sushi? Visiting this site will help you find some of the most amazing sushi restaurants in the world. Search by continent, country, city, restaurant, or address.

Vegetarian Resource Group Travel Articles

http://www.vrg.org/travel

Vegetarians will find this site useful because it has plenty of resources on traveling as a vegetarian. Articles, online resources, vacation guides, dining guides, and more for the vegetarian can be found here. See Vegetarian section.

Shamash Kosher Restaurant

http://shamash.org/kosher

If eating kosher foods is important to you when you dine, this site provides a database of kosher restaurants around the world.

Restaurant.com

http://www.restaurant.com

This is a directory of restaurants nationwide that provides news and information about dining out. It provides information on where you can save on your next meal and dining gift certificates.

Where to Dine

http://www.where-to-dine.com

This is a site dedicated to the art of dining. The goal is to provide a comprehensive directory of restaurants, complete menus, detailed restaurant information, recipe sites, and cooking products.

*Food to Go

http://www.cooking.com/recipes/reweekmp.asp

http://www.deliverme.com

http://www.waiter.com

If you are looking for food to take on the go, then these may help. Check out *Johnny Jet Code: Food to Go*

*Vegetarians

Johnny Jet Code: Vegetarians

About Vegetarians

http://www.vegetarian.about.com

If you are a vegetarian, you will find plenty of vegetarian resources, answers to your questions, articles, and much more.

Happy Cow

http://www.happycow.net

Happy Cow brings vegetarians worldwide a gathering place to find vegetarian and vegan restaurant offerings and locations. There is information on becoming a vegetarian along with a vegetarian message board.

Vegetarian Times

http://www.vegetariantimes.com

This magazine offers plenty of resources for vegetarians, including articles, recipes, a restaurant directory, and bulletin boards.

The Vegetarian Channel

http://www.thevegetarianchannel.com

This channel is a UK directory that will take you to many recipe resources for vegetarians and vegans.

Veg Web

http://www.vegweb.com

Vegetarians unite to enjoy articles, recipes, message boards, and health resources for vegetarians and vegans.

Vegetarian Dining

http://www.vegdining.com

Vegetarian restaurants around the world can be found at this site that caters to the vegetarian. The mission here is "to promote vegetarianism by doing our best to promote vegetarian restaurants around the world."

VegSource Travel

http://www.vegsource.com/travel

Come here to post your comments and read other comments about traveling as a vegetarian?

Vegetarians Abroad

http://www.vegetariansabroad.com

This is a vegetarian resource directory for vegetarian and vegan friendly travel, accommodations, and recipes.

Vegetarian USA

http://www.vegetarianusa.com

This red, white, blue vegetarian site has everything from vegetarian resources, travel, dietary lifestyles, and natural interests from environmental to yoga resources.

*Vegetarian Vacations

For more information on vegetarian vacations, check out *Johnny Jet Code: Veggie Vacations*

Chapter 13

Traveling with the Family

*Family Trips

Johnny Jet Code: Family Travels

Are you taking the family on a vacation? Here are links that will help you plan, ideas to keep the kids busy, airline policies for minors, and how to find your long lost relatives. If you're interested in adoption travel or planning a family reunion, this one is for you.

Travel Boredom Busters from Sesame Workshop

http://www.ctw.org/parents/advice/article/0,4125,759,00.html

Here are a bunch of games that young kids can play while you are on a road trip. Games include: Counting, I spy, picnic basket, twenty questions, license plate bingo, and more.

Great Vacation Advice from Sesame Workshop

http://www.ctw.org/parents/advice/article/0,4125,756,00.html

Here is some advice to keep kids happier on the trip.

Beach in a Bag Kinder Art Littles

http://www.kinderart.com/littles/beach.shtml

This site has a lesson plan that helps explain the beach to children. Make your own beach in a bag.

Beach and Ocean

http://www.preschooleducation.com/beach.shtml

Young kids can learn about the beach and the ocean through interactive crafts.

About.com Travel with Kids

http://www.travelwithkids.about.com

What would you like to know about traveling with kids? This site explains all about family travel. Whether you are looking for vacation ideas, cruises with kids, Disney vacations, things to do in the car or plane, vacations with teens, and more, it can be found here.

Adoption Travel

http://www.adoptiontravel.com

Adoption Travel is a resource for parents planning adoption travel internationally. The site features travel destinations, travel articles, travel tips, and adoption links.

Baby Center Travel

http://www.babycenter.com/travel

Are you traveling with a baby or toddler or traveling while you are pregnant? This site provides tips for the trip to make it a safe and comfortable travel experience with your baby. You'll find answers to your questions on safety, essential gear, and information you need before you take the baby.

Cyber Parent Traveling with Kids

http://www.cyberparent.com/trips

Traveling with kids can be fun, but how do you keep them happy on the trip? This site provides many resources for keeping kids happy while traveling, and enjoying your trip at the same time. The site has tips on relaxing, taking a family cruise, flying with kids, and information on single parent travel.

Family Fun

http://www.familyfun.com

Disney's Family Fun site is filled with activities, parenting advice, recipes, arts and crafts, and family travel. You'll find places for the family to go, things to see, and do, and much more for the whole family to enjoy and explore.

Family Travel Files

http://www.familytravelfiles.com

This site makes family travel a little bit easier by providing family travel resources, various family travel vacations, a directory of family travel, travel tools, and much more.

Family Adventure Travel Directory

http://www.familyadventuretravel.com

This directory features companies that offer adventure travel around the world.

Family Travel Forum

http://www.familytravelforum.com

FTF is devoted to offering family travel savings for its members. There is a family travel newsletter with different family travel articles, family travel advice, bulletin boards, and family travel news.

Family Travel Guides

http://www.familytravelguides.com

This is an excellent resource to find vacation ideas, tips, and special deals for the whole traveling family. The site consists of family travel articles, vacation packages, adventure family travel, a lodging database, food for the road, great outdoors, and more for the traveling family.

Family Travel Network

http://www.familytravelnetwork.com

This is a great online gathering place for families planning a trip. Families of all walks, parents, and kids can talk to others who experienced the trips, and travel experts alike. Trip planning, travel activities for kids and teens, a message board, and much more can be found here.

Family Travel Times

http://www.familytraveltimes.com

This site is subscriber based and it has a bi-monthly newsletter featuring family travel, and articles.

GORP Family

http://www.gorp.com/gorp/eclectic/family.htm

Traveling outdoors with the family? If so, this is an excellent starting point for outdoor family travel. There is information on places to take kids camping, hiking, fishing, biking, and more.

Grand Travel

http://www.grandtrvl.com

Grandparents and grandchildren can enjoy traveling together with this tour operator. A team of teachers, psychologists, and leisure counselors developed the program. The site provides various trips that will make a child have a memorable experience traveling with grandparents.

Family Learning Vacations

http://www.learn.unh.edu/familyhostel

This site takes your family on a learning vacation to learn about a different culture through experience. It's something kids can take from the trip and bring back to their school classrooms, and have memorable times learning while vacationing.

Parent Soup Family Travel

http://www.parentsoup.com/travel

Part of the iVillage.com network, this site provides parents with information they need to know about traveling with kids and keeping them happy on the trip. There are message boards, chats, travel information for families, and more.

Travel for Kids

http://www.travelforkids.com

Before you take your children on your next trip, it's recommended that you visit this site that provides tips on must see tourism selections for kids. The site explains and shows you the various places that most kids will enjoy visiting. You'll also find useful tips on everything from what documents and medicine to take with you to bringing along a favorite stuffed animal.

Traveling Internationally with Your Kids

http://www.travelwithyourkids.com

Long trips with the family can be a great experience, and this site offers a great resource for parents by parents on how to travel long distances with your kids.

Travel and Leisure Family

http://www.tlfamily.com

Travel and Leisure's family division is found here. You can find all sorts of stuff on family travel, whether it may be planning a family trip to Greece, or a backyard campout there is something for the whole family. Check out the perfect vacations section and see some of the best places for your family to travel.

Vacation.com

http://www.vacation.com

Going on a vacation? This site has a network of thousands of travel agencies and agents providing people and families with vacation packages, cruises, tours, and various other travel services.

*Airline Children Policies

Read all about the airline policies devoted to children flying alone. Check out Johnny Jet Code: Child Policy

*Adoption Travel

Planning on adopting out of the country? These sites will help make your trip. Check out Johnny Jet Code: Adoption Travel

*Baby Travel

Everyone knows it's not easy traveling with a baby, but there are some sites that will make it a joy. Check out Johnny Jet Code: Baby Travel

*Family Reunion

Planning a family reunion? We found the sites that were created to help you plan. Check out Johnny Jet Code: Reunion

*Find Lost Relatives

Want to visit those long lost relatives? These sites will help you trace your roots. Check out Johnny Jet Code: Lost Relatives

*Single Parent Travel

Just because you are a single parent doesn't mean you cannot travel. Here are Web sites that are filled with tips and information to point you in the right direction. Check out Johnny Jet Code: Single Parent

*Summer Camps

Want to find the perfect summer camp for your children? We just made it easier for you. Check out Johnny Jet Code: Summer Camp

*Traveling with Children

Be prepared before you go on that long trip with your kids. Driving or flying, we have the sites you need to research. Check out Johnny Jet Code: Travel Kids

Chapter 14

Health, Medical and Safety

Being safe in your travel adventures is more important than ever. We have all the necessary sites to keep safe on your trip, everything from insurance, medical, and actual FAA, and security precautions. Airport security is stricter and that's why it is important to be prepared when you arrive at the airport. Always have a valid picture ID ready and your ticket out at the gate. It's important to be patient if airport security pulls you to the side to inspect you. Let them do their job, they aren't out to get you, they are just making sure everyone has a safe trip.

*Air Rage

Air rage is becoming more common these days. These sites will show you how to be prepared. Check out Johnny Jet Code: Air Rage

*Doctor House Calls

Johnny Jet Code: Doctor Calls

Web MD

http://www.webmd.com

Web MD is a leading provider of medical information to consumers, doctors, and other health providers.

Doctor Directory

http://www.doctordirectory.com

Looking for a doctor while you're traveling? You will find a directory of doctor names, addresses, phone numbers, and maps to physician offices.

MD Hub

http://www.mdhub.com

Contacting your doctor isn't always easy when you're in town or out of town. This service was created so patients and doctors can communicate securely through fax and email.

Docs Online

http://www.docsonline.com

Docs Online offers a premiere health care directory where you can locate dentists, physicians, health care providers, and hospitals based on your health care needs.

Health Central

http://www.healthcentral.com

Health Central provides an information community of easily accessible health-related content concerning today's health issues. It also offers a wide range of health-related products.

London Doctor Call

http://www.doctorcall.co.uk

Doctor Call provides healthcare services in London, for residents, tourists and visitors alike.

Express Doctors

http://www.expressdoctors.com

If you need a doctor for a non-life threatening medical emergency, you can visit this site and find one any time of the day, whether you are on a wireless phone or the Internet.

*First Aid

You can never have enough information on First Aid.
Now it's at your fingertips. Check out Johnny Jet Code: First Aid

Healthy Guides

Armchair World: Your Health Abroad

http://www.armchair.com/info/health.html

Armchair World explains what you need to know about your health when traveling abroad. Topics cover health insurance, medications, health risks with food and drink, injuries, animal related hazards, traveler's diarrhea, bug and mosquito protection, swimming precautions, blood transfusions, HIV/AIDS and travel, and what you should know after you return from your trip. The main domain covers topics on travel, cuisine, and world perspectives.

Healthy Flying

http://www.flyana.com

Diana Fairechild's site is a great resource for information on healthy and safe travel. Some of the topics covered include: airline air, airline meals, crew fatigue, deep vein thrombosis, dehydration, ear pain, fear of flying, stress, and more.

Lonely Planet Health Check

http://www.lonelyplanet.com/health

This site divides health related travel issues into five categories: Predeparture Planning, Keeping Healthy, Women's Health, Diseases and Ailments, and Health Links. For instance, the Diseases and Ailments section explains how to combat cuts, bites, stings, conquering motion sickness, and covers infectious and diseases.

World Health Organization

http://www.who.int/home-page

This international organization is an authority site on health worldwide. Striving to bring everyone maximum health, this site provides news and information on health issues from all people throughout the world.

*Jet Lag

Johnny Jet Code: Jet Lag

Doctor Travel

http://www.doctor-travel.com/jetlag.html
Doctor Travel writes here to help you to avoid and prevent jet lag.

Coping with Jet Lag

http://www.travelassist.com/mag/a81
Here are some tips to help alleviate jet lag.

Jet Lag Eliminator

http://www.jetlag.net
Here is a jet lag solution that works with acupressure.

Litebook

http://www.litebook.com
This book of light may be your cure for jet lag, seasonal affective disorders, and other symptoms that may be cured by light.

Stop Jet Lag

http://www.stopjetlag.com
Learn how to beat jet lag with this proven plan by using bright light, melatonin, sleep cycles, and your diet.

No Jet Lag

http://www.nojetlag.com
This site explains what jet lag is, who gets, it and how you can prevent it. They also have a tablet pill product that you can get and it will combat jet lag.

*Keeping Safe While Traveling

Johnny Jet Code: Health and Safety

Staying Healthy

American Society of Tropical Medicine and Hygiene

http://www.astmh.org

The ASTMH provides information on prevention and control of tropical diseases with medical entomology, frequently asked questions, other resources, and a travel clinic directory.

Centers for Disease Control Travelers' Health

http://www.cdc.gov/travel

The National Center for Infectious Disease presents this site that informs people about issues of outbreaks, diseases, and vaccinations. You'll find detailed health warnings pertaining to every country with information on how to avoid illness from food and water, travelers with special needs, and traveling with children and pets. Find what immunizations you need before you go.

GORP Health

http://www.gorp.com/gorp/health/main.htm

Keeping safe while you are outdoors is the utmost importance at this site. Answers to frequently asked questions such as treating water, identifying poisons, preventing dehydration, hypothermia, acute mountain sickness, and more can be found here.

Health Advice for Travelers

http://www.doh.gov.uk/traveladvice

The UK Department of Health provides a resourceful site on health advice for travelers.

High Altitude Medical Guide

http://www.high-altitude-medicine.com

This site provides current medical information on the prevention, recognition, and treatment of altitude illness, as well as other health issues affecting travelers in high mountainous regions of the world.

International Society of Travel Medicine Clinic Directory

http://www.istm.org

Traveling out of the country can lead to great adventures, but you also take certain health risks. It's necessary to have immunization, and to take the proper medication and antibiotics for the trip. This site provides a directory of over 500 health clinics around the world.

Travel Health Online

http://www.tripprep.com

This all inclusive site gets you prepared for the trip by providing travel information with a guided overview of vaccines, diseases, health and safety, and special needs travel in most places outside the United States. Click on a destination and find valuable health and safety information on where you are going.

CDC National Center for Environmental Health

http://www.cdc.gov/nceh

The environment is everything around us and this site promotes health and the quality of living by preventing diseases, birth defects, disabilities, and deaths resulting from human interaction with the environment. One section of particular interest to travelers is the vessel sanitation page www.cdc.gov/nceh/vsp where you can see what the NCEH is doing to keep cruises sanitized. Find out which cruises scored well.

Virtual Hospital

http://www.vh.org

The virtual hospital provides a digital science library where you can find information related to health care for providers and patients. This site will keep you informed with first aid and what you should know when traveling.

*Medical Air Services

Johnny Jet Code: Med Flight

Air Ambulance

http://www.airambulance.com

This is North America's oldest licensed air ambulance service available 24 hours a day, seven days a week.

Med Jet International

http://www.medjet.com

Headquartered in Birmingham Alabama, Med Jet specializes in medical transports.

Medical Flight Assistance Group

http://www.medflightag.com

This is an annual membership group that provides emergency medical air transportation to members worldwide.

*Motion Sickness

Johnny Jet Code: Motion Sickness

About Motion Sickness

http://www.seasickness.co.uk

This site emphasizes remedies to prevent seasickness. It explains what seasickness is, who gets it, what triggers it, how it can be prevented, what remedies are available, and medical documentation papers for seasickness.

Motion Eaze

http://www.motion-sickness.net

This is a 7 herbal oil-based product that you can apply to your skin to help prevent motion sickness.

Sea Band

http://www.sea-band.com

Sea Band is a product you can wear on your wrist that helps prevent motion and seasickness.

Travel Band

http://www.travelband.com

This is a knitted elastic wristband that helps prevent motion sickness.

Scopace

http://www.motionsickness.net

This is a prescription medication that provides prevention of motion sickness.

Relief Band

http://www.reliefband.com

This wristband offers a patented wrist product remedy for motion sickness.

*Overcoming Travel Fears

Johnny Jet Code: Why Fear

Afraid to Fly

I used to be afraid now look at me, I fly over 150,000 miles a year on 100 different flights. I know how you feel so it's okay, you can get over it. There are many ways you can conquer your travel fears. These sites should help. If not, contact us and we will go from there.

Virtually Better SOAR Conquers Fear of Flying

http://www.fearofflying.com

Overcoming "aviophobia" or fear of flying is a start at this site that offers professional services, and answers to frequently asked questions to conquer flying phobias.

Fear of Flying Clinic

http://www.fofc.com

This Californian based company offers classes to help offset the fear that many have of flying. Although they can't guarantee any miracle cures, you'll find plenty of tools to help you conquer the fear of flying.

Fear of Flying Resources

http://www.celebratetoday.com/airres.html

There is a great deal of fear of flying Web resources here. This site originally created for celebrating calendar events, so if you overcome your fear of flying there are other things to enjoy here.

*Pharmacies

Are you away from home and looking for a pharmacy?
Well, now you can log on and find where the closest one to you.
Check out Johnny Jet Code: Pharmacy

*Safety and Security

Johnny Jet Code: Travel Safety

Airline Safety

http://www.airlinesafety.com

This site provides comprehensive information on airline safety along with a "free-market forum" for the discussion of relevant policies and issues from an editor who believes that government regulation does not help.

Air Safety Online

http://www.airsafetyonline.com

Air Safety Online was founded in 1998 and is a leading provider of aviation safety and news resources dedicated to members of the commercial airline industry, the media, and the flying public.

Airline Safety Information Pages

http://www.airsafe.com

Air safety is becoming a more important issue daily, and this site focus on selected events, accidents in the travel industry, and current aviation issues. Air Safe provides information and resources on fear of flying, aviation books, and other travel-safety resources. Records from over 100 airlines are presented.

Aviation Safety Network

http://www.aviation-safety.net

This site provides a database with listing of all airplane accidents since 1945.

Aviation Health Institute

http://www.aviation-health.org

This is the world's first private non-profit organization dealing with the health and well being of airline passengers. The objective is to "encourage research, educate the public and the industry, and to seek ways of preventing and reducing health risks to the flying public."

Boeing Safety

http://www.boeing.com/safety

Airplane manufacturer Boeing informs people on aviation safety, with information on who is responsible, how accidents are investigated, and how jetliners fly.

FAA Aviation Safety

http://www.faa.gov/aviationsafety

The Federal Aviation Administration is a government held site that provides safety information along with databases created to keep the public aware of aviation safety statistics, investigations of aircraft accidents and incidents. The site links to FAA safety programs, info on keeping safer skies, runway safety, aviation security, safety statistics, and the National Transportation Safety Board.

Flight Safety Foundation

http://www.flightsafety.org

The Flight Safety Foundation is an independent, non-profit international organization that offers information on flight safety with a neutral meeting environment for the aviation industry.

FRAC

http://www.frac.com

Established in 1991, the Foreseeable Risk Analysis Center provides information on traveler safety and security. The main purpose is to analyze safety and security event data to prevent incidents.

Jet Safety

http://www.jetsafety.com

The mission of this site is to inform and assist military and airline pilots with preventing aircraft accidents. It is hosted by a major airline pilot who also flies jets for the National Air Guard. You'll find information on F-16 crashes, links to crash data, mid-air collision info, and accident photos. There is a resourceful section for kids on basic airplane knowledge.

MASTA

http://www.masta.org

The Medical Advisory Services for Travelers Abroad was set up in 1984 at the London School of Hygiene and Tropical Medicine. The mission is to increase awareness of health issues related to travel.

National Air Disaster Alliance/Foundation

http://www.planesafe.org

The mission of this organization is "to raise standard of safety, security and survivability for aviation passengers and to support victims' families."

Planit Safe

http://www.planitsafe.com

You'll find presentations on flying safety along with a section on fun travel facts and anecdotes, cost cutting travel tips, legal rights, rules and regulations, safety and security tips, and more.

Plane Crash Info

http://www.planecrashinfo.com

This is a database of thousands of airplane accidents, composed of information on the crashes, and actual photos of the crashes, and accident statistics. Although this isn't intended for those with weak stomachs, it is quite informative. Some features include: 100 worst, famous deaths, last words, CVR transcripts, unusual accidents, warning sounds, aircraft specs, and a searchable database by aircraft type and airline. For more information you can visit www.airdisaster.com where you will find more news, a photo gallery, actual crash videos, and such on the very unlikely event of an plane accident.

*U.S. Customs

http://www.customs.treas.gov

The U.S. Customs does more than examine your bags when you leave and enter the country. U.S. Customs protects the borders and protects citizens us from people bringing unwanted things into the country. Check out this site if you wanted to learn more about it. *Johnny Jet Code: Customs*

*Travel Insurance

Johnny Jet Code: Travel Insurance

If you are not sure if you will be able to take that dream vacation, cruise, or not sure if the agency will still be in business take out some health or trip cancellation insurance. Tip: Don't buy insurance from the same agency you bought your trip from because if they go out of business so does your insurance.

All Trip Protection

http://www.alltripinsurance.com

This company offers travel protection worldwide with programs including all-inclusive travel protection, trip cancellation and interruption protection, protection with a car rental, travel medical protection, and annual travel protection.

Global One

http://www.g1g.com

Global One offers medical, health, life, disability, and lost baggage insurance for h-1 visa workers, students, and those traveling internationally.

Worldwide Assistance

http://www.worldwideassistance.com

You'll find extensive travel assistance including pre-trip assistance, emergency medical evacuation, travel assistance, communication assistance, roadside assistance, and relocation assistance.

World Travel Center Insurance

http://www.worldtravelcenter.com

This company specializes in all facets of travel insurance, including: international medical insurance, and trip protection plans.

Access America

http://www.accessamerica.com

Access America is a leader in providing travel protection products sold through more than 22,000 travel agencies in the United States. Coverage is focused on domestic and international travel including business travel, cruises, tours, and vacations.

QuickQuote.com Life and Health Insurance

http://www.quickquote.com

Looking to compare insurance carriers? This site offers free comparisons in real time, of automotive, life, travel, health, and others.

CSA Travel Insurance

http://www.csatravelprotection.com

CSA provides travel insurance and assistance services for both travelers and travel agents.

Global Care Travel Insurance

http://www.globalcare-cocco.com

Global Care offers worldwide travel insurance and protection for trip interruption, medical evaluations, accidents, sickness, baggage coverage, and more.

HTH Worldwide

http://www.hthworldwide.com

HTH Worldwide provides health and travel insurance products to leisure travelers and students alike.

International SOS Medical Assistance

http://www.internationalsos.com

International SOS specializes in providing individual and business travelers with medical and emergency evaluation assistance.

Travel Insurance Services

http://www.travelinsure.com

Since 1973 Travel Insurance Services has offered travel insurance and international medical policies for individuals, families, and businesses.

Travelex Insurance

http://www.travelex-insurance.com

Travelex provides travel insurance and assistance services for travelers looking to protect themselves against unplanned occurrences such as interruptions or delays, lost baggage, medical assistance, and trip cancellations.

Travel-Guard Insurance

http://www.travel-guard.com

This leading travel insurance company has serviced many travelers offering protection against trip cancellation penalties, travel interruptions and delays, emergency medical expenses, lost baggage, and more.

Travel Insured Travel Insurance

http://www.travelinsured.com

Travel Insured International, Inc. provides a variety of high quality travel insurance plans and programs designed to protect individuals and groups from travel occurrences such as trip cancellation, interruption, and delay, missed connections, medical and dental, lost baggage, medical evacuation, and 24/7 emergency assistance.

Travel Assistance International

http://www.travelassistance.com

Travel Assistance offers travel insurance coverage for travelers throughout the year.

Insurance for Trips

http://www.insurancefortrips.com

This travel insurance company offers insurance for unforeseen travel emergencies providing a protection plan covering trip cancellation, interruption or delay, medical emergencies, lost luggage, and missed connections.

Travel Insurance Now

http://www.travelinsurancenow.com

Travel Insurance Now offers international travel insurance throughout the world and specializes in medical insurance while including protection for trip cancellation, emergency evacuation, baggage, trip interruption coverage, optional hazardous sports coverage, and more.

Life Insurance Company

http://www.lifeinsuranceadvisor.com

This company offers quotes from other insurance companies.

MEDEX Assistance Travel Insurance

http://www.medexassist.com

MEDEX is a worldwide provider of medical travel assistance for corporations, insurance companies, colleges, and government contractors and associations.

*Travel Vaccines

Get all the shots you need before going abroad.
Check out Johnny Jet Code: Vaccines

*The Art of Yoga

Johnny Jet Code: Yoga

Yoga

http://www.yogabasics.com

http://www.yogasite.com

Yoga is an art as well as a discipline that aims to train the conscious in order to obtain tranquility. It's also a great sport and you don't have to bring equipment with you. It can be taken wherever you are. These sites will connect you with the art of yoga and you will learn the postures. Yoga Basics teaches you the specific basics, breathing techniques, and more. The Yoga Site provides a general overview of yoga.

Yoga Cruise

http://www.yogacruise.com

Join Yoga Journal and enjoy the ultimate yoga vacation as you cruise with worldwide leading yoga instructors.

Yoga Journal

http://www.yogajournal.com

Known as the "voice of yoga online," this journal provides extensive information on yoga and living healthy.

Chapter 15

Guides and Information Resources

*24/7 Reference

Need a reference, a special dictionary, encyclopedia, thesaurus, or you name it? Check out Johnny Jet Code: Reference

*Books That Can Guide You

Johnny Jet Code: Travel Books

It's not necessary to buy a guidebook for every trip, but they can be helpful. Just log on and plug in your destination for up-to-date information and attractions. If you are going to multiple places, buy the book and read it on the plane ride, it makes the flight go so much faster.

Travel Bookstores

http://www.bookpassage.com
http://www.curiouscat.com/travel
http://www.distantlands.com
http://www.getlostbooks.com
http://www.gulliversbooks.com
http://www.literatetraveller.com
http://www.longitudebooks.com
http://www.thesavvytraveller.com
http://www.thetraveler.com
http://www.travelbooks.com
http://www.travelbooksandmaps.com
http://www.travelbooksusa.com
http://www.travelden.com
http://www.travelerspackltd.com
http://www.travelbugbooks.ca
http://www.travelbugbooks.com
If you are looking for a travel book, these sites specialize in travel guides and books. You could also check out *www.amazon.com*, *www.bn.com*, *www.booksamillion.com*, *www.powells.com*, and a variety of bookstores at *www.booksense.com*.

Adventurous Travel Bookstore

http://www.adventuroustraveler.com
This site brought to you by Away.com is an online store that specializes in travel books, maps, and accessories for adventurous travelers. Some of the subjects include hiking, biking, boating, diving, skiing, fishing, mountain climbing, and more.

Hadami Travel eBookstore

http://www.hadami.com
This store offers many travel e-books to download.

Avalon Travel Publishing

http://www.travelmatters.com
Avalon publishes some of the great travel books including Moon Handbooks, Rick Steves, and Foghorn Outdoors. Check out this site to get linked to a variety of Avalon published titles.

Dorling Kindersley Eyewitness Travel Guides

http://www.dk.com

Dorling Kindersley publishes a variety of travel guidebooks filled with pictures. The site offers guides that are packed with vivid photographs, maps, and travel diagrams that bring your travel experiences to life.

Insider's Guides

http://www.insiders.com

Looking for more information on a particular city? You might find an Insider's Guide to be a helpful resource. There are many U.S. cities that already have an Insider's Guide.

Fodor's

http://www.fodors.com

Fodor's offers a comprehensive guide to worldwide travel and has partnered with iExplore.com to offer almost any travel booking need. You'll find plenty of resources including a travel discussion and advice, personal trip planner, hotel and restaurant locators, travel tips, tipping guides, travel picture tips, and a foreign language resource that teaches the basics in French, German, Italian, and Spanish. So whether you are traveling from New York to Los Angeles, or to an exotic destination such as Antigua, this is a great destination site.

The Original Tipping Page

http://www.tipping.org

If you ever had a question about how much you should tip, this site provides you with that information. It covers where and when to tip, and has a tipping calculator. You can purchase a handy tipping card and books on tipping.

Arthur Frommer's Budget Travel

http://www.frommers.com

Arthur Frommer's Budget Travel magazine has become a household name and one of the most visited resources. From the books to the magazine, this site has received many awards. From travel budget tips, message boards, and an online magazine, this site will suite everyone from the beginning traveler to travel experts. Before this book went to print, Arthur Frommer sold Frommer's and took over the MSNBC Web site, which became: *www.budgettravel.msnbc.com* and featured Arthur Frommer's Budget Travel magazine.

Globe Pequot Press

http://www.globepequot.com

Globe Pequot has been publishing since 1947 and specializes in regional travel and recreation guides. You'll find outdoor and recreation guides, domestic and international travel guides, sports guides, language learning tools and more. Finding titles is easy at this well organized site.

Hunter Travel Publishing

http://www.hunterpublishing.com

Hunter specializes in publishing some great travel guides. Some of the well-known guides include adventure guides, weekend guides, hotel guides, and diving guides.

Karen Brown's Bed and Breakfast Guides

http://www.karenbrown.com

Karen offers guide books to preferred bed and breakfasts and inns along with driving itineraries for regions in Europe and the United States.

Insight Guides

http://www.insightguides.com

The German graphic designer Hans Hoefer founded Insight Guides in 1960 and today it has become one of the most reliable sources for finding information on a country's history, culture, people, and politics. Their guides come in various formats of including insight guides, pocket guides, and compact guides. They make dictionaries, maps, and more.

Let's Go Travel Guides

http://www.letsgo.com

Let's Go was founded by a group of Harvard students in 1960 that handed out travel advice pamphlets to students looking to travel to Europe. The students currently research, and revise the books today.

Lonely Planet Online

http://www.lonelyplanet.com

Lonely Planet is a publisher of guidebooks covering all grounds for independent travelers and its site is award-winning and perhaps the most informative guide to road travel. Looking for any destination is within reach at this not so lonely site that gets millions of visitors. From pinpointing your destination, writing and reading the Thorn Tree bulletin board, travel health, finding the latest travel news, reading the travel column, and more, this site is a travel connoisseur's dream come true. If there is somewhere that you haven't traveled yet and you would like to find out more, this is a great site to visit.

National Scenic Byways Online

http://www.byways.org

Where are the real scenic roads on the information superhighway? A byway consists of rustic back roads and more bearable traffic. At this site sponsored by the Federal Highway Administration, you can search for the byways. The site includes maps and is searchable by keyword. Find current and detailed information about the byways throughout the United States.

Net Travel

http://www.nettravel.com

Net Travel is another great resource for those utilizing the Internet for their travel needs. Created by travel journalist Michael Shapiro, this site provides a link for his book that guides you through travel on the Web.

PassPorter Guides to Disney

http://www.passporter.com

PassPorter offers unique, award-winning travel resource guides providing innovative planning systems for all your Disney vacation needs. Whether you are traveling to Disney in California or Florida, there is a PassPorter to make your experience exceptionally easier, and memorable. With original worksheets and "PassPockets" to help you organize your vacation pictures, receipts, and memories, PassPorters make a great asset for any Disney traveler.

Travelers Tales Publishing

http://www.travelerstales.com

Travelers Tales publishes books on travel experiences from all sorts of people and backgrounds. You'll find stories of, "wit and wisdom" to stories on destination, women's travel, spirituality, humor, food, adventure, travel advice, family travel, gift books, and more. Get some travel tips and you can submit your own nonfiction story on the site.

Travel Rough Guides

http://www.roughguides.com

There are a variety of Rough Guides to travel that covers all planes and places that you could imagine. From Amsterdam to Zimbabwe, you'll find guides for countries to regional and city guides. Some of the features of the site include country photos and postcards to email, and pages where you can write and read travel journals.

National Geographic Books

http://www.nationalgeographic.com/books

National Geographic presents us with some of the most interesting books that explore adventure, geography, exploration history, nature, photography, sports recreation, and more. There is a great selection at this site.

Lanier Travel Guides

http://www.travelguides.com

Lanier is known for its award-winning travel guides. Some of the guides consist of family travel, elegant hotels, golf courses, and bed and breakfasts. You will find information on Pamela's Bed and Breakfast Guide, other sites, and much more.

Ulysses Press

http://www.ulyssespress.com

Ulysses Press publishes a series of award winning Hidden travel guides that lead you to explore "off beaten travel path."

Zagat

http://www.zagat.com

Zagat's Survey is well known for its thousands of ratings of restaurants and hotels. Zagat publishes a guidebook based on customer satisfaction, and measures its results through comprehensive surveys. The site gives you more than forty cities within the U.S. to visit along with searches under categories of restaurants, cuisine, popularity, and neighborhoods.

*City Tourism

Johnny Jet Code: City Tourism

A-Z of Tourism

http://www.a-zoftourism.com

Select a country on the map and then you are directed to various tourist attractions within major cities around the world. It's alphabetically organized with everything from accommodations to entertainment.

Boulevards City Guides

http://www.boulevards.com

Choose from a select group of major U.S. and international cities and Boulevards will take you to a site that focuses on the arts, entertainment, history, and more.

Cities Unlimited

http://www.citiesunlimited.com

With a specific focus on U.S. cities, this site takes you to city specific sites. Click on a city or state of your choice and visit the individual page on a particular city. Each city has a business and city guide directory where you can look up different services within the city.

BestPlaces.net

http://www.bestplaces.net

This site offers a side-by-side comparison of thousands of cities throughout the United States. Compare them and find out the crime rates, climate, cost of living, schools, and then find the best place for you.

CitySearch.com

http://www.citysearch.com

Explore general arts and entertainment offerings in over one 100 cities worldwide. Combined with Ticketmaster, Citysearch offers tickets, and information on hotel and restaurant reservations. It's a great place to start learning more about what's happening in the city and to plan your city tour.

CNN Travel

http://www.cnn.com/TRAVEL

AOL Time Warner's Cable News Network offers the latest travel news, city guides, travel destinations, and more for the well-informed traveler. This is a great starting point for finding news on the latest in travel before you go. Check out the travel destination suggestions for some great vacation ideas.

City Travel Guide

http://www.citytravelguide.com

Featuring city travel throughout the United States, and a few cities internationally, this site provides a destination guides and mini destination guides for the cities. You can find restaurants, book hotels, rent cars, and get tickets here, too.

Click City

http://www.clickcity.com

Click City provides a comprehensive directory linking to various travel places and cities in the United States. You can find city info by state and click on one of the cities.

Columbus World City Guide

http://www.cityguide.travel-guides.com

This is a guide to cities worldwide. Click on a city and find overview information about it along with pictures.

Digital City

http://www.digitalcity.com

Digital City features the largest cities in the United States on this site that delivers local entertainment, commerce, news, and more to residents and city visitors. Find your city destination and start exploring.

E Local Network

http://www.elocal.com
Find local information wherever you are.

Ettractions

http://www.ettractions.com
What's the attraction at Ettractions? You will find plenty of them here at this site that focuses on tourist attractions in the United States and Canada. Just click on where you want to go and browse through a variety of attractions in that area.

My Travel Guide

http://www.mytravelguide.com
This membership directory site has a community of users who share their travel experiences, offering advice, and planning their trips. As a member you get free travel advice, view member's travel videos, photos and travelogues, and submit your own.

Official Travel Info

http://www.officialtravelinfo.com
Here is one large tourism site that links you to the official tourism organizations throughout the world. Click on a destination and you will find information on accommodations, attractions, dining, events, entertainment, shopping, sports and recreation, and transportation.

Tourism Offices Worldwide Directory

http://www.towd.com
The TOWD provides searches for every tourism office in the world. Each tourism office has contact information for address, Web site, and phone number.

Travel-Library.com

http://www.travel-library.com
This library contains comprehensive information on travel and tourism with Web links pages, many travelogues, trip reports, travel tips, and more. There is a comprehensive frequently asked questions page for those planning to take a trip around the world.

USA City Link

http://www.usacitylink.com

Looking for a particular city guide in one of the fifty states? Since 1994 this site has provided direct links to the various city guides. Click on Ohio and find Cleveland, California and find Los Angeles, and many more.

VisIT Europe

http://www.visit.ie

This site is specifically for visiting major cities in Europe. By clicking on the map you will be directed to the chosen city and find accommodations, top attractions, and more about the city.

World66.com

http://www.world66.com

This Dutch-German company has over 10,000 destinations to choose from with extensive travel resources. Start by clicking on the map or find a destination and you will have information on the country history, getting around, and much more.

World Travel Guide

http://www.wtgonline.com

There is an abundance of travel information here on trip planning. When you click on the world map you get a complete travel guide to your destination. Whether you are looking for transportation, accommodations, maps, or anything else, you are likely to find it at www.worldtravelguide.net.

*Domestic Destinations

For a listing of domestic destinations, check out Johnny Jet Code: Domestic Destinations

*Pen Pals

Looking for a Pen Pal? Check out Johnny Jet Code: Pen Pals

*Portlets for Cities

Johnny Jet made these detailed city guides.
They have everything from airport links to local guides.
For a listing of city portals with plenty of informative sites on major cities, check out Johnny Jet Code: City Portlets

*States

Johnny Jet Code: 50 States

State and Local Government on the Net

http://www.statelocalgov.net
You will find information on state and local government for all fifty states. Each state shows the official homepage, statewide offices, legislative, executive, and judicial branches. If you are looking for a particular city site, you can find it here too.

50States.com

http://www.50states.com
This site is a comprehensive resource on the fifty states and capitals. It contains an alphabetical list of nations, fast facts and state trivia, a newspaper directory, politics directory, sports directory, and more.

The U.S. 50 States

http://www.theus50.com
This site prominently displays great resources on the states. You'll find a state study guide, states ranked by area, population rankings, state birds, state flowers and trees, state governors, fun and games, and more.

State Government

http://123world.com/usstates
This site provides a listing of all the state government Web sites.

*Starting Points and Destinations

Johnny Jet Code: Starting Points

Yahoo! Get Local

http://local.yahoo.com

Browse by state for each of the fifty states and search for entertainment, events, dining, and other happenings in your local area.

The Bathroom Diaries

http://www.thebathroomdiaries.com

Every traveler knows going to the bathroom on the road may not be the most exciting part of your trip, but if you have to go why not find out where some of the nicest public restrooms are located. Here you'll find clean restrooms around the world, information on the nicest public restrooms known as the "Golden Plunge" and a few travel essays about bathroom experiences. You can even submit your own favorite bathroom.

Country Studies from the Library of Congress

http://lcweb2.loc.gov/frd/cs/cshome.html

Get facts and tidbits of information on various countries around the world and find out about the country's history, culture, and more at this comprehensive site.

ASTA-American Society of Travel Agents

http://www.astanet.com

This is the world's largest association for travel professionals. The globe logo represents travel agent members and represents a degree of professionalism in travel. Travelers can search for ASTA members on the site. There are many tips, information on traveler's rights, and more for travelers and agents on this site.

Bugbog Travel Guide

http://www.bugbog.com

This interesting unbiased online travel guide will keep you briefly informed with concise destination descriptions. Attempting to make your travel decisions quicker, this site provides travel pictures, maps, a destination finder, wildlife, beaches, travel health, safety, world wonders, and more. Overall, it's a great resource.

City Hunt

http://www.cityhunt.com

This online destination site provides a great amount of Web resources for cities in the U.S. Each city has guided information provided on accommodations, events, dining, shopping, and more.

Concierge.com

http://www.concierge.com

This great travel site is the home of Condé Nast Traveler and an ultimate destination place for many popular travel destinations. Visitors can create their own travelogue, find some of the most visited destinations, get travel deals, access mapping resources, and participate in travel forums.

Go Nomad Alternative Travel

http://www.gonomad.com

Known as the "alternative way to travel," Go Nomad provides a comprehensive resource for independent and alternative travelers looking for budget minded adventures and tours, learning and volunteer vacations, women travel, family travel, and more.

Greatest Cities of the World

http://www.greatestcities.com

This destination guide provides information and statistics on major cities throughout the world. Click on a country, state, and then a city. Information may include the city, the metropolitan area, population, education, recreation, points of interest, economy, government, history, and more.

GOGO Worldwide Vacations

http://www.gogowwv.com

Travel agents gather together at this site offering discounts in travel packages.

Uniglobe

http://www.uniglobe.com

Plan your destination; book your flight, car rental, hotel, cruises, and more at this encompassing travel destination hot spot. The specialty here is cruises and you can find some good cruise deals here.

World Almanac

http://www.infoplease.com/world.html

This almanac features an atlas, geography info, countries, current events, world statistics, international relations, travel and more searchable by year.

I Travel, You Travel

http://www.ityt.com

This is a virtual community of frequent travelers worldwide discussing their travel experiences, airlines, various destinations, travel tips, and more. Registration is required.

Locals in the Know

http://www.localsintheknow.com

If you wanted to know something about a particular city, this site will be able to assist you. Who would be better to ask about a city than a person from that city? You can sign up and answer questions, and read about city news and other local information.

U.S. Census Bureau

http://www.census.gov

The mission of the U.S. Census Bureau is to be the preeminent collector and provider of timely, relevant, and quality data about people and the economy of the United States.

A+ Country Reports

http://www.countryreports.org

Looking for country profiles, history, maps, and more information? Here is a site that provides facts and figures on each of the countries.

Online City Guide

http://www.onlinecityguide.com

OLCG.com is a directory providing links to over 30,000 different cities in the United States. Whether you are new to the city or a regular visitor, you can click on the state and the city and find information, along with deals on travel accommodations.

Travelers

http://www.sela-v.com

This site is a resourceful guide for those traveling to Africa, the Middle East and East Asia, East Europe and the former USSR, West Europe, and North America. It offers a place to find a travel companion, a picture of the day, travel gear advice, lectures about traveling, and more.

Synergise INSITE

http://www.synergise.com

You will find humorous travelogues along with pictures to click on and enlarge at this travel gateway. There are also vacation bargains, accommodations, attractions, and travel Web resources.

The Insider Travel Network

http://www.theinsider.com

These guides give you an insider's tour of what to see and what to do in Bermuda, Boston, Hawaii, New York City, Philadelphia, and San Francisco. These guides feature hundreds of photos, a discount hotel guide, airfare and car rental reservations.

Time Out

http://www.timeout.com

Time Out is the world's living guide that takes you straight to where the action is with guides to the top cities in the world. The site offers Time Out guides that review thousands of the best restaurants, clubs, bars, and gives you an evaluation on hotels along with information on shows, and events in cities throughout Asia, Europe, Australia, and the United States. They are known for the Time Out New York site at www.timeoutny.com.

Travelago

http://www.travelago.com

Travelago is one of the largest video and media travel libraries with streaming video destination guides for leisure and business travel worldwide. The site guides you to vacation hot spots. In making your travel plans, this is a great way to interactively view where you are planning to go. Destinations include: U.S, Africa, Antarctica, Asia, Australia, Canada, the Caribbean, Europe, Mexico, and the Middle East.

Travel Facts

http://www.travelfacts.com

This portal is a destination guide to various places in the United States and the Caribbean. It includes everything from basic information on attractions, arts and culture, history, sports and recreation, to shopping, nightlife, and activities.

Underground Travel

http://www.undergroundtravel.com

Here is a travel destination guide to top international destinations including Europe, Asia, and South Pacific. The site contains travel articles, information on being travel savvy, travel passes, information on working abroad, streaming travel videos, and various travel related Web resources for the budget-minded independent traveler.

VisitEurope.com

http://www.visiteurope.com

This is your official gateway to finding information on different countries in Europe. Each company is listed with fast facts and information on country highlights.

What's Going On?

http://www.whatsgoingon.com

Do you find yourself asking this? Here is a site that will explain the events and festivals along with a book that is called "100 Things to Do Before you Die." With the list of events on this site you won't be at a loss for things to do.

Escape Maker

http://www.escapemaker.com

You can plan an escape on the Northeastern side of the United States with this guide. It specializes in finding local trips that don't involve airports.

Hidden New York

http://www.pbs.org/wnet/newyork/hidden

This is a documentary on New York that shows twelve little known, but great places to visit around the state of New York. Take virtual reality of City Hall, Columbus Circle, Coney Island, Orchard Alley, 1964 World Fair, and others.

*Tourist Offices

For a listing of tourist offices in the United States and worldwide, check out Johnny Jet Code: Tourist Office

*Travel Searching

Johnny Jet Code: Searching

10 Best Inc.

http://www.10best.com

According to this membership site, it's a small world that we live and big travel guides are not something you would want to take with you. Why settle with the rest when you can find the best? For a small monthly or annual subscription fee, you can find out where the best places to eat, shop, sleep, and play. It's compatible with many mobile devices as well.

About Travel

http://www.about.com/travel

Where do you want to go? Find out about it here at this site that contains articles and Web resources selected by experts. You'll get travel tips, and more. All you have to do is go here and click and you'll find more about it.

America's Best Online

http://www.americasbestonline.com

Surf through the clutter and go straight to the best online. Find the most popular amusement parks, the top aquariums, most desired bed and breakfasts, the top beaches, the top cycling tours, the best breweries, the top cities to live in, and much more.

Aardvark Travel

http://www.aardvarktravel.net

This is a simple travel search directory that allows you to type in a word and then see some search results.

AOL Anywhere Travel

http://www.aol.com/webcenters/travel

You can be anywhere and AOL will take you to your destination. Airfare, lodging, car rental, and cruise packages, maps and more are all available at AOL's Anywhere Travel powered by Travelocity. There are some great classified ads to look at as well. Check out the index in the back of the book with the AOL Keywords. AOL has many travel related key words for its users.

MSNBC Travel Toolkit

http://www.msnbc.com/modules/travel/toolkit.asp

MSNBC combined with Expedia provides a toolkit with a variety of simple travel tools. Some of the tools include booking flights, room reservation, fare comparisons, vacation packages, a world guide, maps, a currency converter, and more.

Search the Trip

http://search.thetrip.com

There are a variety of useful travel resources here. In addition to finding flights, rentals, and lodging there are some great travel resources including: flight trackers, wireless services, a guide to destinations, street maps, directions, international holiday research, and more.

Hotbot Open Directory

http://dir.hotbot.lycos.com/recreation/travel

Using this directory and search engine you can search by category for various travel information. You can type in your search or go right to the directory and peruse listings.

TravelEze

http://www.traveleze.com

This site offers a comprehensive directory of Web resources for travelers.

I go U go

http://www.igougo.com

This award-winning site presents a unique community of travel enthusiasts who share their travel experiences through travel journals and photos. With over 30,000 photos, you will visualize some of the best travel. You'll find inspiring travel stories, travel tips, journals, and more at this great site.

Johnny Jet

http://www.johnnyjet.com

Johnny knows where you want to travel. Just jet on over to Johnny and find almost anything you are looking for in travel. Tips, numbers, Web resources galore, and almost anything you can imagine is located at Johnny Jet. This is the ultimate online travel portal.

Planet Rider

http://www.planetrider.com

This directory features top Web resources and divides them into sections including: maps, weather, destinations, activities, landscapes, and helpful resources.

Thirty Thousand Feet

http://www.thirtythousandfeet.com

This is a travel directory filled with thousands of online resources linking to aviation related Web sites, aviation news, FAQs, newsgroups, and other commercial and aviation information.

Travel.org

http://www.travel.org

This comprehensive directory has travel resources organized by sections including: continent, lodging, agents, airlines, and auto rentals.

Traveling Directory

http://www.traveling.com

This site is a comprehensive directory of travel resources.

Travel Notes Directory

http://www.travelnotes.org

This well-organized travel directory can lead you in the right direction to finding your destination. You'll find essential travel info, country backgrounds, links, and articles.

Travel Page Interactive Travel Guide

http://www.travelpage.com

This is an interactive travel guide with information on destinations, hotels and resorts, cruises, and air travel. You can make reservations, read travel reviews, and get the latest news.

Travel Source

http://www.travelsource.com

As the Internet's first interactive travel directory, this site gives you a few links to vacations, resorts, tours, cruises, getaways, recreation, and more.

Travelzoo Travel Specials Directory

http://www.travelzoo.com

Where are the special deals online? Check out this site and you will find an abundance of them. From the top specials and deals on travel to getaways, and last minute travel, this site is a great starting point if you are looking for travel deals.

Alexa Web Search

http://www.alexa.com

Alexa provides Google's search engine along with a toolbar that shows Web site traffic rankings. Visit the affiliated Internet Archive at www.archive.org to surf the Web in the past.

Google.com

http://www.google.com

Google provides great search results based on site linkage. Try the famous "I'm feeling lucky" button and you will be directed to the most popular match for your search results.

Look Smart

http://www.looksmart.com

Look Smart is an online directory with plenty of resources, yet not an exhaustive amount of resources for travel, and other topics.

Yahoo! Travel

http://travel.yahoo.com

Yahoo has become one of the most reliable search tools on the Internet. You can find a variety Yahoo travel related search sites as well as a directory. There is much here, and I think it might cover everything related to travel. Check out the popular destinations if you are not sure exactly where you are looking to go, because this will give you some good places to start your travel expedition.

Lycos Travel

http://travel.lycos.com

There are a variety of good tools that Lycos provides. Whether you are looking for a particular destination or a good place to stay, this full service search engine has what you may be looking for.

Netscape Travel

http://www.netscape.com

Netscape users will be happy to know that they have a place to book their flights and look for travel deals and resources powered by Travelocity. Netscape, AOL, IM, and CompuServe, members can create their own travel profile.

Specialty Travel

http://www.specialtytravel.com

This directory of specialized travel features more than 500 adventure travel tour operators indexed by activity and destination. There is an archive of interesting travel stories, and a magazine.

Adventure Guide

http://www.adventureguide.com

This adventure guide focuses on more than 150 of the world's most exciting travel destinations. You can explore outdoor adventures, eco-tours, senior adventures, business adventures, women traveling solo, and more. Everything from wilderness camps to luxury resorts can be found here.

Accommodation Search Engine Network

http://www.ase.net

If you are searching for hotel accommodations, where to stay, and reservations throughout the world, this search engine does a pretty good job. You can search by region and easily compare hotels and lodging. You can change settings for six different languages and currencies. One unique feature is that you can set your own preferences while you search for over 200,000 accommodations worldwide.

Airlines of the Web

http://www.flyaow.com

Airlines of the Web became the first index of airline sites on the Web and it has been online since 1994. At this hub you will find more than just airlines. Now it is a full service travel-booking site with trains, planes, automobiles, and cruises. There are some interesting vacation packages worth checking out. It's definitely a site to see.

Hotels and Travel on the Net

http://www.hotelstravel.com

Don't let the name mislead you. This search engine is for more than just hotels. With over 75,000 resources, you can pinpoint a particular hotel in almost any country. Other features include travel news, travel message board, and flight booking.

Trotty.com

http://www.trotty.com

This is a European holiday and travel directory with accommodations, transportation, itineraries, maps, weather, and more.

Kasbah: The Travel Search Engine

http://www.kasbah.com

Interesting name, but this site is proclaimed as the, "world's largest travel guide..." with tens of thousands of Web resources for over 200 countries. A UK based site, it seems to be intended for a British audience. You'll find trips based on specific activities. For instance, if you are into golf, scuba diving, or winter sports you can choose a specific category and look it up. There is a breaking news section and you can find out about world news before you take the big trip.

Infospace

http://www.infospace.com

Infospace is one of the first well-known people finders online. You can find numbers and addresses from white pages to yellow pages here. It happens to be one of the better online portals and a top site for travel searching. If you spend much time on the road Infospace is great. You may also want to check out:
www.infospace.com/info.zip or *www.zip2.com* for short and search for some businesses, directions, and people.

Island Information

http://www.islandsinfo.com

Are you searching for an island? You'll be sure to find plenty here. If you are looking to travel to a known or a not so known island you should look at this site first. There is information on island accommodations as well. For more useful information on islands, you may want to check out www.islandstudies.org.

Knowhere Britain Guide

http://www.knowhere.co.uk

Going to Britain? If so this site will help you get around. You can search for over 1,000 different places in England online. It's pretty neat, if you don't know where to go. Just go to Knowhere.

Opinionated Traveler

http://www.opinionatedtraveler.com

Looking for an opinion on travel? These "opinionated travelers" who are professional travel writers will surely give you their opinions. Find out what they think are some of the better travel deals of the week. Just click on a country and get a destination review. There is a traveler's forum to post your travel messages. Be sure to check out some of the really neat audio and video flicks.

Traveling USA

http://www.travelingusa.com

Traveling USA just about covers it all when you are in the fifty states. Whether you are looking for attractions, bed and breakfasts, hotels, motels, golf courses, marinas, resorts, restaurants, RV Parks, Campgrounds, Tour Companies, or Transportation, it can be found on this site. Just click on the category and you can see if they have what you are looking for.

Trip Spot

http://www.tripspot.com

There is plenty of information here at this online directory of sites. If you are looking for something related or remotely related to travel, it could probably be found at this spot. Main topics include: travel guides, bargains, getting there, where to stay, what to do, travel library, travel agents, and more.

Virtual Cities

http://www.virtualcities.com

You'll find a site filled with information on bed and breakfasts, vacation rentals, inns, dude ranches, fishing, skiing, getaways, and more throughout North America. Restaurant recommendations kid and pet friendly lodging, and recipes are other pluses to this comprehensive site.

Virtual Tourist

http://www.virtualtourist.com

This online forum will make you feel like a local in almost any city. Become a member, chat about travel, and join in the travel discussion bulletin board. Find out what other travelers have thought about their visits to other lands. You can even keep your own Web page travelogue here. If you like this site you may want to check out www.bootsnall.com and find more discussion boards, travel stories, and travelogues.

World of Travel Network

http://www.worldoftravel.net

This no frills UK-based travel search engine has an extensive listing of categorized sites with everything from accommodations to travel goods.

World Skip

http://www.worldskip.com

Get news, information, products, and services from around the world. Select a nation and you have information and news at your fingertips. There is some neat information on the Seven Wonders of the World and some information on what happened this day in world history.

World Yahoo!

http://dir.yahoo.com/regional/web_directories/yahoo__regional

Yahoo can be found in different countries and in different languages. Check out this site, if you would like to search the famous Yahoo search engine in another country.

*Visitor Bureaus

These are great local sites to help you plan your trip worldwide. Check out Johnny Jet Code: Visitor Bureaus

Chapter 16

International Travel

Going overseas? In this chapter you will find links that will help prepare you for all the necessary documents and helpful tools. Don't forget to use the language translators and electric converters. Also make sure you are going to a safe place. Get all the safety info from the state departments so you know where to go if you get in trouble.

*Caribbean Islands

Johnny Jet Code: Caribbean Islands

Zubby Directory

http://www.zubby.com

This directory and search engine for Caribbean travel provides searches everywhere from Anguilla to the Virgin Islands. So if you don't know where to go in the Caribbean, or just would like to explore your options, this is a great starting place.

#1 Caribbean Villas

http://www.1caribbeanvillas.com

Renting a private villa in the Caribbean could be an adventure within itself. This site searches for villas in the Caribbean. It's completely searchable by region, bedrooms, bathrooms, type, and listing.

Caribbean Travel

http://www.caribbean-on-line.com

This is a comprehensive guide to travel in the Caribbean. It includes car rental tips, cruise suggestions, resort reviews, and more compiled by a Caribbean tourist.

Where to Stay

http://www.wheretostay.com

Where do you want to stay in the Caribbean? This site advises you before you stay there. Here's how they describe it, "For on-line travelers, WhereToStay.com is the advisory service that offers an independent, objective, and up-to-date account of a majority of the properties for many leisure travel destinations." Read reviews, post your own, and check out the message board.

Caribbean Online

http://www.col.com

Get in-depth travel information about your Caribbean dream destination. You'll find expert travel advice to vacation packages. You can even search for a specific Caribbean island by name. Check out the map to see where all the islands are.

Caribbean Travel Roundup

http://www.caribtravelnews.com

Get the latest island news from this newsletter that you can sign up for or check out on the site. Since 1990 this newsletter has been providing travelers with press releases on the latest island happenings. This is a great way to keep informed with real life stories and news on the islands.

Island Connoisseur

http://www.islandconnoisseur.com

If you love the Caribbean islands, it's likely you'll enjoy this site. This gateway to the Caribbean includes historical and cultural information on the Caribbean islands. You will find duty-free shopping, as well as travel and weather information for each of the islands. There is an abundance of links to check out here.

Paradise Destinations

http://www.paradise-destinations.com

Looking to go to Paradise? This online travel agency will help facilitate your travel needs to the islands and it will provide you with some enjoyable music to listen to while you book your trip online. Cancun, Jamaica, Negril, and the Bahamas are just a few of the choices here.

Villas of the World

http://www.villasoftheworld.com

Some of the top luxury and most pristine Villa rentals around the world can be found here. Offering vacations to the Caribbean islands and Anguilla vacation rentals, as well as Europe, this site is a top-notch local site for finding Villas.

*Expatriate Life

Johnny Jet Code: Expatriate Life

Expatriates or "expats" are people who leave one's native country to live elsewhere, and in this section we provide Web sites that our devoted to help make expatriates' lives easier and more enjoyable.

Expat Exchange

http://www.expatexchange.com

Founded in 1997, expatexchange.com is a resource for English speaking expatriates. It features a regional resource guide, classifieds, city reports, forums, chat, a tax and finance center, travel warnings, and more.

Expat Expert

http://www.expatexpert.com

Robin Pasoe's site is designed to inform, advise, and offer online friendship to expatriates relocating to another country.

Expat Index

http://www.expatindex.com

Intended for British expatriates this resourceful index offers a concise guide to inform expatriates with useful services such as shopping, food, toiletries, healthcare, news related information, and more.

Expat Moms

http://www.expat-moms.com

Intended for expatriate moms, this resource provides articles, forums, chats, and more resources that help with raising expatriate children.

Expat News

http://www.expatica.com

Expatica provides news and information sources for expatriates who live, work, or are moving to Holland in the Netherlands, Germany, France, or Belgium.

Expat Search King

http://expats.searchking.com

This is a dedicated Internet search directory and portal for expatriates.

American Citizens Abroad

http://www.aca.ch

This non-profit organization is dedicated to protecting the interests of individual U.S. citizens throughout the world.

Americans in France

http://www.americansinfrance.net

This is a resource for Americans planning on moving, traveling, or living in France. The site has attractions, answers to questions, culture info, a dictionary, and more.

British Expat

http://www.britishexpat.com

This is an online community for British people who are outside the U.K. Topics include people, travel, news, entertainment, technology, and learning.

Foreign Born

http://www.foreignborn.com

This is a resource for foreigners immigrating to the United States. The site features guides to banking, insurance, medical care, social security, car buying and leasing, careers, schooling, travel, and more.

Expat Focus

http://www.expatfocus.com

Here is a resource guide for expatriates including expatriate news, information, and community issues. There are forums, financial advice, and more.

Expatlandia

http://www.expatlandia.com

This site is a resource to making the expatriate experience successful by providing services and information to the global expatriate community. Some of the services include news, country profiles, checklists, and a chat.

Expat Village

http://www.expatvillage.com

This site is operated by a group of expatriates for expatriates. It covers living and visiting abroad, expatriate jobs, mothering, household finance, entertainment, travel, health care, and more.

International Living

http://www.internationalliving.com

This site offers a subscription based monthly newsletter featuring the best places to live, retire, travel, and invest throughout the world. On the site, there is a subscribers only section, a current issue, special reports, and more.

Overseas Digest

http://www.overseasdigest.com

This is a newsletter for Americans living, teaching, and working abroad. There is a directory of living abroad sites, and a global career guide.

Tales From a Small Planet

http://www.talesmag.com

This is a global literary and travel humor magazine for expatriates everywhere. Their mission is to "enrich and share the experiences of living abroad through literature, humor and the arts, as well as providing information and education on what it is really like to live in a foreign country and how to cope with the challenges that may come along."

UK Yankee

http://www.uk-yankee.com

UK Yankee is an expatriate community for Americans and Britains with forums, and information about culture, education and health, housing, moving, and more.

*International Destinations

Check out these helpful sites when planning your trip abroad!
Check out Johnny Jet Code: International Destinations

U.S. Department of State Passport Services

http://travel.state.gov/passport_services.html

Do you have a valid passport? Make sure you do and that you have six months until it expires. You need a passport or a birth certificate to travel outside the U.S. This site explains the passport and tells you all the information about applying for one, where to find a passport agency, and more. There are some helpful travel tips to see here. Don't worry though, you can get passports in 24 hours, and if you have plenty of time, save some money and don't get a rush delivery. Do you need a visa for the country you are visiting? You may want to check out *www.g3visas.com*, *www.traveldocs.com*, *www.travisa.com* or *Johnny Jet Code: Visas* to download some visa and passports applications. For more passport info, you may want to go to www.passportinfo.com. For more information on passports, check out *Johnny Jet Code: Passports*

Passport Offices

http://www.ppt.gc.ca

http://www.passports.gov.au

http://www.ukpa.gov.uk

Here are the passport offices for Canada, Australia, and the United Kingdom.

U.S. Birth Certificate

http://www.usbirthcertificate.com

If you need a copy of your birth certificate, you can order it at this Web site.

*U.S. Customs

http://www.customs.gov

http://www.customs.gov/travel/travel.htm

This is the official site of U.S. Customs along with information on travel. For more on customs, check out *Johnny Jet Code: Customs*

One World Nations Online

http://www.nationsonline.org

Here you will find informational sites on countries around the world.

Embassies

http://www.embassy.org

http://www.embassyweb.com

Get linked to the embassy sites around the world. For more on embassies and consulates, check out *Johnny Jet Code: Embassy*

Rulers of the World

http://www.rulers.org

This is where the rulers of the world are hanging out. If you are looking for a head of state or head of government of a particular country, you may want to check out this site before you travel to their country.

Euro Vacations

http://www.eurovacations.com

http://www.e-vacations.com

Looking for interactive vacation planning tools that will take you to Europe or Latin America? Combine over 85 years of experience of the Rail Europe Group with Avanti Destinations and you will get this great site. Here you will find hundreds of travel packages and vacation plans that you can customize based on your interests.

Euro Trip

http://www.eurotrip.com

If a budget travel trip to Europe is what you have in mind, then this site will suit you well. You'll find European Hostel Reviews, Destinations, Packing and Travel Advice, Travel Bargains, a Newsletter, and more. This site is an excellent online destination before you make it to Europe.

European Ferrari Rental

http://www.europeanferrarirental.com

If you are in Europe or going to Europe and would like to rent a Ferrari, you may want to check out this site that offers a variety of Ferraris to rent and drive on the German Autobahn. Each of the tour packages will begin and end in Munich, Germany, and include five star hotel accommodations, restaurant recommendations and/or reservations, driving maps and directions, and travel insurance.

Indochina Travel Company

http://www.indochinatravel.com

Since 1992, Indochina Travel has researched and organized innovative travel offerings to Vietnam Cambodia and Laos. The site emphasizes providing unique single traveler and small group adventures.

Things Asian

http://www.thingsasian.com

Explore Asian culture online with everything from where to travel and what art to see. Here you will find photo essays, articles, facts, artwork, and maps of various countries in Asia. The emphasis is on art, culture, history, and travel. Places covered include Burma, Cambodia, Hong Kong, Indonesia, Laos, Macau, Malaysia, Singapore, Thailand, and Vietnam.

Traveling with Ed and Julie

http://www.twenj.com

These travel veterans from Europe show you what you need when traveling there. The site provides comprehensive visitor resources for Rome, Switzerland, Bavaria, and much more.

Hotel Travel

http://www.hoteltravel.com

If Asia is your destination, you may want to make this site your travel service. You'll find an abundance of information on travel to Asia. Airlines, airports, reservations, currency exchange, things to do, and more can be found here.

BC Travel

http://www.bctravel.com

If you are traveling to British Columbia, then this is one site to see. Here you will find information on camping and outdoor adventures, hotels, fishing, golf, real estate, shopping, vacation homes, and wineries.

Cancun.com

http://www.cancun.com

Here is your gateway to the Mexican Yucatan Peninsula. This site contains a collection of everything you can imaginably explore in Cancun. You'll find hotels, tours, restaurants, free discount coupons, water activities, general information, ecology tours, sailing charters, bone fishing, diving trips, and more. The photo gallery is really nice to see.

Countries of the World

http://www.tradeport.org/ts/countries

Are you looking for a country to visit? At this convenient Country Library online you can find out more about the countries before you take a trip out there. Find out more about it before you take the trip at this site.

Puchka Peru Cultural Tours

http://www.puchkaperu.com

Tour Peru and its ancient civilizations and see everything from the desert seacoasts to the amazing Andean highlands, the jungles, and the rainforests. The 22-day tours are three-fold guiding you to a nation's breath-taking artistic heritage, taking you deep into the lives and creative spirits of the artists, and supporting the folk-arts communities.

Washington Post World News

http://www.washingtonpost.com/wp-dyn/world

What's happening on the other end of the world? If you ever wanted to know, you can easily find out with the Washington Post's World News Section.

London Walks

http://london.walks.com

The London Walks Company is the original and foremost walking tour company in London. If you are in London, then you can sign up for one of the walking tours that will usually take you 1 to 2 miles in distance. Every Sunday, you can take the "Jack the Ripper"tour.

Britannia

http://www.britannia.com

Britannia started out as "America's Gateway to the British Isles." However, this award-winning site has become a gateway for more than 120 different countries. At this ezine, you will find a wealth of information to help you make the most of your visit to London and the UK. From deals, vacations, to travel guides and tourism, this site provides you with all that you need to make it to Great Britain.

UK Travel

http://www.uktravel.com

Traveling to UK can be fun and interesting. This site is an informative and useful guide to the various cities, hotels, and castles. There is a section on the Royal Family, an online Gallery, and a map of London at this convenient guide.

Travel Europe

http://www.traveleurope.com

Although the site is "Travel Europe," it may as well be called Travel Italy because the focus is on Italy. You will find photos, history, artwork, and tourist attractions about Italy. If you are planning a trip to Italy this is one great place to stop first.

*Entering the United States of America

Make sure you know what's allowed and forbidden before bringing certain goods into the US. Check out *Johnny Jet Code: Enter USA*

*International Holidays

Johnny Jet Code: International Holidays

There is nothing worse than flying all night long and arriving in a city that is on a National Holiday. Click these links to find out what holidays, festivals, and other events are taking place around the world.

Events World Wide

http://www.eventsworldwide.com

This site is your guide to events throughout the world. Find out the details on locations, dates, and where tickets are being sold in some of the most exotic events. Whether you are looking for unique arts, entertainment, sporting, or other special event, it is likely to be found here.

Festivals.com

http://www.festivals.com

You will find festivals, events, and what's happening worldwide. The database here contains thousands of events to search through by location, keyword, or subject.

Festival Finder

http://www.festivalfinder.com

Music festivals are plentiful in North America and this site will help you find them. Genres of music include Alternative, Bluegrass, Blues, Cajun, Classical, Country, Electric, Folk, Jazz, Reggae, Rock, and others.

Film Festivals

http://www.filmfestivals.com

If it's a film festival you are looking for, this site provides a searchable database of international film and television festivals. You'll find news, articles, interviews, film details, and multimedia.

French Quarter

http://www.frenchquarter.com

New Orleans is known for its architecture, music festivals, mardi gras, parties, and is perhaps the most unique city in the U.S. Here is your guide to the streets of New Orleans and the French Quarter.

National Holidays

http://www.bank-holidays.com

This site informs you of all the days when banks are closed due to religious or public events. Major events such as elections, strikes, riots, and more are also listed.

The Worldwide Holiday & Festival Site

http://www.holidayfestival.com

Are you looking for a particular holiday or festival? This site organizes the holidays by country, religion, and month.

Whatsonwhen

http://www.whatsonwhen.com

Founded in 1999, this award winning company provides travel and entertainment happenings. So if you are looking to find when something is happening out and about this site will assist you.

*Language Schools

Want to learn a foreign language? Now you can go to a foreign country, just to learn their language. We have all the schools you can visit from Spanish to Swahili. Check out *Johnny Jet Code: Language School*

*Speaking the Language of the Land

Johnny Jet Code: Native Tongues

Just because English is the primary world language, it doesn't mean everyone speaks it. Check out these sites for some helpful phrases and books. Or you can translate a Web site into English if needed.

National Anthems

http://www.thenationalanthems.com

This site contains the national anthems in MIDI, words, and shows a picture of the flags of 192 countries.

Foreign Word

http://www.foreignword.com

This directory is one of the most popular language sites worldwide with some unmatched translation tools such as Xanadu, the language and translation wizard. You'll find over 170 different on-line dictionaries, machine translation, and more.

Basic Phrases for Eastern European Languages

http://www.cusd.claremont.edu/~tkroll/EastEur

Learn how to say the basic "hello," "yes," "no," and "how are you" in Albanian, Bulgarian, Croatian, Czech, Estonian, Hungarian, Latvian, Lithuanian, Polish, Romanian, Russian, Serbian and Slovenian.

Berlitz International

http://www.berlitz.com

Berlitz is a well-known provider of language instruction for adults, children, and corporations. It offers language tutorial products such as books, tapes, and CDs.

Jennifer's Language Resources

http://www.elite.net/~runner/jennifers

Learning how to say "goodbye" in over 450 languages is just one of the great resources here. Then learn how to say "thank you," "hello," "good afternoon," and more.

Language Translators

http://world.altavista.com

http://www.google.com/language_tools

Translate from English to Spanish, Chinese, French, German, Italian, Japanese, Korean, and Portuguese. Then translate it back, and to other different languages.

Japanese-Online

http://www.japanese-online.com

Learn Japanese online before you go to Japan. This site includes a free online dictionary, Japanese lessons, a discussion board, and more. If you ever wanted to learn Japanese, this is a great place to start.

Aussie Slang Dictionary

http://www.members.tripod.com/~thisthat/slang.html

G'day if you're heading to Australia, this slang and phrase dictionary may come in handy. Learn how the Aussies speak and give it a try. There are words and phrases for every letter in the alphabet. You'll find some other Australian stuff here, too.

Welsh Course

http://www.cs.brown.edu/fun/welsh

Looking to learn some Welsh? This site makes learning fun and easy for beginners. The site includes a lesson-by-lesson way of learning along with English to Welsh translation tools.

Travlang

http://www.travlang.com

Travel and Language products and services are offered at this resourceful site. From translating gadgets to language courses and sound bytes to help you pronounce and useful phrases, this site covers over seventy different languages.

Free Translation

http://www.freetranslation.com

Translate languages like English, French, Spanish, German, Norwegian, Portuguese, and Italian at this site. This site makes a great resource for a quick translation.

Paralink Language Translator

http://translation2.paralink.com

Translate English to French, German, Russian, Spanish, and more.

I Love Languages

http://www.ilovelanguages.com

This is one of the most comprehensive sites on the Web for foreign language resources. Visit this site and you will be headed in the right direction to learn almost any language.

Internet Living Swahili Dictionary

http://www.yale.edu/swahili

If you ever wanted to learn the African language of Swahili, this dictionary may have the answers for you. Translating words is within a click of your mouse.

Language Link

http://www.langlink.com

This company believes you can learn the Spanish language through immersion programs. Programs are offered in Mexico, Peru, Costa Rica, Guatemala, Ecuador, Chile, Argentina or Spain.

Parlo

http://www.parlo.com

Learn to speak a new language with courses in English, Spanish, French, German, and Italian. Overall, this is a great learning site to learn a language within a few weeks.

*Travel Warnings

Johnny Jet Code: Travel Warnings

Going to a foreign country? Want to know if it's safe? Read the warnings from the State Department and other sites. But read them carefully, just because a city or country has a warning doesn't mean it's unsafe to go. It just means our Government is making sure they can't get sued. You can also dial 202-647-5225 for updated "Travel Warnings" or dial 888-407-4747 for the Bureau of Consular Affairs Overseas Citizen Services which serves Americans abroad. You can also visit *www.travel.state.gov* for more detailed information.

Canadian Consular Affairs Bureau

http://www.voyage.gc.ca
At this Canadian government site, you will find information for Canadians traveling abroad, information on travel warnings, safety, country travel reports, passports, and more.

CIA World Fact Book

http://www.odci.gov/cia/publications/factbook
This site contains country profiles along with facts and statistics on the different countries.

Country Watch

http://www.countrywatch.com
Country Watch is a world leader in providing country specific geopolitical intelligence on the countries of the world.

Foreign and Commonwealth Office

http://www.fco.gov.uk/travel
This British government site offers advice for British citizens traveling overseas and information on travel warnings.

Hot Spots by Air Security International

http://www.airsecurity.com/hotspots.htm

Security professionals have found Hot Spots to be a resourceful site that includes a summary and analysis of current air security, aviation and worldwide travel news. You'll find violence, weather, and other events organized by region and rated by a "threat level" to travelers.

I Jet

http://www.ijet.com

This site provides business and leisure travelers with travel intelligence, warning advisories, security, and real time travel alerts on a per trip subscription. Updates can be sent by email or phone, and are accessible via a customized Web site based on information on your destination.

Kroll Security

http://www.krollworldwide.com

Kroll is a risk consulting company offering investigative, security, and technological services.

The World's Most Dangerous Places

http://www.comebackalive.com/df

This danger finder site will guide you to some of the most dangerous places to travel. Not that you would want to go to them, but just keep in mind that they do exist. Danger is explained here with accident facts, and more to be aware of including: religious wars, terrorists, and unknown alleyways. The information on this site is based on Robert Young's book.

*Air Traffic Control System Command Center

http://www.fly.faa.gov

This site offers real time flight checking and delays in various major airports by clicking on the map. For airport codes, check out www.faa.gov/aircodeinfo.htm and you will see the codes for the airports. For more information about airport codes, check out *www.skygod.com/asstd/abc.html* or check out *Johnny Jet Code: Airport Codes*

Australian Department of Foreign Affairs and Trade

http://www.dfat.gov.au/travel

This government site provides information on the foreign affairs and trade, along with travel advice from Australia, and information on travel warnings.

Background Notes

http://www.state.gov/r/pa/bgn

This site provides background notes or a country profile on countries received from regional bureaus and added to the database of the Department of State site.

Bureau of Consular Affairs

http://www.travel.state.gov

The U.S. Department of State provides travel safety information along with legal information on children's issues, passport info, visas, doctors and hospitals abroad, and more governed by the U.S. government. There are information sheets on every country in the world.

The U.S. State Department

http://travel.state.gov/travel_pubs.html

The U.S. State Department provides informative publications with traveler safety tips for different countries. Some subjects include A Safe Trip Abroad, Travel Warnings on Drugs Abroad, Medical Information for Americans Traveling Abroad, and information on travel warnings.

Overseas Security Advisory Council

http://www.ds-osac.org

Created in 1985, the OSAC organization promotes the information exchange between the U.S. Government and the American private sector, including American colleges and universities. It provides security updates for about 2,100 U.S. business and private groups including churches and nonprofits.

Traveling and Living Abroad

http://state.gov/travel

The U.S. Department of State provides travel warnings, information on passports, visas, living abroad info, and other U.S. government related sites.

Travel Management Daily

http://www.tmdaily.com

TMD offers an annual membership for a premium daily newsletter particularly catered toward travel agents and the travel industry professionals.

Travel Warnings

http://www.travel.state.gov/travel_warnings.html

The U.S. Department of State keeps you updated with travel warnings and public announcements on travel, focusing on suggestions on avoiding particular countries. You can also call the toll free number (888) 407-4747 for information on warnings.

Weissmann Travel Reports

http://www.weissmann.com

For an annual subscription, Weissman Travel Report offers an Intelliguide service, which provides up to date advice, warnings, and safety and security information seven days a week and 24 hours a day. You can receive the information through the site or via email, cell phone, or PDA.

Chapter 17

Know Before You Go

**About the Euro*

The euro is the single currency of the European Monetary Union, which was adopted by elevenMember States from 1 January 1999. The eleven Member States are Belgium, Germany, Spain, France, Ireland, Italy, Luxembourg, the Netherlands, Austria, Portugal and Finland. Greece became the 12th Member State to adopt the Euro on 1 January 2001. The name "euro" was chosen by the European Heads of State or Government at the European Council meeting in Madrid in December 1995. For more information on the Euro, check out Johnny Jet Code: About Euro

*Airport Maps

Don't get lost in the airport. From Atlanta, Georgia to Tokyo, Japan, you'll find convenient airport maps, check out Johnny Jet Code: Airport Maps

*Calendars

Not sure what day of the week it is? Now you are only a click away. Check out Johnny Jet Code: Calendars

*Currency Exchange and Money Services

Johnny Jet Code: Money Exchange

Currency Exchange Tips

1. Go to a bank or legal money changer for the best current exchange rates.
2. Exchange some money before you leave so that you don't have to do it at the airport.
3. Some money exchanges don't exchange coins so it is wise to spend your extra change or take it home as a souvenir.

Oanda.com Currency Converter

http://www.oanda.com

http://www.oanda.com/converter/travel

When traveling to a foreign country and you have to convert a pound into a dollar or any other currency conversion, you may not know where to go. OANDA.com provides a quick and easy way to convert online. Select the currency of where you are traveling and choose a rate. Then you will have a conversion chart.

Bank Notes

http://www.banknotes.com

If you ever wondered what a certain bank note or paper currency looks like, this is the site to visit.

Currencies of the World

http://pacific.commerce.ubc.ca/xr/currency_table.html

Here is a list of the different currencies of the world.

International Currency Express Inc.

http://www.foreignmoney.com

You'll find currency exchange services including currency conversion, foreign currency drafts, wire transfers, and travelers checks.

Travelex Exchange

http://www.travelex.com

Travelex offers exchange rates, delivery of travelers checks, insurance services, and coin changing services.

X-Change Rates

http://www.x-rates.com

What's a yen worth in dollars? Find out how many dollars are in a pound. This site is easy to use and it will calculate the conversion for exchange rates and then graph them out for you. All values are gathered from the Federal Reserve Bank.

Universal Currency Conversion

http://www.xe.com/ucc

The Universal Currency Conversion was one of the first interactive foreign exchange rate services available on the Web, and it remains as one of the most popular tools on the Web with over 180 currencies. So next time you wonder how much dinner was in dollars, you'll find it here.

*Maps: Map it up and Route Your Way

Johnny Jet Code: Map It

Yahoo! Maps

http://maps.yahoo.com

Yahoo provides mapping and driving directions in conjunction with turn-by-turn routing.

Oddens' Fascinating World of Maps and Mapping

http://oddens.geog.uu.nl

If there is something related to mapping that you are having difficulties finding, it's likely you will find it at this site with over 20,000 cartographic links.

Atlapedia

http://www.atlapedia.com

Atlapedia has physical and political maps as well as facts and statistics on alphabetized countries throughout the world. This is a great geography and learning resource for anyone looking to travel.

Maps

http://www.earthamaps.com

Locate yourself on the map by longitude and latitude while you get directions from point A to point B. Try some of the map panning and scaling options where you can zoom in and out of the maps.

Expedia Maps

http://www.expediamaps.com

Expedia provides a variety of detailed maps of North America and Europe along with topographic maps of places worldwide. You can search for an address or an intersection or a region. If you are looking driving directions, you can type in your starting and where you would like to go.

Free Trip on Autopilot

http://www.freetrip.com

Want road directions and a place to help plan your trip for free? This award-winning site offers it. Avoid a roadway or take a route. Whichever way you choose, you can make your own itinerary by selecting facilities while planning your route here.

MapBlast!

http://www.mapblast.com

Everyone could use a little direction at this award-winning mapping site where you can quickly get accurate interactive maps and driving directions. MapBlast also provides information on lodging, traffic, and products that help with your travel route.

California Map & Travel Center

http://www.mapper.com

This online version known for their brick and mortar store in Santa Monica, California provides everything you could possibly need to map your trip. Maps, books, globes, GPS and navigation software, audio language tools with hundreds of languages, and travel accessories are some of the great products located here.

MapEasy Guidemaps

http://www.mapeasy.com

These unique colorful guidebooks provide street maps and destination guides together on tear-resistant and waterproof material. Each guide contains useful facts on landmarks including: hotels, restaurants, shopping, museums, cultural events and attractions.

Maps.com

http://www.maps.com

Need a printable map for the road or would you like to get a wall map, or driving map? Maps.com provides one stop shopping for downloadable maps paper atlases, travel accessories, and more.

Mapsco Map and Travel

http://www.mapsco.com

Founded in 1952, Mapsco has served many with maps and mapping products. Specializing in a variety of printed U.S. and World maps, and globes, there is even customized mapping here.

Mapquest.com

http://www.mapquest.com

Mapquest originally started as a map-making company that provided roadmaps at gas stations, and today, online it has become a leading interactive mapping software site for comprehensive door-to-door road directions and trip planning.

Map Science

http://www.mapscience.org

This map site will not tell you how to get from A to Z, but by typing in an address you will find the closest nuclear waste route maps. Typing in your zip will find the latitude and longitude and the approximate distance from the nuclear waste route. Icons show which hospitals and schools are located in the general vicinity.

Maps On Us

http://www.mapsonus.com

A division of Switchboard.com, this award-winning site offers customized mapping along with turn-by-turn driving directions integrated with the yellow pages.

National Geographic Mapping

http://www.nationalgeographic.com/maps

The mapping machine here is quite interesting, providing U.S. and world theme maps, street maps of U.S., Canada, and Europe, a world atlas by continent, historical maps, and other fascinating facts. There's even a map of Mars here, and other downloadable and printed maps.

Navigational Technologies

http://www.navtech.com

A leading provider of GPS mapping software, NavTech provides mapping, driving directions, turn-by-turn routing, fleet management and geographic information systems. You'll find the software installed in vehicles and computing devices.

University of Texas Map Collection

http://www.lib.utexas.edu/maps

This is one of the more extensive collections of online and general interest maps. You'll find maps of the world, Africa, America, Asia, Australia and the Pacific, Europe, The Middle East, Polar Regions and Oceans, United States, National Parks, Historical Maps, and more.

Omni Map Resources

http://www.omnimap.com

There are plenty of maps to be found here. Whether you are looking for travel maps, topographic maps, geologic maps, or any other kind of map, it's likely you will find it here.

Rand McNally

http://www.randmcnally.com

Founded in 1856, Rand McNally is a well-known map publisher providing indispensable printed road atlases and travel guides along with electronic mapping products. You can find everything from Thomas Bros. maps to some of the most reliable Road Atlases. The site offers driving directions, world atlases and downloadable maps, road trip planning, a travel store, and more.

Terra Servers

http://terraserver.microsoft.com

http://www.terraserver.com

These Terra Servers sites offer aerial photographs of digitized satellite images of the globe.

World Atlas

http://www.worldatlas.com

You'll find an abundance of graphic maps, globes, flags, extensive information on countries, and much more at this comprehensive geography and mapping site.

World of Maps

http://www.worldofmaps.com

This retail and mail order store of Canada sells maps, atlases, charts, and aeronautical charts made by the Canada Map Office.

*Money: Find the Cash: ATMs and Credit Cards

Johnny Jet Code: Find Money

Find the closest ATM where you can use your bank or credit card no matter where you are in the world. Make sure your pin is only four digits because that's all many international machines will allow. You can also find out the current currency exchange rates. If you need to wire money, try Western Union, or if you want to buy something over the web use Pay Pal.

MasterCard ATM Locator

http://www.mastercard.com/cardholderservices/atm
Where's the closest MasterCard, Cirrus, or Maestro ATM machine? Search the world here to find it.

Visa Card ATM Locator

http://www.visa.com/atms
Find the closest Visa Card ATM machines around the globe.

American Express ATM Finder

http://maps.americanexpress.com/expresscash/mqinterconnect
Find American Express ATM machines and Express Cash ATMs worldwide.

Credit Cards

http://www.americanexpress.com
http://www.mastercard.com
http://www.visa.com
http://www.discovercard.com
The four major credit cards have some sites to visit.

Stock Quotes

http://www.bloomberg.com
http://www.cnbc.com
Get the latest stock quotes.

Wiring Money

http://www.moneygram.com

http://www.paypal.com

http://www.westernunion.com

Here are sites where you can wire money.

*Money Tracking

Johnny Jet Code: Track Money

Dosh Tracker

http://www.doshtracker.co.uk
Track information about British Pounds.

Euro Bill Tracker

http://www.eurobilltracker.com
Follow information about European notes..

Japanese Yen Tracker

http://www.osatsu.net
Track information about the Yen.

Where's George?

http://www.wheresgeorge.com
Track U.S. dollar bills and any denomination throughout the United States. Enter the bill's serial number and your zip code and you could find out where your bill has been before it reached your hands.

Paying Your Bills

http://www.paymybills.com

http://www.paytrust.com

http://www.piggybills.com

Here are a few bill paying services. You can pay, track and receive all your bills easily online.

*Time: Know the Time Anywhere

Johnny Jet Code: Clock Set

Don't go waking people up one in the middle of the night. Find out what the local time is over there before you start dialing those numbers.

Local Times Around the World

http://times.clari.net.au
Here is a guide to all of the world's countries and many islands with a pointer to the local time in the region.

Greenwich Mean Time

http://www.greenwichmeantime.com
Here is the home of Greenwich Mean Time (GMT) in London, England. The site contains the time for any place in the world.

TimeZoneTicker.com

http://www.timezoneticker.com
This site shows the time in hundreds of places on your desktop.

EconoFinance.com

http://www.econofinance.com/time.htm
EconoFinance.com provides a world time zone converter.

Calendar a History

http://ernie.cummings.net/calendar.htm
This site has a brief history of the Western Calendar and clock.

Complete Sun and Moon Data for One Day

http://aa.usno.navy.mil/data/docs/RS_OneDay.html
The Astronomical Applications of the U.S. Naval Observatory computes the times of sunrise, sunset, moonrise, moonset, and more. Not the most exciting site, but a very interesting way of calculating time.

U.S. Naval Observatory Atomic Master Clock

http://tycho.usno.navy.mil/what.html

What time is it? This site may have the exact answer for you. It will even play it to you.

World Time Server

http://www.worldtimeserver.com

Find out the time in any country around the world. This site also calculates daylight savings time.

Time and Date World Clock

http://www.timeanddate.com/worldclock

This site is a guide to time zones and calendars around the world. See the world clock and check out the time in over 100 different locations. Check out the countdown to the next year.

Time Zone Converter

http://www.timezoneconverter.com

Want to know what time it is in another state or country? This site will tell you.

Time.gov

http://www.time.gov

Find the official U.S. time here.

*Wake Up Services

Johnny Jet Code: Wake Up

Mr. Wake Up

http://www.iping.com

Visit iPing.com or MrWakeUp.com and you'll find a place where you can get wakeup calls and customized reminders via email and the phone for a monthly fee or a flat fee per call.

Tell Me

http://www.tellme.com

Call 1-800-555-TELL or #121 on an AT&T wireless phone and say, "wake up call" and you will get a free wake up call.

Wake Up Land

http://www.wakeupland.com
Get your wake up calls scheduled to you throughout the month.

Wake 123

http://www.wake123.com
Conveniently wake up to this "SmartAlarm" service for a monthly or a flat fee per call.

*Weather: How's the Weather

Johnny Jet Code: Weather

Prepare for your trip! Always check out the weather at your destination and pack accordingly.

Yahoo Weather

http://weather.yahoo.com
Yahoo offers the weather by zip or city.

AccuWeather.com

http://www.accuweather.com
AccuWeather is the world's weather authority. Click on the map and zoom in to see radar images, satellite images, and 5-day weather forecasts throughout the world and U.S. Get storm advisories, news, features, and more at this excellent weather site.

Earth Cam

http://www.earthcam.com
How's the weather in another city, state, country, or your travel destination? Take a look here and all you have to do is preview a picture of the live Earth cams before you leave for your next trip.

Earth Watch Weather on Demand

http://www.earthwatch.com
Earth Watch provides a neat 3-D weather site that is updated continuously. Whether you are looking for weather headlines, storm watch advisories, radar, forecasts, or warnings, it can be found here. It's quite a fascinating way to view the weather.

Intellicast.com

http://www.intellicast.com

What's the weather like around the world? Intellicast.com provides weather reports for active lives. Radar and satellite imagery, along with allergy alert information can be found here. Check out the section, "Weather 101" and learn everything from El Nino terminology to how to read satellite imagery. Overall, it's a great view of the weather.

My Cast

http://www.my-cast.com

My cast provides neighborhood level forecasts as well as severe weather information, satellite and radar imagery through a cell phone service and online.

RoadWeather.com

http://www.roadweather.com

More than how the weather is on the road in the United States, this site tells you how the weather conditions will affect your driving safety. RoadWeather.com will let you know about icy conditions if you are taking a road trip, or keep you updated with the pavement temperature.

*STORMFAX Guide to Fall Foliage

http://www.stormfax.com/foliage.htm

If the weather of the leaves or the changing color of the fall foliage entertains you, this site will certainly be of great use. It contains a comprehensive listing of resources and toll-free numbers to states in the Mid-Atlantic, New England, Midwest and West. For more information on Fall Foliage, check out *Johnny Jet Code: Fall Foliage*

Weather.com for Travel

http://www.weather.com/travel

Traveling and would like to know the weather? Whether you are driving and would like to know the road conditions, the driving forecasts, or if you are flying and would like to know the turbulence potential, this site provides it.

WeatherBug

http://www.weatherbug.com

If you are one who checks the weather frequently, here you can download a little something that will keep you updated on the weather throughout the day.

Washington Post Historical Weather Database

http://www.weatherpost.com/historical/historical.htm

What was the weather like on this day in the past? The site explains weather history by providing the average high and low temperatures along with the average temperature, the average precipitation, wind speed, days of sunshine, humidity, and more.

Weather Underground

http://www.wunderground.com

This colorful weather site provides a map that explains more than just the temperature. Radar, visibility, wind, heat index, wind chill, humidity, dew point, satellite Map, Fronts, Snow, and Jet Stream are all included.. This is a great site to get detailed weather information.

World Climate History

http://www.worldclimate.com

What's the weather normally like elsewhere around the world? Type in the city or town and get temperature averages and precipitation data for that geographic location.

World Meteorological Organization

http://www.wmo.ch

The WMO specializes in focusing on international cooperation in meteorology. Whether the topic is weather prediction, air pollution research, climate change activities, or ozone layer depletion, the WMO organizes global scientific movements to increase accurate weather information provided to public, private, and commercial use. The site provides public info, issues, a library, and more.

*Weight & Measure Conversions

Johnny Jet Code: Conversions

Converters

http://travel.discovery.com/tools/converters/measure.html

http://www-sci.lib.uci.edu/HSG/RefCalculators.html

http://www.calculators.com

http://www.convert-me.com/en

http://www.onlineconversion.com

If you are looking to convert Fahrenheit to Celsius, distance, weight, or volume, these sites provides the tools.

Density Altitude Calculator

http://rshelq.home.sprynet.com/calc_da.htm

This site calculates density altitude or the altitude in the International Standard Atmosphere that has the same air density as the air being evaluated.

Chapter 18

Miles, Points, and Memberships

Do you like to travel for free? Well, then this chapter will help you maximize your miles and points. Make sure you link your credit cards, long distance telephone service providers, and everything that offers miles/points. You can even refinance your home and accrue miles or points. We also list the Web sites that specialize in frequent travel awards and the ones where you can buy or sell your awards.

*Buying and Selling Miles

You have some extra miles you want to sell,
or do you want to buy some from someone selling their miles?
Check out: Johnny Jet Code: Buy Sell Miles

*Cards that Give You Miles

American Express, Diners Club, and some of the airlines, plus many more cards can give you added flyer miles.
This is a great way to get miles before you board the plane.
Check out: Johnny Jet Code: Card Miles

*Check Hotel Enrollment Points

So how many hotel enrollment points do you have?
To check your hotel enrollment points, check out Johnny Jet Code: Check Hotel Points

*Distances for Miles

How many miles are you going to earn?
What route does the pilot take? Find the distance between two zip codes. All your answers here and more, check out Jet Code: Distance

*Donating Miles to Charity

Are you feeling generous to donate miles to charity?
A good site is www.miledonor.com or check out: Johnny Jet Code: Donate Miles

*Frequent Flyer Programs

How can I maximize my miles? Where do I get points?
Find message boards and more about frequent flying programs.
Learn more about joining specific frequent flyer programs, check out Johnny Jet Code: Join Frequent

*Frequent Flyers

Johnny Jet Code: Frequent Flying

Frequent Traveler Programs

http://dir.yahoo.com/Business_and_Economy/Shopping_and_Services/Travel_and_Transportation/Frequent_Travel_Programs
Yahoo has a listing of frequent flyer programs.

Frequent Business Travelers Club

http://www.fbtc.com
If you travel much for business, this site might come in handy. By becoming a club member, you will be able to save at select hotels, restaurants, clubs, and business centers.

Frequent Flier

http://www.frequentflier.com

This site is a great starting place for frequent fliers. Learn how to make the most of your frequent flyer miles and read the frequent flyer newsletter. Compare and contrast frequent flyer programs. There is a frequent flyer message board where you can post comments on frequent flying.

Web Flyer

http://www.webflyer.com

This pioneering site in frequent flying is sponsored by Inside Flyer magazine and has all the information you could possibly want to know about frequent flyer programs and mileage. Learn about deals, programs, and more ways to get the most frequent flyer miles. Tools you can use include in air flight tracking, destination guide, and its Mile Marker distance calculator. Check out Inside Flyer magazine on this site or visit www.insideflyer.com. This site will lead you to other popular sites such as the FlyerTalk frequent flyer community at www.flyertalk.com.

*Hotel Enrollment Points

Many of the larger chain hotels offer enrollment points. You may be able to get a free room or save on your next room. The hotels have sites where you can sign up for its enrollment program. It's a good idea to sign up for hotels that you expect to stay or visit frequently.

Check out: Johnny Jet Code: Hotel Points

*Special Mile Offers

Always check to see if the airline you are flying on has a special offer. (They do this when they are operating a new route, have a low fare competitor in the market, or during hard economic times.) If they do, you will most likely need to either call or go online to register. It only takes a minute and you could get double or triple miles!

Check out Johnny Jet Code: Mile Offers

Chapter 19

Adult Travel and Romantic Vacations

Adults wanting to get away and enjoy a romantic vacation, or celebrate an anniversary will find these sites helpful. If you are going on your honeymoon, you'll also find some great getaways for honeymooners.

*Alternative Lifestyles: Gay and Lesbian Travel

Johnny Jet Code: Gay and Lesbian

Here are sites that are geared towards gay and lesbian travelers.

Coda International Tours

http://www.coda-tours.com

This tour operator is for the intellectual curious gay men and women who enjoy travel together. Each tour brings along a guided expert scholar with gays from ages 30-70 plus gays find Coda-Tours to be great learning experiences where you will travel in style.

Alyson Adventures

http://www.alysonadventures.com

This tour operator offers active and adventurous vacations for gays, lesbians, and friends. Some of the trips include biking, hiking, climbing, diving, and rafting.

Atlantis Gay Vacations

http://www.atlantisevents.com

This tour operator specializes in creating unique gay vacations in an all-gay resort environment. Atlantis is dedicated to providing high standards and trips to exotic places with a focus on friendship and camaraderie.

Gay.com

http://www.gay.com

This specialty membership site for the bisexual, gay, lesbian, and transgender community is one of the leading places online. It features local information, chat, personals, shopping, and more.

Gay Travel

http://www.gaytravel.com

At this site, gays and lesbians are specifically catered with their travel accommodations. There are plenty of trips, getaways, and offerings with everything from small trip getaways to large mainstream cruise ship travel experiences.

Gay Cruise Vacations

http://www.gaycruisevacations.com

This gay owned and operated cruise company offers mainstream cruise vacations exclusively for gay and lesbian travelers. Bookings on major cruise lines along with offerings for small group trips are available.

GayGuide.net Global Gay Guide Network

http://www.gayguide.net

This directory of gay and lesbian destination guides has hundreds of guides throughout the world in almost every country and continent including: Africa, Asia, Canada, Europe, South America, Middle East, and the United States.

Gay Wired

http://www.gaywired.com

The Global Gay and Lesbian Network is an interactive source for today's gay and lesbian community. The site provides news, columns, horoscopes, model contests, information on travel, and more.

Gayellow Pages

http://www.gayellowpages.com

This is a guide to America's gay communities. You can search by state, city, province, and keyword.

IGTLA

http://www.iglta.org

The International Gay and Lesbian Travel Association is a leading trade association committed to growing and enhancing the gay and lesbian tourism business through education, promotion, and networking. Their members are retailers and suppliers of the travel industry.

Now, Voyager Gay and Lesbian Travel

http://www.nowvoyager.com

This leading gay and lesbian owned and operated travel agency specializes in gay cruise trips, gay tourism and resorts, and more gay-friendly vacation destinations at discounted prices.

Olivia Cruises and Resorts

http://www.olivia.com

Olivia provides cruise and resort based vacations exclusively for lesbian and bisexual women.

Our World Publishing

http://www.ourworldpublishing.com

This site is for Our World Magazine, a monthly travel magazine for the gay and lesbian community. It features travel updates, travel resources, back issues, subscription info, and an online edition to purchase.

Out and About

http://www.outandabout.com

This comprehensive gay and lesbian magazine has a gay calendar, gay tour operator resources, gay travel health, info on the magazine, and much more.

Out West Adventures

http://www.outwestadventures.com

The adventurous gay and lesbian will enjoy trekking in Nepal, to rafting through the Grand Canyon. This site offers camping, hiking, rafting, skiing, kayaking, diving, and any other imaginable worldwide adventure getaway packages.

Planetout.com

http://www.planetout.com

Planet Out is a well-known online community for lesbian, gay, bi, and transgender people. It provides a base of well-researched topics in categories such as: news and politics, money and careers, entertainment, families, multimedia, pride, romance, and travel. Travel options are well diversified with plenty of different travel offerings along with a message board.

Pridenet

http://www.pridenet.com

Pridenet proudly serves the gay, lesbian, bi, and transgender community with a g-rated site offering a general e-zine guiding you to various desired locations, and accommodations. Everything on the site is fully organized into categories including: Bars, Camping, Family Issues, History, Senior Citizen, and more.

Rainbow Query

http://www.rainbowquery.com

This is a search engine for the queer Internet community. You can search for anything and read the daily news highlights.

RSVP Gay and Lesbian Vacations

http://www.rsvp.net

This is a well-known travel spot for the gay and lesbian community, offering cruise vacations. RSVP charters large cruise ships, club vacation resorts, and small cruise ships throughout the world.

Travelook.com

http://www.travelook.com

This service provides a way that gay and lesbian travelers can meet other gay and lesbian travelers. You can look for hosts, home exchanges, businesses, and events.

Venture-Out Gay Travel and Tours

http://www.venture-out.com

You will find a place where gay travelers can take small group cultural adventure tours to places in Europe. Whether you are traveling to Italy or Holland, there is something with a cultural and adventure focus.

*Honeymoons and Anniversaries

Johnny Jet Code: Honeymooners

Honeymoons.com

http://www.honeymoons.com

Getting married? Now start planning a honeymoon at this site. From tips to making your honeymoon great, to where to stay and what to do can be found here. After you are finished here, you can head on over to www.thehoneymoon.com and register your honeymoon.

Honeymoon Travel

http://www.honeymoontravel.com

Looking to spend your honeymoon in the Caribbean? If so, this site is a great place to start. It specializes in traveling on your honeymoon and finding a place to go.

Honeymoon Travel & Registry

http://www.honeymoontravel-htr.com

Here they specialize in honeymoons, anniversary trips, and romantic getaways.

Love Tripper

http://www.lovetripper.com

This is a portal for romantic getaways. Whether you are looking for a getaway, honeymoon trip, or wedding destination, this site is for the loving couple. It contains information articles on romantic resorts, couples-only resorts, resort weddings, luxury hotels, spas, cruises, adult-only destinations, and more.

Modern Bride

http://www.modernbride.com/travel

Modern Bride magazine offers travel for honeymooners including beaches, adventure, cultural travel and pampering.

Moon Rings

http://www.moonrings.com

Moon Rings specializes in making personalized and customized honeymoon and anniversary trips according to your budget. Whether your interests are luxury oriented, touring driven, or just for relaxation, Moon Rings offers extraordinary trips.

The Knot

http://www.theknot.com

The Knot is a comprehensive site for couples looking for information and services pertaining to weddings and planning. There is also much information on honeymoons.

Wedding Location

http://www.weddinglocation.com

Beverly Clark's site provides information on planning a wedding, and has a directory of over 10,000 places wedding ceremonies are held. You can plan honeymoons here too.

*Romantic Getaways

Looking for that special place to take that special someone?
Now you know! Check out Johnny Jet Code: Romantic Getaways

*Nudist Camps

Need we explain this? If you want to leave some of your clothes behind, these sites will help explaining the bare necessities. Check out Johnny Jet Code: Nudist Camps

*Naturism Nudist

Johnny Jet Code: Nudism Adult

Fantastic Voyages Nude Tours

http://www.nudetours.com

Looking for a trip to a warm climate area where clothing is optional? This site provides you with that option. This site includes photos, brochures, and answers to your questions about touring unclothed.

No Pockets

http://www.nopockets.com

Sail the Caribbean on a private yacht that allows unclothing as an option.

Naturist Society

http://www.naturist.com

This naturist association believes in the philosophy that, "Body Acceptance is the Idea, Nude Recreation is the Way." Promoting body acceptance, this site promotes trips where clothing is optional. There is a magazine, resources, events, and frequently asked questions.

*Travel for Singles

Johnny Jet Code: Singles Travel

Amazing Singles

http://www.amazingsingles.com

Amazing Singles offers plenty of tours, cruises, and vacations just for singles. There are also many resources for singles available along with personal ads for those singles looking to travel with someone.

Escapade Singles Cruises

http://www.singlescruises-tours.com

Escapade Cruises and Tours specialize in cruise vacations and holiday tours for the solo traveler.

Jewish Singles Connection

http://www.thejewishpeople.org

Jewish singles in the age range of 20-40 plus will find this site interesting. It contains links to groups, travel, and personals.

Vacation Partners

http://www.vacationpartners.com

Singles looking for a vacation partner will find this organization a great place to match up with other singles looking to vacation.

All Singles Travel

http://www.allsinglestravel.com

A division of Travel Services Worldwide, All Singles Travel provides roommate matching services for singles on various adventure getaway trips throughout the world.

Single In Paradise

http://www.singleinparadise.com

Singles going to Maui, Hawaii will find that this site offers a variety of tours and interesting activities to keep the adventurous single traveler entertained.

Singles Tour Groups

http://www.tourgroups.com/singles

Singles in the age range of 35-55 are offered summer vacation packages to places like Cape Cod, Marthas Vineyard, Nantucket Island, and Newport Rhode Island.

Singles On The Go

http://www.singlesonthego.com/travel

This top portal for single travelers contains an abundance of information for busy singles looking to travel and information on dating sites.

Match Travel

http://www.matchtravel.com

This match.com affiliate offers group travel for groups of 50 to 300 singles seeking opportunities to interact with other singles while enjoying numerous vacation packages.

O Solo Mio Singles Travel

http://www.osolomio.com

O Solo Mio is a group of friendly singles throughout the United States who enjoy traveling. The site offers group tours for ages 18-35 and 35 and up to places such as Europe.

*Wineries and Vineyards

Johnny Jet Code: Wine Tastes

Wines.com

http://www.wines.com

Wine enthusiasts will surely enjoy this site. Ask the wine testers a question or post a question on the board, find plenty of wine resources, enter a virtual wine country in California, and try the virtual tasting room.

Ozwine Australian Wineries Directory

http://www.ozwine.com.au

Here is a directory of Australian wineries with a selection of grape varieties, and a glossary of wine tasting terminology. The site also includes wine regions, wineries wines, and wines to try.

Canadian Wine, Wineries, and Vineyards

http://www.vancouver-island-bc.com/canadianwines

If you are going to Canada, there are plenty of wineries to see. This site lists the various wineries by Canadian region. Wineries can be found in Vancouver, North and South Okanagan, Ontario, Quebec, Nova Scotia, and Newfoundland.

Sonoma County Wineries Association

http://www.sonomawine.com

Sonoma provides visitors with plenty of fresh foods, premium wines, and breathtaking scenery within an hour north of San Francisco. Between the rugged western Pacific Coast and the eastern rolling hills, Sonoma presents great landscapes and valleys to explore wine tasting and fresh foods in this premier destination. The site contains history, members, events, and a welcoming center.

France in Your Glass

http://www.inyourglass.com

Since 1986, France in Your Glass has offered trips and wine travel tours in the French countryside. Small-guided tours of groups of six are offered to places like Bordeaux, Burgundy, Rhone and Provence, Champagne and Alsace, and more. Whether you are a wine connoisseur or not it's quite possible you'll find a wine trip here for you.

Napa Valley Wineries

http://www.napavalley.com/wineries

This site features wineries in Napa Valley by region. Each winery has contact information, details, and a small description. There is a comprehensive alphabetical listing as well.

Napa Valley Wine Train

http://www.winetrain.com

You will find a wine adventure via distinguished rail travel. Enjoy culinary delights of gourmet luncheon dining as you travel through Napa Valley's scenic picturesque vineyards and renowned wineries. Each tour is approximately three hours.

Chateau St. Jean

http://www.chateaustjean.com

This vineyard was designed from the ground up to accommodate various types of grapes and separate them in the winemaking process. The wines are bottled with the vineyard name on the label. Chateau St. Jean offers a broad range of Chardonnays.

Chateau Ste. Michelle Winery

http://www.ste-michelle.com

Chateau Ste. Michelle Winery is Washington state's oldest and most prestigious winery. It offers award-winning wines at the chateau and historic grounds near Seattle.

The Hess Collection Winery

http://www.hesscollection.com

The Hess Collection boasts a collection of vineyards, wine, and art with a passion. Hess is committed to quality, which is evident in its contemporary paintings and sculptures throughout the galleries.

Korbel Champagne Cellars

http://www.korbel.com

Established in 1882, and located in Sonoma County Wine Country, Korbel has been known as the exclusive champagne at presidential inaugurations. Today it has been the supporter of various Olympic Games.

Latah Creek Wine Cellars

http://www.latahcreek.com

This is a family owned and operated winery in Spokane, Washington. Since 1982, Latah Creek has been known for its grapes, chardonnays, and red wines.

Matanzas Creek Winery

http://www.matanzascreek.com

Known for its world-class wines and estate-grown lavender products, this site offers the various products that can be found at this Sonoma based winery and information on visiting the winery.

Silverado Vineyards

http://www.silveradovineyards.com

Silverado offers some of the finest wines in the Napa Valley with farms on over 300 acres. Silverado produces Sauvignon Blanc, Chardonnay, Merlot, Sangiovese, and Cabernet Sauvignon.

Tastings

http://www.tastings.com

Originally the Beverage Testing Institute, Tastings was established in 1981 with a mission to produce fair and impartial wine reviews for consumers. Today, it stands behind that philosophy by being a guide to wines, beers, and spirits while publishing their quarterly wine journal.

Beaucastel

http://www.beaucastel.com

Beaucastel offers a selection of fine organically fermented wines.

Chateauneuf-Du-Pape

http://www.chateauneuf-du-pape.com

Located in the beautiful Provence region of southern France, the Chateauneuf-Du-Pape is known in Europe for its full-bodied red wine that has been produced around the town for over eight centuries.

La Cave Du Vergers Des Papes

http://www.pape-verger.com

You will find five different wines to taste on a daily basis.

*Women Travelers

Johnny Jet Code: Women Travel

Here are some sites that are geared towards women travelers with all kinds of safety tips and guides.

Yahoo! Women's Travel Directory

http://dir.yahoo.com/recreation/travel/women

Yahoo provides a listing of many places that help you find women's travel.

Christine Columbus

http://www.christinecolumbus.com

Traveling women will find Christine Columbus to have much of what they need before they travel. All products offered are tested and approved by woman. The online community consists of a packing list, travel resources, travelogues, and travel tips.

Debbie Guide

http://www.debbieguide.com

Guiding women to the inside chic scene, this site provides the latest travel trends and styles for women on the go. Whether you are looking for a women's book to accompany you while you travel, or booking a trip, Debbie's Guide comes in handy as an online guide to the happening inside scene.

Explorations in Travel

http://www.exploretravel.com

Women over 40 or those educationally minded with their travels desiring to explore the world, or participate in a unique volunteering adventure will find this site a great starting place. Whether off the beaten path travel or learning about a new culture is in mind, you can find something here.

Femina Web

http://femina.cybergrrl.com

Since 1995 Femina has provided a Web portal for women worldwide. Wherever you are, you can find plenty of resources specifically suited for girls and women. This is a great starting point for Web site resources for and about women. For the recreation and travel section of Femina, check out:
http://femina.cybergrrl.com/femina/RecreationandLeisure
and you will find more resources.

Gutsy Women Travel

http://www.gutsywomentravel.com

Are you a gutsy woman who would like to take a week of adventure traveling or an excursion just for women? Your tour guide award-winning travel author Marybeth Bond, has the itinerary set and is ready to escort you around the world with her "girls only" packages. Don't leave home without some travel advice and the gutsy women tips.

HERmail.net

http://www.hermail.net

This site is connecting women travelers around the world with its directory. With free email service, women unite and get connected with each other. Suppose you are a traveling woman in New York looking to go to France and need information, this site provides women to meet at your destination.

Journey Woman Travel Magazine

http://www.journeywoman.com

Women who love to travel find this quarterly magazine to be a reliable resource and starting point. Not only does it show you "gal-friendly" cities, you'll find information on everything from what to take and wear to where to go and what to do. Learn about the travel experiences of other women through reading travel tales and stories, and check out the classifieds for deals on different places to go.

Hitchhiking Vietnam: Letters from the trail

http://www.pbs.org/hitchhikingvietnam

Karin shares her personal experiences of trekking through the country in this PBS travelogue documentary. Read her story, view her pictures, and learn from her personal travel tips. The photos are excellent and the story is amazing.

Senior Women's Travel

http://www.poshnosh.com

This site caters to women who are fifty plus and are passionate about touring and traveling. Tours travel to Barcelona, Greece, London, New York, Paris, Venice, and more. There is even a grandma and grandmother tour. The philosophy here is not putting your life "on hold," but rather keep living and traveling while you can.

Sally's Place Travel

http://www.sallys-place.com/travel.htm

At Sally's Place, you'll find articles with an emphasis on food and culture from different nations. Each article is a travelogue or travel experience explained from start to finish. From great recipes, to cultural culinary delights, Sally's Place has something for the "woman food and travel connoisseur."

The Traveling Woman

http://www.travelingsafe.com

Traveling safely is important to any woman looking to make the most of her journey. This site promotes safe travel for women traveling solo by telling you how to fend off crime, peculiar strangers, custom agents, and more. There is also a book available here too.

Travel Lady Magazine

http://www.travellady.com

Women journalists and travel professionals tell their travel stories. The site is filled with plenty of destinations to choose with selections of written photojournalistic travel experiences on specific locations.

Walking Women

http://www.walkingwomen.com

You will find walking tours for women in the UK. Tours are held in the Lake district, Scotland, and abroad. Whether you are a gentle walker or a high impact walker, there is something for you. The site has many photos and information on all types of walking tours held throughout the year.

Wild Women Expeditions

http://www.wildwomenexp.com

These expeditions are for the adventurous woman traveling up north to Ontario. Featuring wilderness canoe trips, and themes oriented with mind, body, and spirit, will challenge and entertain any adventurous outdoors-oriented woman. Trips include gourmet dining, and activities such as swimming, paddling, cycling, campfires, sauna, and after a day massage.

Women On Their Way

http://www.womenbusinesstravelers.com

The Wyndham Hotels and Resorts presents a site for women business travelers that includes travel tips, a book club, annual contests, and information on Wyndham Hotel reservations.

The Women's Travel Club

http://www.womenstravelclub.com

Becoming a member of the club entitles you to enter password protected areas and to take as many as 25 -30 discounted trips per year with a small group of women. Trips are taken to places within the U.S. and overseas.

Women Traveling Together

http://www.women-traveling.com

This membership site specializes in small group travel for women. The tours are all-inclusive and include some exotic lands. The site includes information on the tours, and tour news.

Women.com

http://www.women.com

At this community site dedicated to women, you will find information on entertainment, horoscopes, dating, style, fun, games, girl talk, and more.

Chapter 20

Seniors: Traveling in the Golden Years

If you're over the age of 62, you qualify for a senior discount. This is usually 10% off tickets and sometimes even your companion under 62 will get the same discount. All the major airlines offer senior coupon books, which are 4 one-way coupons. These coupons can be a great savings so make sure you ask. Although they want you to make a 14-day advance notice, you can fly stand by, just call the reservation desk and ask them how flight "such and such" looks to fly stand by.

*Senior Airline Policies

Some airlines offer special perks or discounts to Senior Citizens.
Check out Johnny Jet Code: Senior Policy

Yahoo! Travel for Seniors

http://dir.yahoo.com/recreation/travel/seniors
Yahoo provides a directory for senior travel with a few good sites to click for seniors.

AARP Trips n' Travel

http://www.aarp.org/travel

This popular organization offers a place where you can share your travel stories, various discounts on travel and deals for members. Read the featured travel stories and find out where others find their happy trails traveling.

Discounts for Senior Citizens

http://www.narfe.com/va/discount.htm

http://www.seniorcitizens.com/discounts/airlines.shtml

http://www.seniordiscounts.com

There are many services seniors can get a discount on. These sites explain them with everything from driving, flying to train traveling.

Elder Hostel

http://www.elderhostel.org

The Elder Hostel program is a non-profit organization, with all-inclusive programs providing affordable liberal arts educational opportunities for seniors. Create, learn, and explore is the motto here.

Elder Treks

http://www.eldertreks.com

This is the world's first adventure travel company designed for seniors. Elder Treks is taking you to exotic places in small group adventures to over 50 different countries. Whether you are in for a safari in Kenya, a hike somewhere in Europe, this is a great starting place to find culture, wildlife, and adventure tourism.

Grand Travel

http://www.grandtrvl.com

Grandparents can take a trip with their grandchildren. This program was developed by teachers, psychologists, and leisure counselors to help grandparents create lasting memories for themselves and their grandchildren.

Interhostel Learning Vacations

http://www.learn.unh.edu/interhostel

Traveling, learning about different cultures, expanding your horizons is what Interhostel is about. You will find learning vacations specific for various interests, different cultural awareness, and more. Spanning the globe, these learning experiences can be found taking you to the different continents. This site is provided by the continuing education program at the University of New Hampshire.

Manufactured Mobile Home Marketplace

http://www.mkpmag.com

Here you can find information on RV and mobile homes for seniors in Florida's retirement communities. You can find buyers and sellers and possibly your dream home on this site.

Marco Polo Magazine

http://www.marcopolomagazine.com

Marco Polo Magazine is a national magazine publication that caters to soft adventurous travelers over 50.

The Retirement Net

http://www.retirenet.com

If you are looking to move to a retirement community or a retirement home, this site will come in handy. You can browse active retirement with on-the-go lifestyles, to extended care, or golf communities, RV living or seasonal rentals.

Seniornet

http://www.seniornet.org

Seniornet is a comprehensive online community for seniors who use computer technology. With over 600 discussion topics, including travel, there are plenty of resources here, making it an excellent site.

Travel 50 and Beyond

http://www.travel50andbeyond.com

This magazine is geared for travelers who are 50 and older. This site serves the more thoughtful traveler who demands quality, value, and an inspiring travel experience.

United Airlines Silver Wings Plus

http://www.silverwingsplus.com

United Airlines created this site for senior travelers over the age of 55 to save on travel accommodations. Membership is required and members will get news articles and discounts on trips.

Over The Hill Gang International

http://www.skiersover50.com

Are you over the hill or on the hill skiing? Since 1977, this site has been taking senior skiers on the slopes or hills. Memberships entitle you to greater discounts at ski resorts in the U.S. and Canada, a newsletter, and much more.

Senior Summer School

http://www.seniorsummerschool.com

Seniors wanting to go back to school will find affordable learning opportunities for seniors to enhance their summer are available with this company on campuses throughout the U.S. and Canada. Although there are no grades or mandatory attendance, this program is great for any senior looking to broaden their horizons in the classroom with others.

Travel and Learn

http://www.travelearn.com

Compared to a "luxury field trip," this company provides information on touring vacations where you will explore the past, present, and explain how you can take a trip like this in the future. Group camaraderie is included with all trips. This is a memorable learning adventure, exploring places like Asia, Australia, Europe, and many more exceptional learning tours.

*Senior Tours

Don't worry about traveling on your own. You can take a Senior Tour to pretty much anywhere in the world with people your age and at the pace you can enjoy. Check out Johnny Jet Code: Senior Tours

Chapter 21

Shipping Out and Moving In

*Cargo

Johnny Jet Code: Air Cargo

Arrow Air Inc.

http://www.arrowair.com

Arrow Air Inc. is a leader in providing air cargo between the United States, the Caribbean, South and Central America. Their hubs are in Miami International Airport, San Juan, and Puerto Rico.

DHL Worldwide Express

http://www.dhl-usa.com

With its global system of 36 hubs and 275 gateways, DHL is a leader in providing information on international and local shipping, package tracking, and customs. DHL offers cost efficient services, in addition to offering chartered and commercial moving airlines.

Emery Worldwide

http://www.emeryworld.com

Based in Redwood City, California, Emery Worldwide specializes in global freight transportation services for business-to-business shippers of heavyweight cargo. It also provides global air and ocean freight transportation, logistics management, and customs brokerage services to manufacturing, industrial, retail and government customers.

Evergreen International Aviation

http://www.evergreenaviation.com

Headquartered in McMinnville, Oregon, Evergreen International provides one of the largest shipping cargo fleets worldwide via 747s and DC-9s. Some of their services include helicopters, international airlines, aircraft sales and leasing, an aircraft museum, a nonprofit humanitarian organization, and Evergreen Orchards.

Southeast Airways

http://www.southeastairways.com

This is an all-cargo airline to the Bahamas from Miami with daily Cessna Caravan and DC-3 freighter service offering competitively priced demand charters worldwide.

Amerijet International Inc.

http://www.amerijet.com

As a leader in air cargo throughout Latin America, Mexico, and the Caribbean, Amerijet offers purchasing of quality products and services.

Atlas Air Worldwide Holdings

http://www.atlasair.com

This Purchase, New York based Atlas Air is a worldwide all-cargo carrier that operates a fleet of 747 freighters under long-term contract to the major international airlines.

*Cargo Airlines

Johnny Jet Code: Cargo Airlines

Asiana Cargo

http://www.asianacargo.com

This company focuses on the Asia-Pacific air cargo market. The site offers air cargo reservation and tracking of cargo.

BAXglobal.com

http://www.baxglobal.com

BAX Global offers shipping for business-to-business shippers worldwide through a network of hundreds of offices in 123 countries. Services include guaranteed overnight freight shipping, logistics, and import and export processing.

China Airlines

http://www.china-airlines.com

China Airline's site has online booking, information on its cargo services with delivery around the world.

U.S. Finnair

http://www.us.finnair.com/services/cargo

Finnair offers cargo services on its 747 and MD-11 to northern Europe with airbus freighter service worldwide.

Cargo Carriers Worldwide

http://www.hawaiiag.org/transport/cargocar.htm

This site lists cargo carriers throughout the world.

JAL Cargo

http://www.jalcargo.com

http://www.jal.co.jp/jalcargo/index-e.htm

JAL Cargo of The Americas is the freight and mail division of Japan Airlines Company.

Kitty Hawk

http://www.kha.com

Kitty Hawk is one of the largest non-integrated freight carriers offering air cargo, charter services, and logistics.

Lan Chile Cargo

http://www.lancargo.cl

Founded in 1929, Lan Chile Cargo has become a known name in cargo transportation. The company suits customer's cargo needs through delivery of live animals, general cargo, dangerous goods, valuable goods, and perishables.

Lufthansa Cargo

http://www.lhcargo.com
Lufthansa Cargo offers international air cargo transportation along with environmentally friendly ground transportation. Goods arrive at the Frankfurt Airport and proceed to various European destinations.

Nippon Cargo Airlines

http://www.ananet.or.jp/nca
This company offers cargo transportation to and from Japan.

Polar Air Cargo

http://www.polaraircargo.com
Polar Air was founded in 1993 and offers international logistics through linking centers of commerce in Asia, Europe, Australia, New Zealand, and North and South America.

Qantas Freight

http://www.qantas.com.au/freight/dyn/menu
Qantas can handle any kind of freight, with primary focus on transport of high technology products. They believe in providing the widest possible range of services including cargo, express, airmail, freighters and charters, and customs clearance.

*Moving Companies

Johnny Jet Code: Moving Trucks

Allied Van Lines

http://www.alliedvan.com
Founded in 1928, Allied Van Lines is an industry leader holding more than 600 agent locations throughout North America. Today Allied offers assistance with corporate relocations and household moves.

Bekins Van Lines Agent Locator

http://www.bekinsagent.com
Bekins Van Lines can be found in many locations throughout the nation offering corporate relocations and household moves. This site assists you in finding the nearest Bekins Van Lines agents.

Home Gain

http://www.homegain.com

Home Gain makes buying and selling a home easier. The site boasts that it will save buyers and sellers time and money and assist in finding and comparing realtors. The site consists of thousands of realtors and homes.

Mayflower Transit

http://www.mayflower.com

Since 1927, Mayflower Transit has been specializing in assisting families with quality moving throughout the United States.

United Van Lines

http://www.unitedvanlines.com

Based in Fenton, Missouri, United Van Lines is one of the largest corporate and home movers in the United States.

Shipping and Boxing Your Goods

Shipping and Cargo

http://www.dhl.com

http://www.fedex.com

http://www.mbe.com

http://www.ups.com

http://www.mapsonus.com/db/USPS

http://postcalc.usps.gov

http://www.canadapost.ca

If money is no object, then ship your bags so you don't have to worry about the airline losing anything or straining your back. These companies will get them to your destination and will save you time. DHL, Fed Ex, Mail Boxes Etc., UPS, the United States Postal locator and calculator, and the Canada Post are here to help you with your shipping needs.

*Storage

Johnny Jet Code: Store It

All Boxes Direct

http://www.allboxes.com

This deliver company provides free delivery of moving, storage, shipping, packaging products and accessories.

Door to Door Storage

http://www.doortodoor.com

This company offers both self-storage and moving with security features for both homes and businesses. Door to Door offers packages, then you pack it, and they deliver it.

Movers Guide

http://www.moversguide.com

The U.S. Postal Service offers this comprehensive guide to assist you with moving. Some of the stuff offered includes changing your address, moving supplies, connecting your utilities, moving tips, and more.

Chapter 22

Shop Away

Love to shop? We list all the important travel shops for all your travel gear and trips. We also list the shops where you can send a little love (Flowers, Chocolates...) home while you are away.

Dubai Duty Free

http://www.dubaidutyfree.com
Since starting in 1983, Dubai Duty Free has become a widely recognized airport retailer of duty free products.

Easy Travel Air

http://www.easytravelair.com
This site offers a hands free pouch that carries around your identification and ticket while you are going through airport security.

eZiba.com

http://www.eziba.com
This online gallery has unique handcrafted items that are imported throughout the world. From cultural gifts, to hard to find crafts, you can find things you would normally have to travel far away to get. Shopping here helps prepare you for your trip or get items after you have returned home.

Ghirardelli Square

http://www.ghirardellisq.com

Ghirardelli Square is a historic San Francisco destination known for the famous Ghirardelli Chocolate Company. There is a lot to do here, including shopping, fine dining, and live entertainment. You will find the world famous soda fountain and you can try to win some Ghirardelli chocolate.

Largest Shopping Malls

http://www.mallofamerica.com

http://www.westedmontonmall.com

Shopping is one thing. Going to these malls is another story. The Mall of America is the largest indoor shopping mall in the United States located in Bloomington, Minnesota. The West Edmonton Mall is the largest mall in the world located in the City of Edmonton in Alberta, Canada. Come see what makes these malls extraordinary.

Novica

http://www.novica.com

Novica, in association with National Geographic offers handmade arts and crafts, jewelry, linens, tapestries, masks, paintings, and more creative artwork from Andes, Bali, Brazil, Mexico, Africa, Thailand, and India.

Pike Place Market

http://www.pikeplacemarket.com

Pike Place Market is known as America's Favorite Farmers Market. Located in Seattle, Washington, this nine-acre historic district attracts more than nine million visitors annually. It's quite a site to see virtually online and in person. From farmers to crafts people and performers, there is much happening here.

Click Rewards

http://www.clickrewards.com

At Click Rewards you can earn flyer miles and click miles when you purchase products from their partners.

Sky Mall

http://www.skymall.com

Looking for a gift while you are in the air? Sky Mall is an excellent place to start. It's the leading in-flight catalog marketer on all major U.S. airlines. It provides direct marketing for manufacturers and service providers. You can place orders online or in the air.

Flowers

http://www.1800flowers.com

http://www.florist.com

http://www.flower.com

http://www.ftd.com

http://www.virtualflowers.com

Are you looking for roses or flowers? Here are some great starting places for flowers.

Fragrances

http://www.beautysampling.com

http://www.perfumania.com

http://www.scentiments.com

http://www.sephora.com

Are you looking for some nice scents, colognes, and perfumes for the trip? Here are a few good starting places.

*Bags, Luggage, and Travel Gear

Johnny Jet Code: Luggage Goods

The Complete Carry-on Traveler

http://www.oratory.com/travel

This site is all about packing luggage and traveling light. Forget waiting for the baggage carousels and try packing light. It's easy to pack too much and this site tries to help you avoid doing that. It tells you why you should pack light and gives you packing tips.

Altrec

http://www.altrec.com

Looking for camping, climbing, hiking, cycling, running gear or travel gear is easy to find at Altrec. In addition to gear and gear reviews, you will find great advice, photos, a trip planner, articles, tips, and more for the outdoors traveler.

Bag It

http://www.bagit.com

BagIt.com was one of the first bag and luggage online stores. They have a selection of quality luggage bags, cases, accessories, and leather goods. Specialties include Briggs & Riley, Atlantic and other quality brands.

1-800-LUGGAGE

http://www.1-800-luggage.com

There's so much luggage at this site that can be found at discounted prices. You'll find brand name luggage and briefcases. You can shop by category or manufacturer.

Eagle Creek Travel Gear

http://www.eaglecreek.com

Eagle Creek offers special backpacks made for the adventurous traveler and backpacker. Backpacks are designed especially for easy commuting and preventing back pains. They also carry some interesting travel accessories.

Easy Going

http://www.easygoing.com

We've all heard the words "take it easy" and this site makes shopping easy for travelers by making your shopping options simple. You'll find a little bit of luggage, travel accessories, and guidebooks here.

eBags

http://www.ebags.com

Bags are just one of the many business related accessories you will find at eBags.com. Umbrellas, boxes, luggage, backpacks, wallets, and sports gear are some of the product offerings at this award winning travel shop.

Eddie Bauer

http://www.eddiebauer.com

Since 1920 Eddie Bauer has been offering outdoors products and sporting gear. It offers a wide selection of Eddie Bauer branded bags, duffels, and luggage.

Eastern Mountain Sports

http://www.ems.com

EMS was founded in 1967 by two rock climbers in Wellesley Massachusetts. They felt that there wasn't a good variety and selection of climbing products. EMS specializes in offering climbing and camping equipment based on the founder's hobby of rock climbing. Today, it is a leading provider of outdoor specialty products with many retail outlets nationwide.

eTraveler Gear

http://www.etravelergear.com

This store was created for the business and frequent traveler. It offers an a great variety of different products including hard-to-find travel accessories, smoke hoods, translators, laptop cases, backpacks, luggage, and more.

Going in Style

http://www.goinginstyle.com

You'll find thousands of unique travel accessories, organizers, and luggage at this unique travel store based out of California. There is an in depth catalog to view with an abundance of products to assist your traveling needs.

One Stop Travel Shop

http://www.healthytravel.com

This one stop travel shop in Beverly Hills offers a unique combination of everything you need for your travels. Whether you are looking for travel books, maps, luggage, clothing, health essentials, and more there is something for you. Its Travel Medicine Center provides vaccinations and counseling before you travel and diagnosis when you return.

Lands' End

http://www.landsend.com

A large collection of bags, duffels, and luggage can be found at this well-known outfitter's site.

L.L. Bean

http://www.llbean.com

Since its founding by Leon Leonwood Bean in 1912, L.L. Bean has become a leader in direct mail of outdoor products. Today it provides a great deal of outdoor products including gear, bags, and much more.

Luggage Factory

http://www.luggagefactory.com

The luggage comes straight from the factories and is viewable on your screen. If you are looking for a factory made luggage piece or luggage variety, this is a great place to look, as there is a great selection here. Brands such as Travel Pro, Tumi, and Samsonite are here.

Luggage Online

http://www.luggageonline.com

Covering almost all luggage needs, this site offers personalized service along with a low price guarantee on luggage. There's a selection of accessories, computer cases, and briefcases, too.

Nations Travel Stores

http://www.nationstravelmall.com

Nations Travel Stores of California offer a little bit of everything travel related with luggage, travel clothes,
maps, books, and more for the travel enthusiast.

REI

http://www.rei.com

http://www.rei-outlet.com

REI specializes in products for the outdoor traveler and expands its products into various areas. You'll find a vast selection of gear, products, camping, hiking, climbing, cycling, snow sports, water sports, and more.

Sierra Trading Post

http://www.sierratradingpost.com

The Sierra Trading Post offers a variety of outdoor gear and wear for travelers and outdoors people. Everything from jackets to flashlights can be found at this site.

Magellan's Travel Catalog

http://www.magellans.com

Magellan's offers a great variety of travel supplies and products. If you need it for travel, you will likely find it here. Products include: accessories, appliances, comfort items, luggage and bags, straps, binoculars and cameras, personal care items, electrical adapters, and almost anything else you could imagine.

Passenger Stop

http://www.passengerstop.com

The goal of this Maryland based travel store is to "provide everything for the traveler…but the ticket." You'll find guidebooks, world maps, luggage gear, foreign electricity converters, business cases, and much more.

Sumdex Computer Carrying Cases

http://www.sumdex.com

Sumdex specializes in computer carrying cases of different designs, including backpacks, briefcases, and smaller camera and PDA/mobile phone cases. They are known for their timeless design and quality. This site is a great place to look when you need to travel with your electronics.

Travelite

http://www.travelite.org

This site is all about traveling light. You'll find the basics to more advanced travel tips to make your destination with minimal baggage.

TravelGearNow.com

http://www.travelgearnow.com

Since 1994, Travel Essentials has provided a broad selection of the highest quality travel gear and accessories. With a team of well-seasoned travelers, they know what gear, luggage, and materials that will suit you for your trip. Their online presence meets the standards and guarantees all products.

Travel Smith

http://www.travelsmith.com

Travel Smith has been known for their catalog and online presence of travel products. You will find some comfortable travel outfits from wrinkle-free shirts to hats and footwear as well as luggage.

TravelSupplies.com

http://www.travelsupplies.com

Get the supplies you need for your trip at this one stop for travel supplies. Find appliances, clothing care, luggage, organizers, safety supplies, gifts, and more.

Unclaimed Baggage Center

http://www.unclaimedbaggage.com

Imagine what people are packing and not claiming at the baggage claim? They could wait forever, but after ninety days, it usually is labeled unclaimed. Most of the merchandise consists of clothing, with the rest dedicated to items like cameras, electronics, sporting goods, jewelry, designer optical, books, and you could of guessed it, luggage.

Walkabout Travel Gear

http://www.walkabouttravelgear.com

Travel accessories and gear from safety products to baggage can be found here. There are also very interesting travel tips from travelers. The products here have been tested by seasoned travelers. Overall, this site makes a great shopping experience for all travelers.

World Traveler Luggage and Travel Goods

http://www.worldtraveler.com

This online luggage extravaganza was designed for the modern traveler. With decades of experience in the travel industry, this site offers almost everything you could imagine when it comes to traveling. You can shop by brand name products for discount baggage, briefcases, computer cases, travel outfits, accessories, and more.

Yak Pak Bags

http://www.yakpak.com
Quality backpacks, mini backpacks, bags, duffel bags, shoulder bags, and all sorts of stylish and durable bags at the Yak Pak bag store. They guarantee their bags for life, and there are a variety of brand names to choose from here.

*Factory Outlets

http://www.premiumoutlets.com

http://www.primeoutlets.com

http://www.tangeroutlet.com

http://www.vffo.com

For factory outlets, check out some of these factory outlet shopping centers. *Johnny Jet Code: Factory Outlets*

*Food and Gifts

Instead of lugging gifts home, why not order online and have them shipped? It's also a great way to say "I miss you or wish you were here!" Check out Johnny Jet Code: Gift Shop

*Music and Movies

We list all the best places to buy movies and music online. Check out Johnny Jet Code: Music Shop

*Shaving Supplies

Johnny Jet Code: Smooth Shave

The Art of Shaving

http://www.artofshaving.com
This company provides some of the highest quality shaving products and accessories. Creams, soaps, brushes, stands, and shaving goods are offered here. Check out the shaving tips, and some of the shaving travel bags.

Gillette Company

http://www.gillette.com

The blade company makes more than blades. Razor, shaving gels, creams, toiletry, oral care, and battery products are offered here.

Tend Skin

http://www.tendskin.com

Razor bumps are a thing of the past with the shaving products offered here. You'll find a unique shaving gel as well as deodorant. The company story is quite interesting too.

Quick Shave

http://www.quickshave.com

The philosophy here is that two blades are better than one or quicker. You'll get some shaving tips, a little history of shaving and if nothing else, an interesting product.

*Shopper Assistance

Johnny Jet Code: Shopping Assistance

Bizrate.com

http://www.bizrate.com

Looking for an online shop? This site will help you find some great shops in a variety of categories.

Buy Buddy

http://www.buybuddy.com

You will find price comparisons on books, computers, electronics, games, movies, and music.

Consumer Research

http://www.consumersearch.com

Here is a consumer advocacy site that has product reviews, reports, and ranks products by categories.

Dealtime.com

http://www.dealtime.com

Looking for good deals? Here is a site that searches various retailers, auctions, and classifieds for the lowest prices.

Epinions.com

http://www.epinions.com

See what others recommend and make an informed buying decision.

Froogle

http://www.froogle.com

Froogle is a service from Google that provides information about products for sale online when consumers search for a product.

My Simon

http://www.mysimon.com

My Simon will help you compare products and prices around the Web.

Chapter 23

Staying in Touch

Here are some inexpensive ways to stay in touch. You can buy an international calling card, look up country codes, get online greeting cards, rent an international cell phone or visit one of the many Internet Cafés to send an email.

***Addresses**

http://www.555-1212.com
http://www.addresses.com
http://www.anywho.com
http://www.phonenumbers.net
http://www.superpages.com
http://www.switchboard.com
http://www.teldir.com
http://www.tollfree.att.net
http://www.yellowpages.com
http://yp.yahoo.com
Find someone's address and phone number. At Addresses.com you can search for email addresses. *Johnny Jet Code: Address*

Internet Café Guides

http://www.cybercafes.com

http://www.cybercaptive.com

http://www.netcafeguide.com

Since you're on the Internet you may want to look for the nearest Internet Café in town. Check out these sites where you will be sure to find some great coffee, Web browsing and a great place to check email. The last time I checked, there was over 4,000 Internet cafés in the world.

*Cellular Phones

Johnny Jet Code: Cell Phones

About Cell Phones

http://www.cellphones.about.com

What would you like to know about cell phones that you didn't already know? This site explains cell phones to you with ring tones, information on buying, and the latest cell phones.

Wireless Connection

http://www.boingo.com

http://www.skytel.com

http://www.goamerica.com

http://www.novatelwireless.com

http://www.prontonetworks.com

http://www.ricochet.com

Looking to connect wirelessly to the Internet? Here are a few good places to start. *Johnny Jet Code: Wireless Internet*

Mobile Phone and Wireless Companies

http://www.bluetooth.com

http://www.ericsson.com

http://www.nokia.com

http://www.motorola.com

http://www.qualcomm.com

http://www.sonyericsson.com

Here are some mobile phone and wireless manufacturer Web sites. *Johnny Jet Code: Wireless Companies*

Wireless Service Providers

http://www.attws.com

http://www.cingular.com

http://www.sbc.com

http://www.sprintpcs.com

http://www.verizonwireless.com

http://www.voicestream.com

Here are some wireless service providers. *Johnny Jet Code: Wireless Service*

Your Mobile Phone

http://www.yourmobile.com
Download some mobile phone ring tones.

Planet Fone

http://www.planetfone.com
If you are traveling internationally, your cell phone may not work in the foreign country you are visiting. You can go here to find out more about how you can rent an international cell phone.

Travel Cell

http://www.travelcell.com
Travel Cell offers premiere global cellular rentals at low rates.

*Email

Johnny Jet Code: Email

For more information on places you can go to check email, check out *Johnny Jet Code: Check Email*

Check Email

http://anywhere.aol.com
http://www.eprompter.com
http://netmail.att.net
http://webmail.earthlink.net
http://www.hotmail.com
http://my.msn.com
http://www.usa.net
http://www.mail.yahoo.com
http://mailcafe.net
http://mailstart.com
Here are various places you can go and check your email.

Pocket Email

http://www.pocketmail.com
Don't miss email because you are on the go.

Efax.com

http://www.efax.com
Send faxes over the Internet.

*Greeting Cards

Johnny Jet Code: Send Greetings

Hallmark

http://www.hallmark.com
Known for its paper greeting cards and gifts, Hallmark has e-cards you can attach with a gift certificate.

American Greetings

http://www.ag.com
AmericanGreetings.com has some of the best selections of online and offline paper greeting cards. Becoming a member gives you a greater selection of e-cards to send for every occasion.

Blue Mountain

http://www.bluemountain.com
Some of the world's best personalized animated e-cards can be found on a variety of different subjects.

Disney Cards

http://www.dcards.com
Send Mickey Mouse or any of the other great Disney characters through email. The site contains a wide variety of animated cards featuring the magical world of Disney.

E-Cards

http://www.e-cards.com
There is a broad selection of e-cards and gifts here with a global, educational, and environmental twist.

E Greetings

http://www.egreetings.com
Specializing in animated online greetings, this site has a great collection of online cards to choose from, with a variety of themes.

Here You Go!

http://www.hereyougo.com
You'll find some humorous greetings and gifts, panty grams, and more.

Message Mates

http://www.messagemates.com
There is a collection of funny and free e-cards to send here.

Netcards.com

http://www.netcards.com
There is a broad selection of simple and free animated greetings to send here.

Photocartoonist

http://www.photocartoonist.com
Kat Kaverly certainly shows her stuff here. She really has some of the coolest greeting cards and you got to love her animations. You might also want to visit *www.funnypictureslady.com* to see more of her funny pictures.

Regards.com

http://www.regards.com
At this site you will find a unique collection flash animated greeting cards, games, a reminder service, an invitation service, and more.

Talking Toons

http://www.talkintoons.com
These cartoon characters will deliver your greeting card in a fun flash animated way.

Castle Mountains

http://www.castlemountains.com
You can send some free postcards and greetings here.

*Telephone

Johnny Jet Code: Telephone

Area Code Lookup

http://www.areacodesonlinelookup.com
Look up the area code for any state.

Callwave.com

http://www.callwave.com
Don't miss calls because you are surfing the Web. Callwave offers an Internet answering machine.

Country Calling Codes

http://www.countrycallingcodes.com
http://www.kropla.com/dialcode.htm
Need an international calling code to stay in touch with your friends and family in other countries? This site has the numbers you need.

Internet Toll Free Directory

http://www.inter800.com

Looking for a toll free number? Here you go. This site will direct you to sites like www.internettollfree.com and the toll free pages of www.whitepages.com where you can search for toll free numbers on a variety of businesses. This site is very convenient for the traveler looking for a toll free number.

Kallback

http://www.kallback.com

The discount long distance rates can help you save on long distance rates around the world. The Kallback program allows you to change your callback number as you travel.

Rate Keeper

http://www.ratekeeper.com

This site is dedicated to providing you with up to date information on long distance phone rates.

*Mobile Computing

Johnny Jet Code: Mobile Computing

Yahoo! Mobile Computing Directory

http://dir.yahoo.com/computers_and_internet/mobile_computing

Yahoo has a directory of various mobile computing resources. Check out this site if you would like to see some of the mobile computing resources listed in Yahoo.

Computer Companies

http://www.apple.com
http://www.csd.toshiba.com
http://www.dell.com
http://www.gateway.com
http://www.hp.com
http://www.ibm.com
http://www.ita.sel.sony.com
http://www.sharp-usa.com

Here are some of the larger computer companies.

Microsoft

http://www.microsoft.com

Looking for anything Windows related?

All Net Devices

http://www.allnetdevices.com

Any possible Internet related device can be found here. Looking for handheld computers, Internet enabled PDAs, mobile computing devices, email devices, and other devices that can be connected to the Internet? Find the latest news and what's new. This is a great place to start.

Ask Dr. Tech

http://www.askdrtech.com

Looking for computer tech support and don't know who to call while you're on the go? "Ask Dr. Tech" may have the answer for you. This company offers live phone support for computers.

AvantGo Inc.

http://www.avantgo.com

Would you like to use your PDA to connect to your business? AvantGo provides solutions with software applications that allow you to make the Web work for you when you are on the go.

Go To My PC

http://www.gotomypc.com

If you don't want to bring your PC with you, this service allows you to access your computer from any PC connected to the Internet.

City Sync

http://www.citysync.com

This is a comprehensive travel guide you can download to your handheld device. It's available worldwide from the experts at Lonely Planet and includes hundreds of restaurant reviews, attractions, and entertainment.

Connect Globally Inc.

http://www.connectglobally.com

Different countries use different adapters and plug connections. This site offers a variety of mobile connectivity products such as adapters, accessories, batteries, and other equipment for the mobile computing consumer.

Downloads

http://www.download.com

http://www.tucows.com

If there is something you need to download, these can be helpful.

Laptop Travel

http://www.laptoptravel.com

Mobile computing professionals will find what they need at this site that offers adapters, batteries, converters, and more. The information section provides answers to your frequently asked questions about mobile computing.

Steve Kropla's Help for World Travelers!

http://www.kropla.com

Steve Kropla is helping world travelers hook up their modems in foreign countries, find dialing codes in far away lands, know which plugs work in different countries, a list of worldwide TV formats, and more. No longer will you be lost for which plugs to take along on your foreign travels.

iPass Inc.

http://www.ipass.com

The company iPass provides remote access services to mobile executives so that they can gain secure access to their corporate network and email from anywhere in the world.

Mobile Computing & Communications

http://www.mobilecomputing.com

Mobile Computing magazine contains comprehensive information on laptops, cell phones, notebooks, pages, PDAs, and more for the mobile computing professional. See what's in the latest magazine and what product is featured this week.

Mobile Planet

http://www.mobileplanet.com

Mobile Planet has some of the most unique electronic mobile computing and wireless products available online.

Mobile Info

http://www.mobileinfo.com

This site is a comprehensive resource for mobile computing information, written by wireless networking and mobile computing consultants. If you ever have a question about mobile computing, this is a great place to start.

MobileStart.com

http://www.mobilestart.com

This virtual meeting place is a news arena for mobile computing people. Articles, virtual fairs, product ratings, message boards, and more can be found here.

Palm Inc.

http://www.palm.com

Palm Inc. created the Palm Pilot and Palm operating system. Palm Inc. is the pioneering company in the mobile company arena. This site contains information on the products, support, and anything else you would want to know about this company.

Palm Gear

http://www.palmgear.com

Download the latest software for your Palm Pilot.

Portable Internet

http://www.portableinternet.com/frommers

Get portable Frommer's guides on your portable computing device.

Handango

http://www.handango.com

Handango publishes software for handheld computing devices.

Vindigo

http://www.vindigo.com

Vindigo offers a software program for PDAs that provides directions, restaurant reviews, nightlife, shopping, movie show times, and more.

Techno Travel

http://www.pobox.com/~technotravel

It says, "As the world gets smaller, the Internet gets bigger." This site questions traveling with a computer or traveling without one, and takes you to related resources and places on the Web that show you what you need to know.

RoadNews.com Resources for the Laptop Traveler

http://www.roadnews.com

Traveling with your laptop shouldn't be more work than not taking it at all. This site leads you to help sections that answer your frequently asked questions about traveling with your notebook computer. The site answers questions about power adapters in different countries, local ISP connections, and anything else you can imagine.

Thinkmobile

http://www.thinkmobile.com

This portal contains up-to-date information on news, features, and events within the mobile computing realm.

Rent DVDs on the Net

http://www.netflix.com

Go to Netflix, if you are thinking about renting DVDs online. You can rent DVDs for a flat monthly rate, and you don't have to worry about the late fees. DVDs make great entertainment for the mobile computing enthusiast with a portable DVD player.

Technology Reviews

http://www.beststuff.com
http://www.cnet.com
http://www.computeruser.com
http://www.extremetech.com
http://www.onmagazine.com
http://www.popsci.com
http://www.technologyreview.com
http://www.tweakers.com.au
http://www.wired.com
http://www.zdnet.com

Looking for the latest and greatest technology related stuff and reviews? Try some of these sites.They make great resources to finding what you need to know about it all. *Johnny Jet Code: Tech Reviews*

*Postcards

A postcard is a great way to stay in touch with friends, and family. Check out: Johnny Jet Code: Postcards

*Prepaid Phone Cards

A prepaid phone card is a great way to save on your phone bill and stay in touch when you're on the go. Check out: Johnny Jet Code: Prepaid Phone

Chapter 24

Student Travel

*Student Trips

Johnny Jet Code: Student Travel

Going home for the holidays? Going with your friends for spring break? How about backpacking through Europe? Students take a break from school. This section has links for all of that and places to get an International Student Card (ID card for discounts). We also have learning vacations listed in this section, such as Semester at Sea, educational vacations, studying abroad, and much more...

*College Campus Visits

A campus visit can get you more familiar with what the college has to offer. Check out: Johnny Jet Code: College Visits

*Educational Vacations

Johnny Jet Code: Smart Vacations

Horizons To Go: Artistic Vacations

http://www.horizons-art.com

With this educational travel program, you can take week long artistic travel workshop adventures in New York, France, Ireland, Italy, Mexico, Nepal, and Southern Spain. Trips are taken in small structured groups and accommodate novices to advanced artists who enjoy exploring art, history, and nature.

Learning Vacations

http://www.learningvacations.com

These vacations were meant for learning specified subjects and interests. So if you travel with this site you can expect to be instructed with adventurous and educational trips. The learning vacations include: golf, language, cooking, adventure, culture, and more.

National Geographic Expeditions

http://www.nationalgeographic.com/ngexpeditions

National Geographic offers you the opportunity to live the stories and visit the exotic destinations read about in its well-known magazine. From exploring the "lost city of the Inca" to discovering remote villages of Papua New Guinea, there is something interesting to learn and enjoy.

National Outdoor Leadership School

http://www.nols.edu

NOLS is a non-profit educational leader in wilderness adventure learning expeditions with a professionally trained staff.

Outward Bound

http://www.outwardbound.com

Since the early 1900s, Outward Bound has offered outdoor wilderness education to young adults and adults. The site specializes in five separate wilderness schools and two urban centers providing courses for struggling teens and corporate groups.

Shaw Guides Inc.

http://www.shawguides.com

Founded in 1988, Shaw Guides is a publisher of over 4,500 educational, travel, and creative career directories. Programs include cooking schools, wine courses, golf and tennis programs, film and video workshops and schools, arts and crafts, language vacations, cultural travel, artist and writer retreats.

Smithsonian Study Tours

http://www.smithsonianstudytours.org

Love to travel and learn? Smithsonian Study Tours are for you. This museum based educational travel site reflects the vision and interests of the Smithsonian Institution, the world's largest museum affiliated educational travel organizer. All walks, ages, and people travel and tour with the Smithsonian Institution. Categories ranging from art and history to the sciences can be found in the tours.

The Oxford Experience

http://www.conted.ox.ac.uk

Oxford University offers a broad range of educational, training, and continuing education programs.

Third World Traveler

http://www.thirdworldtraveler.com

Ever planned on making it out to a Third World country, this site provides the information you need to know. What is it like traveling to these countries, what regulations are there, human rights, and so forth can be found here. The site is filled with interesting famous quotes.

TraveLearn

http://www.travelearn.com

As a leading learning tour company, TraveLearn offers people-oriented international learning vacations for adults ages 30-80. These vacations are promoted through more than 300 universities, colleges and associations across the United States.

*Spring Break

Looking for a great Spring Break hangout?
Check out: Johnny Jet Code: Spring Break

Students Take a Break from School

Council for Standards for International Educational Travel

http://www.csiet.org
The CSIET Advisory List is a non-profit organization that provides information about 75 international youth education and exchange programs. The organization listings show countries served, a program overview, financial aid opportunities, and contact information.

ISTC

http://www.istc.org
The International Student Travel Confederation consists of a non-profit network of the world's leading student travel specialists and organizations promoting travel for students.

Smarter Living for Students

http://www.smarterliving.com/student
Smarter Living provides students with travel savings, student travel articles and information, student travel tips, and more.

Student Advantage

http://www.studentadvantage.com
Students can find savings on all sorts of travel when getting this discount card.

Student Ambassador Program

http://www.studentambassadors.org
This site offers international summer educational travel programs for students in middle school through high school.

StudentCity.com

http://www.studentcity.com

Specializing in travel for students, this site offers affordable deals for high school graduation trips to college Spring Break getaways.

Student Universe

http://www.studentuniverse.com

Student Universe offers all sorts of travel information for students, offering low student airfares, local insight, rail passes, and youth hostels for students, faculty, and young adults.

Student Now Travel Resources

http://www.studentnow.com/travel

There are plenty of resources here for students looking to travel.

Spring Break Travel Inc.

http://www.springbreaktravel.com

Spring Break for college students could be one of the best breaks and this company knows it well. Since 1987, this company has been offering different kinds of Spring Break travel. Check out the 360-degree hotel tours, pictures, and video tours.

STA Student Travel

http://www.sta-travel.com

This agency offers special low rates for students traveling in groups or alone. You'll find fares, trip planning services, as well as important travel information and more from these student travel experts.

Student Travel

http://www.studenttravel.com

In conjunction with Council Travel, www.counciltravel.com offers discounts especially for students looking for international travel ID cards, budgeted airfare, railway passes, hostel memberships, car rentals, study abroad, travelers insurance and more.

Student Traveler Magazine

http://www.studenttraveler.com

Whether you are traveling abroad or touring, this magazine is designed to assist students with their travels. It contains tips, student travel info, places to go, and more.

Student Youth Travel Association

http://www.syta.com

The SYTA of North America is a non-profit, professional trade association with a mission to promote student and youth travel. Known as the "Voice of Student & Youth Travel," the members consist of tour operators, travel agencies, and supplier organizations such as hotels, restaurants, and more.

Travel CUTS

http://www.travelcuts.com

Since 1969, Travel CUTS has provided professional travel consultation to help millions of students explore low cost travel opportunities.

Student Travel Tips

http://travel.state.gov/studentinfo.html

Here are tips for students traveling and studying abroad.

Teen Tours

http://www.aave.com

http://www.americantrailswest.com

http://www.eftours.com

http://www.reinteentours.com

http://www.summerfun.com

http://www.teentour.com

http://www.teentravelofamerica.com

http://www.travelselections.com

Here are some sites that offer student teen tours throughout the world.

Studying Abroad

Johnny Jet Code: Travel Abroad

AFS Intercultural Programs

http://www.afs.org

This is a nonprofit volunteer based educational program for students, young adults, and teachers throughout the world. You can learn more about going abroad with AFS in more than fifty countries and read about the history of the program.

American Institute for Foreign Studies

http://www.aifs.com

http://www.aifsabroad.com

The AIFS organizes study abroad programs for thousands of high school and college students annually during the school year and the summer.

Council on International Educational Exchange

http://www.ciee.org

Since 1947, the CIEE has provided information on traveling and studying globally. There are programs for study, working abroad, international volunteer programs, international student ID cards, and more.

Go Abroad

http://www.goabroad.com

Here is a directory for studying abroad, interning abroad, foreign language programs, volunteering abroad, jobs abroad, and eco-adventures. There is a section of travel tools here too.

iAgora.com

http://www.iagora.com

This is a member site filled with articles and forums for college students traveling and living abroad. It's broken down into sections which include iNotes, iClubs, iClassifieds, iWork, iStudy, iTravel, and iPeople.

Institute of International Education

http://www.iie.org

The IIE is the most experienced global higher education and professional exchange agency and the administrator of the Fulbright program. You can search for programs on the site.

Intern Abroad

http://www.internabroad.com

Looking for an internship and going abroad at the same time? If so, this site is for you.

NRCSA

http://www.nrcsa.com

The National Registration Center for Study Abroad contains over 125 foreign schools and adult education centers in over thirty countries welcoming Americans.

Semester at Sea

http://www.semesteratsea.com

The programs offered here allow undergraduate college students to take a semester on a cruise ship with a culturally diverse group of students throughout the world. Through its Continuing Education Program, some non-student travelers can take part in a Semester at Sea.

Study Abroad

http://www.studyabroad.com

This is a directory of colleges and universities offering study abroad programs.

Study Abroad Links

http://www.studyabroadlinks.com

This is a directory of study abroad and educational travel throughout the world.

Transitions Abroad

http://www.transitionsabroad.com

This bimonthly magazine is for anyone interested in an affordable alternative to mass tourism and living, studying, or working abroad.

Chapter 25

Things to Do and See

You will never be bored on another trip after reading this chapter. We list everything you can possibly do from going to a pro sport event or the Zoo. Make sure you check out what's going on in your city before you leave.

*Air Shows and Teams

Have you been to the air show? Some of the tricks are amazing.
Check out: Johnny Jet Code: Air Shows

*Amazing Cathedrals

Visit some of the most precious and amazing cathedrals.
Check out: Johnny Jet Code: Amazing Cathedrals

*Castles and Buildings

The history and architecture behind these castles is quite fascinating.
Check out Johnny Jet Code: Castles

*Concerts, Events, and Tickets

CityPass

http://www.citypass.net

City Pass offers packages of discount tickets to the most popular events and attractions in major U.S. cities. Featuring tourist attractions like the Space Needle in Seattle, the MOMA in San Francisco, the Museum of Science in Boston, the Guggenheim in New York, Universal Studios in Hollywood, Adler Planetarium in Chicago, the Franklin Institute in Philadelphia, and more.

Culture Finder

http://www.culturefinder.com

Get culturally involved at this site where you can find tickets from the performing arts to the visual arts. Looking for the orchestra, music, dance, theater, opera, or what's on Broadway, this site is great for that too. Search for shows and events by name or organization. Or click on a major city and find events nearby.

GoTickets.com

http://www.gotickets.com

Tickets to major sporting events, concerts, and tours can sometimes be hard to find. On this site, they aren't as hard to find. Whether the Masters Golf Tournament is sold out or you are looking to go to the Super Bowl, GoTickets.com is a great place to look. Hotel packages are also offered through this site.

Keith Prowse Entertainment Tickets

http://www.keithprowse.com

Keith Prowse offers travel packages along with tickets to theatre, sporting events, and concerts. From London to New York you can get an email alert with new shows.

Mojam.com

http://www.mojam.com

Get your jam on and search for concerts and tickets in a variety of different genres including, rock, country, classical, and more. Search by artist, city, or venue and see a top ten list and new tours.

AOL Moviefone.com

http://www.moviefone.com

You don't have to call your local theatre to find out what time a movie is showing. Log onto this site and see previews of movies, and where they are playing anywhere in the U.S. Other features include movie news, reviews, a video, and DVD store.

Open Seats

http://www.openseats.com

There are open seats for sports, concerts, and entertainment throughout the United States. Open Seats welcomes buyers and sellers of tickets.

Tickets.com

http://www.tickets.com

You'll find tickets for concerts, sporting events, theater, and more at this nationwide ticketing site.

Ticket Advantage

http://www.ticketadvantage.com

Not every season ticket holder can make it to every game. This site provides a venue where season ticket holders can buy and sell tickets to professional and college sporting events.

Ticket City

http://www.ticketcity.com

Ticket City offers tickets for Broadway theatre, Las Vegas shows, concerts, and college and pro sporting events. Ticket City is unique because tickets are available in live time. Events also include seating chart maps.

Ticket Master

http://www.ticketmaster.com

Ticketmaster is known as the largest ticket resource online with hundreds of thousands of tickets sold annually. Tickets for pro sports, arts, family, events, concerts, comedy, and more can be found here.

Tickets Now

http://www.ticketsnow.com

You will find preferred seating available to major events nationwide. Browse and search for tickets, view seating charts, and order tickets online for concerts, sporting events, and more.

Ticket Solutions

http://www.ticketsolutions.com

Since 1992, Ticket Solutions has provided the Midwest with reputable ticket brokering services for premier sporting events, concerts, theatre, and more. The site offers a guarantee for some of the most sought after seats.

Tickets Up Front

http://www.ticketsupfront.com

One of the largest selections of tickets online can be found here. This site specializes in sports, concerts, theatre, and buying tickets.

Ticket Trader

http://www.tickettrader.com

This was the first company in the U.S. to provide computerized communication between ticket brokers. A list of tickets are shown for concerts, sports, and theatre.

Ticket Vision

http://www.ticketvision.com

Ticket Vision specializes in selling tickets for concerts, theater, and sporting events. Show tickets in Las Vegas are a specialty here. If you can't find a ticket, you can make a request for it.

Web Tickets

http://www.webtickets.com

Web Tickets is a source for all types of tickets including concerts, sporting events, or theatre. You can find a ticket, or at least look for one. Buy tickets and sell them.

TV Tickets

http://www.tvtickets.com

If you are making it out to Hollywood and you would like to be a part of a live studio audience, this site is a great place to start and find free tickets. They want guests at the shows, so here is your opportunity to get them.

*Crop Circles

These crop circle designs are certainly worth a look.
Check out: Johnny Jet Code: Crop Circles

*Factory Tours

Have you ever wondered how chocolate, ice cream or cakes are made? Take a tour of the factories. For more information on factory tours, check out Johnny Jet Code: Factory Tours

*Gambling Trips

Are you up for rolling the dice or are you looking to test your luck on the roulette wheel or play some cards?
Check out: Johnny Jet Code: Gambling Trips

*Hall of Fames

From sports to music, you can see the latest inductees.
Check out: Johnny Jet Code: Hall of Fames

*Pro Sports Hall of Fames

http://www.baseballhalloffame.org
http://www.bowlingmuseum.com
http://www.hhof.com
http://www.hoophall.com
http://www.ibhof.com
http://www.mshf.com
http://www.profootballhof.com
http://www.soccerhall.org
http://www.tennisfame.org
http://www.volleyhall.org
http://www.wbhof.com
Visit the Pro Sport Hall of Fames including: Baseball, Bowling, Hockey, Basketball, Boxing, Auto Racing, Football, Soccer, Tennis, Volleyball, and Women's Basketball.

*Haunted Houses

Johnny Jet Code: Haunted House

Anna's House and Garden

http://www.ghostwalk.net/gardentourinfo.htm
Known for its famous garden walking tours, you can learn more about the tours of some of the most mysterious picturesque mansion gardens in South Carolina. The streets are cobbled filled, and the green foliage is green, and the tours are guaranteed.

Thematic History Tours of Charlestown SC

http://www.charlestonwalks.com
Charlestown, South Carolina is an eerie town and here you will find some of the walking ghost tours in its haunted historic district.

Find a Grave

http://www.findagrave.com

Not quite a haunted house, but if you are looking for a cemetery or a grave you can find it at this site.

Haunted America

http://www.hauntedamerica.com

This is your directory to haunted houses, hayrides, and every kind of Halloween event. There is a section on ghost stories, a haunted radio with the story of the Raven by Edgar Allen Poe, and more for Halloween.

Haunted House

http://www.hauntedhouse.com

Where's the closest haunted house, barn, trail, or other scary hang-out? Come to the ultimate house directory and find out. This site includes a forum, a scary story of the day, and more to keep you frightened.

Haunt Finder

http://www.hauntfinder.com

Here is a directory to all Halloween haunts, all things haunted, haunted houses, and attractions. You'll find thousands of them listed by state across the United States.

Haunted-Places Directory

http://www.haunted-places.com

This directory contains some of the most haunted and paranormal places throughout the United States, and internationally. The site has information on a current paranormal activity, a paranormal travel guide, and haunted tours and events.

Loch Ness Guide

http://www.lochnessguide.com

This is your complete guide to the Loch Ness Monster area. The site contains local and global news, community info, accommodations, eating out, entertainment, forums, and more to this mysterious place.

New Orleans Haunted History Tours

http://www.hauntedhistorytours.com

Perhaps the most haunted city in America, New Orleans has an interesting ghost tour, an eerie garden tour, a vampire tour, and other tours that will certainly bring some scary entertainment to your trip.

Yard Haunts

http://www.yardhaunts.com

You probably know haunted houses exist, yet this site is a directory to haunted yards. You'll find decorated yards throughout the United States and Canada listed.

*Haunted Tours

Some of these tours can be spooky.

Check out: Johnny Jet Code: Haunted Tours

*Historic Places

Looking to explore a little history on your trip?

Check out: Johnny Jet Code: Historic Places

*London Theatre

The land of theatre brings you Shakespeare's Globe and many more.

Check out: Johnny Jet Code: London Theatre

*Movie Filming

Where are those movies filmed? Take a backstage tour of the set.

Check out: Johnny Jet Code: Movie Filming

*Museums

Johnny Jet Code: Museums

Museums Online

http://www.musee-online.org

http://www.museumspot.com

http://www.museumstuff.com

http://www.museumca.org/usa

Do you know of a museum, yet you don't know where to find it online? You never know if there may be a museum out there that suits your interests. While you are here you will get a direct link to any online museum.

Art Atlas Gallery Database

http://www.artatlas.com

This is a directory and search engine for art galleries worldwide.

Artcyclopedia

http://www.artcyclopedia.com

Here is a guide to museum-quality fine art along with a directory for artists and art museums.

Ballparks

http://www.ballparks.com

http://www.baseballparks.com

http://www.digitalballparks.com

Take me out to the ballpark, you know the song. Now visit various ballparks online where you'll find pictures, descriptions, reviews, and more about America's favorite sports pastime.

Virtual Tour of Museums

http://www.virtualfreesites.com/museums.html

Take a virtual tour of a museum online before you go and travel to see the real museum.

Virtual Smithsonian

http://2k.si.edu

Take a virtual walking tour through the Smithsonian Museum and see some of the most famed exhibits that have made this museum what it is today. This site is a fun and interactive learning experience that encourages all to discover, imagine, and remember.

Air Sickness Bags

http://www.airsicknessbags.com

http://www.sicksack.com

Okay, this may not be the most appealing museum to visit, but this is about travel so it makes the book a little bit more interesting. It shows you that airsickness bags can be art. Interestingly enough, some people actually collect these bags.

Napkin Air

http://home.earthlink.net/~napkinair

Someone has collected airplane napkins and for this site. So this is a museum of airplane napkins. It's quite interesting.

Smithsonian National Air and Space Museum

http://www.nasm.si.edu

Visit the Smithsonian National Air and Space Museum online and find out everything you ever wanted to know about space and travel. Find info about tours are being held and exhibits.

Kennedy Space Center

http://www.kennedyspacecenter.com

Get your tickets to the museum online and find out about tours and exhibits. If learning about space is what interests you, this museum is one to visit. The online version has many answers to the questions you'd want to know about it.

Rock and Roll Hall of Fame

http://www.rockhall.com

Visit the official site of the Rock and Roll Hall of Fame and see some rocking music history on the Net. See the latest inductees and the exhibits. Standing right in the heart of Cleveland, Ohio, the Rock and Roll Hall of Fame is in view. Enjoy the various exhibits that keep people rocking to the music.

Monterey Bay Aquarium

http://www.mbayaq.org

Dive in to this aquarium and see some of the most interesting underwater exhibits. Some can be found online whereas others you would have to visit the aquarium to see its greatness.

Castles of the World

http://www.castles-of-britain.com

http://www.castlesontheweb.com

http://www.castles.org

http://www.haunted-castles-and-hotels.com

Visit the most renowned castles in the world on the Web. See architectural pictures, discover their history, and more while you are here.

Great Buildings

http://www.greatbuildings.com

You don't have to travel to see some of the greatest buildings, but this site can point you in the right direction. This site leads the Web in architecture with buildings and structures exhibited around the world. See all architectural types, pictures, drawings, and 3D models.

International Spy Museum

http://www.spymuseum.org

There is much to see about spies here with exhibit information on intelligence. The mission of the museum is to "educate the public about espionage in an engaging manner and to provide a dynamic context that fosters understanding of its important role in and impact on current and historic events."

National Cowgirl Museum & Hall of Fame

http://www.cowgirl.net

Since 1975, this museum founded in the Texas panhandle town of Hereford is dedicated to honoring and documenting the lives of women who have distinguished themselves while exemplifying the pioneer spirit of the American West. See photos and the latest cowgirl exhibits and happenings.

World Record and Believe it or Not

http://www.guinnessrecords.com

http://www.ripleys.com

http://www.ripleysaquarium.com

See the world records and achievements at Guinness and find out about the oddest, weirdest, and most unusual at Ripley's. If you have the talent or the courage you may want to try to break some records. Both have museums to visit. If you would like to see some amazing aquariums, check out Ripley's Aquarium in South Carolina.

Biltmore Estate

http://www.biltmore.com

The Biltmore Estate in Asheville North Carolina was built by George Vanderbilt around the time of 1889 and it remains one of the most fascinating estates in the world. Standing on over 8,000 acres, with 250 rooms, 65 fireplaces, the Biltmore Estate remains a historic attraction. Visit the site and take a virtual reality tour, and find out more about the Biltmore Estate. To see more Vanderbilt museums, check out *www.vanderbiltmuseum.org.*

*Oktoberfest

It originated in Germany and is a huge party that lasts a few weeks. The American's have adopted it, and have big events all around the country. In Europe they celebrate it in September.

Check out: Johnny Jet Code: Oktoberfest

*On and Off Broadway Theatre

Johnny Jet Code: Broadway Theatre

Ballet Co

http://www.ballet.co.uk

This is the site about ballet and dance in the world and the U.K. It has reviews, news, and more.

Kennedy Center for Performing Arts

http://www.kennedy-center.org

The famous Kennedy Center is located in Washington DC and contains information about theatre performances, educational arts, ballet, opera, symphonies, dance, and more. Buy tickets online and find out what events are coming to the center.

New York Theatre

http://www.nytheatre.com

New York City is the home of some of the greatest theatre events. This site covers theatre news and reviews, Broadway, off-Broadway, and more about theatre plays and coming attractions.

Theater Mania

http://www.theatermania.com

If you are looking for something theater-related, Theater Mania probably has it. You'll find nationwide show listings, reviews, a message board, tickets, and a gold membership club.

Theatre Playbill Online and Talkin' Broadway

http://www.playbill.com

http://www.talkinbroadway.com

If you are looking for the latest information on and off Broadway, you will be able to find it at these theatre sites. Everything from news and reviews to technical theatre information can be found. Playbill offers show listings of on and off Broadway. Talkin' Broadway has articles on all types of drama along with Broadway history, actor interviews, and more.

NY Theatre Workshop

http://www.nytw.org

The NY Theatre Workshop is known as an extraordinary off-Broadway theatre with highly acclaimed and innovative productions, and new works from artists

The Public Theater

http://www.publictheater.org

The Public Theater was founded by Joseph Papp in 1954 as the Shakespeare Workshop. Today, it remains one of the nation's foremost cultural institutions where the country's rhythms and cultures converge.

Brooklyn Academy of Music

http://www.bam.org

The BAM is a performing arts institute that presents theater, dance, music, and opera from around the world. BAM is the home of the Rose Cinemas and the BAM kids Film Festival.

The Ontological-Hysteric Theater

http://www.ontological.com

Richard Foreman created this theatrical exploration site that contains resources for play authors and directors.

Playwrights Horizons

http://www.playwrightshorizons.org

This site is dedicated to the creation of new American plays and musicals.

The Vineyard Theatre

http://www.vineyardtheatre.org

The Vineyard is known for creating new, bold, and idiosyncratic theatre artists and encouraging them to create work that matters. It believes in capturing the heart and imagination of the audience.

The New Victory Theater

http://www.newvictory.org

Built in 1900 by Oscar Hammerstein the "Theatre Republic," was described as the "perfect parlor theater…a drawing room of the drama dedicated to all that is best in dramatic and lyric art." Today, it remains as the ultimate theatre experience for kids and families.

P.S. 122

http://www.ps122.org

Performance Space 122 is a non-profit arts center presenting everything from dance to theatre, music, poetry, to opera, and performing arts. P.S. 122 has been an advocate of innovation and creativity since its inception in 1979.

Adobe Theatre Company

http://www.adobe.org

Adobe has been committed to cultivating audiences in their 20s and 30s catapulting American theatre into the 21st century. The theatre provides an artistic home where actors, designers, and directors can develop entertaining and thought-provoking theater.

*On Location Television Tours

Take one or take two, you can get tickets to watch television live on location. Check out Johnny Jet Code: Television Tours

*Party/Bars

Looking for a bar or just want to party and check out the nightlife? Check out Johnny Jet Code: Party Bars

*Presidential Libraries

These libraries and museums honor the United States Presidents. Check out Johnny Jet Code: Presidential Libraries

*Pro Sports Schedules

When does your favorite team play next? Check out Johnny Jet Code: Pro Sport Schedule

*Take a Tour

Johnny Jet Code: Touring It

Perillo Tours

http://www.perillotours.com

Since 1945 Perillo Tours has been a family operated tour company offering tours to Italy and Hawaii. Tours are taken in deluxe motorcoach throughout Italy and helicopter tours are taken through Hawaii.

Alitalia Italy Vacations

http://www.italiatourusa.com

If touring Italy is in your plans, this Italian tour operator may come in handy. There are packaged trips and itineraries to Rome, Florence, and Venetia. For more custom Italian tours, visit http://www.italiatourusa.com/independent/design/index.asp where you can "Design It Your Way."

Apple Vacations

http://www.applevacations.com

Apple Vacations provide affordable vacation packages from over 100 select U.S. departure cities. You can take the Apple Vacations charter plane or other commercial airlines to your vacation destination.

Austravel

http://www.austravel.com

Austravel offers a wide variety of air travel, vacation holiday getaway tours, hotels, and transport options to Australia, Asia, New Zealand, and the South Pacific.

Contiki Tours

http://www.contiki.com

Contiki specializes in vacation tours for 18-35 year olds. You can search for tours, participate in the message boards, read frequently asked questions about the tours, and book a tour.

Far and Wide

http://www.farandwide.com

Far and Wide offers an array of travel experiences, including customized and independent foreign travel, as well as escorted, educational, adventure, and fitness vacations.

Homeric Tours

http://www.homerictours.com

Since 1969, Homeric has been a leader in offering economical and memorable tours to Greece. It also offers tours to Italy, Turkey, Egypt, Israel, Cyprus, Morocco, Spain, Portugal, and Eastern Europe.

Helene Kahn: Tour Guide in San Miguel

http://www.helenekahn.com/tours/tours.html

Helene Kahn is a personalized guide service offering an insider's view of San Miguel and the surrounding "Bajio" area. Featuring folk art, antiques, art history, and architecture, this tour service offers informational guide service.

Tauck World Discovery

http://www.tauck.com

Since 1925, Tauck has offered leading tours and cruises on seven continents. The site includes featured journeys to places including the Yellow Roads of Europe, Autumn Foliage trips, Private Yacht Excursions, Cruise Tours, National Park Trips, and Rail Trips.

Trafalgar Tours

http://www.trafalgartours.com

Trafalgar offers luxury motorcoach bus tours throughout Europe, Britain, the United States, and Canada.

Travelon

http://www.travelon.com

Travelon is an online travel agency that caters to the traveler looking for a little adventure. Packages include adventure tours and excursions, cruises, last minute vacation packages, and more. You will even find unique trips like dog sledding and helicopter rides. Search is available by region, departure month, destination, interest, price, and life style.

Travel Roads

http://www.travelroads.com

This site will assist you with finding free travel brochures from tour operators. You can search by activity, destination, or special interest.

Viator

http://www.viator.com

Viator offers travel booking and tours for travelers and agents. The travel products offered include technology and distribution of services to the whole spectrum of the travel industry including travel sites, and traditional agencies.

Historic Traveler

http://www.historictraveler.com

If traveling throughout history is what you would like to do, this site is a great starting place. You'll find everything needed to make your own journey into the past.

One World Journeys

http://www.oneworldjourneys.com

This site is where people and the planet clicks. There is a focus on environmental education, ecotourism, and preservation of our ecosystems. You will find pictures of the natural world here. Check out the e-postcards.

*Tours and Events

It's easy to book a tour online.
Check out Johnny Jet Code: Tour Events

*Zoos

Alaska Zoo .... http://www.alaskazoo.com
Atlanta Zoo .... http://www.zooatlanta.com
Austin Zoo .... http://www.austinzoo.com
Birmingham Zoo .... http://www.birminghamzoo.com
Boise Zoo .... http://www.animalpark.org/zoo
Bronx Zoo .... http://www.bronxzoo.com
Brownsville Zoo .... http://www.gpz.org
Cheyenne Mountain Zoo .... http://www.cmzoo.org
Cincinnati Zoo .... http://www.cincyzoo.org
Cleveland Zoo .... http://www.clemetzoo.org
Chicago Zoo .... http://www.lpzoo.com
Fort Worth Zoo .... http://www.fortworthzoo.com
Fresno Zoo .... http://www.chaffeezoo.org
Indianapolis Zoo .... http://www.indyzoo.com
Little Rock Zoo .... http://www.littlerockzoo.com
Los Angeles Zoo .... http://www.lazoo.org
Madison Zoo .... http://www.villaszoo.org
Minnesota Zoo .... http://www.mnzoo.com
Nashville Zoo .... http://www.nashvillezoo.org
Northwest Zoo .... http://www.nwtrek.org
Oakland Zoo .... http://www.oaklandzoo.org
Omaha Zoo .... http://www.omaha.org/zoo.htm
Philadelphia Zoo .... http://www.phillyzoo.org
Phoenix Zoo .... http://www.phoenixzoo.org/zoo
Oregon Zoo .... http://www.zooregon.org
South Carolina Zoo .... http://www.riverbanks.org
San Antonio Zoo .... http://www.sazoo-aq.org
San Diego Zoo .... http://www.sandiegozoo.org
Santa Ana Zoo .... http://www.santaanazoo.org

Seattle Zoo ....*http://www.zoo.org*
Toledo Zoo ....*http://www.toledozoo.org*
Toronto Zoo ....*http://www.torontozoo.com*
Washington D.C. Smithsonian Zoo ....*http://www.si.edu/natzoo*
Wichita Zoo ....*http://www.scz.org*

Here we go to the zoo. For more information on good zoos check out *www.goodzoos.com* or this long list of zoo sites can be accessed with *Johnny Jet Code: Zoology*

Chapter 26

Tips

You can never get enough travel tips and in this chapter we have some of the best.

*Discount Cards

Johnny Jet Code: Great Savings

Entertainment Coupon Book

http://www.entertainment.com

This coupon book offers discounts on airplane flights, hotels, restaurants, movie tickets, and savings at vacation spots.

Member Web

http://www.memberweb.com

Membership entitles you to discounts at various hotels, travel, recreation, and more.

Preferred Traveler

http://www.preferredtraveller.com

This membership club provides travelers with discounts on all types of travel.

*FAA Tips

The Federal Aviation Administration is the government body for travel safety and security. Check out Johnny Jet Code: FAA Tips

*Linen Care

Johnny Jet Code: Linen Care

Linen Care - Luxury Linens

http://www.givingtreeonline.com/linencare1.html
This site contains detailed information on caring for bed and bath linens, bed covers, blankets, and other linens. It includes info on washing, shrinkage, drying, care of down products, universal laundering symbols, and stain removal.

Label Talk

http://www.textileaffairs.com
Sponsored by Textile Industry Affairs and The Clorox Company, this site provides detailed information on understanding apparel care instructions and care symbols.

International Fabricare Institute

http://www.ifi.org/consumer/index.html
Since 1833, IFI has been a premier international trade association for garment professionals. The site answers your questions about the garment industry and contains a membership of over 8,000 dry cleaners, wet cleaners, launders, apparel and textile.

*Packing

Johnny Jet created a Men's and Women's printable packing list so you don't forget anything. We also listed great tips on how to pack and little secrets that you may not have thought about. Most important tip of all: Don't check anything that is valuable including prescriptions, sentimental items, and cameras. Also check out that secure wrap for your luggage once at the airport. Check out Johnny Jet Code: Packing

*Passenger Rights

Johnny Jet Code: Passenger Rights

Passenger Rights

http://www.passengerrights.com

Whether you are flying, driving, or cruising, you have rights as a passenger and this site makes your rights clear. Research your rights, voice your opinion, and read horror stories. If you have a complaint let them know. For more information on your flying rights you may want to check out a site that lists various rights at http://www.ifg-inc.com/FlyRights.shtml and read what is said.

*Photography: Take Some Pictures

Johnny Jet Code: Picture Perfect

Picture Tips

http://www.88.com/exposure

http://www.fodors.com/focus

http://webs.kodak.com/global/en/consumer/pictureTaking

http://www.kodak.com/US/en/nav/takingPics.shtml

Visit these sites to get some better picture taking tips. When traveling, you will want to make sure your pictures are keepsakes.

Magical Places

http://www.earthwisdom.com

Ellen has traveled plenty, as a passion she has created this site that will take you on a journey to places like Egypt, Greece, Ireland, Mexico, Hawaii, Scotland, England, and America. Click on a photo, take a virtual tour, and send some awesome postcards.

Travel Photos

http://www.photo.net/travel

If photo travelogues interest you, this photo travelogue by Philip Greenspun is quite amazing. Stories along with photos are featured from almost every continent. Check out Travels with Samantha and the Great North American Road Trip.

Photo Excursions

http://www.photoexcursions.com

Photographer Pam Singleton has taken some fascinating architectural and landscape photo excursions. And you can join in too. You can visit this site to see a preview of the tours, and learn about her resort workshops.

Photo Secrets: Photo Guide for Travel and Outdoor Photography

http://www.photosecrets.com

You will find some great travel pictures in the gallery and tips on travel photography. There's an excellent selection of photography books to choose from here. There's a comprehensive collection of other photography Web resources here to check out.

Pictures of Places

http://www.picturesofplaces.com

Here is a directory of Web sites linking to an abundance of sites offering pictures of geographical pictures and sights. If you are looking to view before you go or just see some of the various places you research when making travel plans, this is one great place to visit. It covers the United States, Canada, Europe, Asia, Central and South America, Africa, Australia and Oceana.

Shutter Chances

http://www.shutterchances.com.au

This Australian photography club organizes special expeditions for travelers interested in the natural photographic world, the wildlife, and Australian natives. International travelers can view what attracts tourists to the picturesque Australian land. If you are a photographer this is quite a photography experience.

Travel Marks

http://www.travelmarks.com

Where do you make your mark around the world? This site provides photos and travel postcards from various places. One person made it around the world. See Asia, Europe, Latin America, the Middle East, and the USA.

Photo Tour Network

http://www.phototournetwork.com

Travel by and designed for photographers is what this site provides. Taking you on a journey of photographic wonders, Voyagers International provides some of the most fascinating photographic trips to Alaska, Australia, China, Africa, Costa Rica, Galapagos, Kenya, New Zealand, and much more. Check out some of the natural history tours at *www.voyagers.com.*

Virtual Guide Books 360 Degree Panoramas

http://www.virtualguidebooks.com

You'll find an expanding collection of thousands of 360 degree panoramic virtual spanning western North America from Baja California to the Canadian Arctic.

Digital Photography

http://www.kodak.com/US/en/digital/dlc

http://www.shortcourses.com

Taking a digital camera on your trip? Learning how to use a digital camera is fun, and these sites will show you everything you ever wanted to know about digital photography. Learn about taking photographs digitally and the different types of digital cameras available.

*Travel Tips

Johnny Jet Code: Travel Tips

Travel Tips

http://www.freetraveltips.com

http://www.henricson.se/mats/upl

http://www.tips4trips.com

Looking for travel tips? Here you will find plenty of tips on everything from planning the trip to where to stay. Checks out what these experts teach hot to travel.

Chapter 27

Travel News, Magazines, Newspapers & Shows

*Travel News

Johnny Jet Code: Travel News

Do you like to read and get as much information as possible? We have every magazine from the In-flight ones, to the city specific. Don't forget to check out all the great newspapers with their helpful Sunday Travel sections. You can never get enough travel info. We even list the TV and radio travel shows!

*Airline News

For airline news, check out Johnny Jet Code: Airline News

*Auto Club Magazines

AAA provides a variety of magazines.
Check out Johnny Jet Code: Auto Club

*Book Reviews

Find a good book to read. Check out Johnny Jet Code: Book Reviews

*British Magazines

Read a little about the British.
Check out Johnny Jet Code: British Mags

*Canadian Magazines

Canada has some great regional magazines.
Check out Johnny Jet Code: Canadian Mags

*In-Room Magazines

You can find a few magazines in your room.
Check out Johnny Jet Code: In-Room

*International Cities Magazines

Find some magazines on International Cities.
Check out Johnny Jet Code: International Cities

*International Newspapers

Get the latest international news.
Check out Johnny Jet Code: International News

*National Geographic Magazines

National Geographic is a renowned publication for travel.
Check out Johnny Jet Code: National Geographic

*News Feeds

Start your day with news releases and press releases.
Check out Johnny Jet Code: News Feeds

*Onboard Magazines

Rail trains have some interesting onboard magazines to read.
Check out Johnny Jet Code: Onboard

*Regional Magazines

Find out what's the latest in your region or the region you are traveling to with a regional magazine. Check out Johnny Jet Code: Regional Mags

*Travel Chat

What's the trip or vacation that everyone is chatting about? Check out Johnny Jet Code: Travel Chat

*Travel Journals

Catch up on travel with a travel journal. Check out Johnny Jet Code: Travel Journals

*Travel Magazines

Johnny Jet Code: Magazine Rack

*Travel News Magazines

Stay up to date in the travel industry and destinations by reading these online travel magazines. Check out Johnny Jet Code: News Mags

Yahoo! Travel Magazine Directory

http://dir.yahoo.com/Recreation/Travel/News_and_Media/Magazines
Yahoo provides a listing of many travel magazines. If you know the name, just find this page for a good starting point.

*In-flight Airline Magazines

http://www.americanwaymag.com

http://www.attachemag.com

http://www.caribbean-beat.com/current/index.html

http://www.delta-sky.com

http://www.electriclink.net/impressions

http://www.enroutemag.com/english/home_eng.htm

http://www.hemispheresmagazine.com

http://www.ontoeurope.com

http://www.skyword.com

http;//www.spiritofaloha.com

Here are some in flight magazines from American, US Air, BWIA, Delta, British Airways, Air Canada, United, Virgin Express, America West, and Aloha. *Johnny Jet Code: Flight Magazines*

News Directory of Travel Magazines

http://www.newsdirectory.com

Here's another good source to find travel magazines by category and interest. Click on travel magazines, and you'll find plenty.

TravelMagazines.com

http://www.travelmagazines.com

Here you will find a variety of travel related magazines. Topics include: skiing, fishing, sailing, climbing, bicycling, backpacking, photography, outdoor and travel, nature and wildlife, scuba and snorkeling, rafting, kayaking, and canoeing.

Travel Weekly Crossroads

http://www.twcrossroads.com

TW provides news, articles, and informative resources for travel professionals.

Africa Travel Association

http://www.africa-ata.org

The Africa Travel Association (ATA) features information on the country, travel destinations, ecotourism, events, safaris, and more. If you are traveling to Africa, this is one site to check before you make your travel arrangements.

Backpacker Magazine

http://www.backpacker.com

As an outdoor and wilderness travel magazine, this site provides in-depth content on wilderness travel information, news articles, trail talk forums, great photos, backpacking gear, and more.

Big World

http://www.bigworld.com

Big World offers a down-to-earth travel magazine for the nomad. So if you're looking for luxury spas and inaccessible extreme travel, don't expect to make your stop here. However, if you are into real adventures taken by real people, then this is your site. Find offbeat, real adventures, cheap travel, and topics that your traditional travel magazines don't begin to touch.

Blue Adventure

http://www.blueadventure.com

This site is calling all adventure travelers. This site seems to fit the "more graphically enhanced category, "featuring snowboarding, skating, biking, camping, and more for the adventuresome type.

The Connected Traveler

http://www.connectedtraveler.com

If you are well connected or just your typical travel aficionado, this site produces a monthly e-zine that offers accommodation and restaurant reviews from travel experts.

Condé Nast Traveler and Concierge.com

http://condenet.com/mags/trav

You will find it on Concierge.com at *www.concierge.com/cntraveler* and at this luxury travel magazine site you will be directed to the best islands, cities, spas, castles and cruises, and more. From the gold list where you will find some of the premier places to stay to the travel forums, this magazine is a great resource for luxurious travel getaways.

Islands Magazine

http://www.islands.com

Bermuda, Jamaica, ooh I want to take you. This site will lead you to the island destination of your choice. This site features the top islands and their Web sites, and more on the islands.

National Geographic Magazines

http://www.nationalgeographic.com/adventure

http://www.nationalgeographic.com/traveler

National Geographic is one of the more known magazines, but these sites exemplify some of the excellence that this fine magazine brings to us. The Adventure magazine focuses on backpacking, skiing, and all sorts of adventures. The Traveler magazine emphasizes all kinds of travel-oriented topics with storytelling and photography by writers who are passionate about traveling. Be sure to check out the Travelwise section for great trip planning.

San Diego Magazine

http://www.sandiegomagazine.com

What's happening in San Diego? Find out with this magazine touching topics such as entertainment, travel, and dining.

Ticked Off Traveler?

http://www.ticked.com

Don't get mad, get ticked, and you will find some tips and advice on travel that you won't find anywhere else online. Some of the leading travel experts give you their opinions on travel, ways to find bargains, how to make the most of your trip, and more.

Travel-Watch

http://www.travel-watch.com

This daily travel news e-zine service will keep you updated with the travel industry throughout the week. This site covers the news, food, entertainment, sports and recreation, and more. It has a sister publication called the Travel Gram.

Travel & Leisure

http://www.travelandleisure.com

You could only expect to find much useful travel information from this well-known and established travel magazine. Deals, travel news, articles, and a variety of travel tools is what you will see on this site. Have a travel question? Ask the travel experts here at this great lifestyle magazine that focuses on vacation and business travel destinations, leisure travel, hotels, restaurants, and entertainment. Check out some of the top destinations, activities, and more.

Yankee Magazine's New England

http://www.newengland.com

Yankee Magazine's guide to New England is here. If you live in New England or are traveling there, this site will help guide you. Find editor's picks and join in the discussion forum.

Outpost Magazine

http://www.outpostmagazine.com

Outpost takes a more adventurous look at the way people travel around the world. See the current issue, travel health, travel news, earth watch, and more.

Outside Magazine

http://www.outsidemag.com

Since 1978 Outside Magazine has been a well established adventure travel and outdoor recreation magazine. It makes going outside so much fun covering subjects of the latest gear, travel, sports, bodywork, and adventure. Check out what's happening outside and plan your adventures with this great magazine.

Travel Holiday

http://www.travelholiday.com

Travel Holiday Magazine covers just about any destination throughout the world. From trip tips to travel talk, this site is for the "all around traveler." Each issue explores exotic destinations, and specializes on the travel enthusiast visiting both foreign and domestic lands.

World Hum

http://www.worldhum.com

Two guys who love to travel, Jim Benning and Mike Yessis came together to create this award-winning site that has many travel resources. Travel writing is at its greatest and you will find some great travel stories here.

*Travel News, Sunday is Here

Johnny Jet Code: Sunday Papers

We have the Sunday Travel Sections for most major US and World cities. This is another great resource to read every week to find out what's going on locally and nationally.

Headline News

http://www.1stheadlines.com

http://www.headlinenews.com

http://www.worldheadlines.com

Top breaking headline news can be found covering headlines from a variety of different news sources.

Associated Press Breaking News

http://wire.ap.org/public_pages/WirePortal.pcgi/us_portal.html

This site contains news from the Associated Press with a U.S. map to click for member newspapers in each state.

Internet Public Library Newspaper

http://www.ipl.org/reading/news

The IPL provides links to online newspapers worldwide.

News Directory

http://www.newsdirectory.com

What's happening in the news? This site is a guide to all the various news resources online. There is a travel section to check out links to many news related travel resources.

The Paperboy Newspaper Directory

http://www.thepaperboy.com

This searchable directory contains thousands of newspapers around the world. Type in your paper or city and find a direct link to that paper.

Newslink

http://www.newslink.org

This is a directory of newspapers that categorizes U.S. newspapers by state and international papers by continent.

Newspapers.com

http://www.newspapers.com

This is a directory and search engine of local, state, college, business, religious, trade journals, and industry related newspapers.

Arizona Republic Surf Guide

http://www.azreporter.com/surfguide

What's happening in Arizona? This Arizona Reporter will keep you up to date with your travel to the desert, what events are happening, and a little Arizona history.

Baltimore Sun

http://www.sunspot.net/travel

Find out what there is to do in the Baltimore Maryland, and what keeps people revisiting here.

Boston Globe Travel

http://travel.boston.com

Find out what's happening on the East coast, New England, and in Boston while you stay up to date with the latest travel news there. Boston residents should like this one.

Charlotte Observer

http://www.charlotte.com

If you're from Charlotte, this newspaper is one that you should check out.

L.A. Times and Calendar Live

http://www.calendarlive.com

http://www.latimes.com

Calendar live is the entertainment section of the L.A. Times, the largest newspaper in Los Angeles. The L.A. Times Travel section can be viewed at www.latimes.com/travel.

Chicago Tribune

http://www.chicagotribune.com/travel

Those living in the Midwest or visiting will find the Chicago Tribune's Travel section a good read. Registration Required.

Christian Science Monitor

http://www.csmonitor.com

In the Arts and Leisure section, you will find a variety of worldly travel news.

Cleveland Plain Dealer Travel

http://www.cleveland.com/travel

Clevelanders will find some great travel spots to visit in the Cleveland Plain Dealer, and those traveling to the city with Rock Hall and the flats will find it to be quite a comprehensive travel section.

Dallas News Travel

http://www.dallasnews.com/travel

How are things in the big southern state of Dallas? Register to see what's new in travel here.

Denver Post Travel

http://www.denverpost.com/travel

Home of the Rocky Mountains, and adventure travel out West, you can be sure to find some great travel articles and travel notes here.

Detroit Free Press Travel

http://www.freep.com/index/travel.htm

Traveling to the Motor City or do you live there? Here is the travel section you'll find yourself reading.

Hartford Courant Travel

http://www.ctnow.com/travel

Traveling through Connecticut, this is the paper you'll pick up. You'll be sure to find a comprehensive travel section here.

Houston Chronicle Travel

http://www.chron.com/travel

Those who live in Houston will find the travel articles, the tips, and trips here worthwhile.

Miami Herald

http://www.miami.com

Heading down to South Beach or do you live there? Check out some of the hot spot destinations that this paper has offer.

Milwaukee Journal Sentinel Travel

http://www.jsonline.com/dd

The Journal Sentinel has a comprehensive travel section for any Wisconsin traveler.

Minnesota Star Tribune Travel

http://www.startribune.com/travel

The home of the Mall of America, the largest mall in the country is in Minnesota, but more importantly this travel section will lead you to some great travel photos, travel talk, articles, and more.

New York Times

http://www.nytimes.com

The New York Times has been one of the most well known newspapers in the world. Its online presence is no different. If you can't get the paper edition, the online presence is a great news resource. The New York Times Travel section can be viewed at *www.nytimes.com/travel.*

N.Y. Newsday Travel

http://www.newsday.com/travel

There are some great travel articles to be found here, whether or not you are traveling to New York.

New York Post Travel

http://www.nypost.com/travel/travel

There are great travel reviews with destinations to lodging covered here. Along the way you'll find tips, advice, and featured travelers.

Newcity.com

http://www.newcity.com

New City is a network of alternative weekly papers. If you are looking for things that you can't find in your daily paper, this is a great place to look.

OregonLive.com Travel

http://www.oregonlive.com/travel

Traveling to Oregon? This paper is one to read before you leave for your trip. There is an excellent visitor's guide to help you discover Oregon.

Pittsburgh Tribune

http://www.pittsburghlive.com

There is a travel section here where you will find leading travel headlines.

Travel Telegraph

http://www.travel.telegraph.co.uk

The Travel Telegraph is the United Kingdom's travel paper. It provides information for those traveling in London and around the world.

Richmond Times-Dispatch Travel

http://www.timesdispatch.com/entertainment/travel

Weekly travel news can be found here.

Sacramento Bee Travel

http://www.sacbee.com/content/travel

What's happening in travel with the Sacramento Bee? Find out here.

San Francisco Gate Bay Area Traveler

http://www.sfgate.com/travel

Traveling to the Bay Area can be fun. This site provides adequate information about Bay Area traveling. You can find where to go and what to do can be found at this San Franciscan travel newspaper.

San Francisco Bay Area Travel

http://www.bayarea.com/travel

This is the home of the Mercury News and the Contra Costa Times.

Salt Lake City Tribune

http://www.sltrib.com/goto/travel.asp

Read Utah's latest travel column and see the archives here.

Seattle Post-Intelligencer

http://www.seattle-pi.com

The Seattle Post-Intelligencer is the oldest newspaper in the state of Washington and it serves hundreds of thousands of people in Washington and the Northwest.

Seattle Times Travel

http://seattletime.nwsource.com/html/travel

The Seattle Times has a great travel section with weekly articles and travel news.

Sun-Sentinel.com Travel

http://www.sun-sentinel.com/travel

Those traveling to South Florida will find this travel section to be quite resourceful with much information on where to stay and what entertainment to enjoy while you are down south.

USA Today

http://www.usatoday.com

http://www.travel.usatoday.com

Perhaps the most well known paper in the United States and it is received in Asia and Europe. USA Today covers News, Sports, Money, Technology, and Weather.

Wall Street Journal

http://www.wsj.com
This major financial oriented paper is keeping many updated in the news.

Washington Post Travel

http://www.washingtonpost.com/wp-dyn/travel
The Washington Post has a special section for travelers. It includes Web Travel, International Travel, DC Visitors Guide, Ski Guide, Beach Guide, Photo Galleries, and more.

*Travel Newsletters

Johnny Jet Code: Newsletters

There's no easier way to stay in the loop of airfare deals, special mile offers, and travel tips. Most of these newsletters are free and provide valuable info. Don't forget to sign up for Johnny Jet's Weekly Newsletter that has all of the above and "Where's Johnny Jet?!"

Alaska Travel Gram

http://www.alaskatravelgram.com
This weekly newsletter is an Alaska specific newsletter with travel tips on Alaska, specials deals, advice, and more about Alaska.

Clark Howard

http://www.clarkhoward.com
Clark has a radio talk show in Atlanta and travel tips, a forum, and a newsletter.

Cool Travel Mail

http://www.cooltravelmail.com
It boasts to be the coolest travel newsletter, with something new everyday of the week. Whether you are looking for discounts or miles, tips, travel freebies, or weekend getaways, this newsletter provides it.

Elliot

http://www.elliott.org

Travel expert, connoisseur, consumer advocate Christopher Elliott, provides a weekly newsletter covering all aspects of travel with advice on becoming a better traveler. Topics cover business travel, commentary, leisure travel, and more.

Hobo Traveler

http://www.hobotraveler.com

Andy has visited more than 25 different countries and offers personal descriptions of places he's been along with photos. He explains how to get there reasonably, avoid theft, plan your trip, and more for the hobo traveler.

Rudy Maxa Traveling in Style for Less

http://www.rudymaxa.com

Have a travel question to ask Rudy? Renowned travel expert, Rudy Maxa offers an online newsletter devoted to traveling in style for less. Visiting Rudy's site can help you locate him, and find out more about his radio and television appearances and his newsletter.

Terry Trippler

http://www.terrytrippler.com

With over thirty years in the travel industry, Terry provides a newsletter with leading information on airlines, flying facts, information on traveler rights, and more.

Travel Skills Group

http://www.travelskills.com

This group offers communication and consulting for business travelers along with a newsletter by travel expert and speaker Chris McGinnis.

Travel-Watch

http://www.travel-watch.com

This is a daily news service with forty writers, photographers, and videographers. It publishes featured travel news stories, food and wine reviews, water, and snow sports and entertainment reviews.

Victoria Brooks' Greatest Escapes

http://www.greatestescapes.com

This is a monthly newsletter and Webzine to adventure, business, and romantic travel.

Weblope

http://www.weblope.com

A Weblope is "an envelope delivered via the Internet." Weblope was created to make life easier for you with a focus on travel and leisure activities such as dining, entertainment, sports, and weekend getaways. This email newsletter provides special offers and discounts weekly.

*Travel and Radio Shows

Johnny Jet Code: Radio Music

Live Radio on the Internet

http://www.live-radio.net/canada_splash.shtml

http://www.live-radio.net/us.shtml

http://www.live-radio.net/worldwide.shtml

You can listen to live radio on the Internet in Canada, the United States, and worldwide.

Live 365

http://www.live365.com

This site revolutionizes radio listening with its online radio.

Radio Free Europe

http://www.rferl.org

Listen to the radio in Europe online.

Radio Locator

http://www.radio-locator.com

Radio-Locator is the most comprehensive radio station search engine online with over 10,000 radio station Web sites and over 2,500 audio streams from radio stations in the U.S. and worldwide.

Satellite Radio

http://www.sirius.com

http://www.xmradio.com

Sirius and XM Radio offer satellite radio listening in your car.

Sky Radio Network

http://www.skyradionet.com

Listen to the radio show airing in major airlines.

The Savvy Traveler

http://www.savvytraveler.org

This is actually a radio program that gives travel advice and on the site you will find a bulletin board, the travel question of the week, a message from the host, and an archive of recent interviews. Try listening to the show online.

The Traveler's Journal

http://www.travelersjournal.com

The Traveler's Journal is a series of two-minute radio programs that broadcast on many public radio stations throughout the U.S. You can listen to it here on the Web in Real Audio.

The Travel Show

http://www.thetravelshow.com

With a name like this, you are destined to find something interesting about travel.

Travel World Radio

http://www.twc.ca

This Canadian show provides a variety of information on travel and travel related topics.

*Travel and Television Shows

Johnny Jet Code: Travel Television

A & E Travel

http://travel.aande.com

A & E offers pre-planned tours to historic places.

CNN Business Traveler

http://www.cnn.com/businesstraveller

This site is for Europe's television program for the business traveler. It covers health, family, and cost conscious travel.

PBS Travel and Expeditions

http://www.pbs.org/neighborhoods/travel

PBS provides a variety of cultural documentaries on the traveling experience. Some include Hoover Dam, New York Underground, Yellowstone, and many more.

International Channel Networks

http://www.internationalchannel.com

This network provides a cable television viewing of cultural sights and sounds and heritage to viewers in the United States.

Travel Channel

http://www.travelchannel.com

From your cable television to the Internet, this site has travel tips, travel newsletters, and programming announcements. You can book a trip, check out the travel cams, explore, and more at this interactive site.

Travel History

http://www.historytravel.com

The History Channel and A & E Television Networks present this site that will add some history to your travel experiences. If you are looking for a trip that is historically driven retracing the historic journeys of great journeys or visiting historic areas, this is one site to check out.

*Travel Writers

Johnny Jet Code: Travel Writers

Read popular travel writers weekly columns and keep up to date with the latest travel writing news.

Literary Traveler

http://www.literarytraveler.com
Are you interested in writing about your travel expeditions? This site is an online magazine dedicated to literary imagination. You will find inspiring and unique articles that showcase information about traveler writers and where they have traveled.

Travel Intelligence

http://www.travelintelligence.net
This UK based publishing company features leading travel writers throughout the world along with a newsletter that will keep you updated with travel information.

Travel Writers

http://www.travelwriters.com
This excellent resource for travel writers provides writing tips, news, information, and press trips for thousands of writers.

*U.S. City Magazines

We list all the major U.S. City Magazines so you can read about your destination before you get there.
Check out Johnny Jet Code: US Magazines

*Worldwide Magazines

You will find all the Worldwide Magazines so you can read about what's going on in that part of the world.
Check out Johnny Jet Code: Worldwide Mags

Chapter 28

Travel Professionals

For all the workers in the Travel Industry! We list all the travel organizations and conferences so you won't miss a beat on what's going on. If you are a writer, we even have travel writing Web sites.

*Travel Conferences

Johnny Jet Code: Conferences

Trade Show Resources

http://www.tsnn.com

http://www.tsnn.com/partner/exhibitormag.cfm

You will find the ultimate online resource for trade shows and exhibitions. You can search for trade show venues, see all the facilities, learn about trade show marketing, learn how to put your trade show online, and more about trade shows. Search for trade shows by industry, state, city, or country.

*National Travel Industry

Johnny Jet Code: Travel Industry

IACVB

http://www.iacvb.org

The mission of the International Association of Convention and Visitors Bureaus is to "enhance the professionalism, effectiveness, and image of destination management organizations worldwide." It offers an abundance of useful information for business and leisure travelers alike.

TIA

http://www.tia.org

The Travel Industry Association of America has been in existence since 1941 and is a unifying non-profit association that serves all components of the U.S. travel industry.

NBTA

http://www.nbta.org

The National Business Travel Association is an authoritative voice on business travel management. The site provides a forum for exchange of information and ideas with its members.

AHMA

http://www.ahma.com

The American Hotel and Lodging Association is the largest national association for the hotel and lodging industry consisting of members from across all segments of the industry.

ACTE

http://www.acte.org

The Association of Corporate Travel Executives consists of corporate practitioners offering travel management techniques and suppliers of business travel services.

ATA

http://www.airlines.org

The Air Transport Association was founded in 1936 by a group of fourteen airlines that met in Chicago. Today, it remains the only trade organization for major U.S. airlines, and plays a role in government decisions for aviation.

ASTA

http://www.astanet.com

The American Society of Travel Agents is the world's largest association of travel professionals. With thousands of members including travel agents and companies offering tours, cruises, hotels, car rentals, and more travel products.

CASMA

http://www.casma.org

The Computerized Airline Sales and Marketing Association has been addressing complex distribution issues. It offers a unique forum of open exchange between airlines and experts in travel distribution.

ICTA

http://www.icta.com

Founded in 1964, the Institute of Certified Travel Agents is an international, non-profit organization educating certified travel industry professionals at all career levels.

IATAN

http://www.iatan.org

The International Airlines Travel Agent Network promotes professionalism, administering business standards, and provides services and educational programs for the travel industry.

IACC

http://www.iacconline.org

The International Association of Conference Centers provides information on conference centers, such as dining, recreation, meeting services, and accommodations.

IHRA

http://www.ih-ra.com

The International Hotel and Restaurant Association represents hundreds of thousands of establishments in over 150 countries, providing a voice at the international level. Members consist of chain operators, national associations, hospitality suppliers, and educational centers in the hotel and restaurant industry.

NTA

http://www.ntaonline.com

The National Tour Association is the premier association for travel professionals who have an interest in the packaged travel sector of the industry. The organization brings together those who are in the packaged travel industry.

PATA

http://www.pata.org

The Pacific Asia Travel Association is the authority on Pacific Asia travel and tourism. The PATA provides marketing, research, and educational opportunities to a membership of government tourist offices, airlines, hotels, travel agencies, and more.

USTOA

http://www.ustoa.com

The United States Tour Operators Association is a professional association representing the tour operator industry. It consists of companies whose packages are worldwide and do business in the United States.

*Travel Writing

For more information on travel writing and sites for travel writers, check out Johnny Jet Code: Travel Writing

Chapter 29

Pets Can Travel Too

Johnny Jet Code: Pet Travel

Don't leave Rufus home alone. Here are airline policies on taking your pet and websites that give you tips and pet friendly places.

APHIS Traveling with Pets

http://www.aphis.usda.gov/travel/pets.html

This site covers what you need to know before you bring your pet along for the trip. It covers the proper procedures for taking your pets on a plane, helpful travel hints, and information on what to do if your pet gets lost. It focuses on a variety of pets including: birds, horses, dogs, cats, and more.

Traveling with Your Pet

http://www.avma.org/care4pets/safetrav.htm

The American Veterinary Medical Association provides safety tips for traveling with your pet in the air and by car. There are topics covered on vaccinations, feeding, cages, grooming, health, and more.

Dog Friendly

http://www.dogfriendly.com

Taking your dog with you when you travel? Dog Friendly is a travel resource for dog lovers who can't leave home without their dog. They have done the research to find places and travel accommodations that are accepting of dogs. There is travel info on dogs, upcoming dog events, a dog store, and more.

Horse Trip

http://www.horsetrip.com

Taking your horse for the ride shouldn't keep you in stall mode. This site features a state-by-state directory of stable listings and Bed and Breakfasts that will board your horse after a long day on the road.

Pets on the Go

http://www.petsonthego.com

Get the inside scoop on traveling with your pet. Travel writers specializing in pet travel give you advice, find accommodations, provide a message board, and more for the dedicated pet enthusiasts.

Pets Welcome

http://www.petswelcome.com

Before you leave for your next trip, come here to find out if your pets are welcomed in your hotel, motel, inn, or bed and breakfast. The site includes a searchable database of over 25,000 places that welcome pets, info on emergency vets, pet stories, and a bulletin board.

Travel Dog

http://www.traveldog.com

Leaving Rover or Spot at home could take a lot out of a dog enthusiast's travel experience and this very unique membership site understands. As a member you will find a variety of saving benefits as well as dog related topics such as accommodations, transportation, and much more that may interest you. If you travel with your dog, this is one site to check out.

Travel Pets

http://www.travelpets.com

This free online directory to pet friendly hotels may have the answer when you are traveling with your pet. Filled with travel tips for pet owners, some great dog pictures, this is a great starting place to learn more about traveling with your pet.

Take Your Pet

http://www.takeyourpet.com

Take your pet with you when you travel. This site is a directory of pet-friendly places. Sign up for the free newsletter and get tips on taking your pet with you when you travel. As a member you can check out the pet bulletin boards.

Tale Waggers-Dogs at the Wheel

http://www.ddc.com/waggers/dogs_at_wheel.html

If you have a dog and take him in the car, you know how it can be driving with your canine friend at your side. This site will give you a few good travel tips for traveling in the car with your dog.

*Airline Pet Info

Traveling with a pet?
Then make sure you log on to these Web sites for information and tips on how to transport or travel with your beloved animal.
Check out: Johnny Jet Code: Airline Pet

*Pet Supplies

Here you can find everything from pet travel gear to food for your pet.
Check out: Johnny Jet Code: Pet Supplies

Chapter 30

Unhappy Traveler

Did the airline tick you off again? Don't just sit there and take it. Complain and get it off your chest! If they lost your luggage, check out the Unclaimed Baggage Center in Alabama, they might have it but you will have to pay to get it back.

*Complaints

Johnny Jet Code: Complaints

Complaints.com

http://www.complaints.com

This database of complaints allows you to post your own and read others. Check out the top complaint of the day, and see what everyone else is complaining about. Your complaints may not be so bad after all.

eComplaints.com

http://www.ecomplaints.com

This award-winning complaint site is not specifically for travel, but at this colorful site you can speak your voice to support this constructive consumer advocacy site. Issue a complaint and read someone's complaints at this one stop complaint place.

Travel Complaints

http://www.travelcomplaints.com

Do you have something to complain about? Here you can speak your voice, see your rights, and read about what other complaints.

Air Travel Consumer Report

http://www.dot.gov/airconsumer

This is the aviation consumer protection division where you can find info on how to cope with flight delays, air travel problems, complaints, travel tips, safety and security.

Planet Feedback

http://www.planetfeedback.com

Here is a consumer advocacy site where you can send feedback to companies.

*Lost and Found

Johnny Jet Code: Lost and Found

Lost and Found

http://www.boomerangit.com

Don't let loosing your possessions scare you. This site offers labels that stick onto products that reward the finder of the product you may have lost. You don't want your possessions ending up at a store like the Unclaimed Baggage Center at www.unclaimedbaggage.com. However, you can purchase some other people's unclaimed baggage there.

Chapter 31

Water Sports: Get Wet

Are you like me and like to go to all the warm places for vacation? Well, in this chapter we have all the hot surfing spots, fishing tours, scuba diving and snorkeling Web sites. You can even research your favorite beaches and find places where you can swim with the dolphins.

*Canoeing, Kayaking, Rafting, and Water Sports

Johnny Jet Code: Water Sports

Adventure Whitewater

http://www.adventure-whitewater.com

Since 1994 they've been taking people on memorable rafting trips to Nepal, Peru, Turkey, Sri Lanka, Bolivia, and New Zealand. All inclusive packages include: transfers, accommodations, permits, river and safety equipment, river and trekking guides, raft support, and safety kayakers. Drinks and laundry may not be included, but you can find everything else.

AllAboutRivers.com

http://www.allaboutrivers.com

The boaters here are passionate about guiding you on the rivers and they show it with their great river rafting photos, video clips, and screensavers. In addition to shopping for river gear and books, you can see detailed information about rivers across the U.S., and bid on a rafting trip.

Beyond Limits Adventure

http://www.rivertrip.com

This site specializes in offering rafting trips in California's Gold Country. There are rafting trips on the American River, Yuba River, Kaweah River, and Stanislaus River. Canoeing and kayaking are also available on various rivers.

Knick Canoers and Kayakers

http://www.kck.org

This Alaskan non-profit organization is a paddling club in Anchorage Alaska. Members of all skill levels are rafting, ocean kayaking, and canoeing with this club that offers various types of instruction in boating, along with a safety emphasis. Meetings, events, and safety classes are all accessible from the site.

Earth River

http://www.earthriver.com

Rafting or kayaking on the Peru's Futaleufu, the Yangtze, or Fiji Sea Kayaking can offer an experience of a lifetime. This site provides exotic whitewater trips to Tibet, Patagonia, Peru, China, Chile, Yukon, and Ecuador. Here you will find comprehensive safety tips, along with breathtaking photos of high end rafting. Whether you are new to rafting or a rafting expert, you'll find something. Check out the comparison chart.

Endless River Adventures

http://www.endlessriveradventures.com

ERA offers private kayaking instruction, whitewater rafting trips, rock climbing adventures, and fly-fishing. Take a whitewater trip to Nantahala River in North Carolina or Ocoee River in Florida. ERA will plan your specialty trip to Costa Rica, Ecuador, and New Mexico, while you take on the whitewater kayaks and mountain bikes.

Friends of the River

http://www.friendsoftheriver.org

FOR is California's statewide river conservation organization. However, it has an impressive rafting program with hundreds of volunteer guides. If you are interested in rafting down some of California's great rivers and going on a spirit filled trip of conservation and environmental restoration, then this is the site for you.

Outdoor Adventures Go Rafting

http://www.gorafting.com

Outdoor Adventures offers whitewater rafting trips on some of the best rivers in the western United States. Find six day river vacations on the Middle Fork and Main Salmon in Idaho, or four day trips on Oregon's Rogue River. This site also offers shorter one to three day trips on the Kern, Tuolumne, and American rivers in California. Check out their other site at www.kernrafting.com.

Outdoor Adventure River Specialists

http://www.oars.com

OARS or Outdoor Adventure River Specialists is a quality tour operator of water sporting and it provides whitewater rafting, sea kayaking, and various wilderness vacations throughout the western United States and rivers of Idaho, Utah, California, Oregon, Wyoming, and the Grand Canyon. Trips are personable and guided with trained and experienced professionals. Trips are specialized for families, youth groups, and corporations.

Rafting.com Outfitter Directory

http://www.rafting.com

Members of the directory are located throughout the U.S. Click on a state to find which area you are interested in finding out more about the rafting experiences.

Whitewater Connection

http://www.whitewaterconnection.com

Rafting in Northern California on the American, Kaweah, and Upper Klamath Rivers can be found here. Whether you are a beginner, rafting with your family, or a more advanced rafter, there is something to be found here.

Whitewater Voyages

http://www.whitewatervoyages.com

This is California's largest rafting outfitter with over twenty whitewater rafting trips. Inexperienced rafters will find classes and summer camps for learning how to raft. The site offers specialized trips for families, river cleanup, and community outreach.

A Better Water Search Directory

http://www.watersportfun.bizland.com
This is one of the most comprehensive Web directories specific to water sports. It contains a simple listing of every topic you can imagine when it comes to water sports.

*Fishing Trips

Johnny Jet Code: Fish Fun

Alaskan Fly Fishing Float Trips

http://www.brightwateralaska.com
Sport fly-fishing by floatplane in Alaska's Bristol Bay is what you will find at this site. The trips here lead by a legendary guide and based on seasonal fishing with top-notch equipment and meals prepared fresh daily.

Fishing Trip USA

http://www.fishingtripsusa.com
Providing resources for fishers, this site helps you plan your next fishing trip. Click on a freshwater, saltwater, or international location and you are directed to various lakes, rivers, and resorts that offer fishing opportunities. The site includes a directory of cabins, cottages, homes, and houseboats, along with maps, guides, fishing reports, and weather resources for fishermen.

Fish Link

http://www.fishlink.com
This site is known as the focused site for fish and fishing, providing a large directory of fish related resources.

Fishing Lines

http://www.fishinglines.com
Specializing in Canadian fishing resorts, books, videos, and software, you will find a variety of fishing resources here. Click on fish species and check the overviews of different fish. Clicking on Canada will take you to a map where you can find fishing resorts and trips in Canada.

Fishing International

http://www.fishinginternational.com

Since 1974, Fishing International has specialized in sports fishing and planning trips to a variety of fishing destinations around the world. The FI staff consists of professionals and believes that its clients are from all walks and appreciate exceptional sport fishing adventures.

Dragonfly Trout Fishing Adventures

http://www.fishingtasmania.com

Tasmania, the capital of Australia is known for beautiful waters, and its plentiful wild trout, which presents an unmatched fishing experience. This site invites you to discover an unforgettable adventure to Tasmania and the fly fishing opportunities. Check out the fishing gallery.

About Fly Fishing

http://www.flyfishing.about.com

The Fly Fisherman On-Line is for the magazine and is a one-stop place for your fishing needs. You can find an archive of magazines. Some of the subjects covered include fishing reports, fly rod building, salt water, conservation, Alaska, Eastern Canada, Florida, Caribbean, Foreign Waters, Rocky Mountains, and more.

Point Loma Sport Fishing

http://www.pointlomasportfishing.com

This site offers a wide variety of deep sea fishing trips in California and Baja Mexico. Trips offered range anywhere between six hours and sixteen days.

Montauk Sport Fishing and Tropical Fishing

http://www.tropicalfishing.com

This site has two sections to visit. The first section has everything you would want to know about fly-fishing in Montauk, New York. The site features articles from the magazine, fishing reports, charter boats, booking service, and more. The second site features trips throughout Central America, including Costa Rica, Belize, Panama, Guatemala, Honduras, Venezuela, and the Yucatan Peninsula.

World Wide Fishing Guide

http://www.worldwidefishing.com

This resource is a guide for saltwater fishing, freshwater fishing, and fly-fishing. You will also find information on charters, and you can watch television clips of the latest fishing shows.

*Life is a Beach

Johnny Jet Code: Best Beaches

All Beaches

http://www.allbeaches.net

Looking for a beach Web site? This site has a directory of many beach sites. Select a state and find a beach.

Amelia Island

http://www.ameliaisland.com

The northernmost barrier island off the Atlantic coast of Florida is Amelia Island. There is something for everyone here. The site contains info on accommodations, dining, weather, history of Fernandina Beach, shopping, and events.

At the Beach

http://www.atbeach.com

This is your Mid Atlantic coastal information resource to Delaware, Florida, Maryland, New Jersey, and Virginia beaches. The site contains a vacation guide, an event information board, beach classified ads, real estate info, shopping, and weather guides.

Beachcomber

http://www.beachcomber.com

Beachcomber is "Unlocking the Treasures" of Cape May, New Jersey and places around the world. From beaches of the world, cities of the world, camping in New Jersey, this site provides much information on tourism.

Canaveral National Seashore

http://www.nps.gov/cana

Near Titusville and New Smyrna Beach in Florida, this national seashore on a barrier island has a beautiful beach, and flatland habitats. Activities on the island include lagoon and surf fishing, boating, canoeing, surfing, sunbathing, swimming, hiking, horseback riding, and camping. The site contains the basics, activities, camping, and the facilities.

Daytona Beach

http://www.daytonabeach.com

Known for its Spring Break parties, but this beach has much to offer throughout the entire year, and especially during the summer seasons. The site has info on events, accommodations, nearby attractions, nightlife, and fun stuff for the whole family to enjoy. Check out the video clips and the postcards.

Delray Beach, Florida

http://www.delraybeach.com

Known as the "village by the sea" and as a first-class resort town, Delray Beach in South Palm Beach is on the Atlantic Ocean. With much to do and see, along with endless stretches of beauty, this site provides info on accommodations, the city, and much more.

South Beach and Miami Beach

http://www.miamiandbeaches.com

Welcome to Miami, and find some of the most beautiful beaches, sunsets, and more. This site keeps you up-to-date with the city events, along with a city guide, and information on booking.

Dewey Beach, Delaware

http://www.deweybeach.com

The most scenic coastline in Delaware is more scenic at this site where you can find out what to see, where to go, and what to eat. The site lays it all out for you in an easy to read fashion.

Assateague Island

http://www.nps.gov/asis

Near Berlin, Maryland and Chincoteague, Virginia, Assateague Island provides great seashore recreation and natural habitats of thirty-seven miles. Whether you are swimming in the ocean, camping, canoeing at bayside, crabbing, or fishing, there is something here for you at this national park. The site contains the basics, activities, camping, and the facilities.

Kiawah Island, South Carolina

http://www.kiawah.com

On the Coast of South Carolina you will find this island between the Atlantic Ocean and mainland. This private resort island is great for any golfing, other sports and recreation enthusiasts. With ten miles of pristine beaches, the historic city of Charleston, and more events and activities, this site provides all that you need and more. Check out www.greatbeach.com for more Charleston Resort Islands.

Old Orchard Beach, Maine

http://www.oldorchardbeachonline.com

This beach is a known hot spot in Maine where families have come to visit and vacation every year. You'll find dining, shopping, street entertainment, and beautiful sandy beaches to hang out and play beach volleyball. Everything you would want to know about Maine's top beach is here.

Nantucket Island Chamber of Commerce

http://www.nantucketchamber.org

Known for its history, Nantucket means "far-away land." However, within thirty miles, it is not too far away from the Massachusetts coast and offers much for the seasonal tourist. The site provides a little history, some trivia, accommodations, events, and information on the beaches.

Cape Cod National Seashore

http://www.nps.gov/caco

With 43,604 acres of shoreline and forty-miles of sandy beach, this continues to be a travel spot for many. Cape Cod has some historic lighthouses, a lifesaving station, and Cap Cod houses to see. The site has the basics, info on camping and lodging, activities, facilities, and a printable guide.

Marine Conservation Society's Good Beach Guide

http://www.goodbeachguide.co.uk

This is the ultimate guide to UK beach bathing. The beaches in this guide have achieved the highest standards for water quality. Information on the beaches and the water quality are described here.

Maui's Fantastic Beaches

http://www.maui.net/~tkern/beaches.html

You'll find some of the most beautiful public beaches on the shoreline of this Hawaiian island. From sun bathing to activities such as jet skiing, fishing, sailing, diving, kayaking, and parasailing, the excitement here is outlined with maps, pictures, and descriptions.

Gulf Islands

http://www.nps.gov/guis

The National Park Service presents a site for the Gulf Islands. It includes beaches, with great blue waters, white beaches, and a picture that makes this worth a visit. Information on the basics, camping, lodging, facilities, and activities are all here on these treasured islands.

Myrtle Beach

http://www.myrtlebeachlive.com

Going to Myrtle Beach in South Carolina? It's a beach, and a whole lot more to keep you entertained. Amusements, underwater adventures in the Ripley's Aquarium, mini golfing, and much more is here at this amazing place.

Padre Island National Seashore

http://www.nps.gov/pais

There about 133,000 acres on this island in Corpus Christi, Texas remaining the longest undeveloped barrier island worldwide. Check out some of the events and read about the history of the island.

Sand Castle Central

http://www.sandcastlecentral.com

Okay, this is not a beach, but you will find some sand castles here, so it's close enough. Have some fun in the sand, get some tips and tricks on building a sand castle masterpiece, find contests, sculptors, sand castle news, and great photos of sand castles.

Surf Sun

http://www.surfsun.com

This directory is a great starting point for those traveling to beaches. You'll find activities, lodging, vacation rentals, and more details on each of the various beaches here. There is a beach discussion board to post questions and a photo album to check out.

Cannon Beach, Oregon

http://www.cannon-beach.net

West of Highway 101, this small beach site has information on the beach, what to do, and a great collection of sunset photos to check out. Lodging, camping, shopping and more are here.

Long Beach, Washington Peninsula

http://www.funbeach.com

Located off Washington's southwestern coast, surrounded by the Pacific Ocean, this peninsula has tradition along with award-winning lodging and dining. The site has good fish and clams. There are plenty of fun attractions on the beach including: boating, fishing, shops, and more.

Best Beaches in the USA

http://www.petrix.com/beaches

Find out which beaches are the best in the United States. A listing of the top twenty beaches is shown here along with a photo. There are different categories to choose from including: Best Beaches with Night Life, Best Romantic Beaches, Best Wild Beaches, and Best Walking Beaches.

Newport Beach, California

http://www.newportbeach.com

The Newport Beach Chamber of Commerce is a site that explains the general accommodations of the beach, dining, entertainment, shopping, and more that can be found in the Newport Harbor area. Check out the slide show and view the pictures.

Top Beaches

http://www.topbeaches.com

This site takes you to a healthy beach campaign where promoting conservation of the coastal resources is emphasized, and a Dr. Beach's top beach site where you will find the best beaches in the U.S. Also see www.drbeach.org.

Virginia Beach

http://www.allaboutvirginiabeach.com

If Virginia Beach is your destination, this site is your answer to all that you would want to do at the beach and the surrounding areas. There are brief explanations of what to do, where to eat, info on boating and fishing, where to stay, and more on the historic landmarks.

*SCUBA: Just Dive It

Johnny Jet Code: Dive Deep

3 Routes Worldwide Scuba Directory

http://www.3routes.com

This is the largest diving directory on the Web with over 5,000 scuba destinations. Click on the map and find your charters and resorts worldwide.

Ambergris Caye

http://www.ambergriscaye.com

Ambergris Caye is the largest and most popular offshore caye in Belize with 25 miles of amazing barrier reef. There is much to do and see underwater and on land at this "kick-back" and relaxing getaway where the motto is "no shirt, no shoes, no problem." The site contains plenty of resources for diving in Belize with great pictures of underwater habitat. Some of the features include articles, postcards, fishing, things to do, and much more.

The Cayman Islands

http://www.cayman.org

The Caymans consist of lovely islands featuring a seven mile beach, a renowned Stingray City, and some of the most fascinating diving. The site explains the Caymans in a nutshell and is divided into six section including getting around, what to do and see, where to stay, the tourism information, dive news, and special perspectives on Cayman.

Diving Australia

http://www.diversionoz.com

Would you like to dive down under in Australia and see the Great Barrier Reef? The specialists here have mapped out extended and day diving excursions in Palau, short cruises to the Coral Sea, tours of Papua New Guinea, the Solomon Islands, and Micronesia. See some pictures of the people, learn about the history, geography, and plan a trip.

Dive Global

http://www.diveglobal.com

This site boasts it's the "ultimate source for scuba divers, snorkelers, and travelers." At Dive Global you can explore some of the finest diving travel, diving locations and destinations, tour operators, resorts, and exquisite underwater photography worldwide. Trip planning along with customized diving trips to some of the most sought after diving spots are offered.

Iguana Reef Inn

http://www.iguanareefinn.com
Explore Caye Calkner, Belize and discover the barrier reefs, scuba diving, fishing, windsurfing, and the ambiance at this laid-back elegant inn. You'll find some of the best diving and water sports here.

Manta Ray Bay Hotel

http://www.mantaray.com
This unique luxury diving resort in Micronesia is devoted to divers and has been voted five stars with Yap Island Divers. The quality assurance of safe diving is available in a full range of diving from beginner to master, and on location it has its exclusive PADI Manta Ray Awareness Course which has gained recognition as, "The Best Little Dive Hotel in the Pacific." In addition to great diving, the site has information on fishing, kayaking, some Yap history, and journeying there.

Reef Environmental Education Foundation

http://www.reef.org
REEF is an organization dedicated to preserving marine life through educating and getting people involved with its Fish Survey Project, which was started in 1990 by The Nature Conservancy (TNC) and has been guided by the Southeast Fisheries Science Center of the National Marine Fisheries Service (NMFS). Volunteering divers collect information on marine populations through the site. In the fish gallery, species can be viewed with descriptions.

Rum Point Inn

http://www.rumpoint.com
This family operated inn is sixty miles south of Belize City on the Placencia Peninsula. Surrounded by some of the best waters and beach side inland tours, the Rum Point Inn offers a personalized environment, and full amenities such as the garden pool, massages, sailing, windsurfing, snorkeling, a nature trail, and beach hangouts.

Scuba Source

http://www.scubasource.com

This abundant source for diving has just about everything a diver could need. It provides classifieds, a scuba poll, photo and postcard gallery, travel articles, forums, and more.

Scuba Yellow Pages

http://www.scubayellowpages.com

This complete directory or scuba diving and related resources has everything for divers from equipment and accessories to resorts, photos, and training.

Sea Saba Dive Center

http://www.seasaba.com

The Sea Saba dive is a unique and exotic world-class diving experience in the Caribbean. This private island is remote from the rest of the highly commercialized world without fast food restaurants, traffic, crowds, or cruise ships. It doesn't have a beach, but it does have an Internet café. When not diving, you'll snorkel, kayak, hike, rock climb, view arts, birding, and shop a little.

Southern Cross Club

http://www.southerncrossclub.com

Dive right in to Caribbean diving on Little Cayman Island at this small resort about 400 miles below Miami. This unpopulated and not highly commercialized island has everything a diving enthusiast can imagine, and then some.

World of Diving and Adventure Vacations

http://www.worldofdiving.com

This tour operator specializes in worldwide diving and adventure packaged vacations including live-aboards to Micronesia, Fiji, Soloman Islands, Papua New Guinea, Australia, Philippines, Galapagos, Bahamas, and more. The site has an excellent photo gallery.

Aqualog Magazine

http://www.aqualog.com

This unique interactive online magazine is dedicated to scuba diving and free diving. It has articles, some great photos, and artwork from scuba enthusiasts around the globe.

Aquaholic

http://www.aquaholic.com

If you are a scuba diving enthusiast, this site has some scuba software to download along with information on how you can have your own scuba page created, scuba training, equipment, and rentals.

Aquanaut

http://www.aquanaut.com

Since 1993, this online magazine has been dedicated to the recreational and technical scuba diving community. There is a club directory, diving images, gear reviews, information on other resources, and more.

Aqua-Trek

http://www.aquatrek.com

Aqua-Trek specializes in diving in the Fiji Islands. PADI Scuba Centers are located in Centra Resort Pacific Harbour, Magna Island, and Matamanoa Island. You will see a great photo gallery marine life, find tips on traveling to the Fiji Islands, and find more about a world-class diving trip.

Bay Islands Beach Resorts

http://www.bibr.com

The BIBR is an all inclusive dive and snorkel resort on Roatan in the Bay Islands of Honduras. Providing a personalized vacation for divers, snorkelers, island explorers and families, this company offers great pictures, and easy accessibility to the oceanfront.

Belize Scuba Diving Resort

http://www.scubabelize.com

This is the only resort on Lighthouse Reef Atoll dedicated to serious divers and has beachfront villas on a private Caribbean island. In addition to some of the best diving in Belize found on this site, you can enter the dive forum, and take a virtual reality tour as if you were there.

Buddha View Diving in Thailand

http://www.buddhaview-diving.com

Experience the island of Koh Tao of South East Asia, a major diving destination in Thailand. Known as one of the top diving educational experiences worldwide, this company suits all tastes, budgets, and divers. When not diving, you can find activities such as rock climbing and wake boarding.

Caradonna Caribbean Tours

http://www.caradonna.com

Divers leisure vacationers will enjoy some of the packages here, where you can find yourself traveling to Aruba, Bay Islands, Belize, Cayman Islands, Costa Rica, Cozumel, the Florida Keys, and more.

Club Kupps

http://www.clubkupps.com

Club Kupps is located off the beautiful Sea of Cortez in San Carlos Mexico offering unique private scuba and snorkeling vacations for families and couples alike. A certified sailing and PADI instructor will guide you throughout your adventure. Additional activities include boating, jet skiing, and fishing. Visit *www.mexicosailingdiving.com* as well.

Crystal Divers

http://www.crystaldivers.com

Catering to the discerning diver, Crystal Divers offers unique personalized diving experiences in the most excellent areas of Fiji, the Bligh Waters. Experienced divers will find a unique marine life experience on the 870-acre Nananu-I-Ra Island. Be sure to check out the photo gallery to see some corals, views, and more.

Cayman Diving Lodge

http://www.divecdl.com

The Cayman Islands are known for the beauty of its underwater diving experiences and Stingray City. This site features a diving lodge operated by dedicated PADI diving instructors exclusively for diving on the East End. Vacation packages are all-inclusive and accommodations are plentiful.

Deeper Blue

http://www.deeperblue.net

This international online magazine for divers features diving information and highlighted diving news. There are editorials, discussion boards, virtual postcards, a dive shop, and more.

Dive Buddy

http://www.divebuddy.com

Are you looking for someone to dive with? You can register at this site and find another diving partner around the world, find out about diving conditions, various diving hot spots, and get connected to the diving world.

Worldwide Diving Encyclopedia

http://www.divefree.net

This diving directory has listings of many online scuba resources, including subjects like photography, training, shops, conservation, operators, and dive travel. It has a discussion board and a monthly dive holiday contest.

Dive Guide International

http://www.diveguide.com

Dive Guide is a definitive diver's resource for diving destinations, accommodations, charters, gear, and more. At this portal you can click on operators, accommodations, or shop in the dive store, or bookstore.

DIVERNET

http://www.divernet.com

This UK Diver magazine has everything diving related in it. It provides archives the magazine back to 1995 and you will find the latest diving news updated every week.

Divers Alert Network

http://www.diversalertnetwork.org

Associated with Duke University Medical Center, DAN is a non-profit organization dedicated to promoting scuba diving safety, education, and recreation for divers. Throughout the years, DAN has offered lifesaving services, as well as educational programs. Find out how you can become a member of this growing diving organization.

Immersed Magazine

http://www.immersed.com

The International Technical Diving Magazine is a quarterly publication featuring new areas of interest to divers, and articles about projects, ideas, developments, and practices in technical diving. You can preview the magazine and see some back issues.

Belize Scuba Diving

http://www.gooddiving.com

Located on the unpopulated island of St. George's Caye about eight miles from Belize City, this NAUI/SSI scuba certified diving vacation spot is a great place for short boat trips to the most desirable diving in Belize. As the first dive resort in Belize, you will find a small living space, catered to private and smaller groups, to make a memorable experience.

Maravu Plantation Resort Diving

http://www.maravu.net/diving.htm

At this aqua adventure site you will experience diving at the Maravu Resort on the Taveuni Island in Fiji which is known as the "world capital of soft corals." See the Rainbow Reef in the Somosoma Strait, which is world renown for diving.

P & O Australian Resorts

http://www.poresorts.com

Create your own dive holiday getaway at some of the most pristine island resorts off the coast of Australia. Silky Oaks Lodge, Lizard Island, Dunk Island, Bedarra Island, Brampton Island, Heron Island, and Cradle Mountain Lodge are some of the places to visit at this extraordinary site. Take a virtual tour, and view some of the great pictures in the photo gallery.

Regal Dive Worldwide

http://www.regal-diving.co.uk

This award-winning diving holiday specialist in the UK offer worldwide scuba diving experiences for beginners and experts alike. At the site you can find dive destinations, take diving courses, get diving news and order a brochure.

Rodale's Scuba Diving

http://www.scubadiving.com

This scuba magazine is a well-regarded name in scuba diving. Featuring 360-degree virtual scuba tours, a message board, safety information, equipment reviews, training, and more for the scuba enthusiast. There are some great photos to check out here.

Scuba Duba

http://www.scubaduba.com

Perhaps the ultimate scuba directory online, this site is fully organized with plenty of scuba resources, discussion boards, scuba essays, articles, games, scuba humor, galleries, dive logs, postcards, and much more.

Scuba Radio

http://www.scubaradio.com

This is the world's first radio show devoted to diving. You can listen live and listen to archived shows.

Undercurrent Online

http://www.undercurrent.org

This is the site for the scuba magazine. Since 1975, it has provided the latest unbiased ad-free reviews of dive resorts, scuba gear, and health and safety issues. Resorts featured are located in places like Australia, the Bahamas, Belize, the Cayman Islands, Bonaire, and Papua New Guinea.

YMCA Scuba

http://www.ymcascuba.org

The YMCA SCUBA program launched the dive training in the United States and remains today as a learning place for scuba diving. Join the YMCA heritage and start learning to dive with the YMCA. Find an instructor in your state and check out some of the courses offered.

*Surfing and Wind Sports

Johnny Jet Code: Wind Surfer

Adventure Productions

http://www.adventurep.com

This multimedia company offers videos, books, and CDs of hang gliding, paragliding, and parachuting.

Evolution Surf

http://www.evolutionsurf.com

This surf company manufacturers custom made Wayne Lynch designed surfboards and accessories. There is a surf shop and a surfer's photo gallery to check out.

PWA World Tour

http://www.pwaworldtour.com

The Professional Windsurfing Association organizes windsurfing competitions worldwide and shows a calendar of windsurfing events. Also featured are results, the latest windsurfing news, profiles of surfers, rankings, and the largest collection of Web resources for windsurfers.

Aussie Surf Adventures

http://www.surfadventures.com.au

Interested in surfing it up in Australia? This all-inclusive surfing trip from Sydney to Byron Bay will set the pace for an adventure. This cool site explains the five day trip itinerary, the equipment, and even has some fun stuff like surfer lingo.

San Diego Surfing Academy

http://www.surfsdsa.com

Looking to learn how to surf? If so, the SDSA offers an instruction camp that will show you the way to San Diego and Baja. The site includes information on lessons, photos, and a surf shop.

International Surfing Museum

http://www.surfingmuseum.org

In Huntington Beach, California, this museum holds a great collection of some of the most significant surfing exhibits containing artifacts of surfing history. The site contains some of the fine works of surfing memorabilia amongst surfing music, surfing legends, and other stuff for the surfing enthusiast.

Swell.com

http://www.swell.com

Swell is a leading surf shop offering brand name surf accessories and apparel.

Windsports Hang Gliding Center

http://www.windsports.com

This is the largest and oldest hang gliding school in southern California. Since 1974, Windsports has provided quality flight training to students worldwide. The site includes getting started information, a beginner's tour, info on flight equipment, frequently asked questions, and more.

World Windsurfing Directory

http://www.worldwindsurf.com

This is a leading directory for windsurfing Web resources worldwide. If you are looking for something windsurfing related, this is the place to find it.

*Swimming with Dolphins

Johnny Jet Code: Dolphins Swim

Dolphin Adventure

http://www.dolphin-adventure.com

Watch, swim, encounter, and enjoy the company of bottlenose dolphins in Puerto Vallarta, Mexico. This is a once in a lifetime experience where you can interact with these fascinating aqua dwellers in their tropical habitat.

Dolphin Cove

http://www.dolphinscove.com

Dolphin Cove is on a five-acre natural lagoon and offers a variety of marine programs for education and enjoyment. The site focuses on preserving marine environmental systems while educating and entertaining dolphin enthusiasts.

Dolphin Quest

http://www.dolphinquest.org

Swim with the dolphins in Hawaii, Bermuda, French Polynesia, and Oaha. The Dolphin Quest program provides an enchanting and memorable dolphin experience to explore.

Dolphin Discovery

http://www.dolphindiscovery.com

Enjoy swimming and scuba diving with dolphins in Isla Mujeres, Cozumel, or Puerto Aventuras. Discoveries are fun and educational experiences featuring swim, encounter, and dive programs. Check out the dolphin photos and make a reservation.

Dolphin Odyssey

http://www.dolphinodyssey.com

The Dolphin Odyssey offers swimming with the dolphins and a group of naturalists and water experts. Dolphin trips are taken to Shell Island between the Gulf of Mexico and St. Andrews Bay in Panama City Beach, Florida.

Dolphin World

http://www.dolphinworld.org

Enjoy a naturally rewarding experience of swimming with the dolphins in the Florida Keys. This is a lifelong lasting experience that offers 1-4 day programs for all.

Divine Dolphin

http://www.divinedolphin.com/dolphinswim5.htm

Enjoy dolphin and whale encounters in the shallow waters just off the Costa Rica coasts. The site is filled with pictures, answers to frequently asked questions, travel info, and rates.

Human Dolphin Institute

http://www.human-dolphin.org

Those who enjoy studying humans and their interactions and relationships with dolphins will enjoy this site. The Human Dolphin Institute is a Conservation Society in Florida dedicated to understanding the relationship between humans and dolphins.

Mayan Riviera

http://www.mayanriviera.com/attractions/dolphins

This Dolphin Discovery site offers a once in a memorable experience of swimming with dolphins in the beautiful waters of Isla Mujeres, about 20 minutes by boat from Cancun.

People Oceans Dolphins

http://www.people-oceans-dolphins.com

POD was created to promote awareness, respect, and contact with whales, dolphins, and porpoises worldwide. The site offers affordable dolphin swimming trips, along with workshops, and seminars.

Unexso

http://www.unexso.com

Unexso offers tropical vacations where you can swim and interact with dolphins. Trips include snorkel and scuba diving in a relaxed atmosphere on Grand Bahamas Island.

Waterplanet USA

http://www.waterplanetusa.com

Waterplanet offers therapeutic dolphin swimming programs for children with special needs. The site contains many pictures with information on the programs.

Wild About Dolphins

http://www.wildaboutdolphins.com

Wild About Dolphins offers daily interactive and educational dolphin experiences with bottlenose dolphin in Key West, Florida. Trips are boat chartered with learning exploration of natural dolphin habitats and sounds of nature.

Wild Quest

http://www.wildquest.com

Wild Quest offers swimming with dolphins in Bimini, and the Bahamas. The site shows weekly trip programs with frequently asked questions, photos, and videos. There are other dolphin resources to check out here.

Chapter 32

Planning

*Vacation Planning

Johnny Jet Code: Vacation Planning

Free To Go

http://www.freetogo.com

Think of all the inconvenient things you have to do before you travel. This site helps you do them. Whether you are putting your newspapers on "vacation hold" or having your mail stopped, researching your destination, telling co-workers your itinerary, or finding a pet sitter, Free To Go is making travel more convenient.

Getting Through Customs

http://www.getcustoms.com

Well this site isn't just about getting through customs, but it provides the tools to help you get through normal practices in different countries. Learn how to greet someone in another land. Should you kiss, bow, or shake hands when you greet someone from another country? The site offers seminars, books, and free articles on the customs of various countries. Advice on drinking, dressing, gestures, greetings, gift giving, and more in different cultures can be learned.

1 Vacation

http://www.1vacation.com

Find a bunch of family vacations, all-inclusive, city stays, tours, and more vacation listings here. You can call in and make a reservation.

Fun Jet Vacations

http://www.funjet.com

Fun Jet is a tour operator that specializes in package trips to the southern climates. Fun Jet has both charter and commercial flights along with accommodations. You can find some good travel savings here.

Great Hawaii Vacations

http://www.greathawaiivacations.com

If Hawaii is your destination, this site will help you find everything from condos and hotel rentals to airfare, rental cars and more. This site serves all Hawaii islands.

Grown Up Camps

http://www.grownupcamps.com

You don't have to be a kid to go to camp, and this site proves it. Here you will find a great directory of camps suited for adults interested in broadening their horizons. Everything from recreational activities to advanced instruction can be found here.

Sunfinder Vacations

http://www.sunfinder.com

Looking to go to the sunny beach? This site finds destinations like Hawaii, Cancun, and the Bahamas and emails vacation packages to you per your request.

Welcome Centers

http://www.welcomecenters.com

This site welcomes you to the United States by providing information on each state. Click on a state, location, or activity and you will find information on tourist attractions and accommodations, shopping, entertainment, arts, and more. It's a great starting place to plan your trip to any of the fifty states.

World Wide Travel Source

http://www.wwtravelsource.com

This directory is filled with information, links, and more related to the travel industry. If you are not sure where you want to go, this site may be a good starting place.

*Luxury Travel Planning

Johnny Jet Code: Luxury Travel

1st Class Ticket Deals

http://www.1st-air.net

This site specializes in premium travel and offering business and first class tickets on international flights at reduced prices. What's the catch you may ask? It's important to book in advance to get the best savings and there is a penalty if you cancel your flight. These sites is good for travelers looking for good international flight rates, and are not looking to change their travel arrangements.

12 Degrees

http://www.12degrees.com

These trips are extraordinary and upscale, but very customizable for the FIT (Foreign Independent Traveler) who is interested in making their trip truly unique. Featuring over 100 travel experts, this site is primarily for travel agents, but travelers may find it useful as well.

Andrew Harper Travel

http://www.harperassociates.com

Andrew Harper is an authority on luxury travel and at his site you can subscribe to his various publications, which include Andrew Harper's Hideaway Report, The Andrew Harper Collection, and Andrew Harper's Q Club.

Elite Traveler

http://www.elite-traveler.com

Elite Traveler is a bimonthly magazine that provides the most affluent with information on planning their trips, along with information that is hard to find in other travel publications. Read by corporate executives, famous celebrities, and the like, you can find more information about this high-end publication and subscribe.

Entrée New

http://www.entreenews.com

This luxury travel newsletter is published monthly and is intended for the discriminating and uncompromising traveler. Similarly, practical and value-conscious travelers read this newsletter as well. Visit the site and see some tips, read some past articles, and get a peak at the headlines.

Extravagance Magazine

http://www.extravagancemagazine.com/home.htm

If you ever wanted a few good suggestions on where luxury travel may lead you, Extravagance certainly has something for you. It conveniently features various journeys, information on spas and pampering, cruises and casinos, villas and castles, information on lifestyle trips including everything from antique, architecture, history, to music and nightlife.

Flight Fantasy

http://www.flightfantasy.com

Total luxury and first class services are offered here. From private air travel and yachts to five star luxury resorts, you can find it here. There are no prices, but if you are visiting this site, prices would be no object. You may just want to look at some of the extravagant stuff here. No request is too outrageous here.

Luxe Life

http://www.luxelife.com

Personalized travel consultants lead you to some of the most extravagant and luxurious vacations and travel adventures imaginable. The belief behind this Internet travel company is that traveling is a personal, creative, and interactive experience.

Luxury Link

http://www.luxurylink.com

Luxury Link contains thousands of products and services keeping the luxury traveler in mind. You can find discounted prices particularly during the off-season. From tours, cruises, specialty travel, hotels, resorts, inns, lodges, yacht charters, villas, spas, and more, you will find your luxury travel needs here. Auctions are featured where you can bid on luxury trips and properties worldwide. So the only catch is that you will know the range of departure dates, but you can't check availability of a specific date until after you've paid.

LuxRes

http://www.luxres.com

This joint venture between the Leading Hotels of the World and McDonald Investments provides an interactive way to book all of your luxury travel desires.

Luxury Traveler

http://www.luxurytraveler.com

This is a leading upscale online travel magazine for European travelers. It includes news and reviews for the luxury traveler, information on London Theatre, Museums and Galleries, Opera, luxury hotels, and more.

Private Jetaway

http://www.privatejetaway.com

Here you'll find super exclusive first class retreats to exotic and luxurious places. Whether you are looking to take a private jet or private yacht, you may find it here.

Chapter 33

Business Travel

Johnny Jet Code: Business Travel

Don't leave town or your office without reading this chapter. We have all the necessary sites to make your meetings and sales calls go smoothly!

About.com Business Travel

http://www.businesstravel.about.com

If you are a business traveler, this site provides an abundance of resources for you. From tips to informational articles, business travelers will find everything from how to avoid the middle seat on the plane to frequent flyer programs.

Inn-Business Travel

http://www.inn-businesstravel.com

This site specializes in helping you find an inn or a bed and breakfast that is well suited for the business traveler. Strict guidelines determine whether or not a bed and breakfast is appropriate for the business traveler. Some of the guidelines include corporate rates, in-room phone, fax, Internet readiness, and more.

Business Forum

http://www.bizforum.org/world.htm

This organization is dedicated to senior decision makers and experts in business and government. The senior decision makers can meet for lunch to discuss innovative technology products. The world section of the site contains business information on many countries, resources, articles, weather, and travel and entertainment.

Biz Traveler

http://www.biztraveler.org

This is an authoritative resource for business travelers. It offers "Road Rules" a section of tips for your trip, the latest news in a section called "Useable News," travel advisories, and a place where you can file travel complaints.

Bradmans

http://www.bradmans.com

Bradmans is an English company that makes guides that are specialized in meeting the needs of the business traveler. This is a site with major cities around the world featuring guides for cities with basic information on what to see, how to get around, shopping, and excursions.

Business Travel

http://www.businesstravel.com

This site was created specifically for the business traveler to book a flight, rent a car, make a hotel reservation, and read some business travel related articles.

Business Traveler Online

http://www.btonline.com

This online magazine caters to the business traveler with special reports, news, destination guides, and general travel data.

CEO Express

http://www.ceoexpress.com

CEO Express is a business Web portal, which was founded in 1998 and was created by a CEO for the busy executive looking for a quick gateway to Web links. Their portal has been designed in a way to save the busy executive time during the workday. The ultimate goal is to be the best executive assistant imaginable.

CNN Money

http://money.cnn.com/services

CNN and MONEY magazine have teamed up to give you this service providing a variety of services including travel news.

Corporate Travel Safety

http://www.corporatetravelsafety.com

Corporate Travel Safety provides travel safety and security information for business and leisure travelers. Through offering training seminars, safety and security products, and consulting, the goal is to reduce the chance of a traveler becoming a victim of a crime while traveling domestically or internationally.

Expedia Business Travel

http://www.expedia.com/daily/business

Expedia has a special section for business travelers. It includes travel tools that will help you plan your trip, make a reservation, and more.

First Class Flyer

http://www.firstclassflyer.com

This is the travel industry's premier monthly newsletter on business and first class air travel. Access Mr. Upgrade's Newsroom to free upgrades, great fares, corporate travel, and more.

Fit for Business Health Clubs

http://www.fitforbusiness.com

Just because you are traveling doesn't mean you have to stop your exercise regimen. This site lists hotels with some of the best gyms and athletic facilities throughout the world. Listings include countries such as Australia, Czech Republic, the UK, and the United States.

Joe Sent Me

http://www.joesentme.com

Joe Brancatelli, a leading business travel expert sends you to his site where business travelers can embark on their travel adventures. Read his latest commentary on traveling, and what the others have to say at this comprehensive business travel e-zine.

Learn About Cultures

http://www.learnaboutcultures.com

This site provides the international business professional with updated cross-cultural information on travel and leisure. It includes culture guides containing dos and don'ts, a culture quiz, hot topics, and articles.

Meeting News

http://www.meetingnews.com

Here you will find the latest news and information on meetings, conventions, and trade shows. There is a searchable archive online along with a paper magazine subscription.

MeetingsNet

http://www.meetingsnet.com

MeetingsNet is the meeting industry's magazine and portal for information related to planning meetings and events. It provides comprehensive coverage of meeting planning issues, trends, and event in six areas including: association, corporate, insurance/financial, technology, religious, and medical.

Official Airline Guide

http://www.oag.com

OAG provides products, information, services for business travelers and the travel industry. It also offers flight booking in addition to checking flight status.

The Internationalist Center for International Business

http://www.internationalist.com

This is an award-winning site and resource for international business and travelers. You will find books, directories, guides, maps, reports, and all sorts of publications for the business minded traveler. There is a very good community board here as well.

ProcurePoint Travel Solutions Inc.

http://www.procurepoint.com

This site is a leader in online sourcing of corporate hotel lodging for offsite meetings and short term travel. The company provides a unique combination of automated online processing tools integrated with its original "OpenBid" reverse auction platform and comprehensive reporting capabilities streamline labor intensive, manual planning processes between corporate travel managers, meeting planners and hoteliers.

Rosenbluth International

http://www.rosenbluth.com

This company is one of the leading travel management providers in the world.

Trade Show News

http://www.tradeshownews.com

Business Wire presents this site that providing the latest news about trade shows.

SkyGuide.net

http://www.skyguide.net

This business travel portal presented by American Express was created for frequent business travelers. The site has an interactive portal and a print magazine that is pocket sized. The publication contains access to more than 75,000 direct and connecting flights. You will find articles, resources, and more.

Worldroom.com International Business Travel Guide

http://www.worldroom.com

Worldroom.com is an ideal site for international business travelers. The site includes travel news, city guides, travel health, trip tech, destination spotlights, and more.

*Business Magazines

http://www.business2.com

http://www.businessweek.com

http://www.economist.com

http://www.entrepreneur.com

http://www.fortune.com

http://www.forbes.com

http://www.inc.com

http://www.money.com

http://www.smartbusinessmag.com

Here are some of the top business magazine sites for the discerning business traveler. Travel may not be the main focus at these sites, but they have overall business content that is interesting. *Johnny Jet Code: Business Magazines*

News Magazines

http://www.newsweek.com

http://www.usnews.com

http://www.time.com

These news magazines will come in handy for the weekly news. If you are looking for world news, you may want to check out these sites.

Chapter 34

Specialty Travel

This chapter covers all the places and helpful Web sites for disabled and volunteer travelers. We also have specific sites for African American travel.

*African American Travel

Johnny Jet Code: Black Travel

Black Travel Online

http://www.blacktravelonline.com

Specializing in travel for the African American community, this site offers an e-zine filled with information, cruise specials, vacation packages, family travel, retreats, a cultural calendar, jazz festivals, and much more.

Festival at Sea

http://www.festivalatsea.com

The Festival at Sea is a popular cruise vacation for many African American travelers. Offering three, seven, and fourteen day cruises in the Caribbean and Brazil, these trips have a little bit of everything to "find your groove."

Pathfinders Travel

http://www.pathfinderstravel.com

This quarterly magazine provides travel information for people of color. There is a feature story section along with recipes called "Chef's Table" and information on the current issue.

Soul of America

http://www.soulofamerica.com

This African American portal publishes travel information addressing online cultural resources, historical sites, shops, hotel accommodations, inns, events, tours, and more for the black online community.

*Disabilities, Handicaps, and Special Needs

Johnny Jet Code: Handicap Source

Global Access Disabled Travel Network

http://www.geocities.com/Paris/1502

This travel network is a comprehensive resource for those with handicaps and special needs while traveling. The site provides resources for accessible hotels, transportation, tips, featured trips, and more.

Access Able Travel Source

http://www.access-able.com

Since 1995, this site has provided access information for mature and disabled travelers. Whatever you may be looking for in accessible travel for those with disabilities can likely be found on this comprehensive site. This site is available in text only and graphics versions.

All Go Here

http://www.allgohere.com

All Go Here is a British directory of hotels and airlines that are accessible to everyone despite their disabilities.

Breathing Easy

http://www.oxygen4travel.com

If you need oxygen, this site offers a resourceful guide to over 2,500 locations where you can refill your oxygen tanks within the fifty states.

World on Wheels

http://www.geocities.com/Heartland/6295

This site is dedicated to travelers who are in a wheelchair. Find info with a first person trip report on wheelchair accessible travel with a focus on various destinations and attractions.

Emerging Horizons Accessible Travel News

http://www.emerginghorizons.com

This quarterly news magazine is devoted to accessible travel, focusing on travel for people with mobility disabilities. Wheelchair users to slow walkers will find the travel resources helpful.

Dialysis Finder

http://www.dialysisfinder.com

Here you can locate dialysis units from wherever you are. Just type in the zip, city, or state, and press find to "find" nearby units.

Global Dialysis

http://www.globaldialysis.com

This comprehensive resource is for dialysis patients traveling throughout the world. Search for centers worldwide, and get information for those traveling with dialysis.

Independent Living

http://www.independentliving.com

Here you'll find products to assist with everyday living.

Wheelchair Getaways Inc.

http://www.wheelchair-getaways.com

This company provides rentals for those in a wheel chair. On the site, you can find rental locations, features of different wheelchair accessible vehicles, and more resources for wheel chair travel.

DisabilityWORLD.com

http://www.disabilityworld.com

Providing a directory of disability resources on the Web, this UK site is visited worldwide, yet it tends to have a European slant to it.

Accessible Journeys

http://www.disabilitytravel.com

This site specializes in designing accessible trips, and escorting groups of slow walkers, wheelchair travelers, and their families. Here they focus on independent travel, cruises, rentals, and more.

ScootAround Inc.

http://www.scootaround.com

This is a national scooter and wheelchair rental company, that offers rentals in over 500 locations throughout North America and worldwide.

Society for Accessible Travel and Hospitality

http://www.sath.org

Since 1976, SATH has been a non-profit educational organization representing travelers with disabilities. The mission is to promote awareness, respect, and accessibility for the disabled and mature travelers and employment in the tourism industry. The site contains resources, events, and more for accessible travel.

Medical Travel on the Cruise

http://www.medicaltravel.org

Looking for a full service Medical Travel Agency catering to the patients along with their friends and families? Specializing in cruises and land vacations for dialysis patients, patients with respiratory problems, ventilator users and wheelchair users, and other special needs, this company makes it easy. Enjoy the background music.

Mobility International USA

http://www.miusa.org

This non-profit was created to empower people with disabilities around the world through international exchange, information, technical assistance and training. They also ensure the inclusion of people with disabilities by offering travel opportunities and programs.

Accessible Japan

http://www.wakakoma.org/aj

This is a guide for wheelchair users traveling in Japan.

*Religious Travel

Johnny Jet Code: Travel Religion

For more information on Christian religious travel, check out *Johnny Jet Code: Christian Travel*

For more information on Jewish religious travel, check out *Johnny Jet Code: Jewish Travel*

For more information on Muslim religious travel, check out *Johnny Jet Code: Muslim Travel*

Christian Traveler

http://www.christiantraveler.com

Your source for Christian Travel and family vacation ideas can be found at this site. There is a book that offers Christian Travelers information along with information on individuals looking for spiritual travel. There are plenty of Web resources here for the Christian Traveler.

Jewish Travel

http://www.jewishtravel.com

Jewish Travel provides meaningful vacations for special holidays. Whether you are experiencing a Bar/Bat Mitzvah or would like to tour around the world, this site offers memorable travel experiences for Jews. Kosher safaris, singles tours, and adventure travel.

Jewish Travel Network

http://www.jewish-travel-net.com

Are you Jewish, looking to travel, but want to keep it kosher, or just want to interact with other Jews? Give this one a try and see what travel Jews have in mind.

*Volunteer Travel

Johnny Jet Code: Travel Volunteers

World Youth International

http://www.worldyouth.com.au

This non-profit is committed to creating unique and exciting travel volunteer opportunities for those contributing to the global community. The organization provides cultural programs for teens, oversees service projects for seniors and youth, hosting programs, and community developing projects.

Campus California TG

http://www.cctg.org

CCTG is an international campus for the humanization of mankind and the care of our planet. A variety of activities take place on this educational campus. Here you can teach yourself about the development of mankind.

Alternative Breaks for College Students

http://www.alternativebreaks.org

Break Away is a program that unites college and high school students to participate in a common goal of community service during their fall, winter, spring, and summer school breaks. Examples of breaks consist of tutoring migrant farm workers, building homes, registering voters in rural areas, and working with homeless.

American Red Cross

http://www.redcross.org

This humanitarian organization helps many people each year prevent, prepare for, and cope with disasters and emergencies. There are many different ways you can volunteer.

Generous Adventures Travel Auctions

http://www.generousadventures.com

This company donates profits from travel auctions to the Natural Resources Defense Council. The site provides auctioneers bidding on lodging, outdoor adventures, safaris, vacation packages, exotic destinations, and more.

The University of California Expeditions Program

http://www.urep.ucdavis.edu

The University of California Research Expeditions Program is focused on improving our understanding on life on earth through partnerships between UC researchers and the general public. Programs are offered throughout the world in animal studies, archeology, geology, environmental studies, and arts and culture.

Sierra Club Outings

http://www.sierraclub.org/outings

This site is for the traveler who wants to explore, enjoy, and protect the natural world around. Sierra Club Outings sponsors hundreds of outings each year. Activities cover everything from backpacking, rafting, and service oriented outings.

SCI International Voluntary Service

http://www.sci-ivs.org

Here you will find volunteering abroad as an option with offerings of 2-3 week summer group work camps in over fifty countries. Also offered are longer year round volunteering trips.

Quaker Information Center

http://www.afsc.org/qic.htm

The QIC is located in Pennsylvania and provides listings of volunteer and service opportunities, internships, and employment opportunities, for Quakers and non-Quakers.

Oceanic Society

http://www.oceanic-society.org

This society offers various conservational expeditions for students and teachers. From natural history expeditions and research expeditions, to workshops and courses, if you are an ocean dweller or a conservation person, this trip may be for you.

Habitat for Humanity

http://www.habitat.org

Habitat for Humanity is an organization where people come together with others and volunteer by building affordable housing for those who are in need of a home.

Global Service Corps

http://www.globalservicecorps.org

Volunteer abroad in developed and underdeveloped countries worldwide. The Global Service Corps is built on the philosophy that personal lives and activities of people throughout the world are becoming more intertwined. Understanding another person's culture and understanding our interconnectedness to help each other's country is at the core of this program.

Global Volunteers

http://www.globalvolunteers.org

This non-profit and non-sectarian development organization was founded in 1984 with a goal of helping to establish a foundation for peace through mutual international understanding. Global Volunteers sends teams of volunteers to live and work with locals on human and economic development projects.

Caribbean Volunteer Expositions

http://www.cvexp.org

The Caribbean is a beautiful paradise, rich in cultural and architectural heritage. Most of the Caribbean's naturalness is destroyed by over development. This non-profit organization, CVE stands to preserve the heritage of the Caribbean and maintain its great architectural heritage through its trips.

Council Exchanges

http://www.councilexchanges.org

Council Travel offers international opportunities for students ages thirteen and up, parents, and teachers to work, study, teach, and volunteer abroad. Each year there is another volunteer project. Past projects included volunteering at an archaeological dig in Rome.

CEDAM International

http://www.cedam.org

Dive into the world of underwater adventure and become a reef explorer. CEDAM stands for Conservation, Education, Diving, Awareness, and Marine Research. Each year the volunteer trips consist of scientist-led marine-conservation and marine research expeditions to help protect our underwater environments.

Archaelogical Institute of America Tours

http://www.archaeological.org

The AIA first started in the Industrial Age in 1879, and it is the oldest and largest organization dedicated to archaeology. Today, it provides professionally guided group study tours and travel opportunities for the archeological minded with first class traveling in mind. You will travel to the most phenomenal archaeological locations, and explore a hands-on experience of the remains of past civilizations.

Cross Cultural Solutions

http://www.crossculturalsolutions.org

CCS is a humanitarian organization offering non-religious international volunteer work in China, Costa Rica, Ghana, India, Peru, and Russia. Their mission is to empower local communities, foster cultural sensitivity and understanding, and contribute grassroots solutions to global challenges. The site is interactive with video clips and detailed information on each program.

Landmark Volunteers

http://www.volunteers.com

High School students and adults ages 25-35 can take a one week getaway during the summer to help improve different cultures, environments, and offer community service throughout the United States.

Amizade Volunteer Programs

http://www.amizade.org

This non-profit organization is devoted to promoting worldwide volunteerism and community service to improve group work, provide community services, and cultural awareness with first hand cultural experiences. Amizade is Portuguese for friendship and was started in 1994. Today, it offers volunteer travel opportunities throughout the world to help make a difference.

American Hiking Society

http://www.americanhiking.org/events/vv

The events and volunteer opportunities are devoted to hikers and those passionate about hiking. Each trip has a goal of revitalizing natural trails. You can expect much shoveling, trimming, and grooming the trails you love to hike.

Peace Corps

http://www.peacecorps.gov

The Peace Corps was established under John F. Kennedy when he said, "Ask not what your country can do for you, ask what you can do for your country." This organization was created to promote world peace. See how you can join and what volunteer opportunities are here.

Volunteers for Peace International Workcamps

http://www.vfp.org

Since 1982, the VFP has offered adults and teens with overseas volunteering projects and workcamps. The workcamps have partnered with U.S. Forest Service, National Park Service, and various affiliates of Americorps and Habitat for Humanity. Their mission has been to promote International Voluntary Service as an effective means of education and community service.

Volunteer Abroad

http://www.volunteerabroad.com

College students looking to study abroad with an emphasis on volunteerism will find many great opportunities here.

Volunteer Match

http://www.volunteermatch.com

You are looking to volunteer, but don't know what community involvement suite you best, or would like to find something in a particular area. Volunteer Match helps you find the volunteer opportunities you are looking for, without searching everywhere.

Wilderness Volunteers

http://www.wildernessvolunteers.org

Founded in 1997, Wilderness Volunteers is a non-profit organization that promotes volunteer services for America's wild lands. They work with the National Park Service and schedule week long volunteer led trips in small groups.

Quick References

Appendix

Destination by State

Listed below are sites based on destination. Some are private sites that feature major attraction areas whereas others are official state and tourism offices or convention and visitor bureaus. Official state and tourism bureaus are denoted with ***bold italics.*** For more information on tourist offices and visitor bureaus, visit *Johnny Jet Code: Visitor Bureaus* and *Johnny Jet Code: Tourist Office* and you will find many resources. If there is a particular city that you are looking for that cannot be found, go to USA City Link *www.usacitylink.com* or visiting the chapter City Tourism will help you find a particular city. If you are looking for specific government related resources, you may also want to visit www.governmentguide.com to get information on government sites for each state.

Alabama, AL
The Cotton State, Capital: Montgomery

http://www.touralabama.org .... **Alabama Bureau of Tourism**
http://www.alabama.gov.................................... **Alabama State Government Site**
http://www.apls.state.al.us .... **Alabama State Library**

Birmingham
http://www.birminghamnet.com .... **Information site for Birmingham**
http://www.northalabama.org .... **North Alabama Tourism Association**
http://www.postherald.com .... **Birmingham Post Herald Newspaper site**

Montgomery
http://www.ci.montgomery.al.us .... **City of Montgomery**
http://www.al.com/montgomery .... **The Montgomery Independent Newspaper site**

Alaska, AK
Land of the Midnight Sun, Capital: Juneau

http://www.360alaska.com ....**Panoramic Tour**
http://www.alaska.com..**Informational site for Alaska**
http://www.adn.com/visitors.............................**Alaska Visitors Guide**
http://www.alaskanet.com/Tourism ....**Alaska Tourism and Travel Guide**
http://www.akrr.com...**Alaska Railroad**
http://www.dced.state.ak.us/tourism/home.htm
....**Alaska Visitor Information**
http://www.library.state.ak.us ....**Alaska State Library**
http://www.state.ak.us ....**State of Alaska**

Anchorage
http://www.muni.org..**The Municipality of Anchorage**
http://www.adn.com...**Anchorage Daily News**

Fairbanks
http://fairbanks-alaska.com ....**Fairbanks, Alaska Information Site**

Inside Passage
http://www.alaskainfo.org ....**Alaska Southeast Tourism Council**

Juneau
http://www.juneau.lib.ak.us ....**City of Juneau**
http://www.juneau.com ....**Information site for Juneau**
http://www.traveljuneau.com ....**Juneau Convention and Visitors Bureau**

Arizona, AR
The Grand Canyon State, Capital: Phoenix

http://www.accessarizona.com ....**Information site for Arizona**
http://www.arizonaguide.com............................**Arizona Office of Tourism**
http://www.arizonatourism.com ....**Arizona Tourism**
http://www.azcentral.com ....**Information site for Arizona**
http://www.az.gov ....**State of Arizona**
http://www.azstarnet.com ....**Arizona Daily Star Newspaper site**
http://www.carizona.com ....**Information site for Arizona cities**
http://www.dlapr.lib.az.us ....**Arizona State Library**
http://www.lakehavasu.com ....**Information site for Lake Havasu, Arizona**

http://www.webcreationsetc.com/Azguide ....**Arizona Vacation Guide**

Flagstaff

http://www.flagguide.com ....**Information site for Flagstaff, Arizona**

Phoenix

http://www.ci.phoenix.az.us ....**City of Phoenix**

http://www.boulevards.com/cities/phoenix.html ....**Phoenix Hotels**

http://phoenix.citysearch.com ....**City Guide to Phoenix**

http://www.allaboutphoenix.com ....**Arizona Travel & Visitors Guide**

Sedona

http://www.sedonachamber.com ....**Sedona-Oak Creek Canyon Chamber of Commerce**

http://www.visitsedona.com **Information site for Sedona**

Tucson

http://www.boulevards.com/cities/tucson.html ....**Information site for Tucson**

http://www.ci.tucson.az.us ....**City of Tucson**

Arkansas, AR
The Natural State, Capital: Little Rock

http://www.ardemgaz.com.................................**Arkansas Democratic Gazette Newspaper site**

http://www.arkansas.com...................................**Arkansas Department of Parks and Tourism**

http://www.arktimes.com ....**Arkansas Times Newspaper site**

http://www.asl.lib.ar.us..**Arkansas State Library**

http://www.state.ar.us..**State of Arkansas**

Fort Smith

http://www.fortsmith.org.....................................**Fort Smith Conventions and Visitors Bureau**

Hot Springs

http://www.hotsprings.com ....**Information site about Hot Springs**

http://www.hotsprings.org ....**Hot Springs Advertising and Promotion Commission**

Little Rock

http://www.littlerock.com...................................**Little Rock Convention and Visitors Bureau**

North Little Rock
http://www.northlittlerock.org ....**North Little Rock Visitors Bureau**

Ozarks
http://www.ozarkmountainregion.com ....**Information site for the Ozark Mountains Region**

California, CA
The Golden State, Capital: Sacramento

http://gocalif.ca.gov ....**California Division of Tourism**
http://gocalifornia.about.com/travel ....**Information site for Southwest California**
http://www.ca.gov ....**State of California**
http://www.library.ca.gov ....**California State Library**

Anaheim
http://www.allaboutanaheim.com ....**Anaheim Travel and Visitors Guide**

Berkley
http://www.ci.berkeley.ca.us ....**City of Berkeley**

Big Sur
http://www.bigsurcalifornia.org ....**Big Sur Chamber of Commerce**

Los Angeles
http://losangeles.citysearch.com ....**Information site for Los Angeles**
http://www.cityofla.org ....**City of Los Angeles**
http://www.la.com ....**Information site for Los Angeles**
http://www.lacvb.com ....**Los Angeles Convention & Visitors Bureau**
http://www.latimes.com ....**Los Angeles Times Newspaper site**
http://www.losangeles.com ....**site for City of Los Angeles**

Monterey
http://www.monterey.com ....**Information site for the Monterey Peninsula**

Oakland
http://www.oakland.com ....**Information site for City of Oakland**

Palm Springs
http://www.allaboutpalmsprings.com ....**Palm Springs, CA Travel and Visitors Guide**

http://www.desert-resorts.com ....Guide to Palm Springs Desert Resorts

Palo Alto

http://www.boulevards.com/paloalto ....Information site for City of Palo Alto

Sacramento

http://www.cityofsacramento.org ....Information site for City of Sacramento

http://sacramento.citysearch.com ....Information site for City of Sacramento

http://www.sacbee.com ....The Sacramento Bee Newspaper site

San Diego

http://www.boulevards.com/sandiego/index.html ....San Diego Hotels

http://sandiego.citysearch.com ....Information site for City of San Diego

http://www.allaboutsandiego.com ....San Diego Travel & Visitors Guide

http://www.gaslamp.com ....Information site for San Diego's Gas Lamp Quarter

http://www.infosandiego.com ....San Diego Visitor Information Center

http://www.sandiego.org ....San Diego Convention and Visitors Bureau

http://www.sannet.gov ....City of San Diego

http://www.sdinsider.com ....Information site for City of San Diego

http://www.sdro.com ....San Diego Restaurants and Entertainment Online

http://www.signonsandiego.com ....The San Diego Union-Tribune

San Fernando

http://www.valleyofthestars.org ....Information site for San Fernando Valley

http://www.economicalliance.org ....Economic Alliance of the San Fernando Valley

San Francisco

http://bayarea.citysearch.com ....Information site for The Bay Area

http://www.bayarea.com ....Information site for The Bay Area

http://www.bayinsider.com ....**Information site for The Bay Area**
http://www.bayinsider.com/partners/ktvu ......**KTVU Bay Area News**
http://www.bayinsider.com/partners/kicu ......**Action 36 Cable 6**
http://www.ci.sf.ca.us ....**City of San Francisco**
http://www.examiner.com ....**San Francisco Examiner Newspaper site**
http://www.fishermanswharf.org ....**Information site for San Francisco's Fisherman's Wharf**
http://www.goldengate.org ....**Golden Gate Bridge, Highway and Transportation District**
http://www.nps.gov/alcatraz ....**National Park Service Government Site for Alcatraz Island**
http://www.sanfrancisco.com ....**Information site for San Francisco**
http://www.sfgate.com/chronicle ....**San Francisco Chronicle Newspaper site**
http://www.sfguide.com ....**San Francisco Guide**
http://www.sfvisitor.org ....**San Francisco Convention & Visitors Bureau**

San Jose

http://sanjose.citysearch.com ....**Information site for City of Silicon Valley**
http://www.sanjose.com ....**Information site for City of San Jose**
http://www.sanjose.org ....**Convention & Visitors Bureau**

San Luis Obispo

http://boulevards.com/cities/sanluisobispo.html
....**Information site for City of San Luis Obispo**

Santa Barbara

http://www.boulevards.com/cities/santabarbara.html
....**Information site for City of Santa Barbara**

Santa Cruz

http://www.boulevards.com/cities/santacruz.html
....**Information site for City of Santa Cruz**

Sonoma County

http://boulevards.com/cities/sonoma.html .....**Information site for City of Sonoma** http://www.sonomacounty.com ....**Sonoma County Tourism Program**

Santa Monica

http://www.santamonica.com ....**Santa Monica Convention & Visitors Bureau**

Colorado, CO – The Centennial State, Capital: Denver

http://www.cde.state.co.us/index_library.htm
....**Colorado State Library**

http://www.colorado.com ....**Colorado Travel and Tourism**

http://www.colorado.gov ....**State of Colorado**

Colorado Springs

http://www.colorado-springs.com ....**Colorado Springs Government Site**

Denver

http://denver.citysearch.com ....**Information site for City of Denver**

http://www.allabout-denver.com ....**Denver, Colorado Travel & Visitors Guide**

http://www.denver.com ....**Information site for City of Denver**

http://www.denver.org ....**Denver Metro Convention & Visitors Bureau**

http://www.denvergov.org ....**City of Denver**

http://www.denverpost.com ....**Denver Post Newspaper site**

http://www.milehighcity.com ....**Denver, Colorado On-line Business & Tourism Guide**

http://insidedenver.com ....**Rocky Mountain News site**

http://web.vail.net ....**Information site for City of Vail Valley**

http://www.visitvailvalley.com ....**Vail Valley Chamber & Tourism Bureau**

Connecticut, CT – The Constitution State, Capital: Hartford

http://www.cslib.org ....**Connecticut State Library**

http://www.state.ct.us ....**State of Connecticut**

http://www.tourism.state.ct.us ....**Connecticut Tourism**

http://www.visitconnecticut.com ....**Information site for Cities of New England**

Hartford

http://www.ctnow.com .... **The Hartford Courant Newspaper site**

Delaware, DE – The Diamond State, Capital: Dover

http://visitors.delawareonline.com .... **Information site for City of Delaware**

http://www.delaware.com .... **Information site for City of Delaware**

http://www.delaware.gov .... **State of Delaware**

http://www.lib.de.us .... **Delaware State Library**

http://www.visitdelaware.com .... **Delaware Tourism Office**

Dover

http://www.cityofdover.com .... **City of Dover**

http://www.doverpost.com .... **Dover Post Newspaper site**

http://www.visitdover.com .... **Kent County Tourism Convention and Visitors Bureau**

Wilmington

http://www.wilmcvb.org .... **Greater Wilmington Convention & Visitors Bureau**

Regions

http://www.delmarweb.com .... **Information site for Delaware and Maryland**

Florida, FL – The Sunshine State, Capital: Tallahassee

http://www.absolutelyflorida.com .... **Information site for Florida**

http://www.dos.state.fl.us/dlis .... **Florida State Library**

http://www.floridainfo.com .... **Information site for Florida**

http://www.floridakeys.com .... **Florida Keys Travel Guide**

http://www.flausa.com .... **Official Tourism for State of Florida**

http://www.funandsun.com .... **Information site for Florida**

http://www.see-florida.com .... **Information site for Florida**

Captiva Island

http://www.captiva.com

Daytona Beach

http://www.daytonabeach.com .... **Daytona Beach Area Convention & Visitors Bureau**

Florida Keys

http://www.floridakeys.org .... **Florida Keys Visitor Centers**

http://www.fla-keys.com .... **Information site for Florida Keys and Key West Kissimmee**

Kissimmee

http://www.floridakiss.com .... **Kissimmee-St. Cloud Convention & Visitors Bureau**

Miami

http://miami.citysearch.com .... **Information site for City of Miami**

http://www.about.com/travel/gomiami .... **Information site for City of Miami**

http://www.allabout-miami.com .... **Miami, Florida Travel & Visitors Guide**

http://www.ci.miami.fl.us .... **City of Miami**

http://www.herald.com .... **Miami Herald Newspaper site**

http://www.miami.com/category/travel_and_visitors
.... **Information site for Miami**

http://www.nps.gov/ever .... **Everglades National Park Service Government site**

Orlando

http://orlando.citysearch.com .... **Information site for City of Orlando**

http://www.allabout-orlando.com .... **Information site for City of Orlando**

http://www.go2orlando.com .... **Information site for City of Orlando**

http://www.orlandocity.com .... **Information site for City of Orlando**

http://www.orlandoinfo.com .... **Orlando/Orange County Convention & Visitors Bureau**

St. Petersburg

http://www.stpetersburg.com .... **Information site for City of St. Petersburg**

http://www.stpete-clearwater.com .... **St. Petersburg/Clearwater Area Convention & Visitors Bureau**

Tallahassee

http://www.talgov.com .... **City of Tallahassee**

http://www.tallahassee.com .... **Tallahassee Democrat Newspaper site**

Tampa Bay
http://tampabay.citysearch.com ....**Information site for City of Tampa Bay**

Georgia, GA – The Peach State, Capital: Atlanta ......

http://www.georgia.org ....**Georgia Department of Industry, Trade & Tourism**
http://www.georgia.gov ....**State of Georgia**
http://www.gpls.public.lib.ga.us ....**Georgia State Library**

Atlanta
http://atlanta.citysearch.com ....**Information site for City of Atlanta**
http://boulevards.com/cities/atlanta.html ....**Information site for City of Atlanta**
http://www.accessatlanta.com/ajc ....**Atlanta Journal Constitution Newspaper site**
http://www.allabout-atlanta.com ....**Atlanta, GA Travel & Visitors Guide**
http://www.ci.atlanta.ga.us ....**City of Atlanta**

Savannah
http://www.savannah-visit.com ....**Savannah Convention & Visitors Bureau**
http://www.savannahnow.com ....**Savannah Morning News**

Hawaii, HI – The Aloha State, Capital: Honolulu
http://www.about.com/travel/gohawaii ....**Information site for Hawaii/South Pacific**
http://www.aloha-hawaii.com ....**Information site for Hawaii**
http://www.ehawaiigov.org ....**State of Hawaii**
http://www.gohawaii.com ....**Hawaii Visitors & Convention Bureau**
http://www.hawaii.com ....**Information site for Hawaii**
http://www.hcc.hawaii.edu/hspls ....**Hawaii State Library**
http://www.konaweb.com ....**Information site for City of Konaweb**
http://www.thisweek.com ....**Information site for Hawaii**

Honolulu
http://www.kauaivisitorsbureau.org ....**Kauai Visitors Bureau**
http://www.starbulletin.com ....**Honolulu Star-Bulletin Newspaper**

Kauai
http://www.travel-kauai.com ....**Information site for Kauai**
Maui
http://www.visitmaui.com ....**Maui Visitors Bureau**

Idaho, ID – The Gem State, Capital: Boise

http://www.accessidaho.org ....**State of Idaho**
http://www.idahostatesman.com ....**Idaho Statesman Newspaper site**
http://www.state.id.us/isl/hp.htm ....**Idaho State Library**
http://www.visitid.org ....**Idaho Department of Commerce**
Boise
http://www.boise.org ....**Boise Convention & Visitors Bureau**
http://www.ci.boise.id.us ....**City of Boise**
Sun Valley
http://www.sunvalley.com ....**Information site for City of Sun Valley**

Illinois, IL – The Prairie State, Capital: Springfield

http://www.cyberdriveillinois.com/library/isl/isl.html
....**Illinois State Library**
http://www.enjoyillinois.com
....**Illinois Department of Commerce & Community Affairs**
http://www.state.il.us ....**State of Illinois**
Chicago
http://boulevards.com/Chicago ....**Information site for Chicago**
http://centerstage.net/chicago/virtual-el ....**Information site for Chicago**
http://chicago.citysearch.com ....**Information site for Chicago**
http://www.allabout-chicago.com ....**Chicago, Illinois Travel & Visitors Guide**
http://www.artic.edu ....**The Art Institute of Chicago**
http://www.chicago.il.org ....**Chicago Convention & Tourism Bureau**
http://www.chicagotribune.com ....**Chicago Tribune Newspaper site**
http://www.cityofchicago.org ....**Official site for City of Chicago**

http://www.sears-tower.com ....**Sears Tower site**
http://www.suntimes.com ....**Chicago Sun-Times Newspaper site**

Springfield
http://www.sj-r.com ....**The State Journal Register Newspaper site**
http://www.springfield.il.us ....**City of Springfield**

Indiana, IN – The Hoosier State, Capital: Indianapolis

http://www.enjoyindiana.com ....**Indiana Tourism Division**
http://www.state.in.us ....**State of Indiana**
http://www.statelib.lib.in.us ....**Indiana State Library**
http://www.visitindiana.net ....**Information site for Indiana**

Indianapolis
http://www.indianapolis.com ....**Information site for City of Indianapolis**
http://www.indy.org ....**Indianapolis Convention & Visitors Association**
http://www.indygov.org ....**City of Indianapolis**
http://www.indystar.com ....**Indianapolis Star Newspaper site**

Iowa, IA – The Hawkeye State, Capital: Des Moines . . .

http://www.jeonet.com/amanas ....**Amana Colonies Convention & Visitors Bureau**
http://www.silo.lib.ia.us ....**Iowa State Library**
http://www.state.ia.us ....**State of Iowa**
http://www.traveliowa.com ....**Iowa Tourism Office**

Des Moines
http://www.ci.des-moines.ia.us ....**City of Des Moines**
http://www.dmregister.com ....**Des Moines Register Newspaper site**

Sioux City
http://www.sioux-city.org ....**City of Sioux City**

Kansas, KS – The Sunflower State, Capital: Topeka

http://skyways.lib.ks.us ....**Kansas State Library**
http://www.accesskansas.org ....**State of Kansas**
http://www.kansascommerce.com ....**Kansas Department of Commerce & Housing**

Kansas City
http://www.experiencekc.com ....Information site for Kansas City

Lawrence
http://www.visitlawrence.com ....Lawrence Convention & Visitors Bureau

Topeka
http://www.cjonline.com ....Topeka Capital Journal Newspaper site
http://www.topeka.org ....City of Topeka

Kentucky, KY – The Bluegrass State, Capital: Frankfort

http://www.kdla.state.ky.us ....Kentucky State Library
http://www.kentuckytourism.com ....Official Kentucky Tourism site
http://www.kydirect.net ....State of Kentucky Official Tourism site
http://www.tourky.com ....Kentucky Tourism Council

Louisville
http://www.courier-journal.com ....The Courier-Journal Newspaper site
http://www.louisville-visitors.com ....Greater Louisville Convention & Visitors Bureau
http://www.louky.org ....City of Louisville

Louisiana, LA – The Pelican State, Capital: Baton Rouge

New Orleans
http://neworleans.citysearch.com ....Information site for City of New Orleans
http://www.allabout-neworleans.com ....New Orleans, LA Travel & Visitors Guide
http://www.bigeasy.com ....New Orleans Guide
http://www.bestofneworleans.com ....Information site for City of New Orleans
http://www.frenchquarter.com ....Information site for French Quarters in New Orleans
http://www.gumbopages.com ....Information site for City of New Orleans
http://www.insideneworleans.com ....Information site for City of New Orleans
http://www.infolouisiana.com ....State of Louisiana

http://www.louisianatravel.com .... **Official site of Louisiana Tourism**
http://www.mardigras.com .... **New Orleans Mardi Gras site**
http://www.neworleansonline.com .... **Official site for the City of New Orleans**
http://www.new-orleans.la.us .... **City of New Orleans**
http://www.nola.com .... **Information site for the City of New Orleans**
http://www.state.lib.la.us .... **Louisiana State Library**
http://www.theadvocate.com .... **The Advocate Newspaper site**

Baton Rouge

http://www.ci.baton-rouge.la.us .... **City of Baton Rouge**

Regions

http://www.crt.state.la.us/crt/tourism.htm ...... **Louisiana Department of Tourism**

Maine, ME – The Pine Tree State, Capital: Augusta

http://maineguide.com/travel .... **Maine Travel Center**
http://www.maine.gov .... **Official Maine Government site**
http://www.chickadee.com/lobster .... **Information site for Southern Maine Seacoast**
http://www.mainetoday.com .... **Blethen Maine Newspapers**
http://www.mainetourism.com .... **Information site for Maine**
http://www.state.me.us/msl/index.html .... **Maine State Library**
http://www.visit-maine.com .... **Information site for New England Coast**
http://www.visitmaine.com .... **Maine Office of Tourism**

Augusta

http://www.ci.augusta.me.us .... **City of Augusta**

Portland

http://www.portland.com .... **Press Herald Online**

Maryland, MD – The Old Line State, Capital: Annapolis

http://www.beach-net.com .... **Information site for Delaware/Maryland Shore**
http://www.delmarweb.com .... **Information site for Delaware/Maryland**
http://www.mdisfun.org .... **Official site of Maryland Tourism**
http://www.mec.state.md.us .... **State of Maryland**

http://www.pratt.lib.md.us/slrc/index.html ....**Maryland State Library**
http://www.tilghmanisland.com ....**Tilghman Island Maryland Official Travel Guide**

Annapolis

http://www.ci.annapolis.md.us ....**City of Annapolis**
http://www.hometownannapolis.com ....**Capital Gazette Newspaper site**

Baltimore

http://baltimore.citysearch.com ....**Information site for City of Baltimore**
http://www.boulevards.com/cities/baltimore.html ....**Information site for City of Baltimore**
http://www.ci.baltimore.md.us ....**City of Baltimore**

Massachusetts, MA – The Bay State, Capital: Boston

http://www.mass.gov ....**State of Massachusetts**
http://www.massvacation.com ....**Massachusetts Office of Travel and Tourism**
http://www.mlin.lib.ma.us ....**Massachusetts State Library**
http://www.visit-massachusetts.com ....**Information site for New England**

Berkshires

http://www.berkshires.org ....**Berkshires Visitors Bureau**

Boston

http://boston.citysearch.com ....**Information site for City of Boston**
http://www.boulevards.com/cities/boston.html ....**Information site for City of Boston**
http://www.allaboutboston.com ....**Boston, MA Travel & Visitors Guide**
http://www.boston.com ....**Information site for City of Boston**
http://www.bostonbyfoot.com ....**Guided Tours of Boston**
http://www.bostonherald.com ....**Boston Herald Newspaper site**
http://www.bostonphoenix.com ....**Information site for Boston Phoenix**
http://www.bostonusa.com ....**Greater Boston Convention & Visitors Bureau**
http://www.bso.org ....**Boston Symphony Orchestra**
http://www.ci.boston.ma.us ....**City of Boston**

Cape Cod

http://www.allcapecod.com ....**The Cape Cod Information Center**

http://www.capecodchamber.org ....**Cape Cod Chamber of Commerce**

Martha's Vineyard

http://www.mvy.com ....**Martha's Vineyard Chamber of Commerce**

Nantucket Island

http://www.allcapecod.com/nantucket ....**Nantucket Island Information Center**

http://www.salem.org ....**Salem Office of Tourism & Cultural Affairs**

Michigan, MI – The Wolverine State, Capital: Lansing

http://www.libofmich.lib.mi.us ....**Michigan State Library**

http://www.michigan.org ....**Information site for Michigan**

http://www.michigan.gov .... **State of Michigan**

http://www.yesmichigan.com/cities **The Michigan Travel Companion**

Detroit

http://detroit.citysearch.com ....**Information site for City of Detroit**

http://www.detroit.com ....**Information site for City of Detroit**

http://www.detnews.com ....**Detroit News Newspaper site**

http://www.freep.com ....**Detroit Free Press Newspaper site**

http://www.visitdetroit.com ....**Official Tourism site for Metro Detroit**

Mackinac Island

http://www.sheplerswww.com ....**Shepler's Mackinac Island Ferry**

South Haven

http://www.bythebigbluewater.com ....**South Haven Visitors Bureau**

Traverse City

http://www.mytraversecity.com ....**Traverse City Convention & Visitors Bureau**

Region

http://www.michiweb.com ....**Northern Michigan Connection**

Minnesota, MN – The North Star State, Capital: St. Paul

http://cfl.state.mn.us/library ....**Minnesota State Library**
http://www.exploreminnesota.com ....**Minnesota Office of Tourism**
http://www.state.mn.us ....**State of Minnesota**
Minneapolis/St. Paul
http://twincities.citysearch.com ....**Information site for Twin Cities**
http://www.citypages.com ....**Twin Cities Online News**
http://www.downtownmpls.com ....**Minneapolis Downtown Council**
http://www.minneapolis.org ....**Greater Minneapolis Convention & Visitors**
http://www.twincities.com ....**Information site for the Twin Cities**
http://www.startribune.com ....**Star Tribune Newspaper site**
http://www.saint-paul.com ....**Saint Paul City Guide**
http://www.stpaul.gov ....**City of Saint Paul**

Mississippi, MS – The Magnolia State, Capital: Jackson

http://www.mlc.lib.ms.us ....**Mississippi State Library**
http://www.ms.gov ....**State of Mississippi**
http://www.visitmississippi.org ....**Mississippi Division of Tourism**

Jackson
http://www.visitjackson.com .... **Convention & Visitors Bureau**
http://www.clarionledger.com ....**Clarion Ledger Newspaper site**
Vicksburg
http://www.vicksburgcvb.org ....**Vicksburg Convention and Visitors Bureau**

Missouri, MO – The Show Me State, Capital: Jefferson City

http://www.sos.state.mo.us/library ....**Missouri State Library**
http://www.missouritourism.com ....**Missouri Tourism**
http://www.mostateparks.com ....**Missouri State Parks and Historic Sites**
http://www.state.mo.us ....**State of Missouri**
Jefferson City
http://www.newstribune.com ....**Jefferson City News Tribune Newspaper site**

Kansas City
http://www.kansascity.com ....**The Kansas City Star Newspaper site**
http://www.kcmo.org ....**City of Kansas City**
St. Louis
http://stlouis.citysearch.com ....**Information site for City of St. Louis**
http://stlouis.missouri.org ....**City of St. Louis**
http://www.allaboutstlouis.com ....**Information site for St. Louis**
http://www.stlouis.com ....**Information site for St. Louis**
http://www.stltoday.com ....**Information site for St. Louis**

Montana, MT – The Treasure State, Capital: Helena

http://msl.state.mt.us ....**Montana State Library**
http://www.visitmt.com ....**Travel Montana Tourist site**
http://www.wintermt.com ....**Winter in Montana**
Helena
http://www.helenair.com ....**The Independent Record Newspaper site**

Nebraska, NE – The Cornhusker State, Capital: Lincoln

http://visitnebraska.org ....**Nebraska Division of Travel and Tourism**
http://www.state.ne.us ....**State of Nebraska**
http://www.nlc.state.ne.us ....**Nebraska State Library**
Lincoln
http://www.lincoln.org ....**Lincoln Convention & Visitors Bureau**
http://www.journalstar.com ....**Journal Star Newspaper site**

Nevada, NV – The Sagebrush State, Capital: Carson City

http://dmla.clan.lib.nv.us/docs/nsla ....**Nevada State Library**
http://www.state.nv.us ....**State of Nevada**
http://www.travelnevada.com ....**Nevada Commission on Tourism**
Carson City
http://www.carson-city.nv.us ....**City of Carson City**
Hoover Dam
http://www.hooverdam.usbr.gov ....**Hoover Dam Government National Historic Landmark**

Las Vegas

http://lasvegas.citysearch.com .... **Information site for Las Vegas**
http://www.allabout-lasvegas.com .... **Information site for Las Vegas**
http://www.a2zlasvegas.com .... **Las Vegas Visitors Guide**
http://www.ilovevegas.com .... **The Las Vegas Guide**
http://www.lasvegas.com .... **Information site for Las Vegas**
http://www.pcap.com .... **Las Vegas Leisure Guide**
http://www.reviewjournal.com .... **Las Vegas Review Journal Newspaper site**
http://www.vegas.com .... **Official Las Vegas Travel Site**
http://www.vegasfreedom.com .... **Las Vegas Convention & Visitors Authority for Las Vegas Vacations**

Reno

http://www.playreno.com .... **Reno-Sparks Convention and Visitors Authority**

New Hampshire, NH – The Granite State, Capital: Concord

http://www.state.nh.us .... **State of New Hampshire**
http://www.state.nh.us/nhsl .... **New Hampshire State Library**
http://www.visitnh.gov... **New Hampshire Division of Travel & Tourism Development**
http://www.visit-newhampshire.com .... **Information site for New England**
http://www.whitemtn.org .... **Official New Hampshire White Mountains Visitors Bureau**

Concord

http://www.ci.concord.nh.us .... **City of Concord**
http://www.cmonitor.com .... **Concord Monitor Newspaper site**
http://www.theunionleader.com .... **The Union Leader Newspaper site**

New Jersey, NJ – The Garden State, Capital: Trenton

http://www.njstatelib.org .... **New Jersey State Library**
http://www.state.nj.us .... **State of New Jersey**
http://www.state.nj.us/travel .... **New Jersey Travel & Tourism**
http://www.virtualnjshore.com .... **Guide to the Jersey Shore**
http://www.weirdnj.com .... **Weird NJ Guide to Local Legends & Best Kept Secrets**

Atlantic City

http://www.acnights.com ....**Atlantic City Hotels and Casinos**

http://www.allabout-atlanticcity.com ....**Information site for Atlantic City**

http://www.atlanticcitynj.com ....**Atlantic City, New Jersey Travel & Visitors Guide**

New Mexico, NM – The Land of Enchantment, Capital: Santa Fe

http://www.newmexico.org ....**New Mexico Department of Tourism Official site**

http://www.nmculture.org ....**The New Mexico Cultural Treasures**

http://www.state.nm.us ....**State of New Mexico**

http://www.stlib.state.nm.us ....**New Mexico State Library**

Albuquerque

http://www.abqcvb.org ....**Albuquerque Convention & Visitors Bureau**

http://www.abqjournal.com ....**Albuquerque Journal Newspaper site**

Santa Fe

http://www.santafe.org ....**Santa Fe Convention & Visitors Bureau**

http://www.sfnewmexican.com ....**Santa Fe New Mexican Newspaper site**

New York, NY – The Empire State, Capital: Albany

http://www.canals.state.ny.us ....**The NY State Canal System**

http://www.iloveny.com ....**Information site for New York City**

http://www.nysl.nysed.gov ....**New York State Library**

Albany

http://www.albany.org ....**Albany County Convention & Visitors Bureau**

http://www.timesunion.com ....**Times Union Newspaper site**

Lake Placid

http://www.lakeplacid.com ....**Lake Placid in the Adirondacks**

New York

http://www.allabout-newyorkcity.com ....**Information site for New York City**

http://www.mostnewyork.com ....**Daily News Newspaper site**
http://www.nationalgeographic.com/features/97/nyunderground
....**New York Underground**
http://www.newyork.com ....**New York City Guide**
http://www.nyc.com ....**Information site for New York City**
http://www.nyc.gov ....**New York City Government site**
http://www.nycvisit.com ....**New York City Official Tourism site**
http://www.nypostonline.com ....**New York Post Newspaper site**
http://www.nytourist.com ....**New York City Tourism**
http://www.nytimes.com ....**New York Times Newspaper site**
http://www.nytoday.com ....**New York Times-NY Today**
http://www.pbs.org/wnet/newyork/hidden ...**Hidden New York**
http://www.timeoutny.com/cityguide ....**Time Out New York**

Western

http://www.westernny.com ....**Western NY Travel Guide**

Upstate

http://www.roundthebend.com ....**Upstate NY Travel Guide**

North Carolina, NC – The Tar Heel State, Capital: Raleigh

http://statelibrary.dcr.state.nc.us ....**North Carolina State Library**
http://www.ncgov.com ....**State of North Carolina**
http://www.visitnc.com ....**North Carolina Department of Commerce**

Ashville

http://www.ashevillechamber.org ....**Asheville Area Chamber of Commerce**

Charlotte

http://charlotte.citysearch.com ....**Information site for City of Charlotte**

Durham

http://www.durham-nc.com ....**Durham Convention & Visitors Bureau**

Greensboro

http://www.greensboronc.org ....**Greensboro Convention & Visitors Bureau**

Outer Banks
http://www.outerbanks.com ....**Outer Banks of North Carolina**
Raleigh
http://www.raleighcvb.org ....**Raleigh Convention & Visitors Bureau**
http://www.newsobserver.com ....**News Observer Newspaper site**
Raleigh/Durham
http://triangle.citysearch.com ....**Information site for the Raleigh/Durham area**
Winston-Salem
http://www.journalnow.com ....**The Winston-Salem Journal Newspaper site**
http://www.wscvb.com ....**Winston-Salem Convention & Visitors Bureau**

North Dakota, ND – The Peace Garden State, Capital: Bismark

http://ndsl.lib.state.nd.us ....**North Dakota State Library**
http://www.bismarcktribune.com ....**Bismark Tribune Newspaper site**
http://www.in-forum.com ....**In-Forum Newspaper site**
http://www.discovernd.com ....**North Dakota's State Government Information**

Ohio, OH – The Buckeye State, Capital: Columbus

http://winslo.state.oh.us ....**Ohio State Library**
http://www.ohiotourism.com ....**Ohio Tourism**
http://www.ohiotravel.org.................................**Ohio Travel Association**
Cincinnati
http://boulevards.com/cities/cincinnati ....**Information site for Cincinnati**
http://cincinnati.citysearch.com ....**Information site for Cincinnati**
http://www.enquirer.com ....**Cincinnati Enquirer Newspaper site**
Cleveland
http://cleveland.citysearch.com ....**Information site for Cleveland**
http://www.cleve-visitors-guide.com...............**Greater Cleveland Visitors Guide**
http://www.cleveland.com ....**Cleveland Plain Dealer Newspaper site**

Columbus

http://columbus.citysearch.com ....**Information site for City of Columbus**

http://www.dispatch.com ....**Columbus Dispatch Newspaper site**

http://www.columbuscvb.org ....**Columbus Convention & Visitors Bureau**

Oklahoma, OK – The Sooner State, Capital: Oklahoma City

http://www.odl.state.ok.us ....**Oklahoma State Library**

http://www.state.ok.us ....**State of Oklahoma**

http://www.travelok.com ....**Official Oklahoma Tourism Site**

Oklahoma City

http://www.newsok.com ....**Oklahoman Newspaper site**

http://www.okccvb.org ....**Oklahoma City Convention & Visitors Bureau**

Tulsa

http://www.tulsaweb.com ....**Information site for Tulsa**

http://www.tulsaworld.com ....**Tulsa World Newspaper site**

Oregon, OR – The Beaver State, Capital: Salem

http://www.oregon.gov ....**State of Oregon**

http://www.osl.state.or.us/home ....**Oregon State Library**

http://www.traveloregon.com ....**Oregon Tourism Commission site**

Portland

http://boulevards.com/cities/portland-or ....**Information site for Portland**

http://www.pova.com ....**Portland Oregon Visitors Association**

http://www.oregonlive.com ....**Information site for Oregon**

http://www.travelportland.com ....**Portland Oregon Visitors Association**

Salem

http://www.statesmanjournal.com ....**Information site for Salem**

Southern Oregon

http://www.sova.org ....**Information site for Southern Oregon**

Roseburg

http://www.visitroseburg.com ....**Roseburg Visitors & Convention Bureau**

Pennsylvania, PA – The Keystone State, Capital: Harrisburg

http://www.experiencepa.com ....**Official Pennsylvania site for Travel & Tourism**
http://www.fallinpa.com ....**Pennsylvania in the Fall**
http://www.state.pa.us/visit ....**Pennsylvania Official State site**
http://www.statelibrary.state.pa.us ....**Pennsylvania State Library**

Erie
http://www.eriepa.com ....**Adventures in Northwest PA**

Gettysburg
http://www.gettysburgaddress.com ....**Gettysburg Tourist site**

Harrisburg
http://www.visithhc.com ....**Harrisburg-Hershey-Carlisle Welcome Center**

Lancaster
http://www.800padutch.com ....**The Pennsylvania Dutch County Welcome Center**
http://www.lancastercounty.com ....**Information site for Lancaster County**
http://www.padutchcountry.com ....**Pennsylvania Dutch Convention & Visitors Bureau**

Philadelphia
http://philadelphia.citysearch.com ....**Information site for Philadelphia**
http://www.pcvb.org ....**Pennsylvania Convention & Visitors Bureau**
http://www.philadelphia.com ....**Information site for Philadelphia**
http://www.phila-tribune.com ....**Philadelphia Tribune Newspaper site**
http://www.philly.com ....**Philadelphia Inquirer Newspaper site**

Pittsburgh
http://boulevards.com/cities/pittsburgh ....**Information site for Pittsburgh**
http://pittsburgh.citysearch.com ....**Information site for Pittsburgh**
http://www.post-gazette.com ....**Pittsburgh Post Gazette Newspaper site**

Rhode Island, RI – The Ocean State, Capital: Providence

http://www.coastalvillages.com ....Coastal Villages of Rhode Island & Massachusetts
http://www.olis.state.ri.us ....Rhode Island State Library
http://www.state.ri.us ....State of Rhode Island
http://www.visitri.com ....Information site for New England
http://www.visitrhodeisland.com ....Official Rhode Island Tourism site

Newport
http://www.gonewport.com ....Official site for Newport, RI

Providence
http://www.projo.com ....The Providence Journal Newspaper site
http://www.providencecvb.com ....The Providence Warwick Convention & Visitors Bureau
http://www.providenceri.com ....City of Providence

South Carolina, SC – The Palmetto State, Capital: Columbia

http://www.beaufortgazette.com ....Beaufort Gazette Newspaper site
http://www.state.sc.us/scsl ....South Carolina State Library
http://www.thestate.com ....The State Newspaper site
http://www.travelsc.com ....South Carolina Department of Parks, Recreation & Tourism

Charleston
http://www.charleston.net ....The Post and Courier Newspaper site
http://www.charlestoncvb.com ....Charleston Convention & Visitors Bureau
http://www.spoletousa.org ....Spoleto Festival USA
http://www.tourcharleston.com ....Walking Tours of Charleston

Hilton Head
http://www.hiltonheadisland.org ....Hilton Head Island Chamber of Commerce

Myrtle Beach
http://www.myrtlebeachlive.com ....Myrtle Beach Area's Official Online Vacation Guide

South Dakota, SD – The Coyote State, Capital: Pierre

http://www.sdstatelibrary.com ....**South Dakota State Library**
http://www.state.sd.us ....**South Dakota Official State site**
http://www.travelsd.com ....**South Dakota Travel Information**

Pierre
http://www.pierre.org ....**Pierre Chamber of Commerce**

Rapid City
http://www.rapidcitycvb.com ....**Rapid City Convention & Visitors Bureau**

Tennessee, TN – The Volunteer State, Capital: Nashville

http://www.state.tn.us/sos/statelib ....**Tennessee State Library**
http://www.tennesseeanytime.org ....**State of Tennessee**
http://www.tennweb.com ....**Information site for Tennessee**
http://www.tourism.state.tn.us ....**Tennessee State Department of Tourism Development**

Chattanooga
http://www.chattanooga.net ....**Information site for City of Chattanooga**

Knoxville
http://www.knoxville.org ....**Knoxville Convention & Visitors Bureau**

Memphis
http://www.cityofmemphis.org ....**City of Memphis**
http://www.gomemphis.com ....**The Commercial Appeal Newspaper site**
http://www.memphis.com ....**Information site for City of Memphis**

Nashville
http://boulevards.com/cities/nashville .... **site for City of Nashville**
http://nashville.citysearch.com ....**Information site for City of Nashville**
http://www.allabout-nashville.com ....**Nashville, Tennessee Travel & Visitors Guide**
http://www.nashville.gov ....**Metropolitan Government of Nashville**
http://www.nashvillecvb.com ....**Nashville Convention & Visitors Bureau**
http://www.tennessean.com ....**The Tennessean Newspaper site**

http://www.tennesseetribune.com ....**Tennessee Tribune Newspaper site**

Smoky Mountains

http://www.rodsguide.com ....**Information site for Smoky Mountains**

http://www.smokymountains.org ....**Information site for City of Townsend, TN**

http://www.thesmokies.com ....**Information site for Smoky Mountains**

Texas, TX – The Lone Star State, Capital: Austin

http://www.state.tx.us ....**State of Texas**

http://www.traveltex.com ....**Texas Travel & Vacation Destinations**

http://www.tsl.state.tx.us ....**Texas State Library**

Abilene

http://www.reporter-news.com ....**Abilene Reporter News Newspaper site**

Amarillo

http://www.amarillo-cvb.org ....**Amarillo Convention & Visitors Bureau**

Arlington

http://www.arlington.org ....**Arlington Convention & Visitors Bureau**

Austin

http://austin.citysearch.com ....**Information site for City of Austin**

http://boulevards.com/Austin ....**Information site for City of Austin**

http://www.austin360.com/acvb ....**Austin Convention & Visitors Bureau**

http://www.austin360.com/aas ....**Austin American Statesman Newspaper site**

http://www.ci.austin.tx.us ....**City of Austin**

Corpus Christi

http://www.corpuschristi-tx-cvb.org ....**Corpus Christi Convention & Visitors Bureau**

Dallas

http://www.allabout-dallas.com ....**Dallas, TX Travel & Visitors Guide**

http://www.dallas.com ....**Information site for Dallas**

http://www.dallascityhall.com ....**City of Dallas**
http://www.dallascvb.com ....**Dallas Convention & Visitors Bureau**
http://www.dallasnews.com ....**The Dallas Morning News Newspaper site**
http://www.dallasobserver.com ....**Dallas Observer Newspaper site**
http://www.guidelive.com ....**Information site for Dallas/Fort Worth area**

East Texas
http://www.easttexasguide.com ....**East Texas Tourism Association**

Fort Worth
http://www.fortworth.com ....**Fort Worth Convention & Visitors Bureau**

Houston
http://houston.citysearch.com ....**Information site for Houston**
http://www.cityofhouston.gov ....**City of Houston**
http://www.houston.com ....**Information site for Houston**
http://www.houstonchronicle.com ....**Houston Chronicle Newspaper site**
http://www.houston-guide.com ....**Official Guide to Houston**

San Antonio
http://sanantonio.citysearch.com ....**Information site for San Antonio**
http://www.sanantonio.com ....**Information site for San Antonio**
http://www.sanantoniocvb.com ....**San Antonio Convention & Visitors Bureau**

South Padre Island
http://www.sopadre.com ....**South Padre Island Official Tourism site**

Utah, UT – The Beehive State, Capital: Salt Lake City

http://library.utah.gov ....**Utah State Library**
http://www.utah.com ....**Utah Adventure Travel**
http://www.utah.gov ....**State of Utah**

Moab
http://www.moab-utah.com ....**Moab, Utah Tourism Information**

Salt Lake City
http://utah.citysearch.com ....**Information site for Utah**

http://www.ci.slc.ut.us ....City of Salt Lake City
http://www.sltrib.com ....The Salt Lake Tribune Newspaper site
http://www.visitsaltlake.com ....Salt Lake Convention & Visitors Bureau

Vermont, VT – The Green Mountain State, Capital: Montpelier

http://dol.state.vt.us ....Vermont State Library
http://www.1-800-vermont.com ....Official Vermont Tourism site
http://www.discover-vermont.com ....Vermont Travel Guide
http://www.state.vt.us ....State of Vermont
http://www.visit-vermont.com ....Information site for New England

Montpelier
http://montpelier-vt.org ....City of Montpelier
http://www.timesargus.com ....Times Argus Newspaper site

Virginia, VA – The Old Dominion State, Capital: Richmond

http://www.lva.lib.va.us ....Virginia State Library
http://www.state.va.us ....State of Virginia
http://www.vatc.org ....Virginia Tourism Corporation
http://www.virginia.org ....Information site for Virginia

Mount Vernon
http://www.mountvernon.org ....George Washington's Mount Vernon Estate & Gardens

Newport News
http://www.newport-news.org ....Newport News Tourism

Richmond
http://richmond.citysearch.com ....Information site for City of Richmond
http://www.richmondva.org ....Richmond Metro Convention & Visitors Bureau

Roanoke
http://www.visitroanoke.com ....Roanoke Valley Convention & Visitors Bureau

Virginia Beach
http://www.allaboutvirginiabeach.com ....Virginia Beach, VA Travel & Visitors Guide

Williamsburg

http://www.history.org .... **Information site to Colonial Williamsburg**

http://www.williamsburg.com .... **Official Guide to Williamsburg, VA**

Washington, WA – The Evergreen State, Capital: Olympia

http://access.wa.gov .... **State of Washington**

http://www.statelib.wa.gov .... **Washington State Library**

http://www.tourism.wa.gov .... **Official site for Washington State Tourism**

http://www.travel-in-wa.com .... **Washington State Travel**

San Juan Islands

http://www.sanjuanguide.com .... **Information site for San Juan Islands, WA**

Seattle

http://seattle.citysearch.com .... **Information site for Seattle**

http://www.allaboutseattle.com .... **Seattle, WA Travel & Visitors Guide**

http://www.seattle.com .... **Information site for Seattle**

http://www.seeseattle.org .... **Seattle's Convention & Visitors Bureau**

Spokane

http://www.spokane.org .... **Information site for City of Spokane**

Washington D.C. – District of Columbia, United States Capital

http://www.dcpages.com .... **Information site for Washington, DC**

http://www.exploredc.org...................................... **Information site for Washington, DC**

http://www.thedistrict.com .... **Washington DC Online Travel Guide**

http://www.washington.org .... **Official Tourism site for Washington DC**

West Virginia, WV – The Mountain State, Capital: Charleston

http://www.callwva.com .... **West Virginia Division of Tourism**
http://www.state.wv.us .... **State of West Virginia**
http://www.westvirginia.com .... **Official West Virginia Vacation Guide**
http://www.wvlc.wvnet.edu .... **West Virginia State Library**

Charleston
http://www.charlestonwv.com .... **Charleston Convention & Visitors Bureau**
http://www.dailymail.com .... **Charleston Daily Mail Newspaper site**
http://www.wvgazette.com .... **The Charleston Gazette Newspaper site**

Harper's Ferry
http://www.nps.gov/hafe .... **Harper's Ferry Historic National Park Service Government Site**

Wisconsin, WI – The Badger State, Capital: Madison

http://tourism.state.wi.us .... **Official Wisconsin Tourism site**
http://www.dpi.state.wi.us/dlcl .... **Wisconsin State Library**
http://www.travelwisconsin.com .... **Wisconsin Department of Tourism**
http://www.wisconsin.gov .... **State of Wisconsin**

Madison
http://www.boulevards.com/cities/madison.html
.... **Information site for Madison**
http://www.ci.madison.wi.us .... **City of Madison**
http://www.visitmadison.com .... **Greater Madison Convention & Visitors**

Milwaukee
http://www.ci.mil.wi.us .... **City of Milwaukee**
http://www.jsonline.com .... **Milwaukee Journal Sentinel Newspaper site**
http://www.milwaukee.com .... **Information site for Milwaukee**
http://www.milwaukee.org .... **Greater Milwaukee Convention & Visitors**

Wisconsin Dells

http://www.dells.com ....**Wisconsin Dells Premier Online Resource**

Wyoming, WY – The Cowboy State

http://www.state.wy.us ....**State of Wyoming**

http://www-wsl.state.wy.us ....**Wyoming State Library**

http://www.wyomingtourism.org ....**Wyoming Tourism**

Cheyenne

http://www.cheyenne.org ....**The Cheyenne Convention & Visitors Bureau**

http://www.cheyennecity.org ....**City of Cheyenne**

http://www.wyomingnews.com ....**Wyoming Tribune Eagle Newspaper site**

Jackson Hole

http://www.jacksonholenet.com ....**Information site for city of Jackson Hole**

Destination by Country

Listed below are sites based on destination by country. Some are private sites that feature major attraction areas whereas others are official U.S. Government sites that start with *http://lcweb2.loc.gov* or convention and visitor bureaus. Official country and tourism bureaus are denoted with ***bold italics.*** Not all countries have official tourism sites, yet it's possible to find tourism information on the Web. For more information on tourism, you can visit *Johnny Jet Code: Tourist Office* and *Johnny Jet Code: Visitor Bureaus* and you will find many resources. If there is a particular city or country that you are looking for that cannot be found, One World Nations Online at *www.nationsonline.org* or a tourism office can be found at *www.towd.com* or visiting the chapter International Travel and looking in the section on International Destinations will help you find a particular country. The section on City Tourism provides much information on specific cities you may find listed.

Countries

Northeastern Africa

http://www.africaguide.com..............................**Guide to Africa**
http://www.africaonline.com ....Information site for Africa
Egypt, EG - Arab Republic of Egypt, Capital: Cairo
http://www.egypttoday.com ....**Egypt Today The Magazine of Egypt**
http://www.touregypt.net...................................**Official Tourism site of Egypt**
Ethiopia, ET - Federal Democratic Republic of Ethiopia, Capital: Addis Ababa
http://lcweb2.loc.gov/frd/cs/ettoc.html .............**U.S. Government Site**
http://www.cyberethiopia.com ....**Information site for Ethiopia**
http://www.visitethiopia.org.............................. **Ethiopian Tourist Commission**
Kenya, KE - Republic of Kenya, Capital: Nairobi
http://www.kenyaweb.com ....**Kenya's Internet Resource**
http://www.magicalkenya.com...........................**Kenya Tourist Board**
http://www.visit-kenya.com..............................**Information site for Kenya**
Mauritius, MU - Republic of Mauritius, Capital: Port Louis

http://www.mauritius.net....................................Information site for Mauritius
http://www.isle-mauritius.com ....Information site for Isle Mauritius

Somalia, SO – Capital: Mogadishu

http://lcweb2.loc.gov/frd/cs/sotoc.html ............U.S. Government Site Information on Somalia
http://www.unsomalia.org ....United Nations Somalia

Sudan, SD - Republic of the Sudan, Capital: Khartoum

http://www.sudanembassy.org ....Embassy Republic of Sudan
http://www.sudan.net ....Information site for Sudan

Tanzania, TZ - United Republic of Tanzania, Capital: Dar Es Salaam

http://www.intotanzania.com ....Tanzania—African Travel Resource
http://www.tanzania-web.com ....Tanzania Travel Board Official Web site

Uganda, UG - Republic of Uganda, Capital: Kampala

http://www.africa-insites.com/uganda ....Uganda Travel Guide
http://www.visituganda.com ....Uganda Tourist Board

Zanzibar

http://www.allaboutzanzibar.com ....Zanzibar—African Travel Resource
http://www.zanzibar.net ....Zanzibar Travel Network

Zaire

http://www.africaguide.com/country/zaire .....The Africa Guide—Zaire

Northern Africa

Algeria, DZ - Democratic and Popular Republic of Algeria, Capital: Algiers

http://i-cias.com/m.s/algeria...............................Information site for Algeria
http://lcweb2.loc.gov/frd/cs/dztoc.html ............U.S. Government site for Algeria

Libya, LY - Socialist People's Libyan Arab Jamahiriya, Capital: Tripoli

http://www.geocities.com/Athens/8744 ....Information site for Libya
http://www.tripoli-city.org................................Tripoli, Libya City Guide

Morocco, MA - Kingdom of Morocco, Capital: Rabat

http://lexicorient.com/morocco ....Adventures of Morocco
http://tayara.com/club/mrocbd1.htm ....Information site for Morocco
http://www.mincom.gov.ma/english/e_page.html
....Information site for Morocco
http://www.morocco.com ....Internet Guide to Morocco
http://www.tourism-in-morocco.com ....Tourism in Morocco

Senegal, SN - Republic of Senegal, Capital: Dakar
http://www.earth2000.com ....**Information site for The Republic of Senegal**
http://www.senegal-online.com ....**Information site for Senegal**
Tunisia
http://www.tourismtunisia.com ....**The Tunisian National Tourism Office**
http://www.tunisiaonline.com ....**News and Information on Tunisia**

Southern Africa

Angola, AO - Republic of Angola, Capital: Luanda
http://lcweb2.loc.gov/frd/cs/aotoc.html ............**U.S. Government site for Angola**
http://www.angola.org ....**The Embassy of The Republic of Angola**
Malawi, MW - Republic of Malawi, Capital: Lilongwe
http://www.malawiholiday.com ....**Your Holiday in Malawi**
Namibia, NA - Republic of Namibia, Capital: Windhoek
http://www.namibia-tourism.com ....**Namibia Tourism Board**
http://www.natron.net/etour.htm......................**Namibia Travel and Information System**
South Africa, ZA - Republic of South Africa, Capital: Pretoria
http://www.capeconnected.co.za ....**Cape Town Travel Guide**
http://www.esafrica.com ....**Guide to Eastern & Southern Africa**
http://www.places.co.za ....**Southern African Places**
http://www.southafrica.net ....**Official South African Tourism website**
Swaziland, SZ - Kingdom of Swaziland, Capital: Mbabane
http://www.sntc.org.sz ....**Swaziland National Trust Commission**
Botswana and Zimbabwe, BW and ZW - Republic of Botswana, Capital: Gaborone and Harare
http://www.afrizim.com......................................**Information site for Zimbabwe and Botswana**
http://www.zimbabwepost.com ....**Zimbabwe Post Newspaper**

Western Africa

Benin, BJ - Republic of Benin, Capital: Porto-Novo
http://www.travelnotes.org/Africa/benin.htm
....**Benin Travel Guide**
Cameroon, CM - Republic of Cameroon, Capital: Yaoundé
http://www.cameroon.gov.cm ....**Office of the Prime Minister**
http://www.douala.com ....**Cameroon News**
http://www.geocities.com/TheTropics/Shores/4051
....**Postcards from Cameroon**
Chad, TD - Republic of Chad, Capital: N'Djamena
http://www.chadembassy.org ....**Embassy of Chad**
http://www.lonelyplanet.com/destinations/africa/chad
....**Information site for Chad**
Congo, CD – Democratic Republic of the Congo, Capital: Kinshasa
http://www.congo-pages.org ....**Information site for Congo**
http://www.un.int/drcongo ....**Democratic Republic of Congo**
Gambia, GM - Republic of The Gambia, Capital: Banjul
http://www.gambia.com ....**The Republic of the Gambia Official site**
http://www.gambianews.com ....**Gambia News**
http://www.gambianet.com................................**Official site for Gambia**
Ghana, GH - Republic of Ghana, Capital: Accra
http://www.ghana-embassy.org ....**Ghana Embassy**
http://www.interknowledge.com/ghana..........**Information site for Ghana**
Mali, ML - Republic of Mali, Capital: Bamako
http://www.care.org/virtual_trip/mali ....**Care USA**
http://www.lonelyplanet.com/dest/afr/mali.htm
....**Destination Mali**
Nigeria, NG – Capital: Abuja
http://lcweb2.loc.gov/frd/cs/ngtoc.html............**US Government site for Nigeria**
http://www.motherlandnigeria.com................**Motherland Nigeria**

Antarctica

http://www.antarctica2000.net..........................**Antarctica 2000 site**
http://www.glacier.rice.edu ....**Glacier site**
http://www.iaato.org ....**International Association of Antarctica Tour Operators**
http://www.theice.org/faq.html ....**Rob Holmes' Cool Antarctic site**

Central Asia

Afghanistan, AF - Islamic State of Afghanistan, Capital: Kabul

http://www.afghan-web.com .... **Afghanistan Online**

http://www.icarp.org/afghan.html .... **Information site for Afghanistan**

Southern Asia

Bangladesh, BD - People's Republic of Bangladesh, Capital: Dhaka

http://lcweb2.loc.gov/frd/cs/bdtoc.html .... **US Government site for Bangladesh**

http://www.virtualbangladesh.com .... **Information site for Bangladesh**

India, IN - Republic of India, Capital: New Delhi

http://www.assam.org .... **Information site for Assam**

http://www.chooseindia.com/tourism .... **Travel & Tourism in India**

http://www.delhigate.com .... **Delhi, India Travel site**

http://www.goacom.com .... **Goa Directory of Information & Services**

http://www.gujaratonline.com .... **Information site for Gujarat**

http://www.punjabonline.com .... **Information site for Punjab**

http://www.timesofindia.com .... **The Times of India Newspaper**

http://www.tourindia.com .... **Tour India site**

http://www.tourismofindia.com .... **India Ministry of Tourism**

http://www.welcometoindia.com .... **Information site for India**

Nepal, NP - Kingdom of Nepal, Capital: Katmandu

http://www.nepalhomepage.com/travel .... **Nepal Travel Guide**

http://www.travel-nepal.com .... **Information site for Nepal**

http://www.viewnepal.com .... **Nepal's Information Directory**

http://www.visitnepal.com .... **Nepal Travel Information Guide**

http://www.welcomenepal.com .... **Nepal Tourism Board**

Pakistan, PK - Islamic Republic of Pakistan, Capital: Islamabad

http://lcweb2.loc.gov/frd/cs/pktoc.html .... **US Government site for Pakistan**

http://www.alephx.com/pakistan .... **Information site for Pakistan**

http://www.islamabad.net .... **Government of Pakistan**

http://www.tourism.gov.pk .... **Pakistan Tourism Development Corporation**

Sri Lanka, LK - Democratic Socialist Republic of Sri Lanka, Capital: Colombo

http://www.lanka.net/ctb .... **Sri Lanka Tourist Board**

South Eastern Asia

Bhutan, BT - Kingdom of Bhutan, Capital: Thimphu

http://www.kingdomofbhutan.com ....**Bhutan Tourism Corporation**

Cambodia, KH - Kingdom of Cambodia, Capital: Phnom Penh

http://lcweb2.loc.gov/frd/cs/khtoc.html ....**US Government site for Cambodia**

China, CN - People's Republic of China, Capital: Beijing

http://lcweb2.loc.gov/frd/cs/cntoc.html ....**US Government site for China**

http://www.chinaetravel.com ....**Hotel & Travel site for China**

http://www.chinapages.com ....**Information site for China**

http://www.chinatour.com ....**China Tours site**

http://www.chinatravelservice.com ....**China Travel Service**

http://www.chinats.com ....**China Travel System**

http://www.china-vacation.com ....**GAT China Vacation**

http://www.chinavista.com/travel ....**China Virtual Tours**

http://www.citsusa.com ....**China International Travel Service**

http://www.cnta.com..**Information site for China (written in Chinese)**

http://www.flashpaper.com/beijing...................**Information site for Beijing**

http://www.shanghaiguide.com ....**Shanghai Guide**

http://www.shenzhenwindow.net ....**Shenzhen Data Communication Bureau**

http://www.zama.com/ontheroad ....**Information site for China**

Hong Kong

http://www.discoverhongkong.com ....**Hong Kong-City of Life**

http://www.totallyhk.com...................................**Information site for Hong Kong**

Indonesia, ID - Republic of Indonesia, Capital: Jakarta

http://www.bali-paradise.com ....**Information site for Bali**

http://www.balinetwork.com ....**Travel Directory for Bali**

http://www.balitravelforum.com ....**The Bali Travel Forum**

http://www.indo.com ....**Bali, Indonesia Travel Portal**

http://www.indonesia-tourism.com ....**Bali & Indonesia Tourism**

http://www.traveljakarta.com ....**Information site for Jakarta**

http://www.tourismindonesia.com ....**Tourism Indonesia**

Japan, JP – Capital: Tokyo

http://www.bento.com/tleisure.html.................**Information site for Tokyo**

http://www.boulevards.com/tokyo ....**Information site for Tokyo**

http://www.fukuoka-now.com............................**Information site for Japan**

http://www.j-heartland.com...............................**Tokai Association for Tourism**

http://www.jnto.go.jp/english ....**Japan National Tourist**

http://www.joho-kyoto.or.jp/~english/index_e.html
....**Kyoto Media Station**
http://www.mydome.or.jp/travel......................**Smart Traveling in Osaka Japan**
http://www.nagasaki-u.ac.jp/nagasaki-city/nagasaki.html
....**Nagasaki Regional Information**

Laos, LA - Lao People's Democratic Republic, Capital: Vientiane
http://lcweb2.loc.gov/frd/cs/latoc.html..............**US Government site for Laos**
http://www.laoembassy.com/discover ....**Laos Embassy**
http://www.visit-laos.com....................................**Laos Hotels & Tours**

Malaysia, MY – Capital: Kuala Lumpur
http://www.malaysianescape.com.....................**Information site for Malaysia**
http://www.sarawaktourism.com.......................**Sarawak Tourism Board Official site**
http://www.tourism.gov.my ....**Tourism Malaysia**
http://www.virtualmalaysia.com ....**Information site for Malaysia**
http://www.visitmalaysia.com ....**Information site for Malaysia**

Myanmar, MM - Union of Burma, Capital: Yangon (Rangoon)
http://www.myanmar.com..................................**Information site for Myanmar**
http://www.travelmyanmar.com ....**Travel Myanmar**

Tibet, Capital: Lhasa
http://www.schneuwly.com/tibet ....**Tibetan Journey**
http://www.tibet.org/Travel ....**Travel in Tibet**
http://www.tibet-tour.com..................................**Tibet Tourism Bureau Shanghai Office**

Philippines, PH - Republic of the Philippines, Capital: Manila
http://www.filipino.com ....**Philippines Information, Business & Tourism**
http://www.philtourism.com.............................**Philippine Tourism Authority Official site**
http://www.wowphilippines.com.ph.................**Philippines Department of Tourism**

Singapore, SG - Republic of Singapore, Capital: Singapore
http://www.makansutra.com ....**Guide to Best Food in Singapore**
http://www.newasia-singapore.com..................**Singapore Tourism Official site**
http://www.serangoonroad.com ....**Information site for Serangoon Road**
http://www.visitsingapore.com ....**Singapore Tourism Official site**

South Korea, KR - Republic of Korea, Seoul
http://www.koreainfogate.com ....**Information site for Korea**
http://www.lifeinkorea.com ....**Life in Korea**
http://www.mapzinekorea.com ....**Mapzine Korea**
http://www.tour2korea.com.................................**Official Korea Travel site**
Taiwan, TW – Capital: Taipei
http://tpe.gov.tw/gateways/en_monument.htm
....**Taiwan Government site**
http://www.tbroc.gov.tw ....**Information site for Taiwan**
Thailand, TH - Kingdom of Thailand, Capital: Bangkok
http://lcweb2.loc.gov/frd/cs/thtoc.html ....**US Government site for Thailand**
http://www.bangkokpost.net ....**Bangkok Post Newspaper**
http://www.chiangmai-chiangrai.com ....**Chiangmai & Chiangrai Magazine**
http://www.phuketgazette.net ....**Phuket Gazette Newspaper**
http://www.sabaidee.com ....**Best sites for Thailand**
http://www.siam.net ....**Thailand Hotels Directory**
http://www1.thaimain.org/en ....**Thailand's Official Information Center**
http://www.tourismthailand.org ....**Tourism Authority of Thailand**

Vietnam, VN - Socialist Republic of Vietnam, Capital: Hanoi
http://lcweb2.loc.gov/frd/cs/vntoc.html............**US Government site for Vietnam**
http://www.vietnamembassy-usa.org ....**US Embassy for Vietnam**
Australia, AU - Commonwealth of Australia, Capital: Canberra
http://www.about-australia.com ....**Information site for Australia**
http://www.australia.com ....**Australian Tourist Commission**
http://www.bridgeclimb.com.au ....**The Sydney Harbour Bridge**
http://www.canberratourism.com.au................**Australia's National Capital**
http://www.citysearch.com.au ....**Information site for Australia**
http://www.destinationqueensland.com ....**Tourism Queensland**
http://www.discovertasmania.com.au ....**Discover Tasmania**
http://www.melbournevisit.com ....**Melbourne Visitors Guide**
http://www.ntholidays.com...............................**Australia's Outback Northern Territory**
http://www.nttc.com.au ....**Northern Territory Tourist Commission**
http://www.pacific-destinations.com ....**Pacific Destination Center**
http://www.soh.nsw.gov.au ....**Sydney Opera House**

http://www.sydney.visitorsbureau.com.au......**Sydney Travel Bureau.**
http://www.tourism.nsw.gov.au ....**Tourism New South Wales**
http://www.tourism.vic.gov.au ....**Tourism Victoria State Government**
http://www.tq.com.au ....**Information site for Queensland**
http://www.queensland-holidays.com.au **The Complete Travel Guide to Queensland**
http://www.seeaustralia.com.au ....**Information site for Australia**
http://www.visitvictoria.com ....**Tourism Victoria**
http://www.visitnsw.com.au...............................**Tourism New South Wales**
http://www.westernaustralia.net.......................**Western Australian Tourism Commission**

Caribbean

Anguilla

http://www.anguilla-vacation.com ....**Anguilla Tourist Board Official site**
http://www.turq.com/anguilla ....**Anguilla Online Tourist Guide**

Aruba

http://www.aruba.com..**Information site for Aruba**
http://www.arubaonline.com ....**Information site for Aruba**
http://www.visitaruba.com ....**Visit Aruba**

Bahamas, BS – Commonwealth of The Bahamas, Capital: Nassau

http://www.atlantis.com ....**Atlantis, Paradise Island, Bahamas**
http://www.bahamas.com...................................**Bahamas Ministry of Tourism**
http://www.bahamas-on-line.com ....**Information site for Bahamas**
http://www.bahamasvg.com ....**Bahamas Vacation Guide**
http://www.thebahamas.com.............................**Information site for Bahamas**

Barbados, BB – Capital: Bridgetown

http://www.barbados.org ....**Official Barbados Tourism Authority site**
http://www.barbadosguide.com ....**Barbados Travel Guide**
http://www.funbarbados.com ....**Fun Barbados Travel Guide**
http://www.turq.com/barbados ....**Quick Guide to Barbados**

Bermuda

http://www.bermuda.com ....**Information site for Bermuda**
http://www.bermudatourism.com......................**Bermuda Department of Tourism**

British Virgin Islands

http://www.britishvirginislands.com .... **Information site for British Virgin Islands**

http://www.bviwelcome.com .... **The British Virgin Islands Welcome Tourist Guide**

http://www.ultimatebvi.com .... **Information site for British Virgin Islands**

Cayman Islands

http://www.caribbeansupersite.com/cayman .. **Destinations—Island Connoisseur**

http://www.digiportal.com .... **Digiportal Software site**

http://www.caymanislands.ky .... **Cayman Islands Department of Tourism**

Cuba, CU - Republic of Cuba, Capital: Havana

http://www.cuba.tc .... **The Cuba Connection**

http://www.cubanadventures.com .... **Cuban Adventures**

http://www.cubavip.com .... **Cuba Travel Resources**

http://www.infocubana.com/cu/e .... **Info Cuba**

Curacao

http://www.curacao.com .... **Curacao Dutch Caribbean Tourism**

http://www.curacao-tourism.com .... **Curacao Tourism Development Bureau**

http://www.interknowledge.com/curacao .... **Curacao Tourism Development Bureau Official site**

Grenada, GD – Capital: Saint George's

http://www.grenada.org .... **Grenada Official Travel Guide**

http://www.grenadaexplorer.com .... **Grenada Explorer Travel Guide**

http://www.travelgrenada.com .... **Travel Grenada**

http://www.turq.com/grenada .... **Grenada Online Tourist Guide**

Haiti, HT - Republic of Haiti, Capital: Port-au-Prince

http://lcweb2.loc.gov/frd/cs/httoc.html .... **US Government site for Haiti**

http://www.caribbeansupersite.com/haiti .... **Destinations—Island Connoisseur**

http://www.haititourisme.org .... **Official site for Tourism in Haiti**

Jamaica, JM – Capital: Kingston

http://www.jamaicatravel.com .... **Official site of the Jamaica Tourist Board**

http://www.turq.com/jamaica .... **Jamaica Online Tourist Guide**

http://www.virtualjamaica.com .... **Information site for Jamaica**

Martinique
http://www.martinique.org ....**Martinique Promotion Bureau**

Puerto Rico
http://escape.topuertorico.com ....**Internet Guide to Puerto Rico**
http://Welcome.toPuertoRico.org ....**Information site to Puerto Rico**
http://www.caribbeansupersite.com/puertorico
....**Destinations—Island Connoisseur**
http://www.gotopuertorico.com ....**Puerto Rico Tourism Company**
http://www.spiderlink.net/citiview ....**Citiview of Puerto Rico Community Tourist Guide**
http://www.meetpuertorico.com ....**Puerto Rico Convention Bureau**
Saba
http://www.sabatourism.com.............................**Saba Tourist Office**
St. Barthelemy
http://www.st-barths.com ....**Official St. Barthelemy site**
http://www.saint-barths.com ....**Information site for St. Barths**
St. Croix
http://www.st-croix.net ....**St. Croix US Virgin Islands site**
http://www.stcroixguidebook.com......................**St. Croix Chamber of Commerce**
St. Eustatius
http://www.statiatourism.com...........................**St. Eustatius Tourist Office**
St. Kitts and Nevis, KN - Federation of Saint Kitts and Nevis, Capital: Basseterre
http://www.interknowledge.com/stkitts-nevis
....**St. Kitts & Nevis Official Travel Guide**
http://www.nevisweb.kn ....**Nevis Island Government Ministry of Finance**
http://www.stkitts-nevis.com.............................**Official St. Kitts Tourism Authority site**
St. John
http://www.st-john.com ....**Guide to St. John's US Virgin Islands**
http://www.stjohnusvi.com ....**Guide to St. John Vacation**
St. Lucia, LC – Capital: Castries
http://www.st-lucia.com ....**Official St. Lucia Tourist Board**
http://www.stluciatravelnet.com ....**St. Lucia Travel Guide, Resort & Activity Information**

http://www.stlucia.org .... **Official St. Lucia Tourist Board site**
http://www.turq.com/stlucia.html .... **St. Lucia Online Tourist Guide**
St. Martin/ St. Maarten
http://www.interknowledge.com/st-martin .... **St. Martin's Official Tourist site**
http://www.saint-martin.com .... **Destination St. Martin/St. Maarten**
http://www.sxmtravelguide.com .... **The St. Maarten & St. Martin Travel Guide**
St. Thomas
http://www.st-thomas.com .... **Virtual Guide to St. Thomas**
St. Vincent and The Grenadines, VC – Capital: Kingstown
http://www.svgtourism.com .... **Official St. Vincent & The Grenadines Dept. of Tourism**
http://www.turq.com/stvincent.......................... **St. Vincent & The Grenadines Online Tourist Guide**
Trinidad & Tobago, TT - Republic of Trinidad and Tobago, Capital: Port-of-Spain
http://www.visittnt.com .... **Information site to Trinidad & Tobago**
Turks and Caicos
http://www.atsea.com/islands/tciall.htm .... **Information site for Turks and Caicos Islands**
http://www.grand-turk.com .... **The Best of Grand Turk Guide**
http://www.turksandcaicostourism.com .... **Official Turks and Caicos Tourist Board**
U.S. Virgin Islands
http://www.usvi.net... **US Virgin Islands Guide**
http://www.usvi-info.com................................. **US Virgin Islands Information Guide**
http://www.virginislandsparadise.com .... **Virgin Islands Paradise**

Central And South America

Argentina, AR - Argentine Republic, Capital: Buenos Aires
http://www.argentinatravel.com .... **Information site for Argentina**
http://www.argentour.com .... **Information site for Argentina**
http://www.info-argentina.net/ar/e .... **Info Argentina**
http://www.sectur.gov.ar .... **Official Argentina Department of Tourism site**
Belize, BZ – Capital: Belmopan
http://www.belize.com .... **Belize Tourism and Investment**

Guide

http://www.belizenet.com ....**Information site for Belize**

http://www.infobelize.net/be/e ....**Info Belize**

http://www.travelbelize.org...................................**The Belize Tourism Board**

Bolivia, BO - Republic of Bolivia, Capital: La Paz

http://lcweb2.loc.gov/frd/cs/botoc.html ....**US Government site for Bolivia**

http://www.infobolivia.net ....**Info Bolivia**

Brazil, BR - Federative Republic of Brazil, Capital: Brasilia

http://www.bitourism.com ....**Brazilian Incentive and Tourism site**

http://www.brazilinfo.com ....**Guide to Brazil**

http://www.brazilsite.com ....**Information site for Brazil**

http://www.civila.com/brasilia ....**Information site for Brazil (Written in Spanish)**

http://www.embratur.gov.br ....**Brazil Government site**

http://www.infobrazil.net/br/e ....**Info Brazil**

http://www.ipanema.com ....**Insider's Guide to Rio De Janeiro**

http://www.vivabrazil.com ....**Virtual Trip to Brazil**

Chile, CL - Republic of Chile, Capital: Santiago

http://lcweb2.loc.gov/frd/cs/cltoc.html..............**US Government site for Chile**

http://www.chile.com ....**Information site for Chile**

http://www.chile-travel.com ....**Chile Travel Information**

http://www.infochilena.com ....**Info Chile**

Columbia, CO - Republic of Colombia, Capital: Bogotá

http://lcweb2.loc.gov/frd/cs/cotoc.html ....**US Government site for Columbia**

http://www.infocolombia.com ....**Info Columbia**

Costa Rica, CR - Republic of Costa Rica, Capital: San José

http://www.centralamerica.com ....**Costa Rica Tourism site**

http://www.infocostarica.net ....**Info Costa Rica**

http://www.tourism-costarica.com......................**Official Costa Rica Travel site**

Dominican Republic, DO – Dominican Republic, Capital: Santo Domingo

http://www.dominicana.com.do..........................**Official Dominican Republic site**

http://www.hispaniola.com ....**Dominican Republic Travel Guide**

http://www.infodominicana.com ....**Info Dominican Republic**

Ecuador, EC - Republic of Ecuador, Capital: Quito

http://lcweb2.loc.gov/frd/cs/ectoc.html ....**US Government site for Ecuador**

http://www.ecuadorexplorer.com ....**Ecuador Travel Guide**
http://www.exploringecuador.com ....**Information site for Ecuador**
http://www.infoecuador.com .... **Info Ecuador**
El Salvador, SV - Republic of El Salvador, Capital: San Salvador
http://lcweb2.loc.gov/frd/cs/svtoc.html ....**US Government site for El Salvador**
http://www.infoelsalvador.com ....**Info El Salvador**
French Guiana
http://www.guyanetourisme.com........................**Official French Guiana Tourism site**
http://www.worldtravelguide.net/data/guf/guf.asp
....**World Travel Guide—French Guiana**
Guatemala, GT - Republic of Guatemala, Capital: Guatemala (City)
http://www.guatemala.travel.com.gt ....**Official Guatemala Travel site**
http://www.infoguatemala.com ....**Info Guatemala**
Guyana, GY - Co-operative Republic of Guyana, Capital: Georgetown
http://www.turq.com/guyana ....**Guyana Online Tourist Guide**
Honduras, HN - Republic of Honduras, Capital: Tegucigalpa
http://www.honduras.com ....**Information site for Honduras**
http://www.infohonduras.com ....**Info Honduras**
Nicaragua, NI - Republic of Nicaragua, Capital: Managua
http://lcweb2.loc.gov/frd/cs/nitoc.html ....**US Government site for Nicaragua**
http://www.infonicaragua.com ....**Info Nicaragua**
http://www.intur.gob.ni.......................................**Official Nicaraguan Institute of Tourism**
http://www.nicaragua-online.com ....**Information site for Nicaragua**
Panama, PA -Republic of Panama, Capital: Panama City
http://www.infopanama.net ....**Info Panama**
http://www.panamatours.com ....**Official Panama Virtual Tourism Center**
http://www.panamatravel.com ....**Information site for Panama**
http://www.pancanal.com ....**The Panama Canal site**
Paraguay, PY - Republic of Paraguay, Capital: Asunción
http://www.infoparaguay.com ....**Info Paraguay**
http://www.lanic.utexas.edu/la/sa/paraguay ..**Information site for Paraguay**
Peru, PE - Republic of Peru, Capital: Lima
http://www.infoperu.net ....**Information site for Peru**
http://www.peruexplorer.com ....**Information site for Peru**
Suriname, SR - Republic of Suriname, Capital: Paramaribo
http://www.surinametourism.com....................**Suriname Online Tourist Guide**

Uruguay, UY - Oriental Republic of Uruguay, Montevideo
http://lcweb2.loc.gov/frd/cs/uytoc.html .... **US Government site for Uruguay**
http://www.infouruguay.net .... **Info Uruguay**
http://www.turismo.gub.uy .... **Official Uruguay Tourism site**
http://www.visit-uruguay.com .... **Online Source for Hotels in Uruguay**

Venezuela, VE - Republic of Venezuela, Capital: Caracas
http://lcweb2.loc.gov/frd/cs/vetoc.html .... **US Government site for Venezuela**
http://think-venezuela.net .... **The Tourism Directory of Venezuela**
http://www.infovenezuela.net .... **Info Venezuela**

Europe

Austria, AT - Republic of Austria, Capital: Vienna
http://www.abnet.at/tourist .... **Austrian National Tourist Guide**
http://www.austria-tourism.at .... **Official Austria Tourism site**
http://www.salzburginfo.at .... **Salzburg Information & Tourism**

Belgium, BE - Kingdom of Belgium, Capital: Brussels
http://www.belgium.com/travel .... **Belgium Travel**
http://www.belgium-tourism.com .... **Information site for Belgium**
http://www.belgiumpost.com .... **Belgium Post Newspaper**
http://www.expatica.com/belgium .... **Living or Moving to Belgium site**
http://www.visitbelgium.com .... **Official Belgium Tourist Office in the Americas**

Bosnia and Herzegovina, BA – Capital: Sarajevo
http://www.travelnotes.org/Europe/bosnia.htm **Bosnia Travel Guide**

Bulgaria
http://www.bulgaria.com .... **Information site for Bulgaria**
http://www.travel-bulgaria.com .... **Bulgarian Travel Guide**

Czech Republic, CZ - Czech Republic, Capital: Prague
http://www.a-zprague.cz .... **Prague City Guide**
http://www.czech-tourism.com .... **Czech Tourism**
http://www.czechsite.com .... **Czech Site Travel Guide**
http://www.czechcenter.com .... **Czech Center New York**

Cyprus, CY - Republic of Cyprus, Capital: Nicosia (Lefkosia)
http://www.cyprustourism.org .... **Official Cyprus Tourism**

Organization site

http://www.cyprusexplorer.com ....**Information site for Cyprus**

http://www.traveltocyprus.com.cy....................**Travel to Cyprus site**

http://www.cosmosnet.net/azias/cyprus ....**Cyprus Guide**

Croatia, HR - Republic of Croatia, Capital: Zagreb

http://www.croatia.net ....**Information site for Croatia**

http://www.htz.hr ....**Official Croatian National Tourist Board**

http://www.mint.hr..**Official Ministry of Tourism in Croatia**

Denmark, DK - Kingdom of Denmark, Capital: Copenhagen

http://www.alltraveldenmark.com....................**Denmark Travel & Tourism**

http://www.denmarkguide.com ....**The Ultimate Travel Guide to Denmark**

http://www.visitdenmark.com...........................**Official Tourism site to Denmark**

England, UK - United Kingdom of Great Britain and Northern Ireland, Capital: London

http://llanfairpwllgwyngyllgogerychwyrndrobwllllantysiliogogogoch.info (longest Web site try http://hythe.com)............**Hythe Kent England Information site**

http://www.allofengland.com ....**Information site for England**

http://www.blackpooltourism.com ....**Official Blackpool Tourism site**

http://www.cambridgevirtualcity.co.uk............**Cambridge Virtual City**

http://www.londontouristboard.com................**Official London Tourism site**

http://www.londontown.com ....**Information site for London**

http://www.manchesteronline.co.uk ....**Information site for Manchester**

http://www.newcastle.gov.uk ....**Official Newcastle City Council Web site**

http://www.oxfordcity.co.uk...............................**City of Oxford**

http://www.southeastengland.uk.com ....**South East England Tourist Board**

http://www.thisislondon.co.uk ....**Information site for London**

http://www.timesonline.co.uk .... **London Times Newspaper site**

http://www.toweroflondontour.com ....**The Tower of London Virtual Tour**

http://www.travelbritain.org ....**Official Travel to England Guide**

http://www.travelengland.org.uk......................**Official Online Guide to England**

http://www.visitbritain.com ....**Official Travel Guide to Britain**

http://www.visitheartofengland.co.uk .... **Online Visitors Guide to England**
http://www.yorkonline.co.uk .... **Information site for York**

Estonia, EE - Republic of Estonia, Capital: Tallinn

http://lcweb2.loc.gov/frd/cs/eetoc.html .... **US Government site for Estonia**
http://www.visitestonia.com .... **Official Etonian Tourist Board**

Finland, FI - Republic of Finland, Capital: Helsinki

http://virtual.finland.fi .... **Information about Finland**
http://www.finland-tourism.com .... **Official Travel Guide to Finland**
http://www.thekingsroad.com .... **Finland Kings Road site**
http://www.hel.fi/english .... **City of Helsinki**

France, FR - French Republic, Capital: Paris

http://www.alloffrance.com .... **France Directory site**
http://www.bordeaux.com .... **Official site of Bordeaux Wines**
http://www.cannes.com .... **Official Cannes site**
http://www.france.com .... **Information site for France**
http://www.franceguide.com .... **Official site of the French Government Tourist Office**
http://www.francetourism.com .... **French Government Tourist Office**
http://www.mairie-toulouse.fr .... **Official Site of Toulouse**
http://www.nice-coteazur.org .... **Official City of Nice site**
http://www.parisnotes.com .... **Paris Notes Newsletter**
http://www.paris-touristoffice.com .... **Official Paris Tourism site**
http://www.paris.org .... **The Paris Pages**
http://www.eviantourism.com .... **Information site for Evian**

Germany, DE - Federal Republic of Germany, Capital: Berlin

http://www.germany-tourism.de .... **Official Germany Tourism site**
http://www.berlin.de/home/English .... **Information site for Berlin**
http://www.frankfurt.de/sis/English.html .... **Information site for Frankfurt**
http://www.hamburg-tourism.de .... **Hamburg Tourist Board**
http://www.muenchen-tourist.de .... **Information site for Muenchen**
http://www.stuttgart-tourist.de .... **Information site for Stuttgart**

Gibraltar

http://www.gibraltar.gi .... **Information site for Gibraltar**
http://www.gibraltar.gov.gi .... **Official Government of Gibraltar site**

Greece, GR - Hellenic Republic, Capital: Athens

http://www.alltravelgreece.com .... **Greece Travel & Tourism**
http://www.athensguide.com .... **Athens Survival Guide**

http://www.gnto.gr .... **Official Greek National Tourism Organization**
http://www.greekinternet.com .... **Guide to Greece**
http://www.greektravel.com .... **A Greece Travel Guide**
http://www.travelling.gr .... **Greece Travel**

Hungary, HU - Republic of Hungary, Capital: Budapest

http://lcweb2.loc.gov/frd/cs/hutoc.html .... **US Government site for Hungary**
http://www.budapest.com .... **Official Budapest site**
http://www.gotohungary.com .... **Hungary National Tourist Office**
http://www.hungarytourism.hu .... **Official Hungary Tourism Site**

Iceland, IS - Republic of Iceland, Capital: Reykjavik

http://tourist.reykjavik.is...................................... **Reykjavik Tourism**
http://www.icetourist.is .... **Official Icelandic Tourist Board site**

Ireland, IE – Capital: Dublin

http://www.askireland.com .... **Ireland's Government Directory**
http://www.discovernorthernireland.com........ **Northern Ireland Tourist Board**
http://www.irlgov.ie .... **Government of Ireland**
http://www.irelandseye.com .... **The Culture, History & Tradition of Ireland**
http://www.ireland.travel.ie .... **Official Irish Travel & Tourism Information**
http://www.irelandvacations.com .... **Tourism Ireland**
http://www.galwayguide.com .... **Information site for Galway**
http://www.goireland.com .... **Ireland's National Tourism Service**
http://www.travel-ireland.com .... **Travel Ireland Reservations Service**

Italy, IT - Italian Republic, Capital: Rome

http://www.allofitaly.com .... **Italian Directory**
http://www.alltravelitaly.com .... **European Travel Bureau**
http://www.dolcevita.com .... **Insider's Guide to Italy**
http://www.dreamofitaly.com .... **Dream of Italy site**
http://www.enit.it .... **Official Italy Tourism site**
http://www.initaly.com .... **Travel & Information site for Italy**
http://www.italycyberguide.com .... **Information site for Italy**
http://www.italytour.com .... **Virtual Tour of Italy**

http://www.italiansrus.com ....Italy Culture Online Guide
http://www.italiantourism.com ....Italian Government Tourism Board
http://www.realitaly.com ....Information site for Italy
http://www.travel.it ....Travel Information for Italy
http://www.traveleurope.it/milano.htm ....Travel Europe Guide to Italy & Hotels
http://www.virtualvenice.com ....Map of Venice site
http://www.wandering.com ....Information site for Italy

Latvia, LV - Republic of Latvia, Capital: Riga

http://www.inyourpocket.com/Latvia ....In Your Pocket City Guides
http://www.latviatravel.com ....Latvia Travel site

Lithuania, LT - Republic of Lithuania, Capital: Vilnius

http://lcweb2.loc.gov/frd/cs/lttoc.html ....US Government for Lithuania
http://www.tourism.lt ....Lithuanian State Department of Tourism

Luxembourg, LU - Grand Duchy of Luxembourg, Capital: Luxembourg

http://www.luxembourg.co.uk............................Luxembourg Tourist Office in London
http://www.luxembourg-city.lu ....Luxembourg City Tourist Office
http://www.ont.lu ....National Tourist Office & the Ministry of Tourism Luxembourg

Malta, MT – Capital: Valletta

http://www.aboutmalta.com ....Information site for Maltese Islands
http://www.visitmalta.com ....Information site for Maltese Islands

Monaco, MC - Principality of Monaco, Capital: Monaco

http://www.monaco-congres.com ....Monaco Congress site
http://www.monaco-tourism.com ....Official Monaco Tourism site
http://www.montecarloresort.com ....Monte Carlo Resort

Netherlands, NL - Kingdom of the Netherlands, Capital: Amsterdam

http://www.holland.com.......................................Official Netherlands Board of Tourism site
http://www.noord-holland-tourist.nl................North Holland Tourist Board
http://www.rotterdam.nl ....Information site for Rotterdam

Northern Ireland

http://www.coastofdown.com...........................Kingdoms of Down Accommodation & Visitors Guide

http://www.countyarmagh.com ....Armagh Ireland Tourism
http://www.discovernorthernireland.com ....**Northern Ireland Tourist Board Official site**
http://www.interknowledge.com/northern-ireland
....**Official Guide to Northern Ireland**

Norway, NO - Kingdom of Norway, Capital: Oslo

http://www.norway.org ....**Royal Norwegian Embassy**
http://www.norwegian-scenery.com ....**Norwegian Scenery**
http://www.trondheim.com/engelsk.................**Official Trondheim site**
http://www.virtualoslo.com ....**Oslo Online Travel Guide**
http://www.visitnorway.com.............................**Norwegian Tourist Board**

Poland, PL - Republic of Poland, Capital: Warsaw

http://www.krakow.pl/en ....**Information site for Krakow**
http://www.poland.net ....**Information site on Poland**
http://www.polandtour.org.................................**Polish National Tourist Office**

Portugal, PT - Portuguese Republic, Capital: Lisbon

http://www.infoportugal.net ....**Info Portugal**
http://www.lisbon.cx ....**Information site for Lisbon**
http://www.portugalinsite.pt.............................**Official Portugal Tourism site**
http://www.portugal.org....................................**Information site for Portugal**
http://www.portugalvirtual.pt ....**Information site for Portugal**

Romania, RO – Capital: Bucharest

http://www.rotravel.com ....**Romanian Travel Guide**
http://www.romaniatourism.com.......................**Romanian National Tourist Office**

Russia, RU - Russian Federation, Capital: Moscow

http://www.cityvision2000.com ....**St. Petersburg City Guide & Travel Information Service**
http://www.moscow-guide.ru ....**Official Tourist Moscow Government site**
http://www.russiatravel.com..............................**The Russia Travel Official Guide**
http://www.traveleastrussia.com .... **East Russia Travel Market**
http://www.guide.spb.ru ....**Russia Travel & Limo Services**

Scotland

http://www.destination-scotland.com ....**Destination Scotland**
http://www.visitscotland.com ....**Scottish Tourist Board**
http://www.seeglasgow.com ....**Greater Glasgow & Clyde Valley Tourist Board**
http://www.welcome-scotland.com ....**Holiday Travel to Scotland**

http://www.virtualglasgow.com ....Information site for Glasgow
Slovakia, SK - Slovak Republic, Capital: Bratislava
http://www.our-slovakia.com ....**Slovakia Tours**
http://www.sacr.sk..**Official Slovak Tourist Board**
http://www.slovakia.org/tourism........................**Slovakia Travel Guide & Information for Tourists**
http://www.tanap.sk ....**The High Tatra Mountains**
http://www.travelguide.sk..................................**Travel Guide**
Slovenia, SI - Republic of Slovenia, Capital: Ljubljana
http://www.matkurja.com/eng/country info ....**A Guide to Virtual Slovenia**
Spain, ES - Kingdom of Spain, Capital: Madrid
http://www.barcelona-on-line.es/eng ....**Barcelona Hotels & Travel Guide**
http://www.bcn.es/english/turisme/ivisitar.htm **Barcelona Tourism City**
http://www.cyberspain.com ....**Information site for Spain**
http://www.discoverspain.com ....**Information site for Spain**
http://www.infoiberia.net ....**Info Spain**
http://www.madridman.com ....**Madrid Man's Yankee site**
http://www.tourspain.es ....**Information site for Spain**
http://www.okspain.org ....**Information site for Spain**
Sweden, SE - Kingdom of Sweden, Capital: Stockholm
http://www.alltravelsweden.com ....**Sweden Tourism & Travel with Maps**
http://www.gosweden.org...................................**Travel Guide to Sweden for Americans**
http://www.stockholm.se/english.......................**The City of Stockholm**
http://www.sverigeturism.se/smorgasbord ....**Sweden Information Smorgasbord**
http://www.visit-sweden.com ....**Sweden Tourism Information**
Switzerland, CH - Swiss Confederation, Capital: Bern
http://www.berntourismus.ch ....**Information site for Switzerland**
http://www.geneve.ch ....**Official Genève site**
http://www.luzern.org/index_e.html ....**Tourist Board Luzern**
http://www.myswitzerland.com ....**Switzerland Tourism**
http://www.zuerich.ch ....**Zurich News**
http://www.zurichtourism.ch ....**Zurich Tourism**
Ukraine, UA – Capital: Kiev
http://pages.prodigy.net/euroscope/guidetoc.html
....**Ukraine Online Guide**
http://www.brama.com ....**Gateway Ukraine**

http://www.ukremb.com .... **Embassy of Ukraine**

Vatican City, VA - Holy See, Capital: Vatican City

http://www.vatican.va .... **Vatican Official site**

Wales

http://www.croeso.com .... **Information site for Wales**

http://www.llandudno.cwc.net .... **Llandudno Guide**

http://www.swansea-gower.demon.co.uk ...... **Swansea Mumbles & Gower Visitor Information**

http://www.virtualportmeirion.com .... **Information site for Portmeirion**

Yugoslavia, YU – Federal Republic of Yugoslavia, Capital: Belgrade

http://www.gov.yu .... **Official Yugoslavia Government site**

Middle East

Armenia, AM - Republic of Armenia, Capital: Yerevan

http://www.armgate.com/travel .... **Armenia Travel Guide**

Brunei, BN - Negara Brunei Darussalam, Capital: Bandar Seri Begawan

http://www.brunet.bn .... **Information site for Brunei**

http://www.brunei.gov.bn .... **Official Brunei Government site**

Iran, IR - Islamic Republic of Iran, Capital: Tehran

http://www.itto.org.. **Iran Touring & Tourism Organization**

Iraq, IQ - Republic of Iraq, Capital: Baghdad

http://www.arab.net/iraq................................... **Information site for Iraq**

Israel, IL - State of Israel, Capital: Jerusalem

http://lcweb2.loc.gov/frd/cs/iltoc.html .... **US Government site for Israel**

http://www.dead-sea.net .... **Dead Sea Tourist site**

http://www.goisrael.com .... **Israel Ministry of Tourism**

http://www.helloisrael.net .... **Israel Ministry of Tourism**

http://www.inisrael.com .... **Israel Travel & Hotels Guide**

http://www.infotour.co.il .... **Israeli Tourism & Recreation site**

http://www.israelvisit.co.il .... **Information site for Israel**

http://www.virtualjerusalem.com .... **Information site for Jerusalem**

Jordan, JO- Hashemite Kingdom of Jordan, Capital: Amman

http://lcweb2.loc.gov/frd/cs/jotoc.html .... **US Government site for Jordan**

http://www.arab.net/Jordan .... **Information site for Jordan**

http://www.seejordan.org .... **Jordan Tourism Board North America**

Lebanon, LB - Lebanese Republic, Capital: Beirut

http://lcweb2.loc.gov/frd/cs/lbtoc.html ....**US Government site for Lebanon**
http://www.arabia.com/lebanon/english ....**Information site for Lebanon**
http://www.bookinn.com ....**Information site for Bookinn**
http://www.lebanon-tourism.gov.lb ....**Lebanese Ministry of Tourism**

Palestine, Palestinian Authority
http://www.palestineremembered.com ....**Information site for Palestine**
http://www.visit-palestine.com..........................**Palestine Ministry of Tourism & Antiquities**

Saudi Arabia, SA - Kingdom of Saudi Arabia, Capital: Riyadh
http://lcweb2.loc.gov/frd/cs/satoc.html ....**US Government site for Saudi Arabia**
http://www.arab.net/Saudi ....**Information site for Saudi Arabia**
http://www.saudinf.com ....**Saudi Arabia Information Resource**

Syria, SY - Syrian Arab Republic, Capital: Damascus
http://lcweb2.loc.gov/frd/cs/sytoc.html ....US Government site for Syria
http://www.syriatourism.org ....**Syria Ministry of Tourism**
http://www.visit-syria.com ....**Information site for Syria**

Turkey, TR - Republic of Turkey, Capital: Ankara
http://www.exploreturkey.com ....**Hotels in Turkey**
http://www.istanbulcityguide.com....................**Istanbul City Guide**
http://www.tourismturkey.org ....**Turkey Ministry of Tourism**
http://www.travelturkey.com ....**Turkey Travel Guide**
http://www.turkishpress.com ....**Turkish Daily News**

United Arab Emirates, AE – United Arab Emirates, Capital: Abu Dhabi
http://www.emirates.org ....**United Arab Emirates site**

Yemen, YE – Capital: Sanaa
http://www.arab.net/yemen ....**Information site for Yemen**
http://www.yementimes.com ....**Yemen Times Online Newspaper**

North America

Canada, CA – Capital: Ottawa
http://www.attractionscanada.com ....**Information site on Canada**
http://www.bcadventure.com ....**British Columbia Travel Information**
http://www.bobthetourist.com ....**Travel in Canada**
http://www.bonjourquebec.com ....**Official Quebec Government Site**

http://www.calgaryplus.ca ....**Information site for Calgary**
http://www.canadiangeographic.ca/snapshots
....**Canadian Geographic Online**
http://www.destination-ns.com ....**Destination Nova Scotia**
http://www.discoveralberta.com ....**Alberta Travel & Tourism**
http://www.discovercalgary.com ....**Calgary Travel & Tourism**
http://www.discoveredmonton.com ....**Edmonton Travel & Tourism**
http://www.discoverjasper.com ....**Jasper Travel & Tourism**
http://www.edmontonplus.ca ....**Information site for Edmonton**
http://www.explore.gov.ns.ca ....**Explore Nova Scotia**
http://www.gov.nf.ca/tourism ....**New Foundland & Labrador Tourism Official site**
http://www.hellobc.com ....**Official site of Tourism British Columbia**
http://www.montrealplus.ca ....**Information site for Montreal**
http://www.moremontreal.com ....**The Montreal Directory**
http://www.northernfrontier.com ....**Northern Frontier Visitors Association**
http://www.nwttravel.nt.ca ....**NWT Arctic Tourism**
http://www.onroute.com ....**The Travel Source**
http://www.peiplay.com ....**Official site for Prince Edward Island Visitors Guide**
http://www.quebecplus.ca ....**Information site for Quebec**
http://www.spirit-of-canada.com ....**Information site for Canada**
http://www.tourism.gov.on.ca ....**Government of Ontario**
http://www.tourottawa.org ....**Ottawa Tourism and Convention Authority**
http://www.transcanadahighway.com ....**Canada's Nation-Wide Web Information Source**
http://www.travelalberta.com ....**Government of Alberta**
http://www.travelcanada.ca ....**Official site for Canadian Tourism Commission**
http://www.toronto.com (private).....................**Toronto City Guide**
http://www.torontotourism.com ....**Toronto Convention & Visitors Association**
http://www.tourisme-montreal.org...................**Tourism Montreal**
http://www.tourismvancouver.com ....**Official travel resource for Vancouver.**
http://www.tourismvictoria.com ....**Victoria Visitor & Convention Bureau Official site**
http://www.touryukon.com .... **Official site for Yukon**

http://www.wherecanada.com ....**Information site for Canada**
Mexico, MX - United Mexican States, Capital: Mexico City
http://www.acapulco.com ....**Information site for Acapulco**
http://www.acapulco-cvb.org.............................**Acapulco Convention & Visitors Bureau**
http://www.bajaexpo.com/cities/sanjose.htm
....**Information site for San Jose Del Cabo**
http://www.caboland.com ....**Complete Guide to Cabo San Lucas**
http://www.cozumelfanclub.org ....**Information site for Cozumel**
http://www.gocancun.com ....**Cancun Convention and Visitors Bureau**
http://www.go2mexico.com ....**Mexico Travel Guide**
http://www.infomexicana.com/mx/e ....**Information site for Mexico**
http://www.mayanriviera.com ....**Information site for Mayan Riviera**
http://www.maztravel.com ....**Mazatlán Travel Guide**
http://www.mexconnect.com ....**Access Mexico Connect Magazine**
http://www.mexico-city-mexico.com ....**Information site for Mexico City**
http://www.oaxaca-travel.com ....**State and City of Oaxaca**
http://www.puertovallarta.net ....**Puerto Vallarta Vacations**
http://www.infosma.com ....**Travel Guide to San Miguel**
United States, US – United States of America, Capital: Washington D.C.
http://www.seeamerica.org ....**Travel Industry Association of America**

Miscellaneous

American Samoa, WS - Independent State of Samoa, Capital: Apia
http://www.amsamoa.com..................................**Department of Commerce**
http://www.ipacific.com/samoa/samoa.html ...**Information site for American Samoa**
http://www.samoa.co.uk ....**Information site for Samoa**
Antigua and Barbuda, AG Capital: Saint John's
http://www.geographia.com/antigua-barbuda
....**Antigua and Barbuda Official Travel Guide**
http://www.turq.com/antigua ....**Antigua Tourist Guide**

British Channel Islands

http://tourism.guernsey.net .... **The Guernsey Hotel and Tourism Association**

http://www.jersey.co.uk .... **Information site for Jersey, Channel Islands**

http://www.sark-tourism.com .... **Sark Tourism**

Cook Islands

http://www.cook-islands.com **Official site for Cook Islands Tourism Corporation**

Fiji Islands, FJ - Republic of the Fiji Islands, Capital: Suva

http://www.bulafiji.com .... **Fiji Visitors Bureau**

http://www.fijiguide.com .... **Rob Kay's Fiji Islands Travel Guide**

http://www.internetfiji.com .... **Information site for Fiji**

French Polynesia

http://www.polynesianislands.com/fp .... **Information site for French Polynesia**

Guam

http://ns.gov.gu.. **Official Guam USA site**

http://www.visitguam.org .... **Guam Visitors Bureau**

Maldives, MV - Republic of Maldives, Capital: Male

http://www.visitmaldives.com .... **Maldives Tourism Promotion Board**

Marshall Islands, MH - Republic of the Marshall Islands, Capital: Majuro

http://www.rmiembassyus.org .... **Republic of the Marshall Islands Embassy, USA**

Micronesia, FM - Federated States of Micronesia, Capital: Palikir

http://www.destmic.com .... **Destination Micronesia**

http://www.visit-fsm.org.................................. **Federated States of Micronesia Visitors Board**

Nauru, NR - Republic of Nauru, Capital: Yaren District (no capital city)

http://www.hideawayholidays.com.au/nauru.htm
.... **Information site for Nauru**

http://www.tbc.gov.bc.ca/cwgames/country/Nauru/nauru.html
.... **Government of British Columbia Niue Island**

http://www.niueisland.com .... **Niue Tourism site**

New Caledonia

http://www.sponline.com/nc/anglais/ncen.htm
.... **South Pacific Online**

New Zealand, NZ – Capital: Wellington

http://www.mtcook.org.nz ....Mackenzie Tourism and Development Board
http://www.nelson.net.nz ....Nelson, New Zealand Official Visitors Guide
http://www.newzealand.com ....Internet Guide to New Zealand
http://www.purenz.com ....Official Tourism New Zealand site
http://www.tourisminfo.govt.nz ....Tourism New Zealand
http://www.wellingtonnz.com ....Wellington, New Zealand Travel site

Palau, PW - Republic of Palau, Koror

http://www.destmic.com/palau.html ....Welcome to Palau site
http://www.pbs.org/edens/palau ....Paradise of the Pacific-Palau
http://www.visit-palau.com ....Adventures in Palau

Papau New Guinea, PG - Independent State of Papua New Guinea, Capital: Port Moresby

http://www.niugini.com ....Papau New Guinea site

Seychelles, SC - Republic of Seychelles, Capital: Victoria

http://www.sey.net ....Information site for Seychelles
http://www.seychelles.uk.com ....Seychelles Tourist Office

Solomon Islands, SB – Capital: Honiara

http://www.commerce.gov.sb.............................Solomon Islands Ministry of Commerce, Employment & Tourism
http://www.janeresture.com/solhome ....Jane's Solomon Islands site

Tahiti

http://www.gototahiti.com ....Official Tahiti Tourism site
http://www.tahiti-explorer.com ....The Ultimate Tahiti Travel & Tourism Guide
http://www.tahiti-tourisme.com ....Tahiti Tourism
http://www.papeete.com ....Tahiti Travel & Tourism Guide

Tonga, TO - Kingdom of Tonga, Capital: Nuku'alofa

http://www.tongaholiday.com .... Tonga during the Holidays website
http://www.tongatapu.net.to ....Information site for Tonga

Tuvalu, TV – Capital: Funafuti

http://www.emulateme.com/tuvalu.htm ....Information site for Tuvalu
http://www.janeresture.com/tuvcom...............Tuvalu Travel & Accommodation Guide

Vanuatu, VU - Republic of Vanuatu, Capital: Port-Vila

http://www.vanuatutourism.com ....Vanuatu National Tourism

Here is a listing of automobile rental companies with toll-free numbers and Web sites. You can book online for discounts.

Automobile Rentals:

Alamo Rent-A-Car..800-GOALAMO
USA & Canada 800-424-3687
http://www.alamo.com
Americar USA & Canada..............................800-633-1331
http://www.americar.com
Auto Europe.. 888-223-5555
http://www.autoeurope.com
Avis Rent-A-Car USA 800-230-4898
Canada..800-272-5871
http://www.avis.com
Budget Rent-A-Car USA..............................800-527-0700
Canada..800-472-3325
http://www.drivebudget.com
Dollar Rent-A-Car 800-800-3665
http://www.dollarcar.com
Enterprise Rent-A-Car................................800-566-9249
800-736-8227
http://www.enterprise.com
Hertz Rent-A-Car USA................................800-654-3131
Canada 800-263-0600
http://www.hertz.com
National Car Rental 800-227-7368
USA & Canada ....*http://www.nationalcar.com*
Thrifty Car Rental..800-THRIFTY
USA & Canada 800-847-4389
http://www.thrifty.com
Zip Car 866-4ZIPCAR ....*http://www.zipcar.com*

Hotels and Motels:

Johnny Jet's Hotel Numbers

Visit http://www.hotelnumbers.com for a clickable view on lodging and more.

Here is a list of the many hotel numbers and Web sites.

Adam's Mark Hotels 800-444-2326
http://www.adamsmark.com

Admiral Benbow Inns 800-451-1986
http://www.admiralbenbow.com

AmericInn 800-634-3444
http://www.americinn.com

Amerihost Inn 800-996-2087
http://www.amerihostinn.com

Ameri Suites 800-833-1516
http://www.amerisuites.com

Aston Hotels 800-922-7866
http://www.astonhotels.com

Baymont 800-428-3438
http://www.baymont.com

Best Inn & Suites 800-237-8466
http://www.bestinn.com

Best Western Intl. USA & Canada 800-780-7234
http://www.bestwestern.com

Bradford Suites 800-486-7829
http://www.bradfordsuites.com

Bridge Street 800-278-7338
http://www.bridgestreet.com

Budget Host 800-283-4678
http://www.budgethost.com

Candlewood Suites 800-946-6200
http://www.candlewoodsuites.com

Choice Hotels
(Clarion, Comforts, Econolodge,
Quality Inns, Sleep Inn, Main Stay,
Rodeway Inn) 800-4-CHOICE
USA & Canada 800-424-6423
http://www.choicehotels.com

Club Med 800-258-2633
http://www.clubmed.com

Concorde Hotels 800-888-4747
http://www.concorde-hotels.com

Country Hearth Inns ....800-443-2784 *http://www.countryhearth.com*

Country Inns...800-443-2784
http://www.countryinns.com

Courtyard by Marriot..800-228-9290
http://www.courtyard.com/toc

Crown Plaza..800-227-6963
http://www.sixcontinentshotels.com/crowneplaza

Days Inn USA & Canada 800-DAYS-INN
800-329-7466
800-325-2525
http://www.daysinn.com

Doubletree Guest Suites & 800-222-TREE
Hotels USA...*http://www.doubletreehotels.com*

Drury Inn 800-325-8300
http://www.druryinn.com

Embassy Suites 800-EMBASSY
USA & Canada...800-362-2779

Extended Stay America......................................800-398-7829
http://www.extstay.com

Fairmont Hotels & Resorts 800-866-5577
USA & Canada ....*http://www.fairmont.com*

Family Inns of America 800-251-9752
http://www.familyinnsofamerica.com

Fairfield Inn...800-228-2800
http://www.fairfieldinn.com/toc

Fiesta Americana 800-343-7821
http://www.fiestaamericana.com

Four Points 800-325-3535
http://www.fourpoints.com

Four Seasons 800-332-3442
http://www.fourseasons.com

Hampton Inns 800-426-7866
http://www.hamptoninn.com

Hawthorne Suites 800-527-1133
http://www.hawthorn.com

Hilton Hotels USA & Canada 800-HILTONS
800-445-8667
http://www.hilton.com

Holiday Inns USA & Canada............................888-224-2424
http://www.holiday-inn.com

Homewood Suites..800-225-5466
http://www.homewood-suites.com

Howard Johnson Motor Lodge ....800-I GO HOJO
USA & Canada..800-406-1411
http://www.hojo.com

Hyatt Hotels & Resorts 800-633-7313
USA & Canada..*http://www.hyatt.com*

Ian Schrager Hotels
Call Individual Hotel ....*http://www.ianschragerhotels.com*

Inns of America 800-826-0778
http://www.innsamerica.com

Inter-Continental Hotels...................................800-327-0200
USA & Canada ....*http://www.interconti.com*

ITT Sheraton Hotels & Inns 800-325-3535
USA & Canada ....*http://www.sheraton.com*

Jameson Inns..800-526-3766
http://www.jamesoninns.com

Kimpton Group...800-546-7866
http://www.kimptongroup.com

Knights Inn 800-682-1071
http://www.knightsinn.com

La Quinta Inns 800-531-5900
http://www.lq.com

Leading Hotels of the World.............................800-223-6800
http://www.lhw.com

Loews Hotels 800-223-0888
http://www.loewshotels.com

Main Stay Suites...800-660-6246
http://www.mainstaysuites.com

Marriott Hotels USA & Canada.........................800-228-9290
http://www.marriott.com

Microtel Inn..800-771-7171
http://www.microtellin.com

Motel 6 800-466-8356
http://www.motel6.com

New Otani Hotels...800-421-8795
http://www.newotani.co.jp/en

Nikko Hotels 800-NIKKO-US
http://www.nikkohotels.com

Omni Hotels Worldwide...................................800-THE OMNI

800-843-6664
http://www.omnihotels.com
Outrigger Hotels Hawaii 800-733-7777
http://www.outrigger.com
Pan Pacific Hotels 800-327-8585
http://www.panpac.com
Preferred Hotels 800-323-7500
http://www.preferredhotels.com
Premier Resorts 888-211-7710
http://www.premier-resorts.com
Radisson Hotels International 800-333-3333
USA & Canada ....*http://www.radisson.com*
Ramada Inns 800-228-2828
USA & Canada 800-2-RAMADA
800-272-6232
http://www.ramada.com
Red Roof Inns ....800-RED ROOF
800-733-7663
http://www.redroof.com
Regal Hotels International 800-222-8888
http://www.regal-hotels.com
Renaissance Hotels & Resorts 800-HOTELS-1
800-468-3571
http://www.renaissancehotels.com
Residence Inns by Marriott 800-331-3131
http://www.residenceinn.com
Ritz-Carlton Hotels 800-241-3333
USA & Canada ....*http://www.ritzcarlton.com*
Shangri La 800-942-5050
http://www.shangri-la.com
Sheraton 800-325-3535
http://www.sheraton.com
Shilo Inns 800-222-2244
http://www.shiloinns.com
Shoney Inns (Guest House) 800-552-4667
http://www.shoneysinn.com
Signature Inns 800-822-5252
http://www.signature-inns.com
Small Luxury Hotels 800-345-3457
http://www.slh.com
Staybridge Suites 800-238-8000

http://www.staybridge.com

Sofitel 800-763-4835
http://www.sofitel.com

Sonesta Intl. Hotels..800-SONESTA
USA & Canada 800-766-3782
SRS World Hotels..800-223-5652
http://www.srs-worldhotels.com

St. Regis..888-625-5144
http://www.starwood.com/stregis

Summerfield Suites by Wyndham 800-833-4353
http://www.summerfield.com

Super 8 Hotels 800-800-8000
USA & Canada *http://www.super8.com*
Swissotel Hotels & Resorts 800-63-SWISS
USA & Canada ....*http://www.swissotel.com*
Thistle Hotels..800-847-4358
http://www.thistlehotels.com

Travelers Inn 800-643-5566
http://www.travelersinn.com

Trump Hotels and Casino Resorts.....................877-DJTRUMP
http://www.trump.com

Vagabond Inns...800-522-1555
http://www.vagabondinn.com

Villager...888-821-5779
http://www.villager.com

W Hotels...877-946-8357
http://www.whotels.com

Travelodge Hotels Intl. 888-515-6375
USA & Canada ....*http://www.travelodge.com*
Westin Hotels & Resorts 888-625-5144
USA & Canada 800-782-9488
http://www.starwood.com/westin

Westmark Hotels 800-544-0970
http://www.westmarkhotels.com

Wingate Inns..877-202-8814
http://www.wingateinns.com

Wyndham Hotels 800-822-4200
http://www.wyndham.com

U.S. Airlines:

Visit *www.airlinenumbers.com* for a clickable view on airlines and more.

America West 800-235-9292
Main site ....*http://www.americawest.com*
Vacation site ....*http://www.americawestvacations.com*
American 800-433-7300
http://www.www.aa.com
Continental 800-525-0280
Main site ....*http://www.continental.com*
Vacation site ....*http://www.coolvacations.com*
Delta 800-221-1212
Main site ....*http://www.delta.com*
Vacation site ....*http://www.deltavacations.com*
Jet Blue ....800-JET BLUE
http://www.jetblue.com
Northwest..800-225-2525
http://www.nwa.com
Vacation site ....*http://www.nwaworldvacations.com*
Southwest..800-I FLY SWA
800-435-9792
Main site ....*http://www.southwest.com*
Vacation site ....*http://www.swavacations.com*
TWA..800-221-2000
http://www.twa.com
United 800-241-6522
Main site ....*http://www.ual.com*
Vacation site ....*http://www.unitedvacations.com*
US Airways..800-428-4322
Main site ....*http://www.usairways.com*
Vacation site ....*http://www.usairwaysvacations.com*

International Airlines:

Air Canada 888-247-2262
http://www.aircanada.ca
Air France 800-237-2747
http://www.airfrance.com
British Airways 800-AIRWAYS
800-247-9297
http://www.british-airways.com

Canadian Airlines:

From Canada: 800-665-1177
From USA:...800-426-7000
Canada, French/English:...................................800-363-7530
http://www.cdnair.ca

Finnair USA..800-950-5000
Canada 800-461-8651
http://www.us.finnair.com

KLM..800-447-4747
http://www.klm.com

Lufthansa USA...800-645-3880
Canada 800-563-5954
http://www.lufthansa.com

Qantas Airways 800-227-4500
http://www.qantas.com

Sabena Belgian World Airlines 800-955-2000
http://www.sabena.com

Scandinavian Airlines (SAS).............................800-221-2350
http://www.scandinavian.net

Airfreight Companies:

Airborne Express...800-247-2676
http://www.airborneexpress.com

Bax Global 800-225-5229
Outside USA...480-966-5094
http://www.baxglobal.com

DHL Worldwide Express..................................800-225-5345
Canada..800-387-7783
Outside USA...480-303-5797
http://www.dhl.com

Emery Worldwide USA....................................800-443-6379
800-367-3592
http://www.emeryworld.com

FedEx 800-463-3339
http://www.fedex.com

Mail Boxes Etc..888-346-3623
http://www.mbe.com

United Parcel Service..800-PICK-UPS
800-742-5877
http://www.ups.com

Virtual Bellhop..*http://www.virtualbellhop.com*

Traveler's Checks (Report Lost or Stolen):

American Express 800-221-7282
http://www.americanexpress.com

Thomas Cook 800-223-7373
http://www.thomascookholdings.com

Visa 800-227-6811
Cont. USA, Canada & Caribbean ....http://www.visa.com

Credit Cards (Report Lost or Stolen):

American Express..800-AXP-1234
Outside USA ....Collect 336-393-1111
Diners Club USA..800-234-6377
Outside USA ....Collect 303-799-1504
Canada: Silver..800-363-3333
Gold 800-563-GOLD
Maple 800-663-0284
Outside Canada ....Collect
Discover Card..800-347-2683
Outside USA..Collect 801-902-3100
MasterCard..800-307-7309
http://www.mastercard.com
Visa 800-847-2911
Outside USA & Canada 410-581-3836
http://www.visa.com

Index

D

Johnny Jet Code Index

AOL Keywords Guide:

AOL has become a leader and a reliable Internet service provider with millions of users. You can access many travel sites and travel related material by using AOL keywords. This is one quick reference to AOL travel related keywords AOL users can type in. If you are looking for a particular state or country, you could type in the state or country name and find news on that country. For instance, if you were looking for news from California or Ohio, just type in the state names as an AOL Keyword and you will be prompted with a screen. For more information on AOL Keywords, you can visit Keyword Easy and learn from AOL's Online Advisor.

Keyword: Destination — Meaning

Acapulco: Travel Guides: Acapulco .... Guide to Acapulco
Access: Access .... Different ways to connect to AOL
AdventureVacations: Vacations .... Shop AOL vacations from Travelocity
Airline: Air Travel .... Book fares from Travelocity
Alerts: Alert .... Don't forget reminders and alerts
Amazon: Amazon.com *(www.amazon.com)* .... Amazon.com online superstore
AOL Anywhere: Anywhere *(http://anywhere.aol.com)* .... AOL services anywhere you are
AOLTipsNewsletter: AOL Tips .... AOL tips and tricks
AnchorageAlaska: Travel Guides: Anchorage, AK .... Guide to Anchorage
AspenColorado: Travel Guides: Aspen, CO .... Guide to Aspen
BaggageGuidelines: Baggage Guidelines .... Airline baggage guidelines
Baja: Travel Guides: Baja .... Guide to the Baja Peninsula
Bali: Travel Guides: Bali .... Guide to Bali
Barcelona: Travel Guides: Barcelona .... Guide to Barcelona
BN: Barnes & Noble .... Barnes & Noble Bookstores
Beaches: Beaches .... Beach finder
BestCruises: Best Cruises .... Top cruise offers
Bonaire: Travel Guides: Bonaire .... Guide to Bonaire
BoxOffice: Ticketmaster *(www.ticketmaster.com)* .... Tickets from Ticketmaster
BransonMissouri: Travel Guides: Branson, MO .... Guide to Branson Missouri
CaboSanLucas: Travel Guides: Cabo San Lucas, Mexico .... Guide to Cabo San Lucas
CarRental: Car Rental Center .... Rent a Car
CasinoVacations: Casino Resorts .... Casino Resort Packages
ContinentalAirlines: Continental Airlines Inc. .... Continental Airlines Booking

CostaRicaTravel: Costa Rica Travel Guides .... Guide to Costa Rica
CrownePlaza: Crowne Plaza
(www.sixcontinentshotels.com/crowneplaza) .... Crowne Plaza Hotels
CruiseCritic: Cruises
(www.cruisecritic.com) .... Cruise reviews, bargains, news
Cruises: Cruise Packages .... Cruise Packages
DaytonaBeachFlorida: Daytona Beach Travel Guides . Guide to Daytona Beach
Destinations: Travel Guides .... World destination guides
drivebudget: Budget Rent a Car
(www.drivebudget.com) .... Budget Rent a Car
Ebay: Ebay .... Ebay auction site
EgyptTravel: Travel Guides: Egypt .... Guide to Egypts
Entertainment: Entertainment .... Entertainment guide
FamilyVacations: Family Vacation Packages .... Family Vacation Packages
Flighttracker: Flight Tracker .... Flight Arrival/Departure Request
Florence: Florence, Italy Travel Guides .... Guide to Florence
Food: Food & Recipes .... Food and Recipe Guide
GayTravel: Gay and Lesbian Travel .... Gay and Lesbian from PlanetOut
GolfVacations: Golf Vacations .... Golf Packages
Google: Google Search .... Google Search Engine
Government: Government Guide
(www.governmentguide.com) .... Guide to Government sites
HardRockHotel: Hard Rock Hotel .... Universal Studios Orlando Resort
Hertz: Hertz Corp. *(www.hertz.com)* .... Hertz Rent a Car
HolidayInn: Holiday Inn
(www.sixcontinentshotels.com) .... Holiday Inn Hotels
HolidayInnExpress: Holiday Inn Express .... Holiday Inn Express Hotels
Horoscopes: Horoscopes .... Astrology
Hotel: Hotels .... Lodging and Hotels
Hostel: Student Travel .... Student Travel Guide
IndependentTraveler: Independent Traveler
(www.independenttraveler.com) .... Travel Bargains
Inn: Inns and Bed and Breakfasts
(www.placestostay.com) .... Inn and B&B Guide
InsideFlyer: InsideFlyer Online
(www.webflyer.com) .... Frequent Flyer site
Inter-Continental: Inter Continental
(www.intercontinental.com) .... Intercontinental Hotels
InternationalAccess: International Access
.... How to access AOL internationally
Istanbul: Travel Guides: Istanbul .... Guide to Istanbul

Ithaca: Travel Guides: Ithaca, NY .... Guide to Ithaca
JacksonHole: Travel Guides: Jackson Hole WY ....Guide to Jackson Hole
Kauai: Travel Guides: Kauai, HI..Guide to Kauai
Kissimmee: Travel Guides: Kissimmee, FL ....Guide to Kissimmee
LakeTahoe: Travel Guides: Lake Tahoe ....Guide to Lake Tahoe
LastMinuteTravel: Last Minute Travel..................................Late Ticket Booking
LearningTravel: Educational Travel......................................Learning and Culture
Local: Local Guide..Local Guide to your City
LocalAir: Local Airfare Deals..Local Deals for Select Days
Lodging: Lodging ....Lodging
London: Travel Guides: London ....Guide to London
LonelyPlanet: Lonely Planet *(www.lonelyplanet.com)* ....Destination Guides
Maps: MapQuest *(www.mapquest.com)* ....Driving Directions
MauiHawaii: Travel Guides: Maui, HI..Guide to Maui
Melbourne: Travel Guides: Melbourne ....Guide to Melbourne
MemberOpinions: Travelers' Opinions............Travel Chat and Message Boards
Miles: Miles Manager ....Track Frequent Flier Miles
Monterey: Travel Guides: Monterey, CA ....Guide to Monterey
Montreal: Travel Guides: Montreal ....Guide to Montreal
Mothman: The Mothman ....Strange Creature Mothman
Moviefone: Moviefone *(www.moviefone.com)*Check Movie Times and Showings
Munich: Travel Guides: Munich.. Guide to Munich
Naples: Travel Guides: Naples .... Guide to Naples
NorthMyrtleBeach: Travel Guides: Myrtle Beach, SC .....Guide to Myrtle Beach
Norwegiancruiseline: Norwegian Cruise Line ....Norwegian Cruise Line
OnlineReunion: Online Reunion......................Reunite with Friends and Family
Ontario: Travel Guides: Ontario..Guide to Ontario
ParisFrance: Travel Guides: Paris ....Guide to Paris
ParksAndCamping: Parks and Camping ....Find a Park
PetTravel: Traveling with Pets ....Pet Travel Tips
PNOTravel: PlanetOut Travel *(www.planetout.com)* ....Gay and Lesbian
PortlandOregon: Travel Guides: Portland, OR..........................Guide to Portland
PuertoVallarta: Travel Guides: Puerto Vallarta, Mexico Guide to Puerto Vallarta
Resort: Resorts and Lodges
(www.placestostay.com)..Resorts and Lodges
Restaurants: Restaurant Guide
(www.digitalcity.com/dining) .... Restaurant Guides
RoadTrips: Road Trips.. Road Trip Resource
RiodeJaneiro: Travel Guides: Rio de Janeiro....................Guide to Rio de Janeiro
RomanticVacations: Romantic Vacations ....Romantic Vacation Booking
RomeItaly: Travel Guides: Rome ....Guide to Rome

RV: RVs ....Recreational Vehicle Guide
Safaris: Safari and Zoo Vacations ....Zoo and Safari Finder
Sedona: Travel Guides: Sedona, AZ ....Guide to Sedona
Shanghai: Travel Guides: Shanghai ....Guide to Shanghai
SinglesTravel: The Single Traveler ....Single Traveler Resource
SixFlags: Six Flags *(www.sixflags.com)*..........................Six Flags Amusement Park
SkiTravel: Ski Trips ....Ski Resort Booking
SouthBeach: Travel Guides: South Beach, Miami..............Guide to South Beach
Spa: Spas ....Spa Travel
StMartin: Travel Guides: St. Martin ....Guide to St. Martin
StThomas: Travel Guides: St. Thomas ....Guide to St. Thomas
StudentTravel: Student Travel... Student Travel Resource
ThemeParks: Theme Parks .... Find a Theme Park
Travel: AOL Travel .... AOL Travel Guide
TravelersAdvantage: Traveler's Advantage ....AOL Travel Discount Program
TravelAndLeisure: Travel and Leisure
(www.travelandleisure.com) ....Travel Magazine
TravelBargains: Travel Bargains...AOL Travel Bargains
Travel Cafe: Travel Chat Information ....Travel Chat
TravelClassifieds: Travel Classifieds ....Classified ads
Travel Community: Travel Community ....Travel Chat and Message Boards
TravelNews: Travel News .... News for Travelers
TravelPhotography: Travel Photography ....Travel Pictures Tips
TravelPhotos: Travel Photos .... Travel Photo Gallery
TravelReservation: Travel Reservations Center ....Travel Booking
Tuscany: Travel Guides: Tuscany ....Guide to Tuscany
VacationHomes: Vacation Rental Homes...........................Vacation Rental Finder
Vacations: Vacation Packages and Cruises ....Vacations from Travelocity
VailColorado: Travel Guides: Vail, CO ....Guide to Vail
Vancouver: Travel Guides: Vancouver, BC ....Guide to Vancouver
Venice: Travel Guides: Venice...Guide to Venice
Weather: The Weather Channel *(www.weather.com)* ....Weather News
Weddings: The Knot Honeymoons/Weddings
(www.theknot.com) ....Wedding Information
Wineries: Food and Wine Travel...Wine Tasting
YellowPages: AOL Yellow Pages ....Search for Addresses
Yoga: Yoga ....Yoga Information
Zagat: Zagat *(www.zagat.com)*..Zagat Restaurant Guides

Travel Notes

Travel Notes

Travel Notes

Travel Notes

Travel Notes

Travel Notes

Travel Notes

Travel Notes

Travel Notes

Travel Notes

Travel Notes

Travel Notes

Travel Notes

Travel Notes

Travel Notes

Travel Notes

Quick Order Form

Give the gift of the "You Are Here" series!

Friends, Family, and Loved Ones Can Enjoy Surfing the Internet.

CHECK YOUR LEADING BOOKSTORE OR ORDER HERE

Telephone Orders: Call 866-YAHBOOKS (924-2665) toll free. Please have your credit card ready.
Online Orders: Visit *www.yahbooks.com* to place an order on our secure server.
Postal Orders: Please make check payable and return to: Yahbooks Publishing, 30799 Pinetree Road #356, Cleveland, OH 44124

Visit *www.yahbooks.com* for pricing (Ohio residents please add 7% sales tax per book)

____ copies of ***You Are Here Traveling with JohnnyJet.com***

____ copies of ***You Are Here College Internet Guide***

____ copies of ***You Are Here High School Internet Guide***

____ copies of ***You Are Here Kids & Family Internet Guide***

____ copies of ***You Are Here Internet Planners*** (check Web site for availability)

My check or money order for $________is enclosed.

Please charge my __ Visa __ MasterCard __ Discover __ Amex

Name ____

Address ____

City______________________________State____ ZIP________- ______

Phone ___________________________Email ___________________

Card #__________________________________Exp. Date ____/_____

Name on card ______________________________________

Quick Order Form

Give the gift of the "You Are Here" series!

Friends, Family, and Loved Ones Can Enjoy Surfing the Internet.

CHECK YOUR LEADING BOOKSTORE OR ORDER HERE

Telephone Orders: Call 866-YAHBOOKS (924-2665) toll free. Please have your credit card ready.
Online Orders: Visit *www.yahbooks.com* to place an order on our secure server.
Postal Orders: Please make check payable and return to: Yahbooks Publishing, 30799 Pinetree Road #356, Cleveland, OH 44124

Visit *www.yahbooks.com* for pricing (Ohio residents please add 7% sales tax per book)

____ copies of ***You Are Here Traveling with JohnnyJet.com***

____ copies of ***You Are Here College Internet Guide***

____ copies of ***You Are Here High School Internet Guide***

____ copies of ***You Are Here Kids & Family Internet Guide***

____ copies of ***You Are Here Internet Planners*** (check Web site for availability)

My check or money order for $________is enclosed.

Please charge my __ Visa __ MasterCard __ Discover __ Amex

Name ____

Address ____

City____________________________State_____ ZIP________- ______

Phone ___________________________Email ___________________

Card #___________________________________Exp. Date ____/_____

Name on card _______________________________________